JOURNALISM
1908

University of Missouri Press   Columbia and London

JOURNALISM
1908
BIRTH OF A PROFESSION

Edited by
Betty Houchin Winfield

Library of Congress Cataloging-in-Publication Data

Journalism, 1908 : birth of a profession / edited by Betty Houchin Winfield.
    p. cm.
  Includes bibliographical references and index.
  Summary: "A team of media scholars with personal ties to the University of
Missouri's School of Journalism explore the state of news organizations in 1908,
the year in which the first university-based school of journalism was founded,
and illustrate the profound impact journalism education has had on the news
media"—Provided by publisher.
  ISBN 978-0-8262-1811-7 (cloth : alk. paper)
  ISBN 978-0-8262-1813-1 (pbk. : alk. paper)
  1. Journalism—United States—History—20th century.   2. Journalism—Study and
teaching (Higher)—United States—History—20th century.   I. Winfield, Betty
Houchin, 1939–
  PN4867.J67 2008
  071'.3—dc22

                        2008015841

Designer: Jennifer Cropp
Typesetter: BookComp, Inc.
Printer and binder: Thomson-Shore, Inc.
Typefaces: Palatino and Berkeley

*The University of Missouri Press gratefully acknowledges the support
of the Missouri School of Journalism in the publication of this book.*

To all who took history,

continued to study history,

loved history and remained curious

Contents

Acknowledgments

Several years ago journalism historians at Missouri had become enough of a critical mass to have monthly lunch meetings to share ideas, talk about primary source holdings, discuss our individual research, and invite campus colleagues to join us. We at the J-School mused about how we might do a collaborative historical project when our research emphases were each so dissimilar. Out of those discussions came the kernel of this book for a one-year focus, then unknown in our field. The year 1908 was particularly salient when the school's upcoming centennial was a distant blip on the far horizon. The status of journalism in all its forms in the year of 1908 became a gleam in our eyes.

From our small original group we added former Missouri School of Journalism faculty and students, now stretched across the country at other universities. In the meantime, a couple of our original group moved to other universities as newer faculty arrived, but our vision remained stalwart. The authors of all the chapters here have or have had a Missouri connection at one time or another.

Many thanks to those who made this edited book happen. Each author, as a part of the whole, wrote and rewrote a chapter that was a unique contribution, yet fit the project as an entirety. Journalism Dean Dean R. Mills generously supported the project from the idea to the publication. The School's Frank Luther Mott History Fund paid for Eve Kidd Crawford's initial excellent copyediting. She painstakingly went through each chapter, paragraph by paragraph, to clarify areas and cut out the redundancy from previous chapters as well as to polish the prose. University of Missouri Press Director Beverly Jarrett kept encouraging us from origination to publication. Those unnamed reviewers should be commended for their detailed useful propositions as to format, chapter placement, and missing parts. We did our best to incorporate as many of their suggestions as possible. Managing Editor Jane Lago and Editor John Brenner helped our manuscript prose sing and aided our responses to a timetable.

Others too assisted. Doug Crews of the Missouri Press Association gave us several century-old Missouri photographs to use. Undergraduates Linda Waterborg and Elise Crawley helped us find sources, locate suitable images, and get them ready for publication. Doctoral student David Freman and J-Net Director John Meyer raised the image resolution for publishing.

Lastly, we thank our families and friends and colleagues who heard more about journalism in 1908 than they ever imagined possible.

Betty Houchin Winfield
Editor

JOURNALISM
1908

Introduction

Emerging Professionalism and Modernity

Betty Houchin Winfield

The year 1908 is not one of those readily recalled American historical years, such as 1776, 1812, 1941, and 1964; nor is 1908 one of those heralded journalism years, such as 1690, or 1734, 1798, 1833, 1898, 1951, or 1971. Rather, we argue that 1908 marks a watershed year for a modern, professionalized mass media, originating after the fits and starts of late nineteenth-century state press associations' educational efforts and culminating with formalized university education in journalism. The year 1908 points to a change in the field, a time when journalism professionalism becomes officially established by formal university instruction and organization. This year marks the beginning of university schools and departments of journalism. The Missouri School of Journalism at the University of Missouri was only the first before many more began.

This year of 1908 was rooted in a long national discussion of what journalism was, what it could be, would be, and should offer, and whether journalism was a trade fitting a major American business, or whether it was a profession with a greater calling and social responsibility in a democracy. After the first school of journalism was established at the University of Missouri in 1908, a floodgate opened: during the next two decades some two dozen American journalism programs became separate university departments and schools.

With a spotlight on the year 1908, this book will offer a fresh look at the state of journalism early in the twentieth century and the transformations it was in the midst of undergoing. The news media at the beginning of the twentieth century were primarily print media: newspapers and magazines, filled with advertising, graphic designs, and visual images. This book follows the methodological frame of focusing on 1908 as a point within the trajectory of American journalism professionalism, a development shaped by the larger social, cultural, and political currents of American society. As literary scholar Michael North argued about year studies, "The numbers given to particular years are used to measure historical change . . . [and] can stand for something . . . a year can be used as a date, as if it were punctual and precise, or as a period containing many other dates."[1] This book is about a specific time period, yet containing other dates, but culminating in 1908 as a point of transformation for journalism.

Similar to other studies that spotlight a time, this book focuses on 1908 to understand more completely a microlevel of history within the context of a single period. These chapters offer what Scott Heller calls a time-related focus, "a manageable way to narrow the scope, deal in specifics, yet still works with a beginning, middle and end."[2] To give a more accurate picture of the mass media world in one year and to avoid being too narrow, the chapters place various aspects of journalism in 1908 within the context of the first decade of the twentieth century,[3] while still seeking to clarify trends, issues, and developments that otherwise may be obscured in the sweep of larger historical studies. Where other historical studies have emphasized specific dates and places, this study emphasizes many impressions that became instantaneous by a one-year focus, annihilating a specific time and space. In 1908, journalism was on the cusp of significant change through formalized education, giving promise for professional legitimization.

Why 1908?

By focusing on 1908, there is a risk of historicizing a very brief period in time. Yet, we argue that those early twentieth-century years were ripe for

1. Michael North, "Virtual Histories: The Year as Literary Period," *Modern Language Quarterly* 62, no. 4 (December 2001): 404.
2. Scott Heller, "What a Difference a Year Makes," *Chronicle of Higher Education*, 5 January 2001, A17.
3. Margaret Blanchard, "The Ossification of Journalism History: A Challenge for the Twenty-First Century," *Journalism History* 25, no. 3 (Autumn 1999): 110. See too James W. Carey's "The Problem with Journalism History," *Journalism History* 1, no. 1 (Spring 1974): 3–5, 27.

exposed societal issues, Sometimes in a sensational manner — took aim @ institutions - often served public interest

major changes in journalism. After the previous decades of big-city yellow journalism and circulation wars where many journalists who were paid by the inch embellished the news for larger, more sensational stories, journalism leaders by 1908 had had enough. They sought solutions to journalism extremes, especially following the journalistic frenzy surrounding the 1898 Spanish-American War and the subsequent sensational muckraking reportage on America's societal ills: the shame of the cities, the corruption of big business, and the taint of the country's food and prescription medicines. Muckrakers such as Lincoln Steffens, Ida Tarbell, and Upton Sinclair saw themselves as crusaders for the American worker against industrial greed and corruption, but their critics, including President Theodore Roosevelt, thought they went too far. Journalism must be accountable to its critics; professionalism would be a solution.

The year 1908 was a propitious time because the country was at the height of what has since been called the Progressive Era, not specifically dated, but rather as a spirit perceived. That spirit took shape in a broad movement for reform, as many people thought that the country had not lived up to its democratic ideals. In the various occupations and callings, professionalism was part of that reform; training for occupations crucial to a democratic society would rely less on the previous system of apprenticeships and more on formal education and particular standards. With reform as the character of the era, the question became how to effect change that would lead to demonstrable improvement.

Professionalism

Journalism was one of the many areas that needed improvement. In fact, reformers had begun questioning the normative behavior of journalists. Many journalists were guided by definite beliefs about responsibility and the ethical conduct of a free press. Too, journalists were no longer content to be thought of as hacks, and began evaluating themselves as compared to other established professions, such as medicine, law, the clergy, engineering, and education.[4] Those professions already had particular standards, educational demands and ideals about their societal roles; so too should journalism. One solution to extremes such as yellow journalism, many thought, would be prescribed professionalism through university education and training about obligations, correct practices, and knowledge of historical

features eye-catching

4. Patrick Lee Plaisance, "A Gang of Piucksniffs Grows Up: The Evolution of Journalism Ethics Discourse in *The Journalist* and *Editor and Publisher*," *Journalism Studies* 6, no. 4 (2005): 480.

headlines instead of legit news

roots and acceptable principles. Universities could define the terms, indicate the acceptable behavior necessary for a professional class, and provide the credentials of academic degrees and membership in alumni organizations and networks.[5] With formal education, journalists would be legitimized, and their field's status would increase.

The first decade of the twentieth century marked an important intellectual point at which, asserted one sociologist, there was an intermediate movement between the extremes of individualism and socialism. In 1908 University of Missouri sociologist W. B. Elkin wrote that the problem was how to move from the rights of individuals and the rights of society to a harmonious blending of both. His solution would be education and organization: "education in order to secure for the individual the largest degree of development; organization in order to secure for the community the results of individual progress." Neither force alone would be sufficient, he argued. Organizations differ greatly in development, he emphasized; some are at the beginning of the chaotic stage, some approach the reign of law, and a very few are almost rationalized. He saw journalism at an early, chaotic stage. The year 1908 highlights journalism at that early stage, but about to change.

Elkin summarized the intellectual thinking then about organizations and professionalism by stressing that the rational element as found in various social organs was expected to make more progress in the new century as professions. Among the fields of medicine, law, and religion, he listed journalism as a "modern profession, only just emerging from the biological stage of development." Journalism as an organization grew, not by nature, but by chance. Elkin stated that, as a consequence, "malformation has been one of its predominant characteristics." Formalized education would be a solution, but it must have experiential learning. Journalism cannot be satisfactorily taught by means of theory alone, he wrote; every journalism department should edit a daily paper, "for the journalist, like the scientist, requires to have his laboratory and testing apparatus always at hand."[6] Almost seventy years later, sociologists would see the culture of professionalism as being enormously satisfying to the human ego, even aiding in the rise of the American middle class, but taking an inestimable toll on individualism.[7]

5. See for example Burton Bledstein, *The Culture of Professionalism: The Middle Class and the Development of Higher Education in America* (New York: Norton, 1976).

6. W. B. Elkin, "The Problem of Civilization in the Twentieth Century," *American Journal of Sociology* 13, no. 4 (1908): 541, 554.

7. Bledstein, *The Culture of Professionalism*, xi.

Educational Plan

Elkin was not alone in 1908 in discussing journalism as a profession with particular educational demands. Missouri press leader Walter Williams, in an address before the Missouri Press Association in May 1908, acknowledged that "[t]he word journalist is not held in high esteem by some newspaper folk—and I confess to being one of those who thus lightly regard it." He envisioned a new professional status with the opening of the School of Journalism that fall at the University of Missouri. This educational advance "seeks to do for journalism what schools of law, medicine, agriculture, engineering and normal schools have done for these vocations," he said. As far as its status within the university, Williams told the association, "The School is co-ordinate, equal in rank, with the schools of colleges of law, medicine, engineering, agriculture and the teachers' college." He went on to explain that the school's educational goal "adds the laboratory to the lecture method, the clinic supplementing of the classroom. It trains by doing." He emphasized that the distinct feature of the school, besides "its recognition of journalism as a profession, is this employment of the laboratory plan."[8] By emphasizing the educational component of practical apprenticeship, Williams was counteracting the critics who surmised that journalism could only be a trade and would have to be learned on the job. The new school would be both classroom and laboratory.

Conflicting Views on
Professionalism through Education

Williams, a former president of the Missouri Press Association, knew that the MPA was fully behind a university school of journalism. As an organization, the MPA had long called for university training for journalists, as had other state press associations, legislatures, and college presidents. In fact, the students at the University of Missouri had for years petitioned the university for formalized professional training in journalism.[9] Their views had greatly contrasted with the standard nineteenth-century opinion about the training of journalists, which echoed the views of famed midcentury *New York Tribune* publisher Horace Greeley, who was reported to have said,

8. Walter Williams Address Delivered before the Missouri Press Association at Excelsior Springs, Mo., May 29, 1908, as found in Sara Lockwood Williams, *Twenty Years of Education for Journalism* (Columbia, Mo.: E. W. Stephens Company, 1929), 411, 412.
9. Lockwood Williams, *Twenty Years of Education*, 3.

"Of all horned cattle, deliver me from a college graduate."[10] Unlike well-known late nineteenth-century publishers such as Charles Dana (*New York Sun*) and Arthur S. Ochs (*New York Times*) who would hire those who had college newspaper experience, such as at the *Harvard Crimson*, Greeley refused to employ young college graduates as reporters.[11]

Following the Civil War, others had made a public cry for professionalism as journalism grew into a powerful institution and educational agent without obvious societal responsibility. In an 1869 *Overland Monthly* article, George F. Parsons cited few traces of calm and dispassionate coverage when he noted that the focus was on a business mission, which was being fulfilled in "a very unsatisfactory manner." Parsons acknowledged that there were a few leading journals in the land, but he argued a future historian reading the American newspapers of 1868 would form an erroneous opinion about the condition of the country:

> For he would find facts distorted, occurrences misrepresented, men maligned or lauded . . . according to the political views of the journal he was perusing. He would find intolerance and prejudice soiling the pages under his hand where he turned. He would find that in the main, rant and declamation, frothy philippics and gross personal abuse, stood for argument; and that but few traces of calm and dispassionate reasoning could be found.[12]

[handwritten annotation: verbal denunciation characterized by harsh language]

Parsons's assessment was that journalism "has come to be a kind of alms house for decayed business men . . . who have failed in half a dozen callings . . ." His solution to these many faults prescribed education. He argued, "political licentiousness is one of the worst features of modern journalism, and it is directly traceable to lack of education . . . the more a man is educated, the less inclined will he be to leave the broad pathway of honorable argument for the foul slums of invective and personal abuse." This early call for education asked for modern journalists to have special training "fully as much as do physics or law" and be "well versed in all subjects in a sound nineteenth century education."[13]

By the twentieth century, momentum for change had increased. More and more editors and publishers were college educated. Well-known publish-

10. Ibid., 15.

11. E. J. Carpenter of the *Boston Advertiser*, "Journalism as a Profession," *Education* 7 (February 1887): 410.

12. George F. Parsons, "Journalism as a Profession," *Overland Monthly* 2 (January 1869): 25–26.

13. Ibid., 28–29.

MISSOURI, STATE UNIVERSITY,

Academic Hall with its columns was the site of the first
course in journalism at the University of Missouri in
1879. Courtesy of the University of Missouri Archives.

ers, such as Joseph Pulitzer, touted the idea of a professional school of journalism. Pulitzer predicted in 1904, "Before the century closes schools of journalism will be generally accepted as a feature of specialized higher education, like schools of law or of medicine."[14] Eight years later, in 1912, his efforts would culminate in the birth of Columbia University's School of Journalism, although he would not live to witness it.

Pulitzer's optimism for the twentieth century came despite the previous decades of difficulty in raising journalism to "one of the learned professions." To answer the critics who still saw newspapermen as "born, not made," Pulitzer said he had never met anyone who did not need training: "all intelligence requires development." An apprenticeship is only "incidental training," he said. He also pointed out a practical constraint on apprenticeships: "Nobody in a newspaper office has the time or the inclination to teach a raw reporter the things he ought to know."[15]

In an article for the *North American Review*, Pulitzer addressed other journalism issues, such as potential class conflicts between those with college

14. Joseph Pulitzer, "The College of Journalism," *North American Review* (May 1904): 642.
15. Ibid., 678, 642–43, 647.

educations and those without, and organizational controls over professionalism. For workplace educational differences, Pulitzer wrote, "I sincerely hope it will create a class distinction between the fit and the unfit." What was now needed, this former practitioner of yellow journalism argued, was a class feeling among journalists, based "not upon money, but upon morals, education and character." Pulitzer foresaw organizational controls; educated journalists would gather at a future recognized professional meeting, discuss matters of common interest, and "develop a professional pride that would enable them to work in concert for the public good, and react to the black sheep of the profession." The aim of university education was legitimization for journalists: "a man who has the advantage, honor and pleasure of addressing the public every day as a writer or thinker is a professional man." Pulitzer argued that a college of journalism would make better journalists, "who would make a better newspaper, which will better serve the public."[16]

Pulitzer's ideas complemented Walter Williams's vision for the University of Missouri's School of Journalism: that it would make better journalists to serve society. The Missouri school began eight years earlier than Pulitzer's school at Columbia, with wide-ranging public support from many groups, particularly the Missouri Press Association. Williams's plan was part of a nationwide movement toward professionalism and a statewide movement toward journalism education, an idea that had simmered for decades. Public service would be a major component.

In 1908, the argument for professionalism was apparent elsewhere within the journalism world as well. In Britain the National Journalists Union began the magazine the *Journalist* that year. In the United States, one reaction to the sensational news coverage in much of the urban press was the establishment of the *Christian Science Monitor* by Mary Baker Eddy, not as a religious organ of her Christian Science Church, but rather as a source of thoughtful, high-quality journalism. The *Monitor*'s thoughtful news coverage and journalistic principles became widely known, and its circulation grew to more than 120,000 by World War I.[17]

Previous Journalism College Courses

Journalism higher education was not a sudden inspiration. Prior to 1908, a few journalism classes had been taught in English departments around

16. Ibid., 650, 657, 678–79.
17. Maurine H. Beasley, "The Emergence of Modern Media, 1900–1945," in William David Sloan, ed., *The Media in America: A History*, 6th ed. (Northport, Ala.: Vision Press, 2005), 290.

the country. Right after the Civil War, Washington College (later, Washington and Lee) added technical training in journalism to its curriculum in 1869 because President Robert E. Lee sought to train southern youth in journalism as one way to confront the postwar problems facing the South. He proposed offering university courses in printing and journalism, hoping it would lead to improved regional newspapers. Yet, without broader support and with Lee's death in 1870, the idea did not last beyond 1878. It was not until 1925 that Washington and Lee appointed a professor of journalism and established a laboratory for a program that still exists today.[18]

Nineteenth-century universities began offering singular journalism courses. In 1879, the University of Missouri English Department began a credit course with lectures on the history of journalism and explanations of newspaper practice and writing. So, too, did Cornell in 1888, Pennsylvania since 1893, and Kansas since 1903.[19] Yet, at the same time, journalism leaders in different state press associations pushed for more than singular courses. The Missouri Press Association went on record calling for a "chair of journalism" with a bachelor degree, long before the School of Journalism was established in 1908. Prominent Missouri leaders, such as Norman J. Colman of *Colman's Rural World,* and the Missouri legislature actively sought journalism education at the University of Missouri.[20]

Missouri School of Journalism

By 1905, key supporters of a journalism school held significant clout in Missouri politics and higher education: Walter Williams, president of a model weekly, the *Columbia Herald,* became chair of the Executive Board of the University of Missouri Curators, and the state's governor, Lon V. Stephens, was a banker who also owned the *Boonville Advertiser.*[21] By the end of 1906, the university board recommended the establishment of a college or school of journalism with adequate laboratory equipment for practical journalistic training, a course of study of at least four years, entrance requirements equal to any other university academic department, and a multifaceted curriculum with many courses in the College of Arts and Sciences together with some strictly professional courses for a degree or certificate in journalism. After a year-long

18. Lockwood Williams, *Twenty Years of Education,* 5–6.
19. Ronald T. Farrar, *A Creed for My Profession: Walter Williams, Journalist to the World* (Columbia: University of Missouri Press, 1998), 132–33.
20. William H. Taft, "Establishing the School of Journalism," *Missouri Historical Review* 84 (October 1989): 68.
21. Farrar, *A Creed for My Profession,* 98, 115, 121.

abortive search for an inaugural dean, the university's outgoing and incoming presidents convinced Walter Williams to take the job, despite the fact that he had no college education.[22] Williams was well known because of his editorship, state and national journalism leadership, and international promotion of the 1904 St. Louis World's Fair.

Williams relied on the fact that education for journalists had evolved and was not a sudden inspiration. Already, a few trade books were in the field, such as Benjamin Drew's *Hints and Helps for Those Who Write Print or Read* (1872)[23] and some press histories. To add to an earlier American historical study, Isaiah Thomas's *The History of Printing in America, with a Biography of Printers and an Account of Newspapers* (1810), former *New York Herald* editor Frederic Hudson published *Journalism in the United States, 1690–1872* in 1873. Although the Missouri School of Journalism faculty would write their own textbooks, Williams relied on these two histories in his 1908 "History and Principles in Journalism," a required year-long journalism course.[24]

The Missouri School of Journalism would put into place educational standards for journalism professionalism with its curriculum, expectations, and university standing. While other universities had offered singular courses and even a full curriculum, none had established a separate academic unit with a dean or director or chairman, a separate faculty, and specific terms for a degree in journalism until the University of Missouri in 1908.[25] Missouri's example and leadership opened the gate for professionalizing the field through the establishment of separate university units of journalism throughout the country.

Journalism Academic Units

By 1910, three other U.S. departments or schools of journalism were established, at the universities of Wisconsin, New York, and Washington. Within two years they produced twenty-five graduates.[26] By 1920, the uni-

---

22. Ibid., 94–95, 134, 161–62.
23. Ibid., 161–62.
24. Ibid., 161.
25. Lockwood Williams, *Twenty Years of Education*, 5.
26. Ibid., 6. Sara Lockwood Williams quotes the editorial by Lawrence W. Murphy in the *Journalism Bulletin* (American Association of Schools and Departments of Journalism and the American Association of Teachers of Journalism, November 1927) but points out that one or more classes in journalism were at Ohio, Nebraska, Cornell, Michigan, Indiana, Illinois, Kansas, Kansas State, Pennsylvania, North Dakota, Bessie Tift, DePauw, Oklahoma, and Colorado.

versities of Georgia, Indiana, Iowa, Kansas, Minnesota, Nebraska, and Ohio State had added departments and schools, which grew out their existing journalism instruction. Together with the earlier schools, they added hundreds of journalism graduates.[27]

The results of good journalism with standards would serve the need of a democratic society for information and knowledge. Even Pulitzer argued that a popular government depended upon an educated population.[28] With newspapers and magazines, there was a public trust for the kind of information that free people needed to make political, economic, and personal decisions. Formalized education of journalists would make that happen.

Aim for Standards and Ethics

Organizations were also part of the professionalization of journalism. The year 1908 was also an auspicious time for both professional organization and agreed-upon ethics. Publishers such as Dana and Ochs had articulated standards in the late nineteenth century.[29] Press associations held continuing discussions about the expectations for journalists, but 1908 marked the founding of the National Press Club on May 12. Such a national organization, with its building in the capital, was to be not just a club to attend after the D.C. bars closed at midnight, but a place that would "foster the ethical standards of the profession." As an organization, the new National Press Club meant a community for networking as well as learning, albeit limited to white males for almost seventy years. The club soon became known for its continuing education for journalists through its luncheon speeches by major leaders and scholars. The speeches provided club members with background on world events and issues and policies, as well as discussions about a free press and the current status of journalism. By being situated near the important newsmakers in the nation's capital, the National Press Club would also add to professional legitimization. In fact, the NPC's constitution explained, "The club shall provide people who gather and disseminate news a center for the advancement of their professional standards and skills." Following the leadership of the Missouri School of Journalism, the club added as its ethical standards Walter Williams's Journalists' Creed.[30]

27. See Lockwood Williams's table on the number of schools, departments, and professional four-year courses in order of establishment. *Twenty Years of Education,* 8.
28. Pulitzer, "The College of Journalism," 680.
29. Farrar, *A Creed for My Profession,* 201–2.
30. See http://www.npc.press.org/about/history.

As a moral basis for professionalism, Williams had for years enunciated a type of "Journalists' Creed" in speeches and in his "History and Principles" class. By 1914, Williams wrote down those beliefs as a moral code, as the terms for professionalism, and as commandments for journalistic behavior. He began with an affirmation, "I believe in the profession of journalism." He asserted that a public journal was a public trust and that journalists were "trustees for the public," and that anything less than "public service is a betrayal of public trust." Williams's Creed demanded clear thinking, clear statements, accuracy, and fairness as fundamental to good journalism. He directed that the moral obligation of the journalist was to "write only what he holds in his heart to be true." On the societal level, he argued that "the suppression of news, for any consideration other than the welfare of society is indefensible." The Creed also forbade the noxious practices of bribery, language unfit for a gentleman, lies, careless writing, dependence on other institutions, greed, pride, and deceptive advertising practices. Williams's Creed was one of the first codes of ethics, to be followed by those of the American Society of Newspaper Editors (1922) and the Society for Professional Journalists (1926). For decades, Missouri students memorized the Journalists' Creed, and it was adopted by newspapers and international journalists.[31] Today, it continues to be part of the National Press Club Web site.

No Going Back

Thus, 1908 was indeed a turning point in American journalism. After the foundation of professionalism, journalism would never be the same. Accuracy, fairness, honesty, public service, and responsibility were articulated, expected, and enforced. In the *University Missourian*'s first issue, on September 14, 1908, was the announcement of the opening of the new school, with stacked sub-headlines reading "Idea Was Long Contemplated," "Practical Instruction Will Be Given, Leading to a B.S. Degree." The article gave the history behind the school's establishment, the Missouri Press Association connection, and the legislative support for the school. The article highlighted the new faculty, the adjuncts of other university professors, and the journalism curriculum of history and principles of journalism, reporting, correspondence, editorial writing, newspaper jurisprudence, illustration and newspaper publishing, advertising, circulation, magazine and class

31. Frank W. Rucker, *Walter Williams* (Columbia, Mo.: Missourian Publishing Association, 1964), 114; Farrar, *A Creed for My Profession*, 203–4.

journalism, competitive journalism office equipment, and newspaper administration. The courses gave the terms for the credentials of a professional degree.

The article also emphasized that "the University Missourian will give the students actual laboratory work, the training of a real newspaper office." The justification was "the constant call of reporters, editors, special writers, correspondents, publishers and writers, men in all departments of journalism in city and country, in daily, weekly and monthly journals." The goal was to train *for* journalism, "not to make journalists." The four-year study for a Bachelor's Degree in Journalism would include classes in Arts and Sciences, plus the journalism courses. The article pointed out a dual possibility, combining a journalism degree with a Bachelor of Arts degree by staying in school for a fifth year to take more Arts and Sciences classes.[32]

Later, in a 1915 *Journalism Bulletin*, Williams refined the purpose of the school: 1) to provide instruction necessary to a well-rounded education; 2) to train students for newspaper work through professional instruction; 3) to publish a series of bulletins dealing with various phases of newspaper work; 4) to hold an annual Journalism Week; and 5) to serve the press of the state, and the whole citizenship of the state.[33] Such articulation gave the required credentials for professional training.

Thus, the year 1908 was the start of a new era of professionalism within journalism, but it was also in many ways a routine year in the field's gradual movement from the past to the present. In an article on the year 1897, media scholar W. Joseph Campbell argues that year studies offer insight into what may be considered familiar or even mundane.[34] Here, by focusing on journalism in 1908, what it was, did, covered, was impacted by, and justified, we offer insight into the field, the familiar and mundane, through a rather self-consciously flexible topical manner. By focusing on a study of a single year, depth follows. North, author of *Reading 1922*, asks, "What does it mean for a date to work?"[35] The aim of the authors of this book is that the date of 1908 will "work" as we examine various aspects of journalism at that time. At the same time, we argue that the year cannot be separated from the major events of the time, or the prevailing spirit of the era, and the Progressive reform agenda that affected all early twentieth-century institutions, including journalism.

32. "School for Journalism," *Columbia University Missourian*, 14 September 1908, 1.

33. Lockwood Williams, *Twenty Years of Education*, 54.

34. W. Joseph Campbell, "1897: American Journalism's Exceptional Year," *Journalism History* 19, no. 4 (Winter 2004): 3.

35. Michael North, *Reading 1922: A Return to the Scene of the Modern* (New York: Oxford University Press, 1999); North, "Virtual History: The Year as Literary Period," 415.

In *Journalism—1908: Birth of a Profession*, we give, chapter by chapter, much like unpeeling the proverbial onion, an exploration of those different parts of journalism and place them within the country's history and the reform movement toward professionalism. While the authors come from universities across the United States, they all at one time or another had some connection with the Missouri School of Journalism, either as students or faculty. As will be noted, each chapter is introduced by events connected to journalism in 1908 and also to the founding of the Missouri School of Journalism. The effort here is to reach an understanding of the various aspects of journalism existing when the field came of age as a profession. *Journalism—1908: Birth of a Profession* will examine these various factors of journalism in that one trajectory year.

PART I

The Scene in 1908

The year 1908 provided major newsworthy events, giving neophyte and seasoned general-assignment journalists a lot to report. The year had both presidential and congressional elections, muckraking journalism and responses to it by the courts and legislatures, and the movement in transportation from horse to car and, experimentally, to the airplane. Issues surrounding the status of women, immigrants, African Americans, and the laboring classes pushed their way into the nation's consciousness. And more leisure time for sports and the arts led to expanding coverage of these pursuits.

The year 1908 encompassed newsworthy, Industrial Age inventions. Henry Ford introduced his Model T, generally regarded as the first automobile affordable to the average American, which sold at a price of $850. General Electric patented the electric iron and toaster, the Wright brothers kept testing their new airplane, which the *University Missourian* kept reporting, and America gained its first skyscraper, the forty-seven-story Singer Building in New York City.[1] New York City replaced its horsecars with motorbuses.[2] Nobel Prizes were given for producing the first color photographic plate, for work on immunology, and for the breakdown of elements by X-ray.

The new inventions meant changes to the country's way of life, often noted in America's press. With Model T's, roads had to be improved and

1. Laurence Urdang, ed., *The Timetables of American History* (New York: A Touchstone Book, Simon and Schuster, 1981), 278–79.
2. *The New York Public Library American History Reference*, 2nd ed. (New York: Hyperion, 2003), 254.

more streets and highways built. With the rise of airplanes, the military immediately noted the implications for warfare, and by 1907 the U.S. Army established the Aeronautical Division of the Army Signal Corps.[3]

The fallout from the Spanish American War in 1898 meant that in 1908 the U.S. military still occupied Cuba. Wake Island and Hawaii had been annexed, and the Philippine Islands, Puerto Rico, Guam, and American Samoa were held by treaty. Secretary of State Elihu Root reached an agreement with the Japanese to respect each others' Pacific possessions and uphold an Open Door policy in China.[4]

Other 1908 happenings were there for the press to notice. With public concern growing over the uses of the nation's natural resources, President Theodore Roosevelt called the First National Conservation Congress, which began an environmental resource inventory.[5]

As a continuous part of newspaper reportage, political coverage in 1908 was focused on the local, state, and national elections, and also on state and city reform legislation. The first issues of the *Missourian* relied on the United Press for small clips on the presidential candidates, such as "Taft will Dash South," and on the state conventions, such as "State Conventions for New York and Conn. for Governors."[6] Under "Breaking News" the *Missourian* carried one national response to muckraking: President Roosevelt's accusations that Standard Oil "is seeking to control both political parties and shape legislation and judicial opinions."[7]

Another noteworthy development in 1908 was journalism's growing legal issues having to do with privacy and libel. The first year's curriculum of the Missouri School of Journalism included "Newspaper Jurisprudence" as a required course. In October, a *Missourian* feature on John Davison Lawson, dean of the University of Missouri Law School, named him as "one of the most learned men in the world as far as technical law." The article included a photo portrait and emphasized Lawson's popularity on campus, ending with, "Professor Lawson will deliver a course of lectures on the libel laws in the School of Journalism during the second semester."[8]

The next two chapters, "1908: A Very Political Year for the Press," by Betty Houchin Winfield, and "From Whiskey Ads to the Reverent Jellyfish: Media Law in 1908" by Sandy Davidson, will cover the political and legal landscape of 1908.

3. Ibid., 164.
4. Ibid., 89, 283.
5. Ibid, 279–80.
6. "Taft Dashes South," *University Missourian,* 16 September 1908, 1; "State Conventions for NY and Conn. Governors," *University Missourian,* 14 September 1908, 1.
7. "Breaking News," *University Missourian,* 21 September 1908, 1.
8. "Dean of the Law Department, Author and Former Judge," *University Missourian,* 15 October 1908, 2.

CHAPTER 1

1908

A Very Political Year for the Press

Betty Houchin Winfield

The watchdog role of the American press lingered from Jefferson's 1792 dictum, "No government ought to be without its censors, and where the press is free, none ever will."[1] And, it lingered in 1908 with coverage of politics and editorial advocacy and strong connections between the press and the government. This chapter will discuss the press as a type of censor at the turn of the century, show the symbiotic relationship between the new-century journalists and politicians, and the connecting support system.

In the first issue of the *University Missourian* on September 14, 1908, the editors explained that the newspaper's purpose was not just to serve as a laboratory for students to cover the news field but also to give editorial interpretation and comment upon public questions. Such interpretation and comment would most often concern political and governmental news. The newspaper would provide a public service, as "a foe to wrong doing, an aid to education, a force for moral progress, and an exponent of true Americanism."[2] As a "foe

---

1. Thomas Jefferson to George Washington, September 9, 1792, *Writings of Thomas Jefferson*, vol. 9 (Monticello, Va.: Thomas Jefferson Memorial Association, 1905), 406.
2. "The Purpose of This Paper," *University Missourian*, 14 September 1908, 2.

to wrong doing" the press would be a watchdog over government, and its "aid to education" would be to enlighten the public on the events of the day with local, regional, and national political news stories. The "force for moral progress" could include the journalistic purpose of seeking truth. The "exponent for true Americanism" would be journalism playing a powerful role in a democracy.

In fact, the *Missourian*'s first issue carried out several of these public service ideals. The front page highlighted a major local investigation of tainted food and substandard conditions at the Columbia city jail as well as other local stories, such as a lawsuit over the indebtedness of a local playhouse. For the public's political enlightenment, the front page included a short announcement about an alumnus's candidacy that fall for the Second Congressional District. The four-page newspaper also included national political stories, such as a United Press wire story about the response of presidential candidate William Jennings Bryant to President Theodore Roosevelt's designation of his war secretary as his rightful heir. The *University Missourian* would be a democratic force by serving as a public service, so said an editorial, with interpretation and comment.[3]

If all politics is reportedly local, then local, state, and national political news might be part of this first School of Journalism daily newspaper; with the state and national news, a local connection would be highlighted. For example, another September 14 article discussed presidential candidates and their local associations: "The good town of Columbia has a friendly personal interest in all the prominent candidates for high public office." The paper recollected Columbia's relations to the 1908 national political figures, such as when the GOP candidate William H. Taft, a trustee for the University of Cincinnati, came to Columbia to interview biologist Dr. Howard Ayers as a possible Ohio college president and then stayed at the home of philosophy professor Dr. Frank Thilly. So, too, did the same story remind readers that Democratic presidential candidate William Jennings Bryan had previously visited the university area several times. Moreover, this issue of the *Missourian* and others pointed out that Columbia had connections with the candidates for governor, senator, attorney general, and lieutenant governor, either as alumni or as previous campus speakers.[4]

Similar to other newspapers of 1908, the *Missourian* covered local political news daily with reporter-generated stories based upon complaints of corruption, votes taken, or candidacies. National news, particularly, in the fall of 1908, of presidential campaigns, was provided through wire-service

3. Ibid.
4. Ibid., 1.

coverage, usually via the United Press or later the Associated Press; international news came from other wire-service reports about political leaders, such as when Kaiser Wilhelm II of Germany changed travel plans to escape anarchists' plots.

During that same week in September 1908 a rival newspaper, the *Columbia Daily Tribune,* had primarily local stories on its front page: the opening of the various schools in Columbia, as well as the organizational meetings of the Democratic clubs for presidential candidate William Jennings Bryan. The *Tribune* highlighted a "new technology": the club played two records with "the wonderful tone and carry power of Mr. Bryan's matchless voice." Later that week, the *Tribune* noted the organization of a "Negro Taft Club" with an enrollment of seventy-three.[5]

Other *Tribune* front-page stories that week contained a variety of political coverage, ranging from court arraignments and fines (September 14) to street speakers attacking Sunday blue laws (September 16), from county commissioners' decisions over road construction (September 15) to a city council meeting taking up sewer requests and street and sidewalk improvements (September 16). The paper announced the upcoming speech by Virginia Senator John W. Daniels to the county Democrats. Daniels "is of a type of statesman that is fast passing away . . . his personality is most striking and his oratory is brilliant and convincing."[6]

These small-town front-page articles indicate the type of political coverage found then in both large and small dailies. The Columbia papers reported on local and state governmental actions, candidacies, and elections, and did investigations urging reform. The connections between the institutions of journalism and government were mighty strong, indeed, and the partisan press of the early nineteenth century lingered with interpretations. The community newspapers at the turn of the century usually had local newspaper competitors and thus remained largely partisan; they vied for local printing patronage given by the party in power. The financial support from the political party kept the newspaper alive. Too, trends and issues affected the news, regardless of party.

In addition, the century's first decade was the height of the reform era in American politics, including political reform. These new-century years were a time of many political and legislative progressive actions. The American temperament included an idealistic, "can do" spirit, a willingness to dismiss the old and try the new, wrote Mark Sullivan.[7] Such optimism

5. *Columbia Tribune,* 14 September 1908, 1.
6. Ibid., 17 September 1908, 1.
7. Mark Sullivan, *Our Times, The United States 1900–1925, Vol. I, The Turn of the Century* (New York: Charles Scribner's Sons, 1926), 40.

became part of Progressive Era legislation. For example, the Direct Election Primary of 1900 gave people more control of the selection of their officials and greatly reduced the power of the party machines to choose candidates. Other government actions were the enforcement of the Sherman Anti-Trust Act; an establishment of a permanent Census Bureau; the adoption of land conservation with the Reclamation Act, which reversed the previous policy of transferring public lands into private ownership; regulation of child labor; the Pure Food and Drug and the Meat Inspection Acts; a federal railroad rates law; and protective import tariffs. States had begun regulating the life insurance business and limiting women's working hours. Slowly, too, the states also began approving a constitutional amendment to grant Congress the power to levy and collect an income tax to pay for the progressive enforcement and changes.

There were other political events and issues that warranted news coverage. Within twelve years of the new century, settlement in the Western territories increased population enough so that they could be admitted as states, Oklahoma in 1907 and then Arizona and Nevada in 1912. Indian wars had ended, but remained part of the nation's recent recollections. Consistent issues during the first twentieth-century years were prohibition, women's suffrage, and the direct election of senators, all to become constitutional amendments little more than a decade later. These reform issues became part of the news discussions, editorials, and other related coverage.

Little escaped progressive transformation, and journalism would play a role in enlightening the public. Muckrakers in magazines investigated and published stories that called for reform. Newspapers copied the magazines' investigative efforts, even locally. A case in point was the *Missourian*'s front-page article about local citizens asking that the city jail be investigated. The story, without a byline, gave the background context: the jailer was paid by the number of boarders, but with local prohibition, there were fewer arrests for drunkenness than expected. The reporter quoted "Uncle Mike," the jailer, who pointed out that the problem was that the number of daily boarders had dropped by half, thus cutting financial resources for operating the jail. Twenty former prisoners had petitioned the city council to address the declining food conditions of the jail.[8]

Such an article was part of the era's focus on local political reporting. After all, nationally, muckrakers in popular magazines had investigated corruption in cities, including St. Louis. One such magazine, *McClure's*, had only six years earlier published the first installment of Lincoln Steffens's

---

8. "Jailer Tyson Bewails 'Dry' Era More Than Tainted Meat Charge," *University Missourian*, 14 September 1908, 1.

The role of a watchdog press was evident on the front page of the University Missourian's first issue: "Jailer Tyson Bewails 'Dry' Era More Than Tainted Meat Charge." Note also the front-page cartoon, in which "Journalism" has been added to the other University Columns, remainders of the burned University Hall. University Missourian, September 14, 1908, courtesy of the State Historical Society of Missouri Newspaper Collection.

Shame of the Cities with investigations of the "Tweed Days in St. Louis," in which a courageous district attorney tried to prosecute corrupt city officials. As Steffens wrote, "The corruption of St. Louis came from the top."[9] By the time of Steffens's next installment, "The Shame of Minneapolis," three months later, national attention became so great that the January 1903 issue of *McClure's* in which it appeared immediately sold out. In March, Steffens said the previous St. Louis article had not told "half that the St. Louisans know of the condition of the city" and added a second St. Louis installment,

9. Lincoln Steffens, "Tweed Days in St. Louis," *McClure's Magazine* (October 1902), reprinted in *The Shame of the Cities* (New York: Hill and Wang, 1957), 20.

"The Shamelessness of St. Louis." He quotes the district attorney as saying: "Ninety-nine per cent of the people are honest; only one per cent is dishonest. But the one per cent is perniciously active."[10]

Steffens's contribution had a pattern; he synthesized uneven local newspaper stories, added interviews with local people, and gave the topic national coverage. His formula worked, and he continued to "shame" other cities by examining their politics, finding patterns of governmental corruption and police graft, and then showing the connections with state and local government. Such investigations increased the public's awareness of malfeasance and then depended upon local institutions to remove dishonest office holders. Exposure was a moral force; muckrakers expected political institutions to be more responsive to the public will. One aspect of the movement was the successful direct primary. Within the decade, constitutional amendments were passed to increase the direct participation of people in government. Such muckraker investigators alerted the public and pressured lawmakers, and in response, Congress passed many legislative acts. Yet, by 1908, muckraking was beginning to ebb.[11]

For local newspapers, news from the nation's capital came via the wire services or, if the newspaper was large enough, from the paper's own Washington correspondent. One of the first Missouri School of Journalism professors hired, Charles Ross, later became a Washington correspondent for the *St. Louis Post-Dispatch*. Initially, the *Missourian* relied upon the United Press and later the Associated Press for such stories. In those early twentieth-century years, the dynamic presidency of Theodore Roosevelt impacted the focus of capital coverage.

During Roosevelt's tenure in office, the press continued to move toward greater interest in the presidency as opposed to Congress. Even before Roosevelt took office, journalists had been attending White House receptions in multitudes; in fact, when Roosevelt's predecessor William McKinley held a reception for Washington correspondents in March 1897, 120 attended. Yet, Roosevelt, who became president upon McKinley's death in 1901, would make a difference. He was more available to individuals and to the press in general, and he talked more freely than any of his predecessors in memory. With interested correspondents, he held informal sessions on Sundays to take advantage of the fact that Mondays are traditionally slow news days. The country learned what the president was doing, so much so that the

---

10. Steffens, "The Shamelessness of St. Louis," *McClure's Magazine* (March 1902), in *The Shame of the Cities*, 98.

11. James Aucoin, "The Media and Reform, 1900–1917," in William David Sloan, ed., *The Media in America, A History*, 6th ed., 308–9, 113.

news focus shifted from Congress to the White House. Even so, much of what Roosevelt said was not for direct attribution, though his actions and the statements surrounding them were colorful and newsworthy.[12]

Theodore Roosevelt's presidency dramatically changed newsgathering in the capital. By the early years of the new century, this aggressive president with a colorful persona and decisive leadership style was welcomed by reporters interested in the human-interest aspects of political news. Roosevelt made political coverage effortless. He was available, he always had something to say, and he acted forcefully—all important aspects of news. At the same time, correspondents began demanding greater and greater access to the White House itself. By 1904, the West Wing added a room available to the waiting press.[13] A presidential assistant prepared press releases to distribute to journalists, making their newsgathering easier but also controlling the message.

Roosevelt held strict control over the release of information. As the master of the trial balloon, a type of off-the-record statement given to the correspondents, Roosevelt would wait and see how the people, the press, and Congress responded, and then have a prepared denial for the press if the reaction was unfavorable.[14] Journalists who disregarded his attribution rule were assigned to an "Ananias Club" and had their access restricted.[15] While Roosevelt used the press to further his programs, he also attacked disagreeable journalists, especially muckraker David Graham Phillips. In 1906 Phillips published a series on political corruption, "The Treason of the Senate," in the Hearst magazine *Cosmopolitan*. In the first of two speeches, the president denounced Phillips and the magazine as a "Man with the Muck-Rake," referring to Bunyan's *Pilgrim's Progress* and the man who "continued to rake the filth of the floor."[16] For journalists, the term "muckraker" became a badge of honor; in fact, newspapers began competing with the muckraker magazines by escalating their own rhetoric. Their effort, along with the Phillips series, added to the public movement for a direct, popular election of senators.[17]

---

12. Michael Emery and Edwin Emery, *The Press and America: An Interpretive History of the Mass Media*, 7th ed. (Englewood Cliffs, N.J.: Prentice Hall, 1992), 211.

13. F. B. Marbut, *News from the Capital: The Story of Washington Reporting* (Carbondale: Southern Illinois University Press, 1971), 170.

14. Ibid.

15. This is a biblical reference to Ananias, a man struck dead for lying. Acts 5:15.

16. Arthur Weinberg and Lila Weinberg, eds., *The Muckrakers: The Era in Journalism That Moved America to Reform, the Most Significant Magazine Articles of 1902–1912* (New York: Simon and Schuster, 1961), xiii.

17. Donald A. Ritchie, *Press Gallery: Congress and the Washington Correspondents* (Cambridge, Mass.: Harvard University Press, 1991), 190, 192.

In 1908, Roosevelt handpicked his heir, Secretary of War William Howard Taft, as the Republican presidential nominee. Taft campaigned against the well-known Democratic nominee, William Jennings Bryan, who had twice previously run unsuccessfully. Unlike today's huge entourage of Washington correspondents that follow a candidate around, only wire-service reporters and a few big-city daily correspondents traveled with the candidates; obviously, then, presidential campaign speeches were covered extensively at the local level via the wire services.

Taft had been cordial and friendly toward journalists during his days as a cabinet official, but that changed once he became a presidential candidate. He grew reticent and took little notice of the traveling press or the people, unlike President Roosevelt, who, with his bigger-than-life personality, was known to play to the crowd. While Taft mostly rested in Hot Springs, Virginia, during the last campaigning months, William Jennings Bryan raced vigorously throughout the country, addressing huge crowds with as many as thirty speeches a day.[18] These speeches, too, were reported in the newspapers. Yet by November 4, 1908, it was clear that the popular support of Roosevelt encompassed William Howard Taft, who won almost twice as many electoral votes as his opponent. For newspapers, regardless of Taft's poor showing with the press during the campaign, the expectations for his presidency remained high.

In 1908, a presidential election was the big national news. Even small-town dailies put out election extras. For example, in Columbia, the *Missourian* published an extra on November 4, 1908, reporting on the presidential election results and featuring a drawing of Taft, entitled: "Here's Next President of the United States."[19]

After Taft was inaugurated in 1909, his interactions with the Washington correspondents were reticent and difficult; thus, the journalists were disappointed. Washington correspondents had been used to the easy White House access and colorful quotes and human-interest responses of the Roosevelt era. In fact, they had expected that Taft would continue the 4 p.m. meetings he had held when he was Roosevelt's secretary of war, in which

18. Paolo E. Colette, "Election of 1908," in Arthur M. Schlesinger, Jr., ed., *History of American Presidential Elections, 1789–1968*, vol. 3 (New York: Chelsea House Publishers: 1971), 2082–83.

19. "Extra"; "Taft Defeats Bryan by 1,000,000 Majority; Congress Republican"; "Cowherd, Alumnus of M.U., Next Governor; Stone Defeats Folk"; "Electoral Vote as Indicated by Returns"; "Stone Defeats Folk in Boone in a Close Race"; "Perfect Weather Brings Out Voters"; "Winning Candidates in State, in Blackface" [bold type], *University Missourian*, 4 November 1908, 1. See for a discussion, William H. Taft, "Establishing the School of Journalism," *Missouri Historical Review* 84 (October 1989): 80.

he talked freely as a cabinet secretary. Yet the responsibilities of the presidency cooled Taft's former geniality, and he appeared aloof. Although he tried to hold twice-weekly meetings, they were ultimately abandoned as worthless. Taft could not shake Roosevelt's shadow; he was not as quotable or interesting as his predecessor. Thus, he would say little and refuse interviews. Instead, he gave his confidence to the correspondent who represented his brother's newspaper, the *Cincinnati Times-Star.* Unhappy with this exclusivity, the correspondents began turning their attention back to Congress, where members were quick to divulge White House news.[20] Even though Taft had been around journalists all his life because his family owned newspapers, as president he became increasingly uncomfortable, sensitive, and discouraged by the lackluster and negative press coverage that lasted until he left office. By the waning days of his administration, Taft especially incurred the ire of magazine and newspaper publishers when he pushed a raise in periodical postal rates to help alleviate the postal deficit.[21]

Many journalists had a pay system that affected the way and the amount they wrote. Away from the capital, journalists writing local political news more than likely were paid by the space-rate system, which established payments according to the number of column inches printed. While the turn of the century saw many journalists salaried from seventeen to twenty dollars a week at smaller newspapers,[22] the space system persisted, thereby reinforcing the reporters' tendencies toward sensationalism and invasion of private lives, which often led to unethical actions, such as misappropriation of their identities. Thus, journalists overwrote, writing longer stories in the hope of being compensated more. To make sure all the columns were published, they were sensationalized as features.

Scholar Ted Smythe found one such example. A *New York World* reporter and his colleague were introduced to the governor of Mississippi and his aides as "New York lawyers, who would act as guides." After they had had a rousing good time in the city, with only the governor returning to his hotel early that night, the reporters then wrote up a story so long and colorful that it filled a page of the Sunday paper.[23]

20. Ritchie, *Press Gallery,* 204.

21. James E. Pollard, "William Howard Taft," in *The Presidents and the Press* (New York: Octagon Books, 1973, reprint of 1947 edition), 607–12, 614, 618–19.

22. Jean Folkerts and Dwight L. Teeter, Jr., *Voices of the Nation: A History of Mass Media in the United States,* 2nd ed. (New York: Macmillan College Publishing Co., 1994), 273.

23. Ted Smythe, "The Reporter, 1880–1900: Working Conditions and Their Influence on the News," in Jean Folkerts, ed., *Media Voices, an Historical Perspective* (New York: Macmillan Co., 1992), 223–24.

The space system continued into the next decade, as Woodrow Wilson found during his 1912 presidential campaign. While he was resting on the New Jersey shore, reporters were tiring of no news to report. One reporter asked about the huge increase in mail and then, fishing for a story, said, "We're on space down here, Governor. What about all those letters you're getting?" Wilson replied that it was overwhelming and that he felt like a frog that had fallen into a well and "every time he jumped up one foot, he fell back two." The next morning, the candidate was shocked with the sensational headline: "Wilson Feels Like a Frog."[24]

In addition, coverage was affected by the political party connections to the newspapers. From the early national period, partisan newspapers had financial support through patronage printing and gave public support to particular party politicians. Media historian William David Sloan writes that this relationship remained widespread until World War II: "Still, the ideological relationship between parties and papers remained strong, and a majority of newspapers continued to identify with and work for partisan political goals."[25] Historian David Nord found that among the Chicago newspapers, the *Chicago Tribune* devoted about one-fourth of its coverage to local government and political stands on utility matters.[26] Political news was major, especially during a national election.

During a late nineteenth-century national election, the *St. Louis Globe-Democrat* not only carried the convention proceedings on the front page in 1884 but also on the inside pages, which included scenes and incidents from the convention; a biography of James G. Blaine, the nominee; and columns filled with what other newspapers were saying. Moreover, the paper operated a large bulletin board in front of its buildings where the crowds could watch the tabulation of the balloting. Later, the big board was used for election returns, writes James Allee Hart.[27]

Moreover, a large proportion of the party bosses maintained strong connections with newspapers in their locales. For example, only the *New York Times* and *Harper's Weekly* initially exposed "Boss Tweed" in the 1870s in New York City. Party boss William Marcy Tweed and his circle of powerful

24. John Tebbel and Sarah Miles Watts, *The Press and the Presidency, from George Washington to Ronald Reagan* (New York and Oxford: Oxford University Press, 1985), 366.

25. William David Sloan, "Party Press, Close Attachment between Newspapers and Political Parties," in Margaret Blanchard, ed., *History of the Mass Media in the United States* (Chicago: Fitzroy, Dearborn Publishers, 1998), 498.

26. David Paul Nord, *Communities of Journalism: A History of American Newspapers and Their Readers* (Urbana: University of Illinois Press, 2001), 158.

27. James Allee Hart, *A History of the St. Louis Globe-Democrat* (Columbia: University of Missouri Press, 1961), 150.

political operatives bought off the other newspapers through lucrative advertising contracts with the city, which Tweed's cohorts administered. When the patronage stopped, twenty-seven New York newspapers died, noted *Harper's New Monthly Magazine*.[28]

The line separating journalism and politicians blurred throughout the nineteenth century and into the twentieth. Aides to presidents and governors, as well as the politicians themselves, were often experienced journalists. In fact, elected officials often owned newspapers, such as Montana's Senator William Clark, who secretly owned a string of newspapers and used them for control over the region's Democratic Party.[29] Many journalists began at such newspapers, became publishers, and then ran for office. Joseph Pulitzer once served as a Missouri state legislator; William Randolph Hearst ran twice for Congress, twice for New York City mayor, and once for the New York governorship. While Hearst did serve two terms in Congress, he never reached his goal of being president. In fact, his unrelenting criticism of President McKinley backfired after the president was assassinated and Hearst newspapers were boycotted.[30]

Indeed, the division between politicians and journalists was mighty thin. By the end of the nineteenth century, well-known publishers had become recognized for their political stances and involvement. Henry Raymond of the *New York Times*, known for his political interest, served in the New York legislature and U.S. Congress and was elected lieutenant governor of New York. The editor of *Harper's Weekly*, George Harvey, wrote in 1908 of Raymond's strong political interest: "No threat of controversy was too absurd, no source thereof too insignificant, to distract his attention from public affairs and absorb his entire interest." Moreover, Harvey pointed out the contrast to James Gordon Bennett of the *New York Herald*, who "had personal integrity; he never sold any opinion." And, as far as other publishers, Harvey acknowledged that Samuel Bowles of the *Springfield Republican* "was free," without the shackles of personal political ambition. On the other hand, Horace Greeley of the *New York Tribune* aspired to public office from the day his journal became powerful, unsuccessfully ran for president on the Democratic Party ticket in 1872, and died "broken-hearted by

28. James Parton, "Falsehood in the Daily Press," *Harper's New Monthly Magazine* 49 (July 1874): 274, as found in Paulette D. Kilmer, "The Press and Industrial America, 1865–1883," in Sloan, ed., *The Media in America, A History*, 6th ed., 214.

29. Will Irwin, "The American Newspaper, A Study of Journalism and Its Relation to the Public," 12, "The Foe from Within," in "The American Newspaper," first appearing in *Colliers Magazine* (January-July 1911), as found in *The American Newspaper*, comments by Clifford F. Weigle and David G. Clark (Ames: Iowa State University Press, 1969), 18.

30. Folkerts and Teeter, *Voices of the Nation*, 266.

his inability to attain the Presidency, for which hardly a man then living was less fitted," wrote Harvey.[31]

By 1908, editors such as Harvey were calling for journalists to be independent, not only of politics but also of all powerful local interests. In his same critique, Harvey said of a journalist, "His interest is its interest, but his entire obligation is not fulfilled by mere representation of that interest, however accurate it may be." Here, Harvey argues for strict standards, that the journalist must be subservient to none, but must "stand as the guardian of all, the vigilant watchman on the tower ever ready to sound the alarm of danger, from whatever source, to the liberties and the laws of this great union of free individuals."[32]

In general, in its quest for political reform, the journalism of 1908 aggressively sought change. One example was the *Kansas City Star,* whose owner-publisher William Rockhill Nelson pushed for taxes to pay for city beautification, parks, and other improvements. The *Star* campaigned against the street-railway system, city corruption, election fraud, and saloons. Nelson, originally a Democrat, ran an independent newspaper, but supported Theodore Roosevelt.[33]

Local newspapers became part of the business community, though they tackled municipal reform issues of the day and remained party-oriented. Media historian Frank Luther Mott writes that while there were a considerable number of independent weeklies, partisanship was, on the whole, stronger in the weeklies than in the country's dailies.[34] In fact, often prominent in local politics were small-town editors.

One prime example was William Allen White of the *Emporia* (Kansas) *Gazette,* who wrote to his readers his goals in 1895: "The new editor of the Gazette desires to make a clean, honest local paper. He is a Republican and will support Republican nominees first, last, and all the time." White's purpose in covering politics was informing, interpreting, and cajoling readers to support nonpartisan reform and vote for particular candidates. He explained, "We were chatty, colloquial, incisive, impertinent, ribald, and enterprising in our treatment of local events."[35]

---

31. George Harvey, "Journalism, Politics, and the University. Browley Lectures Delivered by George Harvey, at Yale University, on March 12 and 16, 1908," *Harper's Weekly* (April 1908): 1, 2.

32. Ibid., 2, 3.

33. Ibid., 257.

34. Frank Luther Mott, *American Journalism: A History of Newspapers in the United States through 260 Years: 1690 to 1950* (New York: Macmillan Co., 1950), 590.

35. William Allen White, *The Autobiography of William Allen White* (New York: Macmillan Co., 1946), 261, 269.

As for White's own political bias, he recalled: "Editorially, from the very first week the *Gazette* was a conservative Republican newspaper. I had no use for the protective tariff, but I tolerated it because I wished to advocate the Gold Standard."[36] He wrote of rubbing shoulders with many local, state, and national political figures. He recalled seeing the new president, Theodore Roosevelt, informally speak after a dinner party following the McKinley funeral:

> I was most uncomfortable sitting on a chair, my hands on my knees, agape probably as I heard the young President, who was in his very early forties; tell of his plans and his hopes, his dangers and his fears. Theodore Roosevelt was a most candid man, and I was shocked at the casual way in which he considered affairs of state. I could not get used to it. What he said I do not remember, except that he feared Hanna and was frankly out to beat him for the nomination in 1904. That would stick in my memory.[37]

Roosevelt's influence was strong enough for that 1904 nomination and successful bid for the presidency for another term. In 1912, he unsuccessfully ran again on the Progressive "Bull Moose" party ticket. Afterward, he entered the journalistic ranks as a "contributing editor" of the *Kansas City Star* and *Outlook* magazine.

White's *Emporia Gazette* and other local newspapers used political stands as a way to distinguish themselves among their competition. The national campaign committees provided a wealth of partisan propaganda in the form of both boilerplate and readyprint forms that editors printed during elections, albeit in decreasing cooperation in later campaigns, according to Mott.[38]

Party ties were strong, especially both in Missouri and Kansas at the turn of the century. Chad Stebbins found that when Arthur Aull assumed control of the *Lamar* (Missouri) *Democrat* in 1900, ideology was still stalwart and the competition was financial, with a newspaper's income deriving from not just subscriptions but also job printing, legal advertising, and local and national advertising. The most lucrative was legal advertising, which was also the most cutthroat. Most towns at the turn of the century had at least two newspapers, if not more, which often had ties to the competing political factions, so the reward for publishing political news about a controlling party was ample legal advertising, safeguarded by the party's

36. Ibid.
37. Ibid, 339.
38. Mott, *American Journalism*, 590.

elected officials.[39] In Kansas, White became caught up in such a newspaper war right after he purchased the *Emporia Gazette* in 1895. As the newcomer, he was initially left out but later reached an agreement to split the city printing contract equally.[40]

Such rivalry over printing patronage became contentious enough for legal actions. Arthur Aull's exchanges with his two Missouri newspaper rivals became so malicious by 1901 that libel suits were filed with the Barton County prosecuting attorney. The trial attracted the attention of the entire state, wrote biographer Stebbins.[41] The fight was carried out in the rival presses, and vicious personal attacks were made to the point that the county prosecutor filed criminal libel suits against all three Lamar editors for flagrantly disturbing the peace and good order of the community. In his *Boonville Weekly Advertiser* column, former governor Lon Stephens reproached one of the publishers, his former political appointee as a state labor commissioner. Stephens publicly chided himself for "stupidity and credulity" for such an appointment and for the man's suit against a "brother editor" for libel. The public was entertained for months with the back-and-forth columns, with Aull reprinting Stephens's columns in his *Democrat* and his rival publisher Arthur Rozelle responding. Finally, Rozelle sold his newspaper to the prosecutor who had brought the charges. When the trial was held, and Aull ended up being found not guilty, he applauded his attorneys in a hyperbolic column, "No men ever made a braver fight; undismayed and undaunted, they stood boldly for justice of their cause, winning in the end one of the most notable legal victories ever achieved in the whole history of Southwest Missouri."[42]

Political journalism, whether local, muckraking, investigative, campaign coverage, or White House coverage, was part of the early twentieth-century age of realism about how things actually were, but at the same time idealistically about what could be. It was realism versus reform; progressive civic consciousness affected journalism and swept over the nation, down to small towns. Journalists of the first decade of the twentieth century were not only critical of institutions but also, in one degree or another, espoused moral indignation toward others.

In describing the era as an age of reform, historian Richard Hofstadter wrote, "It was in a great and critical measure directed inward. Contempo-

39. Chad Stebbins, *All the News Is Fit to Print: Profile of a Country Editor* (Columbia: University of Missouri Press, 1998), 11.

40. White, *Autobiography*, 269.

41. Stebbins, *All the News Is Fit to Print*, 12.

42. "Verdict of Acquittal," *Lamar Democrat*, 30 January 1902, as found in Stebbins, *All the News Is Fit to Print*, 23.

raries who spoke of the movement as an affair of the conscience were not mistaken."[43] William Allen White wrote that the progressive impulse was innately religious at the time: "in the soul of the people there is a conviction of their past unrighteousness."[44] The political coverage not only highlighted the need for reform but also reflected the impulse of the nation toward change. Political news went from political party loyalty to political education and reform for an informed public. The journalists' efforts were necessary for the legislative changes, and, as Hofstadter writes, "a wholesome catharsis."[45]

The reform impulse spurred journalists to separate themselves more from political parties and keep a neutral stance on the news pages. The newspapers would gradually lessen the publishing of the political parties' boilerplates. And the pay space system would die a lingering death. As the early issues of the *Missourian* indicated, the Missouri School of Journalism laboratory newspaper followed Jefferson's watchdog directive, such as for the Boone County jail conditions, but also in the informative nature of its political coverage. The era's political coverage was the best of times for what could be in the nation's political life, while it was the worst of times of what actually was in local and national government.

43. Richard Hofstadter, *The Age of Reform from Bryant to FDR* (New York: Vintage Books, 1955), 207.
44. White, *Autobiography*, 428.
45. Hofstadter, *The Age of Reform*, 214.

CHAPTER 2

From Whiskey Ads to the Reverend Jellyfish

Media Law in 1908

Sandra Davidson

One week after the first *University Missourian* appeared on September 14, 1908, a front-page story told of a public execution in Kingston, Missouri. "Crowd Cheers as Murderer Hangs," the headline proclaimed. The United Press story said, in part, that several hundred people "clamored" outside the jail as Albert Filley was hanged for murdering his wife, daughter, and brother: "Cheers went up when the death was announced. . . . His neck was unbroken by the drop and he hung for fifteen minutes before dying." The last public execution in the United States would also take place in Missouri, in Galena in 1937, with hundreds of people watching.[1] Reporters had easy access to these executions—they could just join the crowd and witness the state asserting its power.

This chapter will demonstrate how various aspects of mass media law, including privacy and libel, operated in 1908. The law in general controlling

1. United Press, "Crowd Cheers as Murderer Hangs," *University Missourian*, 21 September 1908, 1; Tim O'Neal, "Galena's Gruesome Claim to Fame," *St. Louis Post-Dispatch*, 20 March 2001, E1; Adam C. Smith, "Journalist Argues for Executions on TV," *St. Petersburg Times* (Florida), 9 April 1998, 1A.

journalists and the media at that time was not as complex as it is today. In part, the media themselves were not so complex. For example, in 1908, motion pictures were not yet a major part of the American scene, although the year before Bell and Howell had created the first system for projecting films onto a big screen. Thomas Edison had copyrighted the first motion picture, *The Kinetoscopic Record of a Sneeze,* in 1894.[2]

Broadcasting had not come of age, either. In 1901, Marconi had transmitted the letter "S" in Morse code from Cornwall, England, across the Atlantic Ocean to Newfoundland, Canada. On Christmas Eve in 1906 in Brant Rock, Massachusetts, Reginald Fessenden made the first radio broadcast—of himself reading the Bible and playing "O Holy Night" on the violin. And television had not yet been invented. In 1927 in San Francisco, Philo T. Farnsworth would transmit the first TV image—a horizontal line—to an adjacent room. In 1939, RCA's David Sarnoff would demonstrate TV to the world at the 1939 World's Fair in New York.[3]

And in 1908, the Internet was not even a gleam in anyone's eye.

Obscenity

The written word, however, let people communicate freely in 1908. Well, maybe not so freely. Courts took obscenity seriously, arguably to the point of being ridiculous. Take, for example, the case of poor Mr. Musgrave. A federal judge in Arkansas handed down the *Musgrave* decision on April 1, but it was no April fool's joke. The judge found Musgrave guilty of violating federal law against mailing anything "obscene, lewd, and lascivious." Indeed, Musgrave had mailed a lusty letter—to his wife. The judge rightly pointed out that Congress, in exercising its power to regulate the mail, had declared that mail "shall not be used for any purposes which are detrimental to the morals of the people or against public policy." But did Congress intend to censor zesty missives from passionate spouses? Yes, it did, according to the judge: "The language of the statute is clear and free from ambiguities; it makes no exceptions in favor of any persons. The language used is 'any person who shall knowingly deposit,' etc. There is no exception in

2. Ken Mingis, "The Rhode Island Century 1910–1920," *Providence Journal Bulletin* (Rhode Island), 28 March 1999, 15A; Paul Nicholls, ". . . I'm Ready for My Close-Up," *Information Today* 16, no. 4 (1 April 1999): 52.

3. Adam Sherwin, "Wireless Is Just Not on Our Wavelength in This Digital Age," *The Times* (London), 17 August 2006, 9; "TV Inventor Shorted on Fame," *Northern Territory News* (Australia), 28 August 2006, 17; David Olive, "A High-Tech Trance," *Toronto Star,* 28 August 2002, C01.

favor of husband and wife."[4] And, thus the hard-nosed judge endeavored, apparently, to make the blushing bride blush a little less.

Privacy

Of little concern in 1908 were privacy suits. Privacy law was still in its infancy. Despite the 1890 publication in the *Harvard Law Review* of "The Right to Privacy" by Lewis Brandeis and Samuel Warren,[5] only a few cases charging invasion of privacy had occurred by 1908. The right to privacy decried intrusion into seclusion and publication of lurid, private facts, as well as appropriation of plaintiffs' names and likenesses, which is also called the "right of publicity." It was appropriation cases that first gained some traction.

Among the sparse privacy cases was a 1907 appropriation case, *Peck v. Tribune Co.* The plaintiff's face appeared in an ad hawking a so-called medicine, namely, Duffy's Pure Malt Whiskey. The federal Seventh Circuit Court of Appeals said: "The plaintiff . . . indisputably has suffered a wrong, the gist of which is that by the publication of her picture in connection with a patent medicine advertisement, people who recognize the portrait will be led to think that she has loaned her face, and perhaps her name, in a way that a self respecting person would not have consented to." Had her attorney done a better job, the court in effect said, she would have won. She could have gotten an injunction against further use of her image, or she could have successfully sued the persons who produced the ad. Instead, she was trying to sue the newspaper, the *Tribune,* which merely operated as an innocent distributor of the ad. The court also rejected her claim that she had been libeled, saying the court could not assume it was libelous wrongly to say a person used or recommended use of Duffy's Malt Whiskey.[6]

In a 1905 case, *Pavesich v. New England Life Insurance Co.,* the plaintiff's attorney had done a better job, suing the life insurance company that appropriated his image instead of the newspaper that printed it, the *Atlanta Constitution.* Under the picture of the healthy-looking plaintiff Pavesich appeared these words: "Do it now. The man who did." Beside his picture was that of an unhealthy man with this caption: "Do it while you can. The man who didn't." Pavesich had not purchased New England Life Insur-

---

4. *United States v. Musgrave,* 160 F. 700, 702, 703 (E.D. Arkansas, 1908).
5. Lewis D. Brandeis and Samuel D. Warren, "The Right to Privacy," *Harvard Law Review* (December 1890): 193.
6. 154 F. 330, 332, 333 (7th Cir. 1907).

ance. In upholding Pavesich's right to sue the insurance company, the Supreme Court of Georgia said, in part, in its lengthy opinion: "All will admit that the individual who desires to live a life of seclusion can not be compelled, against his consent, to exhibit his person in any public place, unless such exhibition is demanded by the law of the land. . . . Subject to the limitation above referred to, the body of a person can not be put on exhibition at any time or at any place without his consent. . . . If personal liberty embraces the right of publicity, it no less embraces the correlative right of privacy." In ruling for Pavesich, the Georgia Supreme Court favorably discussed the influential 1890 Brandeis and Warren article, "The Right to Privacy." The court also permitted Pavesich to sue for libel.[7]

Libel and Dean Lawson

In 1908, the greatest threat to free expression came not from appropriation cases, but in the form of libel suits. Many newspapers were sued, and many lost. So great was the threat that the new Missouri School of Journalism had the dean of the School of Law teaching a course on libel law. The October 15 *University Missourian* announced that Professor John Davison Lawson would be presenting the course during the second semester. The January 12, 1909, edition gave a few more details: The class would be for one hour of credit and meet on Tuesday afternoons in the law building. Of more significance, the newspaper announced: "It . . . is the first time such a course has been given in any American University."[8]

The year 1908 alone offered many examples of libel cases against newspapers.

Libel and Public Officials

The U.S. Supreme Court decided an evidentiary matter in the 1908 libel case of *Pickford v. Talbott*. A prosecuting attorney had won an eighty-five-hundred-dollar judgment after a Washington, D.C., journal, the *Sunday Globe*, published an article titled "History of a Crime in which District Attorney Talbott, of Maryland, Enacts a Leading Role." The journal accused the prosecu-

---

7. 122 Ga. 190, 50 S.E. 68, 196, 204, 222; at 196, 50 S.E., 68, 70, 74, 81 (1905).

8. "Dean of the Law Department, Author and Former Judge," *University Missourian*, 15 October 1908, 2; "Dean of Law School, Who Is to Lecture on Libel Law," *University Missourian*, 12 January 1909, 2.

tor of entering a "criminal scheme" to blackmail Pickford and another man. According to the story, the prosecutor had gotten a grand jury indictment against two men for setting fire to a building and collecting insurance money, based on the testimony of one of the prosecutor's alleged co-conspirators. But the prosecutor wanted to drop the "nefarious indictment" if Pickford would pay up. Pickford did, with "marked bills." The whole scheme unraveled, the prosecutor folded the arson case, "and the great conspiracy thus came to an inglorious end," the journal reported. The prosecutor sued for libel, and at trial, the lawyer for defendant Pickford wanted to question the prosecutor about whether he had "investigated the character of the man" whose testimony had led to the indictment. The judge did not allow that line of questioning, ruling it irrelevant. The Supreme Court agreed, saying, "A charge of using an office to procure an indictment as part of a conspiracy to blackmail could not be justified or in any degree excused by the facts offered to be proved."[9] The Court affirmed the prosecutor's win.

The U.S. Supreme Court would not start its revolution of libel law, giving journalists relief from the "chilling effect" of libel cases brought by public officials, until 1964 in the case of *New York Times Co. v. Sullivan*. In *Sullivan*, the Court talks about the inevitability of error and the imperative of "breathing space": ". . . erroneous statement is inevitable in free debate, and . . . it must be protected if the freedoms of expression are to have the 'breathing space' that they need to survive." The Court says that "neither factual error nor defamatory content remove the constitutional shield from criticism of official conduct." The most crucial language in the case comes when the Court concludes: "The constitutional guarantees [of freedom of speech and press] require . . . a federal rule that prohibits a public official from recovering damages for a defamatory falsehood relating to his official conduct unless he proves that the statement was made with 'actual malice'— this is, with knowledge that it was false or with reckless disregard of whether it was false or not." Further, the Court requires that the plaintiff bear the burden of proving not only that statements were false but also that the defendant acted with actual malice.[10]

But in 1908, the Supreme Court of Kansas was making statements similar to those that would come from the U.S. Supreme Court in 1964. In *Coleman v. Maclennan*,[11] the attorney general of Kansas was a candidate for reelection. As attorney general, he was a member of a commission that managed a state school fund. A newspaper, the *Topeka State Journal*, criticized the

9. 211 U.S. 199, 204, 207, 209 (1908).
10. 376 U.S. 254, 271, 273, 279, 285 (1964).
11. 78 Kan. 711; 98 P. 281 (1908).

John Davison Lawson, dean of the law school, taught the first
ever journalism law course. Courtesy of the School of Law
Archives, University of Missouri.

attorney general's official conduct concerning a school-fund transaction.
The attorney general sued the newspaper, and the newspaper argued that
its article was privileged. At the trial, the judge's instructions to the jury
gave the following definition of "privileged":

> And where an article is published and circulated among voters for the sole
> purpose of giving what the defendant believes to be truthful information
> concerning a candidate for public office and for the purpose of enabling

such voters to cast their ballot more intelligently, and the whole thing is done in good faith and without malice, *the article is privileged, although the principal matters contained in the article may be untrue in fact and derogatory to the character of the plaintiff; and in such a case the burden is on the plaintiff to show actual malice in the publication of the article.*[12] (Emphasis added.)

The jury brought back a verdict in favor of the newspaper. The attorney general appealed, and the Supreme Court of Kansas stated the question posed by the case: "What are the limitations upon the right of a newspaper to discuss the official character and conduct of a public official who is a candidate for reelection by popular vote to the office which he holds?" The question is one of balancing, the court concludes: "the balance of public good against private hurt." The court recognizes the need to protect reputations, saying, "Even in these days, when the amassing of wealth absorbs so much of the energy of the race, it may still be said that a good name is rather to be chosen than great riches."[13] But counterbalanced against this need to protect reputations is the public's need to know. The public, in order to fulfill its obligation to cast an informed vote, must know about the candidate's character, qualifications, and performance. And thus a candidate for office subjects himself or herself to public scrutiny. In the court's words:

> Under a form of government like our own there must be freedom to canvass in good faith the worth of character and qualifications of candidates for office, whether elective or appointive, and by becoming a candidate, or allowing himself to be the candidate of others, a man tenders as an issue to be tried out publicly before the people or the appointing power his honesty, integrity, and fitness for the office to be filled.[14]

The balance thus tips in favor of a free press—a press that is privileged to discuss a candidate's qualifications:

> The importance to the state and to society of such discussions is so vast, and the advantages derived are so great, that they more than counterbalance the inconvenience of private persons whose conduct may be involved, and occasional injury to the reputations of individuals great. The public benefit from publicity is so great, and the chance of injury to private character so small, that such discussion must be privileged.[15]

12. 78 Kan. at 712–13; 98 P., 281–82.
13. 78 Kan. 715, 98 P., 283; at 731, 98 P., 288; at 721, 98 P., 284–85.
14. 78 Kan. 723, 98 P., 285.
15. 78 Kan. 724, 98 P., 286.

The court's ringing endorsement of the necessity of a free press in a demo-cratic society sent a powerful message to political candidates and newspaper editors alike. Kansas politicians must accept the fact that newspapers have an important job to do, and Kansas courts will not throttle newspapers that are doing their job. The Kansas courts will not even stifle newspapers that pub-lish falsehoods that defame political candidates—so long as the news-papers act in good faith. The court fairly well summed up its position by quoting from one of its earlier opinions, *State v. Balch* (1884), a criminal libel case: "Generally, we think a person may in good faith publish whatever he may honestly believe to be true, and essential to the protection of his own interests or the interests of the person or persons to whom he makes the publication, without committing any public offense, although what he publishes may in fact not be true and may be injurious to the character of others."[16] And so, in Kansas in 1908, newspapers covering elections were faring well in libel wars.

Other newspapers besides the *Topeka State Journal* also won libel suits in 1908, on a variety of grounds.

Libel and Wine, "Larceny," Murder, and Betting on Horses

In Arkansas, the *Morrillton Democrat* won a libel suit brought by a man who grew grapes and sold "pure grape wine." The winemaker was incensed by an article the newspaper ran after a man had been murdered by drowning in the nearby Arkansas River. The article said, "The killing near the river Saturday evening was the result of the wine joints that are now in operation here." The article also questioned the purity of the wine being sold at "wine saloons," saying that "it is adulterated and much of it possibly never saw a grape." The winemaker lost his five-thousand-dollar libel suit on the simple grounds that the article did not identify him.[17] Iden-tification was a requirement in any libel suit because a person who is not identified cannot have his or her reputation damaged.

Yet, identification was not nearly enough. In Ashland County, Ohio, the News Printing Company won a suit brought by a man who was part of a trio identified in a story that talked about "unparalleled larceny" of tax-payers' money. This case involved rhetorical hyperbole, although the Ohio

---

16. 78 Kan. 728–29, 98 P., 287 (quoting *State v. Balch*, 31 Kan. 465, 472, 2 P. 609, 614 [1884]).

17. *Comes v. Cruce*, 85 Ark. 79; 107 S.W. 185 (1908).

court did not employ that phrase. Language such as "larceny" that cannot be taken in its literal sense but is used in a loose, figurative, hyperbolic manner does not amount to libel. As the court said:

> ... the publication did not charge the plaintiff with larceny. It charged, in substance, that the plaintiff and his associates retained out of the $35,000 collected for the county treasurer all of said sum, less $18,421. This statement was admittedly true, but the publication speaks of it as a larceny. This, plaintiff insists, it was not. But whatever it was, the exact facts were stated in this publication, and it could not have been understood by anyone who heard it as being other than the published fact showed it to be. It was not a larceny, nor did the characterization of it as such change its character in any wise.[18]

The losing plaintiff walked away empty-handed, except for his share of the $18,421 in taxpayers' money.

A juror in Louisiana also ultimately walked away empty-handed after winning a ten-thousand-dollar libel judgment against the *Daily Picayune*. The newspaper had published a story that quoted Bud Caron and Hines Hughes, two convicted murderers who were sentenced to life imprisonment, as saying that their jury was "jobbed."[19] The Supreme Court of Louisiana found no libel and reversed the trial court's decision. The newspaper did not espouse what the convicted murderers had said. To the contrary, the newspaper painted a negative picture of the murderers, not the jurors. The Supreme Court of Louisiana pointed to the headline above the article: "Caron and Hughes Are Sore Over the Verdict in Their Case and Abuse the Jury Instead of Expressing Regret Over the Kentwood Killing." Then the court concluded that the headline made apparent that instead of agreeing with the convicted murderers, the newspaper was referring to the bribed-jury claims as "remarks discredited by the situation of the parties who made them." So, the court said, instead of injuring the jury's reputation, the article condemned the murderers "for indulging in the abuse customarily heaped by convicted men upon . . . juries, instead of expressing regret for the crime of which they had just been convicted."[20]

The Supreme Court of Louisiana also ruled in favor of a newspaper's right to publish reports of an administrative hearing. The case began on a

---

18. *Mengert v. The News Printing Co.*, 1908 Ohio Misc. LEXIS 295; 16 Ohio C.C. (n.s.) 34, 37–38.
19. *Tate v. Nicholson Pub. Co.*, 122 La. 472, 473; 47 So. 774 (1908).
20. 122 La. 480–81; 47 So. 776–77.

Parish of Orleans racetrack when a bettor got the boot for allegedly con-
spiring to cheat. Racetrack judges heard testimony and then ruled the plaintiff off the track. Four newspapers published the accusations and the
racetrack judges' ruling. The plaintiff sought twenty-five thousand dollars
from a host of defendants. On the question of whether the newspapers
could be held liable, the Supreme Court of Louisiana opined that "fraudulent racing" is of concern to the public and that racetrack proprietors are
"duty bound to keep the public posted" about actions taken in cases in
order to protect both the proprietors and their patrons. The court said flatly
that "the public were as much entitled to be informed of what was going on
as the plaintiff himself, or the proprietors of the race track." Further, the
court declared, "We see no reason, therefore, why the rule applied to the
proceedings of a town council should not be applied to the proceedings of
a court of racing judges."[21] In short, the bettor lost.

Libel and Judicial and Quasi-Judicial Proceedings

In 1908, invoking the privilege to inform the public had its limits, however, even when newspapers were covering court proceedings. A Pennsylvania case pitted "Good" against "Grit." The *Pennsylvania Grit* reported
about a case involving charges that two brothers named Good had robbed
their father's estate and then attempted to "cover their tracks by forgeries
and frauds of various kinds." The charges came in the form of "exceptions"
to the account of the estate. The Superior Court of Pennsylvania said, "The
question arises whether the article . . . was a fair statement of what had been
charged in the exceptions."[22] Had the newspaper published the exceptions
in full, then there would have been no problem. But the court explained:

> When, however, a publisher of a newspaper undertakes to give an abstract
> of such exceptions, instead of pursuing the more prudent course of pub-
> lishing the exceptions themselves and leaving the public to judge of their
> import, he is bound to publish an accurate, truthful and impartial abstract.
> As the learned trial judge well said, he is bound to be truthful and fair in
> his statements as to what is or has been going on in court; he is privileged
> only to tell the truth; he is not privileged to exaggerate. If he uses words dif-
> ferent from those used in the legal document to describe the allegations

21. *Rabb v. Trevelyan*, 122 La. 174, 175, 186, 187–88; 47 So. 455, 459, 460.
22. *Good v. Grit Pub. Co.*, 36 Pa. Super. 238, 238, 256; 1908 Pa. Super. LEXIS 145 *1-*4,
*30.

against the accountant, he must take care that the words he selects, the form in which they are placed and the comments that he makes do not convey to the minds of ordinary readers an impression that the alleged wrongdoings of the accountant are more flagitious than the exceptions themselves show them to be. Failing in this, he forfeits his privilege, and is held liable to action, as he would be if the charges he represents as having been made by the exceptant were made by himself.[23]

In short, failure to produce an "accurate, truthful and impartial" report results in the loss of privilege. After the defendant won at trial, the Superior Court of Pennsylvania granted the plaintiff a new trial to determine if the newspaper had indeed lost its privilege.

The most positive language for newspapers in *Good* arguably came from words the original trial judge spoke to the jury. He spoke of the public's "right to know" what goes on in courtrooms and then said: "Newspapers are the recognized means of informing the general public of the transactions of courts of justice in any community, and they have, as such, a right to publish any and all things transacted before the court and such publication is what the law terms privileged." Newspapers are privileged to report what happens in courts "no difference whom it may hurt," he said. But he immediately added that newspapers are only privileged to tell the truth. If they do not and someone is harmed, then the newspaper is liable for the misinformation.[24]

The Supreme Court of Missouri in 1908 twice hammered newspapers for not publishing a fair article about an extradition proceeding, a quasi-judicial proceeding. In one of the cases, the Globe Printing Company lost its privilege as well as two thousand dollars in actual damages and ten thousand dollars in punitive damages.[25] The case started in Missouri's capital city, Jefferson City, when Cole County Prosecuting Attorney Brown attempted to get William Ziegler extradited from New York. Brown's attempt failed, and the *St. Louis Globe-Democrat,* with a circulation of more than one hundred thousand, distributed a story about the situation under the following headlines on February 3, 1908: "ZIEGLER'S LAWYER CALLS BROWN LIAR. Accuses Him of Perjury. Declares if Missourian Visits New York He Will Be Arrested. Insists Cole County Prosecutor Made Affidavit He Knew Was False."

The story gives an account of the extradition fight, which demonstrates how Ziegler's attorney apparently decided that the best defense was a good offense:

23. 36 Pa. Super 252; 1908 Pa. Super LEXIS 145 *26.
24. 36 Pa. Super 238; 1908 Pa. Super LEXIS 145 *2.
25. *Brown v. Globe Printing Co.,* 213 Mo. 611, 621; 112 S.W. 462, 463 (1908).

New York, February 2.—Gov. Odell's decision, made public yesterday, denying the request of Gov. Dockery of Missouri to surrender William Ziegler of New York to the Missouri authorities for extradition, has for the present at least brought to a definite and unsuccessful end the attempts to get the New York capitalist into the State of Missouri to stand trial on the charge of perjury. . . .

In fighting the application for extradition, Mr. Ziegler employed the most eminent available counsel. . . . The brief of John M. Bowers, which was followed very closely by Attorney-General Cuneen in the opinion upon which the Governor based his decision, is an interesting one. Charges Brown With Perjury . . . In his brief, Mr. Bowers openly charges [Cole County Prosecuting Attorney] Brown with deliberate and criminal perjury, and Mr. Bowers does not hesitate to say that upon his advent into this State, Brown will be instantly arrested and his indictment for perjury sought for.[26]

The *Globe-Democrat*'s story then lists what, "among other things," the brief charged, including statements that the Cole County prosecuting attorney "made an affidavit upon which was put in motion the machinery of the Constitution under which Mr. Ziegler's extradition was sought" and that the affidavit was "false as to every allegation as to Ziegler's flight." Furthermore, Ziegler had sent the governor of Missouri a "respectful message" requesting that the prosecuting attorney appear before the governor of New York to repeat the affidavit's allegation, but that the prosecuting attorney "declined to come." The brief also said that "at page 76 of the stenographer's minutes of the proceedings before your Excellency [the governor of New York], it was openly conceded that he had no knowledge of the matters he swore in this regard." Who did the conceding? The brief did not say.

The story continues, driving home the brief's major point: "Makes Open Charges . . . We openly charged before your Excellency upon the hearing that an official of a state had committed perjury pure and simple upon which he instituted a procedure of this nature, committed a crime of the highest grade." The main issue presented by this case, according to the Supreme Court of Missouri, was whether the *Globe-Democrat*'s publication was privileged. The court acknowledged that if the newspaper's account of a quasi-judicial proceeding was a "full, fair and impartial report," then it was privileged. Likewise, an "abridged and condensed" report can remain privileged if it is also "fair and impartial." And headlines may be privileged but only "if they are a fair index of a truthful report." The court ruled against

26. 213 Mo. 622–23; 112 S.W. 464.

the newspaper, saying flatly, "In the case at bar, the defendant did not publish the entire brief of Mr. Bowers and his associates, but only such portions thereof as seemed to reflect upon the character and integrity of the plaintiff and to impute to him crime or moral turpitude. This was not privileged."[27]

In the second case spawned by the Ziegler extradition proceeding, the Cole County prosecutor sued the *St. Louis Republic,* another newspaper with circulation of more than one hundred thousand. Like in the case against the *Globe-Democrat,* the story appeared on February 3, 1908. The verdict, again, was against the newspaper, with actual damages of five thousand dollars and punitive damages of another five thousand.[28] The *St. Louis Republic,* like the *Globe-Democrat,* argued privilege. The Supreme Court of Missouri echoed its decision in the *Globe-Democrat* case:

> . . . the publication upon which this action is based is not and does not purport to be a fair and accurate report of the proceedings before the Governor of New York for the extradition of Ziegler. It is a reproduction of a part only of Mr. Bowers' brief, filed over a month after that hearing had ended, with comments by the defendant and sensational headlines of its own. It is not even a report of all of Mr. Bowers' brief but of an extract only which reflects upon plaintiff's character and integrity.[29]

Basically, the Supreme Court of Missouri could just have said "ditto" in the second libel suit brought by the Cole County prosecuting attorney. The court referred to the *Globe-Democrat* action as the "companion case" to the *St. Louis Republic* case and referred to the first case multiple times in its second opinion.[30]

In yet another 1908 case where a newspaper claiming a privilege lost, the *San Antonio Light* claimed in a story that a customs official had confiscated goods smuggled by Dora Lewy. She sued and won twenty-five hundred dollars.[31] The story, under headlines that included "SMUGGLED GOODS ARE SEIZED BY THE CUSTOMS OFFICERS" and "Several Official Heads May Fall," arguably read like a novella, with the customs inspector hot on the trail of hand-painted china and glassware, lace, and Oriental and Turkish rugs:

> What has proved the largest seizure of smuggled goods that has occurred in San Antonio in fifteen years, involving the identity of one of the best-

27. 213 Mo. 624, 634, 640, 644; 112 S.W. 464, 467, 469, 471.

28. *Brown v. Publishers George Knapp and Co.,* 123 Mo. 655, 664, 671; 112 S.W. 474, 475, 477 (1908).

29. 123 Mo. 687; 112 S.W. 482.

30. 123 Mo. 688; 112 S.W. 482.

31. *San Antonio Light Pub. Co. v. Lewy,* 52 Tex. Civ. App. 22, 26; 113 S.W. 574, 577 (1908).

known ladies of this city, came to light yesterday when Customs Inspec‐
tor C. M. Ferguson disclosed $1,870 worth of miscellaneous bric-a-brac, in
his office, confiscated from Mrs. Dora C. Lewy, widow of the late Augus‐
tus Lewy. It is claimed that the seized merchandise was smuggled through
the port of Galveston, either with or without the knowledge of the Galve‐
ston authorities.

As a result of the disclosure the Galveston customs service is greatly
agitated, and several official heads will probably fall. . . .

Several years ago Customs Inspector C. M. Ferguson suspected that
smuggled goods of the nature just seized were brought into this city and
sold to local merchants and private purchasers. . . .

Early in January of the current year Mr. Ferguson read an advertise‐
ment in a local paper saying that fine hand-painted china was for sale by
a certain party in the city, who also had established a studio where repro‐
ductions of the work would be taught. Believing he knew who the lady
was who had thus inserted the advertisement, and not wishing to excite
undue suspicion, Mr. Ferguson called in the assistance of Special Treasury
Agent H. C. Smith. . . .

It happened that Special Agent Smith had his wife with him while in the
city, and, by prearrangement, she accompanied her husband to the studio
the following day to make a thorough examination of the imported mer‐
chandise.

Representing themselves as tourists from the north, the pair presented
themselves at the studio.

"This display is perfectly exquisite," exclaimed Mrs. Smith to the owner
of the property. . . . "You have these plates marked at from $25 to $35
apiece. . . . . If I had them back home I could easily get from $75 to $100
apiece for them. Those rugs which you price to me at $150 I could sell for
$300 in my native city."

"Suppose we buy the entire lot, take them back home and sell them
again," interposed Mr. Smith to his wife.

"How perfectly lovely" cried Mrs. Smith, enraptured.[32]

The story continued, including the statement that "Two and two were put
together, and, apparently, the result was four." Apparently, the Court of
Civil Appeals of Texas could add, too. The newspaper argued that it had
published the article in "good faith," believing it to be a "true, fair and
impartial account" of official proceedings of customs officials and "reason‐
able and fair comments upon a matter of public concern." The court flatly

32. 52 Tex. Civ. App. 27–28; 113 S.W. 577–78.

nents of truth, fairness, and impartiality and concluded
"a libel."[33]

me Judicial Court of Massachusetts, Suffolks, made a
ivilege for a newspaper published by the Post Publish-
ory concerned fraud in a corporation whose financial
affairs were, in the newspaper's words, "in a badly tangled condition."
Insofar as the articles related only to court proceedings, the articles were
privileged, the court said. But the court pointed out that there was "something more" in those articles—a report of a stockholders meeting.[34]

> The meeting was simply that of a private corporation invested with no
> privileges and owing no special duties to the public. It was an ordinary
> business meeting.
>   Whether any member was in fraudulent possession of stock, or had
> mismanaged the affairs of the corporation, or whether the plaintiffs were
> unfit to continue as officers, or the corporation had been made bankrupt,
> were matters with which the public were in no way concerned. The meet-
> ing was for the stockholders alone. Only they or their duly constituted
> agents were entitled to be present. The meeting was neither public nor for
> a public purpose.[35]

So privilege existed concerning court proceedings, but no privilege
existed concerning coverage of the private corporation's meeting. Clearly
this could cause a difficulty in sorting out the damages, but the court concluded: "The difficulty of separating the damages gives no immunity to the
defendants."[36]

Libel and "the Rev. Jellyfish" and a "Queen"

In Washington, D.C., a minister who was awarded one dollar in nominal
damages got a new trial and a second bite at the proverbial apple in 1908.[37]
His first attempt at winning damages had been compromised by the trial
judge permitting the jury to consider whether a privilege of "fair comment
on matters of public concern" applied.

---

33. 52 Tex. Civ. App. 26, 30; 113 S.W. 577, 579.
34. *Kimball v. Post Pub. Co.*, 199 Mass. 248, 251; 85 N.E. 103, 104 (1908).
35. 199 Mass. 253; 85 N.E. 105.
36. 199 Mass. 254; 85 N.E. 105.
37. *Russell v. Washington Post Co.*, 31 App. D.C. 277 (1908).

The minister was embroiled in a bitter, colorful divorce trial. The newspaper printed a story about it under the headline of "The Rev. Jellyfish Russell":

> . . . When the Rev. Charles T. Russell made the opening statement in his own defense, he riveted the attention of the entire reading public. "I am like a jellyfish," said the reverend culprit; "I float all around and I touch this one and that one, and, if they respond, I embrace them."
>
> Who will deny that this alluring overture opens many vistas to the disciples of physical research? The Rev. Russell is the founder of a new faith.
>
> He calls his congregation the "Russellites." He doesn't believe there is any hell except right here on earth, and this doctrine he preaches to a very zealous and devoted congregation.
>
> We gather, too, that he monopolizes the jellyfish business in his capacity as head of the church. He floats around among the faithful, touching them here and there. Those who respond he promptly embraces. When they don't respond, that is, presumably, his idea of hell.
>
> . . . The particular case which precipitated the divorce suit appears not to have been at all hellish. In that instance the jellyfish touched one Rose Ball, who must have "responded" very promptly, since Mrs. Marie Frances Russell, the plaintiff in the divorce suit, was an eyewitness to the embrace which followed.
>
> . . . Of course, it's a pity that the jellyfish's wife came on the scene just at the critical moment. Those accidents will occur, however, even in the most carefully arranged schemes of exaltation. The great truth remains that the Rev. Jellyfish Russell has opened up a mighty attractive pathway to the higher life, and that, barring unforeseen catastrophes, he will get there with enviable frequency.[38]

In rejecting the argument that this story was protected by the privilege of "fair comment on matters of public concern," the Court of Appeals for the District of Columbia noted the newspaper did not state its sources but instead stated on its own that the minister engaged in "scandalous and grossly improper conduct." Further, according to the court, the article "is not confined to comment and criticism on his acts as a public man or his public life, but . . . falsely asserts that he has committed certain acts of an immoral nature in his private life." There was "no question of privilege to be submitted to the jury," the court concluded, and so it granted the "Rev. Jellyfish" a second attempt to sting the newspaper.[39]

38. 31 App. D.C. 278.
39. 31 App. D.C. 282, 286.

In a 1908 libel case in California, it was a female reporter's honor that was at issue. Apparently giving one of its own no slack, a Los Angeles newspaper portrayed her as the consort of a Chinese prizefighter named Ah Wing.[40] Mabel Clare Ervin, nicknamed "Queen Mab," took exception to the story headlined "Too Early for the Queen":

> Mab Ervin, "Queen Mab," has a great admirer in one, Ah Wing, champion Chinese pugilist of the world. Ah Wing arrived in Los Angeles Monday morning from his home in Sacramento, to put the finishing touches to his condition for his battle Friday night with Eddie Menny at the pavilion of the Pacific Athletic Club.
>
> Before he left home, he wired "Queen Mab," asking her to meet him at the depot at 7 a.m., but the hour was too early for her majesty and Ah Wing came into town with nobody to welcome him. . . .
>
> . . . He forgot that one of the prerogatives of royalty is to do as you please, and Ah Wing was sad as he came into The Record office to find Queen Mab.
>
> There are some things which are better left unsaid, so it is best to pass over the meeting between the queen and her humble subject. Some things are too sacred for mere words.[41]

The newspaper's only defense was that the facts were insufficient to constitute libel. The Supreme Court of California disagreed. This story, according to the court, could be read as "implying" that Mab was "a member of the underworld, familiar with the Chinese prize-fighter, and upon such terms of intimacy with him, that when they met things took place between them that were not proper for publication, implying that they were of an indecent or improper character." Understood in that way, the article was unquestionably libelous, the court concluded, and it affirmed the judgment for the "Queen."[42]

Criminal Libel

Damage awards for civil suits were not the only concern for newspapers in 1908. Occasionally, criminal libel reared its head. In Lonaconing, Maryland, the *Lonaconing Star* published an anonymous letter signed "Retired

---

40. *Ervin v. Record Pub. Co.*, 154 Cal. 79; 97 P. 21 (1908).
41. 154 Cal. 80; 97 P. 21–22.
42. 154 Cal. 81; 97 P. 22.

Miner" that criticized the city treasurer, calling him, among other things, "a blundering, stuttering ninny" with an "empty, rickety head." The letter also said the city treasurer's "avocation politically has been constantly that of a slimy, wriggling, biting, treacherous snake in the grass." The Court of Appeals of Maryland affirmed a fifteen-day jail sentence and a fine for the newspaper's publisher.[43]

In another case in Ada County, Idaho, the editor of the *Evening Capital News* was charged with criminal libel because the newspaper said this about the governor of Idaho, Frank Gooding: "Gooding and graft have become so thoroughly known as synonymous terms that the rank and file will have no more of it." The editor argued that the charge was insufficient because it did not allege publication of any libelous language. The trial court agreed and dismissed the case. But the Supreme Court of Idaho decided otherwise and remanded the case for trial.[44]

Dean Lawson: Practicing What He Preached

Libel cases such as those covered in this chapter were ready fodder for the first-time class in libel law offered to students of the fledgling School of Journalism in 1909 by Dean John Lawson. Perhaps Dean Lawson was wise to emphasize libel law, to protect himself as well as journalism students. The importance of being able to freely criticize public officials was something Dean Lawson practiced as well as preached, as illustrated in a front-page article of the *University Missourian* on February 8, 1909. Under the headline of "The Silly Rot in Court Decisions," the story quoted Dean Lawson's presentation to the Kansas City Bar two days before. He said: "I have found some of the decisions of the Missouri Supreme Court to be silly stuff and some cases are reversed for reasons that appear childish."[45] It was fair comment and thus privileged, it was gutsy, and arguably it was just what the new School of Journalism needed from its new law professor.

43. *Robinson v. Maryland*, 108 Md. 644, 648; 71 A. 433, 355 (1908).
44. *State v. Sheridan*, 14 Idaho 222, 226, 228, 237; 93 P. 656, 656–57, 661 (1908).
45. "The Silly Rot in Court Decisions," *University Missourian*, 8 February 1909, 1.

PART II

Modernization

Journalism Comes of Age

Newspapers in 1908 were primarily country newspapers. Their editors and publishers belonged to state press associations. The Missouri Press Association, similar to other state press associations, had a membership primarily made up of editors and publishers of small community weeklies run as family businesses with wives, children, and relatives involved. Their newspapers were part of the nation's rural society, at a time when more than 50 percent of the population was still living in the countryside. The *Missourian* reprinted one editorial that satirically told of a successful country editor. "A country editor to be a success must understand everything about a printing office, from making fires to washing rollers to telling lies about candidates and society leaders." With a university education, the *Dunkin County Democrat* cautioned the new journalism school, "Of course, we all should use better English and write better rounded sentences, but even this will not take the place of experience and this can come alone, from contact with the people the editor, or reporter has to please or influence."[1] That hands-on experience would be part of the first journalism school.

In September 1908, the Missouri Press Association passed a resolution in support of the new school, as did the Editorial Association of the Eighth Congressional District. As a regular column, the new *University Missourian* quoted congratulations from the Board of Curators, "for great stride in progress it made in establishing a practical forum, a state school

1. "About Journalism," *University Missourian,* 23 September 1908, 1.

of journalism."[2] Press associations originally were founded to discuss common goals and garner cheaper newsprint after the Civil War, but they also thought of their public responsibilities and place in a democracy. At their annual meetings, they would have speakers to review their histories, from the founding of the American colonies' first newspaper in 1690 to the plight of John Peter Zenger, the role of the press during the Revolutionary War, the hated Alien and Sedition Acts of 1798, the rise of the penny press, and the emergence of the then modern press. The press association members also were reminded about the role of the American press in a democracy: it was to be a free press, providing an expected public service for a viable democracy.

An expectation for greater journalism principles was found in the reaction to the new school. The congratulatory letters published in the *Missourian* reflected high hopes for the impact of a university education in journalism. The *New York Sun* wrote that the new School of Journalism would "start your young men with an understanding . . . [of the] dignity of the profession and the requirements of personal self-respect as to tips or blackmail."[3] Later in October, the *Missourian* reiterated the school's high standards and reprinted Colonel George Harvey's Yale University Bromley lecture about ethics. Harvey, the editor of *Harper's Magazine,* attested that the "journalist must have a Soul above the money that is in his newspaper to win honor in his profession."[4] The following three chapters explore the various aspects within the business of community journalism, and "the soul" or ethical standards of the period.

The authors of the following three chapters describe the historical origins and place of the nation's country or community newspapers, show the connections between state press associations and journalism education, and explain the editors' and publishers' philosophical tenets in 1908: William Howard Taft, "Community Journalism: A Continuous Objective"; Stephen Banning, "Press Clubs Champion Journalism Education"; and Hans Ibold and Lee Wilkins, "Philosophy at Work: Ideas Make a Difference."

2. "About Schools of Journalism," *University Missourian,* 16 September 1908, 2.
3. "About School of Journalism," *University Missourian,* 21 September 1908, 2.
4. "Journalist Stands Nearest Universal Heart, William Dean Howells Writes," *University Missourian,* 6 October 1908, 2.

CHAPTER 3

Community Journalism

A Continuous Objective

William Howard Taft

A merican editors and publishers of smaller newspapers in 1908 had a lot in common with their journalism ancestors as to news topics and their community emphases. This chapter will show how previous American news definitions, news content, and conditions were both alike and different from those in community newspapers in 1908; it will then focus on what was being discussed and taught as community journalism in the early twentieth century when journalism education began.

The traditions for local news had gone on since the founding of the country. The first American journalists set the initial standards for printing community news, much like their London predecessors. Benjamin Harris, who had been a London printer, started *Publick Occurrences: Both Forreign and Domestick* in 1690 in Boston before authorities stopped it after one issue. John Campbell followed him with the *Boston News-Letter* in 1704, printed with permission. Then, William Brooker began a livelier independent *Boston Gazette* in 1719; followed by James Franklin, with his critical *New-England Courant* in 1721. They, among many others, all gave the local news in the midst of foreign coverage to their readers.

Historically, local citizens also depended on official proclamations, broadsides, word-of-mouth, and other sources for news pertaining to their daily lives. During the American colonial era, a few of the more influential and economically sufficient persons received newspapers from "home," which in this instance, was England. People no doubt wanted to learn what was occurring in their previous homeland; to them, "local" was their familiar home country. But, as time went on, it was community news that connected the New England residents.

From the beginning of American newspapers in Boston, the editors produced community-oriented newspapers. Content-wise and goal-wise, editors of the eighteenth century and editors of the early twentieth century shared similar interests and a common objective: to provide information that was interesting and useful for their readers. Although the local content was similar on colonial government, dangers from the nearby Indians, accidents, and fires, the editors' news definitions and presentations differed considerably.

Their news definitions varied by time and space. The earliest newspapers in the seventeenth century published information as soon as it became known, even if a report of a major battle in Europe was six months old. The international news arrived via ships that took from two to four weeks to cross the Atlantic Ocean. However, by 1908, the speed of the telegraph and telephone and improved transportation made timeliness an important news component. The speed of information became very important, especially when there were competing newspapers hawking the latest news on the streets. Even newspapers in smaller communities had access to the newer communication and transportation technologies of the telegraph, the train, the telephone, and cooperative news associations.

Yet, regardless of the era, the purposes for starting a newspaper remained constant. The very first American newspaper editor, Benjamin Harris, expressed his overall news purpose in several ways. In his *Publick Occurrences*, Harris subtitled his paper *Both Forreign and Domestick*, meaning that he would emphasize local as well as international news. Such an emphasis lasted. Harris proposed other aspects of news that continued for his newspaper editor offspring: events, celebrations, and human interest. He said that he would report affairs "both abroad and at home" that would affect the "thought at all times, but at sometimes also to affect business and negotiations." For many colonists, especially from England and the continent, news from abroad resonated and was of local interest. Accuracy was a standard for Harris, just as it would be for later journalists. He made a major point to overcome "that spirit of Lying, which prevails amongst us."

He promised to print the truth while exposing "a malicious raiser of a false report."[1]

Although Harris's initial newspaper was stopped by the colonial government, his news examples of relevance to local readers continued for well over two hundred years and especially for the community newspaper editors and publishers. Powerful political forces stopped Harris's attempt and tried to stop his journalistic offspring.

Forty years later, printer John Peter Zenger, who would gain lasting fame for carrying critical views in his paper, ran news stories in serial form in his *New-York Weekly Journal* rather than expanding the number of printed pages as did the more commercial newspapers, which were filled with classified advertisements, even of houses for sale. These accounts often generally involved governmental affairs as well as what Zenger and his backers thought his community readers wanted to and should know. With information critical of the colonial governor, Zenger was jailed for nine months for seditious libel, before being acquitted by a jury of his peers. Certainly, opinionated journalism about governmental affairs, much like that found in Zenger's publication, continued during the next two centuries.

Subsequent American newspapers added to the types of news found in the early twentieth-century U.S. newspapers. The *Gazette of the United States* in the early national capital of Philadelphia printed not just items on topics of local interest, but also about national political happenings. Its late 1790 edition carried President George Washington's speech to the Congress located in Philadelphia. Too, there were reports of the actions of Congress on various issues. On the front page, foreign news stories became scarcer as the news focus had shifted from what was going on in England and Europe to what was happening locally and nationally in the new United States. Such was the case during the nineteenth century. By 1908 community newspapers reflected a more nearby geographical emphasis, rather than international stories.

These early publications show that newspapers would have more of a role than just informing the public about events; the press would also be educational by transmitting the customs and culture to future generations. For example, the *Connecticut Courant* in Hartford opened its 1764 initial edition with a proposal:

> Of all the arts which have been introduced amongst mankind, for the civilizing human-nature, and rendering life agreeable and happy, none appear of greater advantage than that of printing: for hereby the greatest

1. *Publick Occurrences: Both Foreign and Domestick,* 25 September 1690.

genius's of all ages, and, nations, live and speak for the benefit of future generations—Was it not for the Press, we should be left almost entirely ignorant of all these sentiments which the ancients were endowed with.[2]

Throughout the next two centuries, newspapers continued to transmit culture to readers, both locally and nationally, whether focusing on literary arts or sports, gender mores or fashion, the arts or festivals, or parades or fairs. Community newspapers in many American small towns in the early twentieth century had the same news values.

The Community Press's Objectives

Just as the earliest American newspapers saw their purpose as providing news coverage with a more local focus, early twentieth-century community journalism would follow the same purpose. This priority had sprung from the colonies' independence and the newspaper's growing nationalism. For example, such an emphasis was given by *Hartford Courant* publisher Thomas Green in 1764, who pointed out the benefit of a weekly paper as "... the channel which conveys the history of the present times to every part of the world." He promised "to collect . . . domestic occurrences that are worthy the notice of the public."[3] And he did, as did his successors more and more for the next two centuries.

As Green demonstrated, news from far away had to be taken from a reputable source. While he reprinted news from Boston newspapers that had earlier copied the London periodical, he made sure that local news was also covered. For example, in his first newspaper, Green ran brief items on the death of a local woman, the sailing of a ship to England with some well-known local officials aboard and their names listed, and a notice that the Colonial General Assembly had "appointed the 15th of November next, to be observed as a day of public thanksgiving throughout the Colony." The inside two pages of Green's four-page weekly were devoted to places distant: foreign affairs, along with shorter items from other American regions, New York and Charleston, South Carolina.[4]

These early journalists knew their communities. Acting much like the well-known colonist Benjamin Franklin, who had been a postmaster, local postmasters edited local weeklies for many decades. Who else would have

2. *Connecticut Courant,* 20 October 1764.
3. Ibid.
4. Ibid.

been better qualified to produce a community-oriented newspaper than the postmaster, who knew most of his customers?

Longtime Missouri media historian Frank Luther Mott referred to the worth of "small-city" and "village" journalism when he recorded the spread of such publications throughout the colonies.[5] Throughout the country's history, successful community-directed publications sought to meet the demands of their readers. And such readers continued to want to learn of the local happenings, whether they lived in a hamlet of a few hundred or in a larger area with millions. When wars took the familiar local men, hometown readers wanted to know what happened in the far-off battles, and especially valued information concerning the involvement of the local troops.

Recognition

Authors of the early histories of American journalism tended to focus on the major large-city publishers and editors of the nineteenth century and early twentieth century, first Horace Greeley and James Gordon Bennett, then William Randolph Hearst and Joseph Pulitzer.[6] Unfortunately, small-town publishers received only limited historical attention. What acknowledgment they had usually came much later from local groups and organizations, historical and genealogical societies, and anniversary editions of such publications. As one example, James M. Lee referred to "rural journalism" in his famed *History of American Journalism* (1917). Yet his reference was directed to publisher Horace Greeley, known for his *New York Tribune* and its popular weekly edition mailed across the continent. Lee noted Greeley's "tremendous influence over the country weekly that . . . bears his imprint." In fact, he pointed to Greeley's advice to country editors and publishers.[7] Greeley's lasting influence appeared to have come from an 1860 letter-writer seeking information about starting a newspaper. Greeley's guidelines for the next generations of publishers stressed an emphasis on the local community: "Begin with a clear conception that the subject of deepest interest to an average human being is himself; next to that he is most concerned about his neighbors—Asia and the Tonga Islands stand a long way after these in his regard." Pertinent to the status of community

5. Mott, *American Journalism,* 3rd ed. (New York: Macmillan Company, 1962), 135.

6. See, for example, Frederic Hudson, *Journalism in the United States, 1690–1872* (New York: Harper and Brothers, Publishers, 1873) and James M. Lee, *History of American Journalism* (Boston: Houghton Mifflin, 1917).

7. Lee, *History of American Journalism,* 404–5.

newspapers in 1908, Greeley gave his own truths about how to gather local news:

> Secure a wide-awake, judicious correspondent in each village and township of your county—some young lawyer, doctor, clerk in a store, or assistant in a post office—who will promptly send you whatever of moment occurs in his vicinity. . . . Do not let a new church be organized, or new members added to one already existing, a farm be sold, a new house to be raised, a mill be set in motion, a store opened, nor anything of interest to a dozen families occur, without having the fact duly though briefly chronicled in your columns.

Successful community newspapers in the early twentieth century followed these truths, Including Walter Williams's *Columbia Herald* and then the *University Missourian* in 1908. The famed editor Greeley also advised, "Take an earnest and active, if not a leading, part in the advancement of home industry. Do your utmost to promote not only an annual county fair, but town fairs as well." Leaders in the Missouri Press Association did this, including Williams.

Greeley further advised the young man to seek out connections. He said, "If anyone undertakes a new branch of industry in the county, especially if it be a manufacture, do not wait to be solicited; but hasten to give him a helping hand." A new editor was to be a booster of the community, yet also self-sufficient. Subsequent editors into the twentieth century did likewise.

Greeley advised independence from the power structure. He wrote:

> Don't let politicians and aspirants of the county own you. They may be clever fellows, as they often are, but, if you keep your eyes open, you will see something that they seem blind to and must speak out accordingly. Do your best to keep the number of public trusts, the amount of official emoluments, and the consequent rate exhortation, other than for common schools as low as may be.

He ended his letter, "That you may *deserve and* achieve success is the earnest prayer of yours truly."[8] Greeley might have been writing for all future community journalists.

In fact, Greeley's letter provided a guidebook for those aspiring newspaper publishers, then and later. If they followed these instructions, they

---

8. Horace Greeley, *Reflections of a Busy Life* (1868, reprt., New York: J. B. Ford and Co., 1970), 91–93.

would be publishing diaries of their hometowns as a weekly publication. That was the best thing in town, the source of community pride and information.

Following Greeley, the best-known country editor through the early twentieth century was the Kansan William Allen White, editor of the *Emporia Gazette* since 1895. He explained what community newspapers looked like as well as what they did:

> Our papers, our little country papers, seem drab and miserably provincial to strangers, yet we who read them read in their lines the sweet, intimate story of life. . . . It is the country newspaper, bringing together daily the threads of the town's life, weaving them into something rich and strange, and setting the pattern as it weaves, directing the loom, and giving the cloth its color by mixing the lives of all the people in its color-pot.[9]

Another famous country editor was Walter Williams, who had edited mid-Missouri newspapers for decades before becoming the first dean of the Missouri School of Journalism in 1908. He often touted the newspaper as a community organ. For one of the early School of Journalism bulletins, Williams explained:

> The newspaper is the greatest public utility institution—He serves his newspaper best who serves his *community* best. The chief end of good journalism is helpful public service. The good journalist is the attorney-at-large for the people, the US-sworn conservator of the public peace. Every good journalist seeks first the favor of the right-thinking public through public service.[10]

The Missouri School of Journalism would follow Williams's ideals. Behind him were the supportive Missouri Press Association members who wanted to hire college-trained journalists. There is no doubt that the faculty focused on providing qualified graduates to assist community newspapers, initially called "Rural" or "Country" newspapers; actual classes called "Community Journalism" were not listed until four decades later. Although not an initial course offering, by the time of the 1912–1914 class, the catalog

9. William Allen White, *The Autobiography of William Allen White* (New York: Macmillan Co., 1946), 126–27.

10. Walter Williams quoted in John B. Powell, "Building a Circulation: Methods and Ideas for Small Town Newspapers," *University of Missouri Bulletin*, Journalism Series 15, no. 6 (February 20, 1914).

included a course called "Rural Newspaper Management," which was explained as "an emphasis on the advertising, circulation and business phases of community newspapering."[11] The teacher of the course, journalism graduate John B. Powell, would later spend much of his life in Shanghai as a publisher, only later to become a World War II prisoner of war, held by the Japanese.

By 1913, the Missouri School of Journalism's second catalog offered a course called "The Country Newspaper," taught by Charles G. Ross. Ross, one of the three original faculty members in 1908, was born in Independence, Missouri, and had been a University of Missouri Phi Beta Kappa graduate and a former high school classmate of President Harry S. Truman. He would later become known as Truman's presidential press secretary. Ross's course included a practice, long followed at many journalism schools, of on-the-scene training in community newspapers as part of students' preparation for the outside world.

In 1913, Ross wrote a thirty-four-page monograph as a guidebook for rural journalists: "The News in the Country Papers." He recommended: "The country paper must stand on its own legs, something radically different from and not a weak imitation of the city daily. The two should supplement each other." Ross called for attractive make-up for the newspaper's appearance, for "sane counsel and analysis in its editorials, and most important of all, it should thoroughly cover its local news field." He directed, "And there should be *more* than politics on the editorial page." Always, he stressed "simply, tensely, accurately written" stories, adding, "The reader does not care for exercises in word gymnastics: he wants news."[12] Ross's directive may have echoed the past, but these standards continue today.

The Missouri journalism curriculum indicated both the importance and the expansion of community journalism courses. By 1920, "The Country Newspaper" was taught by Williams, a possible reflection of the course's status. Four years later, the course offerings included a laboratory course, "Country Newspaper Production," which involved student work on the weekly *Columbia Herald-Statesman*, where Williams had been the editor. There, students were exposed to newsgathering, editing, and editorial tasks. Such classes continued, with the additions of circulation, organization, and management, and suburban press offerings with Missouri Press Association directors acting as instructors. Williams and other faculty directed field trips to local newspapers as part of the curriculum; too, they encouraged a summer hands-on experience.

11. Sara Lockwood Williams, *Twenty Years of Journalism Education*, 9.
12. Charles G. Ross, *The Writing of News* (New York: Henry Holt and Co., 1911).

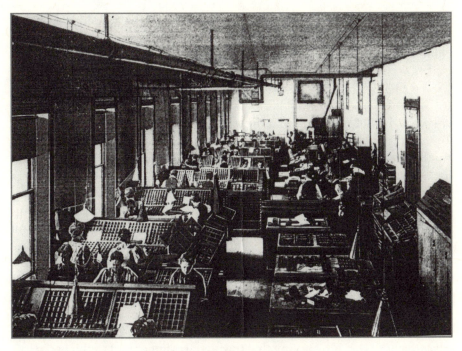

The *Columbia Herald* was typical of early twentieth-century community newspapers. Courtesy of the State Historical Society of Missouri Newspaper Collection.

The importance of community journalism continued. By the time of the twenty-first century, the Missouri Press Association funded one of the country's first endowed chairs in the field.

The purpose of modern community papers remains similar to those earlier country newspapers. As Morris Janowitz wrote about the tremendous press growth in the suburbs and central city, "The unique character of the community press arises from the fact that it has as its audience the residents of a specific sector of the urban metropolis. In the local community the audience conditions its content, determines its appeal, and facilitates its impact."[13]

Origin of the Title "Community Journalism"

Country and then community journalism was nationally a part of the journalism curriculum, though the title as known today did not exist. Kenneth R.

13. Morris Janovich, *The Community Press in an Urban Setting, the Social Elements of Urbanism* (Chicago: University of Chicago Press, 1967), xxi.

Byerly, a Montana editor and publisher who joined the academic world as a professor of journalism at the University of North Carolina in 1957, coined the term "community journalism." In a letter reflecting on his original title, Byerly, then eighty-nine, explained that when he inherited a course called "Country Weekly Newspaper Production," he did not like the narrowness of the title. Because of the growing number of suburban weeklies, he did not think that the common name "Hometown" fit either. Too, he thought that "weekly" did not match as he recognized that many small towns had good dailies, which were successful because they stressed local and area news, editorials, pictures, and features that their readers couldn't get from big-city dailies.[14]

He said, "So I mulled over the idea of a better name, and finally came up with 'Community Journalism.' It seemed to fit these weeklies and small dailies. Anyway, the dean agreed with me and the name of that course was changed to 'Community Journalism.'" Byerly explained that after his new book, *Community Journalism,* sold well, the name caught on. "It became the name for the small dailies as well as weeklies and semi-weeklies."[15]

Byerly further justified his community journalism concept in a book chapter in *The Newspaper: Everything You Need to Know to Make It in the Newspaper Business* (1981) by noting that the big-city dailies had problems covering subjects the community newspapers cover because "they no longer have space for stories on every tea, bridge club and child's birthday." He also added, "A community newspaper should share in the hopes, heartaches, laughs, sorrows, accomplishments, disappointments and joys of its readers. There are times, though, when an editor must be a watchdog, take his gloves off: and report harmful things as they are."[16] His words echo his journalistic ancestors who created by practice the roles of a local newspaper from three hundred years ago.

The contents of these latter-day publications have changed little since Benjamin Harris published *Publick Occurrences* in 1690. Harris's focus is similar to what Lauterer wrote about today's newspaper as the earlier journalist's legacy: "These are the newspapers of the Blue Highways, off the Interstates, perhaps, journalism as practiced by weeklies and small dailies with an intensely local focus. Fully 97 percent of U.S. newspapers fit this

---

14. Byerly Letter to Lauterer; Jock Lauterer, *Community Journalism, the Personal Approach,* 2nd ed. (Ames: Iowa State University Press, 2000), xxiii-xiv.
   15. Ibid.
   16. D. Earl Newsom, ed., *The Newspaper: Everything You Need to Know to Make It in the Newspaper Business* (Englewood Cliffs, N.J.: National Newspaper Foundation, Prentice Hall, Inc., 1981), 7.

description. So—if you're a student of journalism, it's very likely you will be working on a community newspaper."[17]

Lauterer stressed the personal approach found in community journalism, rejecting the often-voiced view that such "a paper is a small version of the big-city daily."[18] Although some critics predicted the doom of newspapers with the advent of television, Lauterer expressed a different view, seeing these publications as "insulated, not only from the vicissitudes of the economy but also from TV's insidious influence. Most of these newspapers have joined the computer era with online editions, 'cracking out local news—our bread and butter.'"[19]

Others have their own interpretations of what community journalism represents, though the majority tend to focus on the characteristics stressed here. They view a community where "the people who live there have certain things in common, a common frame of reference, common knowledge about infrastructures and people and systems—it also implies a certain interactiveness, an accessibility to all." And at their best, "community newspapers satisfy a basic human craving that most big dailies can't touch, no matter how large their budgets."

Some additional identifications of community newspapers have been summarized by Lauterer, as he notes concepts such as "small is beautiful" and "less is more" that can become a boon for the enlightened community newspaper with flexibility, access, and size:

> A community newspaper can turn on a dime—make major decisions about coverage, editorial policy, news judgment, editing, cropping and advertising—without going through layers of needless bureaucracy and personnel. Because of the lack of layers just mentioned, the access to the top is usually clear. Unless it's a poorly run slack chain operation, the editor or publisher is Norm or Nancy in the next room, empowered to make decisions quickly.
>
> Because it is small, it doesn't cost a fortune to staff and equip a community paper—especially now with the revolution in desktop publishing and online publishing.

And this smallness, he adds, "is beautiful because you can limit your coverage area."[20]

17. Lauterer, *Community Journalism*, xiv.
18. Ibid., xv.
19. Ibid., 6.
20. Ibid., 15.

Community newspapers, he says, give us "the affirmation of the sense of community, a positive and intimate reflection of the sense of place, a stroke for our us-ness, our extended family-ness and our profound and interlocking connectedness, what Stanford's Nadinne Cruz calls 'the big WE.'"[21]

Conclusions

"Community Journalism" and the beginning of journalism education are intertwined. The state of Missouri newspaper numbers at the time tell the story. When the Missouri School of Journalism was established in 1908, there were 91 dailies, 11 semi-weeklies, and 774 weekly newspapers in the state, according to the Ayer Directory.[22] Many of these editors and publishers, as active members of the Missouri Press Association, for the most part supported journalism education at a university. They expected an experienced community newspaperman, Walter Williams, and his faculty to train future staffers in the best manner possible. Thus, the school gradually offered such courses as editing, copyediting, and advertising, and as new needs appeared, new courses were added, such as courses in management, circulation, photoengraving, and on and on.

Other state press associations also wanted trained journalists and took leadership roles in making that happen, such as in Kansas, Washington, and Wisconsin. Their universities also added new courses to fulfill technological and industry needs. Drawing from a rich historical background from the country's earliest newspapers, what became known as "community journalism" by whatever name remained a constant focus for the readers.

21. Ibid., 14.
22. *N. W. Ayer and Son's Directory of Newspapers* (Philadelphia: Ayer Publishing Co., 1909).

CHAPTER 4

Press Clubs Champion Journalism Education

Stephen Banning

The first year of the University of Missouri School of Journalism's laboratory newspaper (1908–1909) was one of high expectations and high ideals. Some of those ideals appear to have had their origins in press associations. Amidst stories in the *Missourian* of the new President Lincoln postage stamp, resigning professors, and ads for wool clothing and self-indexing ledgers were numerous references to press association activities, suggesting press associations were not only extremely prominent when the University of Missouri School of Journalism began, but instrumental in its success as well.

For example, on February 2, 1909, University of Missouri Journalism School Dean Walter Williams spoke in Kansas City about the school of journalism. His audience was the Kansas Press Club and the executive committee of the National Editorial Association, the same National Editorial Association founded a few years earlier in New Orleans, where the constitution of the Missouri Press Association had served as a template for the constitution of the larger organization. The next day, the Kansas Editorial Association wrote a proclamation recognizing the importance of the University of Missouri School of Journalism. Two and a half weeks later, the *Missourian* ran a story regarding journalism education efforts in Wisconsin that were being pushed by three different press associations there. Five days later, the *Missourian* published another story about University of Missouri

School of Journalism inquiries from France, Scotland, and New Zealand, in the context of support of the school by the World Press Congress as a means of professionalizing journalism. The *Missourian* also found it significant to mention that the first journalism student from California was a member of the California Press Association.[1]

Press associations had been supporting formal journalism education for some time as a way of helping journalism professionalize in the same way doctors, lawyers, and the clergy had in the previous century. The connection between formal education and professionalization is evident in an article in the *Missourian* on a journalism program getting underway in Colorado. The reporter notes: "Another step in the recognition of newspaper writing as a profession—equal in importance and usefulness with medicine, law or engineering—is indicated by the decision of the faculty of the University of Colorado to add a Department of Journalism to the College of Liberal Arts." Less than a week later, another article in the *Missourian* referred to the school of journalism as a profession in the class of doctors, lawyers, and theology. Two days later, the *Missourian* quoted presidential candidate William Howard Taft as calling journalism a profession at one point and as distinguishing trades from professions in another. A few days later, *Collier's Magazine* editor in chief Norman Hapgood, in speaking to journalism students at the University of Missouri, commented that journalism was a profession, adding, "I regard the newspapers today as more important than the law or the clergy."[2] The roots of this interest in professions, however, began much earlier.

Regular gatherings of newspaper publishers, reporters, and printers began in earnest by the mid-nineteenth century. Prior to this, colonial news purveyors identified more with partisan politics than with each other or a group.

One of the first gatherings of reporters was the Harbor News Association, a mid-nineteenth-century cooperative that eventually evolved into the

---

1. "Williams on Journalism: Talks about Newspaper [*sic*] by the Dean in Topeka and Kansas City," *University Missourian*, 2 February 1909, 1; "To M.U. Journalism: A Resolution by the Kansas Editors Congratulates the Department," *University Missourian*, 8 February 1909, 3; "Journalism at Wisconsin U.," *University Missourian*, 10 February 1909, 2; "From Three Nations: Inquiries About School of Journalism From France, Scotland, New Zealand," *University Missourian*, 24 February 1909, 1; "California Editor Enters University: F. W. Cooke, 49 Years Old, New Student in School of Journalism," *University Missourian*, 2 February 1909, 1.

2. "Journalism in Colorado," *University Missourian*, 16 February 1909, 2; "How Universities Train for Service," 17 February 1909, 2; "Journalism Ranks High, Says Taft," *University Missourian*, 26 February 2007, 3; "Press Popular University Says Norman Hapgood," *University Missourian*, 19 January 1909, 3.

Associated Press. This group was formed entirely for financial reasons with not so much as a nod to social concern or professional interest. It did, however, set the stage for the news disseminators to begin to see that they had common interests.

Also, by the mid-nineteenth century, publishers began to congregate on a regular basis, with the New York Press Club meeting periodically at the famous Delmonico's restaurant in New York City. Author Augustus Maverick noted in 1870 that the clubs discussed little of substance and were designed to improve social graces, contrasting the clubs with professional associations organized by doctors, lawyers, and the clergy. Maverick valued professionalization for the "higher interests" of journalism; he saw professional associations as a key component to journalistic professionalization:

> But while each great printing establishment in New York possesses an internal economy which is smooth in its operation, and nearly perfect in its results, the men themselves know little of each other, and in this respect the profession of Journalism differs from all others. In medicine, members of societies meet at stated times for comparisons of views and for general discussion. In the ranks of the Clergy, and among the members of the Bar, there is a greater or less degree of affiliation. But, unfortunately for the higher interests of journalism, the rivalries of business too often remain operative after the hours of routine duty expire. Frequent attempts have been made to organize Press Clubs in New York. . . . But this experiment faded away.[3]

Three years later, in the first published general history of reporters, Frederic Hudson also was not impressed with the journalism clubs, seeing them as conflict-filled and little more than opportunities to imbibe. Hudson wrote in 1873: "We don't suppose its dinners or its speeches or the intercourse of its members improved the tone of the Press. . . . They continued to criticize and abuse each other, as they always did and always will. . . . The Clubs are social gatherings. . . . None of these social circles are destined for long life but they are useful while they last." Still later, historian John Weeks Moore in the 1886 book *Historical Notes on Printers and Printing* suggested the New York Press Club was the first in a series of city and state organizations: "There exists in New York what is known as the Press Club; and similar organizations have been established in Boston, Baltimore, Philadelphia,

3. Augustus Maverick, *Henry J. Raymond and the New York Press for Thirty Years: Progress of American Journalism from 1840 to 1870* (Hartford, Conn.: A. S. Hale and Company, 1870), 328, 129.

Chicago, and other cities." Moore also mentioned that press clubs had been established in Alabama, Arkansas, Maine, Massachusetts, New Hampshire, Vermont, Wisconsin, Rhode Island, New Jersey, Illinois, Colorado, Minnesota, and Michigan.[4]

There could be business and economic advantages; some early press clubs sought to fix advertising rates for their members. For instance, the Ohio Editorial Association, which began in 1849, and the Wisconsin Press Association, which began in 1853, were both formed to promote a variety of business interests ranging from uniform prices for job work to state printing contracts, increased rates for legal printing, and, of course, advertising rates. For a discussion of professional issues, some press associations would have to wait.

In contrast, shortly after earlier organizational financial purposes, the Missouri Press Association drew up its charter with completely different goals.[5] The time and place for such efforts fit the latter nineteenth-century era for organizational efforts. Nationally, newspaper credibility was low in those years following the Civil War. The war not only divided the country but also reflected the distinct partisan divisions and reporting. Advertising for concoctions composed mostly of alcohol and cocaine kept many papers in business. Merchants' under-the-table payments routinely resulted in complimentary editorials, while a multitude of untutored and inexperienced war correspondents submitted inaccurate stories and demonstrated outlandish behavior in their pursuit of war stories.

Context also provides clues to the deeper motivations for the formation of the Missouri Press Association. After the Civil War, ill sentiment among many publishers continued to smolder, when at the same time the western frontier opened. Perhaps it was this circumstance in addition to the rise of other professions that led midwestern publishers to feel a need to gather together. Professionalization could have been seen as a way to bring cohesiveness and progress to an area of the country lacking in unity. The fact that midwestern publishers tended to be what we would today call small-town community journalists may have made them more open to professionalization than publishers on the East Coast where individual newspaper publishers were already satisfied with their status.

It was also in the mid-nineteenth century that the concept of professionalism began to gain popularity and stature in other fields. By the turn of the

4. Frederic Hudson, *Journalism in the United States: From 1690 to 1870* (New York: Harper and Brothers Publishers, 1873), 666; John W. Moore, *Historical Notes on Printers and Printing: 1420 to 1886* (Concord: Republican Press Association, 1886), 251–62.

5. Stephen A. Banning, "The Professionalization of Journalism: A Nineteenth-Century Beginning," *Journalism History* 24, no. 4 (Winter 1998–1999): 157.

century, doctors, lawyers, and the clergy were considered the models of professionalism, with associations, specialized education, and codes of ethics established as hallmarks of professionalization. Teachers, soldiers, and engineers were considered secondary associations because their efforts to professionalize began later.[6]

Associations were a unique aspect of the American scene, as noted by Alexis de Tocqueville, author of *Democracy in America*. In the 1860s, according to historian Floyd Shoemaker, Missouri was characterized by the formation of numerous associations, many professional in nature. In fact, these organizations were often given complete credit for an occupation's rise to professional status. Sociologist W. J. Reader in *Professional Men* notes: "An occupation's rise to professional standing can be pretty accurately charted by reference to the progress of its professional institute or association. In the early stages it is usually purely an unofficial body—in the eighteenth century, often a dining club—without any legal authority at all and dependent on itself for any authority it may acquire." Associations can be a forum for fraternal bonds, the bedrock of professionalization, according to sociologists A. M. Carr-Saunders and P. A. Wilson, who noted: "A number of men, though they perform similar functions, do not make a profession if they remain in isolation. A profession can only be said to exist when there are bonds between the practitioners, and these bonds can take but one shape— that of formal association."[7]

The state press associations wanted journalists to be considered professionals, much like attorneys, physicians, and the clergy. Law, as the first profession, had in medieval times set educational requirements before attorneys could practice. A facsimile of the bar associations came into existence two hundred years later with English organizations, called inns, and by 1729, a British act required attorneys not only to pass an exam, but to hold a five-year apprenticeship as well. A century later, judges in England decreed that lawyers were required to pass a test before they could practice law, an act that mandated more specialized training. In 1854, the "inns" or associations were recognized as university colleges of law, and by 1869 an

---

6. Stephen A. Banning, "Unearthing the Origin of Journalistic Professionalization in the Mid-Nineteenth Century," Master's thesis, University of Missouri, 1993, 2.

7. Alexis de Tocqueville, *Democracy in America* (New York: Vintage Books, 1945), 138; Richard Taub, *American Society in Tocqueville's Time and Today* (Chicago: Rand McNally College Publishing Company, 1974), 90; Floyd Calvin Shoemaker, *Missouri and Missourians: Land of Contrast and People of Achievement* (Chicago: Lewis Publishing Company, 1943), 1: 1008, 1010; W. J. Reader, *Professional Men* (London: Weidenfeld and Nicolson, 1966), 161, 163–64; A. M. Carr-Saunders and P. A. Wilson, *The Professions*, 2nd ed. (London: Frank Cass and Co., 1964), 298.

accrediting association, the Legal Education Association, further enhanced the credibility of these colleges. Such a progression emerged in the United States; attorneys formed associations in the eighteenth century, but were not fully organized until the second half of the nineteenth century.[8]

Other professions had similar early beginnings. Medieval university educators in England did not consider medicine a liberal art, but it was studied nonetheless, and it was possible to get a university degree in medicine. By 1518, British physicians were required to have medical licenses. In the United States, the professionalization of medicine came to the fore in the mid-nineteenth century as a means of overcoming disrepute from rogue practitioners. Specifically, the American Medical Association became organized in 1847. The clergy had their own means of professionalization as well. The clergy set the structure of education when the colonies were founded, which law and medicine would follow. In fact, both law and medicine emerged from the clergy as the university system was under ecclesiastical control. By the nineteenth century, the clergy had already achieved a high level of status and as a whole sought to maintain it, rather than elevate it.[9]

The growing interest in professionalization through associations in the eighteenth and nineteenth centuries also reflected a greater societal emphasis in urbanization. As people gravitated toward cities during the Industrial Revolution, there appeared to be erosion in communal standards; professionalization was thought to be an antidote. A product of urban centers, professionalism's impact soon began to be felt in rural areas as well. The move from a close-knit rural society to an urban society marked by isolationism also led to a need for trusted professional standards. As people began to be less familiar with their neighbors, there arose a need for a trusted system to produce reliable practitioners in those fields deemed important to society. Journalism would be among them.

Such changes did not come from above, from the government, but rather from individual groups of practitioners. They made the case that their fields were worthy of esteem. The clergy traditionally had held this position, physicians and attorneys followed, then so too did soldiers, teachers, and engineers. Thus, it was against this backdrop that the public understood professions in the mid-nineteenth century. They were few, they were respected, and they were envied.

As an embryonic beginning of professionalism through organizing, the first U.S. press clubs originated along the East Coast and were designed to be social or business gatherings. There has been no evidence that journal-

---

8. See Reader, *Professional Men,* and Carr-Saunders and Wilson, *The Professions.*
9. Ibid.

Missouri Press Association members enjoy a convention cruise down the Mississippi River to Cape Girardeau. Courtesy of the Missouri Press Association.

ism education, ethics, or any professional topics were broached. In short, they initially would not have been mistaken for professional associations. A similar situation seems to have been present in most early clubs in the South and Midwest; the West at this time was largely unsettled. In contrast, the Missouri Press Association did meet semiregularly with other state press clubs. This suggests that through the sharing of ideas, other press clubs, if they had not become interested in professionalization already, would at least have heard the goals of those in the Missouri Press Association who were pressing for it. The MPA minutes indicate MPA members fraternized with members of the Kentucky Press Association in 1874, and Floyd Shoemaker's 1917 history indicates the MPA had joint meetings with the state press associations of Mississippi, Texas, and Arkansas.[10] Certainly professionalization of accepted standards and education would have been discussed at some level.

10. J. W. Barrett, *History and Transactions* (Canton, Mo.: Canton Press, 1867/1876), 102; Floyd Calvin Shoemaker, "History of the First Fifty Years of the Missouri Press Association," 1917, unpublished manuscript, Missouri Historical Society, 151.

There is much evidence the Missouri Press Association was founded as a professional association. The first ten years of the MPA's existence consisted of what Shoemaker called the "golden years" of the MPA due to the eloquence and influence of the members during that time. Shoemaker explains:

> From obscurity and weakness it [the Missouri Press Association] has become one of the great powers of the State. The perfecting of a publisher's and an editorial fraternity; the moral and intellectual elevation of the press; the founding of the State Historical Society of Missouri; the promotion and establishment of the first State School of Journalism in America, and in attendance, the largest; [and] the creation and continuance of the largest Journalism Week in the nation.[11]

While it should not be surprising to find the press forming an association during this period, the environment and time were ripe. According to Shoemaker, "one of the characteristics of the decade of 1860–1870 was the organization of various associations." During this decade, those associations included the Missouri State Medical Association, the St. Louis Institute of Architects, the St. Louis Microscopical Society, the Missouri State Dental Association, the St. Louis Local Steam Engineers Association, and the Engineers Club of St. Louis.[12] These were practitioners in their particular fields.

Several Missouri Press Association members were either members of the traditional professions or very familiar with them. Such connections could explain why they wished to professionalize journalism, too, by organizing an association and pushing for higher standards of ethics and specialized training for all journalists.

Three individuals in particular, Norman Colman, John Marmaduke, and J. C. Moore, well exemplify the sophistication of some of the editors who made up the Missouri Press Association. Norman J. Colman was extremely active in the Missouri Press Association as a founding member in 1867, recording secretary in 1868, and chair of the Committee on Arrangements in 1869. His publishing status stemmed from his position as editor and publisher of the *Rural World* (a periodical still published today). However, he also had achieved professional rank. At the age of sixteen, he received his teaching license and several years later received a license to practice law. He also spent time working with the clergy at a seminary. His professional expertise led first to statewide and then to national prominence. The gov-

11. Shoemaker, "History of the First Fifty Years," Introduction.
12. Shoemaker, *Missouri and Missourians,* vol. 1, 1008, 1010–11.

ernor of Missouri appointed Colman to the University of Missouri Board of Curators in 1868. Also in 1868, Colman ran for the office of state lieutenant governor. Although Colman failed to win that statewide office, he did win an appointment as the United States' first secretary of the Department of Agriculture, and he pushed for federally funded experimental farms in cooperation with universities.

Colman also helped to organize the Missouri State Historical Society. This was accomplished by asking each newspaper in the state to donate one copy of each issue to the society's archives. These documents form the foundation of the society's holdings today in Columbia, Missouri. Coleman also helped organize the St. Louis Historical Society and the St. Louis Fair Association.

Colman's training in the professions of teaching and law made him familiar with the benefits of professionalization, and his experience in politics helped him motivate others. Colman also advocated various aspects of professionalization, including forming professional associations.[13]

John Marmaduke was another multifaceted Missouri Press Association member, both well educated and politically adept. Educated at Harvard and Yale, Marmaduke had served as a major general for the Confederacy during the Civil War. In *Battles and Biographies of Missourians*, W. L. Webb noted, "[Marmaduke's] scholarship in all branches of learning was surpassed by few men in the service of the Southern Confederacy." Marmaduke's father had been governor of Missouri before the war, and his grandfather had been a well-known doctor. In 1885, Marmaduke would follow in his father's footsteps and become governor of Missouri, as well. As grandson of a physician, as son of a governor, and later governor himself, Marmaduke would have been familiar with professional standards of conduct and practice.

J. C. Moore was another Missouri Press Association member very familiar with professions. Moore had served for the Confederacy as a colonel and later was licensed to practice law. Interestingly, his immediate superior during the Civil War was John Marmaduke. Moore is known in journalism history as the cofounder of the *Kansas City Times*. However, prior to joining the Missouri Press Association, he had worked at the *St. Louis Times*, moved to Colorado and won a seat in the Colorado legislature, and served as Denver's first mayor.

Such state leaders would have an impact on the Missouri Press Association's interest in education and focus on being a professional rather than a trade or social organization. There is strong evidence that the MPA did wish

13. Ibid.

to establish professional education for journalists in the latter half of the nineteenth century.[14]

The Missouri Press Association is one of the few journalist clubs for which records exist from the nineteenth century, and it appears to be among those few whose records indicate a desire to professionalize. Too, the MPA was a leader in this effort as the national press association based part of its constitution on the Missouri Press Association's. This is not to say that other press associations were not interested in professionalization at an early point as well. However, there is no evidence of professionalization in other associations in the few records available.

Because many clubs saw their meetings as social meetings, they saw no need to record their conversations. The New York City Press Club fell into this category; it kept no minutes. Frederic Hudson expressed mild irritation at the club's attitude: "The dinners of the Press Club were always considered private. It was never mentioned in the newspapers who dined with them, or what was said. Thus, much wit was lost to the world. All was always under the beautiful rose that hung over the table—the scent went no farther."[15]

Historian Alfred McClung Lee was also frustrated in his research. In *The Daily Newspaper in America,* Lee expressed irritation with press club secrecy: "One difficulty in presenting a summary of trends in newspaper association activities arises from the fact that these bodies—so insistent upon free access by reporters to the affairs of other groups with widespread social connections—protect themselves from reporters."[16]

Such secrecy contrasts directly with the Missouri Press Association's policy of recording its proceedings; a resolution in its 1867 constitution even stated that complete copies of the proceedings should be furnished to newspapers throughout the state with the request that the minutes be published. Missouri Press Association charter member J. W. Barrett was assigned this task, a job he took to heart by rendering complete reconstructions of the meetings. Barrett was the Missouri Press Association president for the first two years of its existence and was influential enough in Missouri that he later was appointed to the University of Missouri Board of Curators. Barrett had built the *Canton Press* out of a printing press that occupying Union Army soldiers had tried to destroy during the Civil War. Barrett thought the

14. Stephen Banning, "The Cradle of Professional Journalistic Education in the Mid-Nineteenth Century," *Media History Monographs* 4, no. 1 (2000–2001): 4.

15. Ibid., 660.

16. Alfred McClung Lee, *The Daily Newspaper in America* (New York: Macmillan Co., 1937), 233.

Missouri Press Association proceedings extremely important, claiming: "To present a brief account of the origin and several meetings of the Association would, perhaps, have involved but little labor and expense, but in view of the many able addresses, poems and essays presented at these interesting re-unions during the first decade of our history, it seemed desirable to preserve these 'gems of purest ray serene,' from threatened oblivion."[17]

The Missouri Press Association members thought the meeting proceedings so important that they later commissioned Barrett to bind and publish three hundred copies of the complete minutes of the first ten years. The hardback copies, 136 pages long, were given to Missouri Press Association members. Three of these copies have survived and are found at the Missouri State Archives, the Missouri School of Journalism Library, and in a private collection of media historian William Howard Taft. Those MPA records reveal that the Missouri Press Association members repeatedly referred to themselves as professionals and that the field of journalism was a profession from the time they formed in 1867. There are some clear examples that help illustrate this.

In 1872, John Marmaduke gave the annual oration and focused on how the profession of journalism had benefited society. Marmaduke noted:

> Before discussing American journalism it may not be amiss to here take a very brief notice of the origin of the profession. . . . New arts and sciences have given man his greatest blessings; and who can say how much of this is justly attributable to that profession of which we today are humble members.[18]

Others outside the Missouri Press Association also understood that the association saw itself as professional in nature. In 1874, Lexington, Missouri, city official John Reid spoke at the annual Missouri Press Association convention to welcome them to the city of Lexington. At a time when journalism was seen almost universally as a trade, Reid specifically refers to the Missouri Press Association members as professionals, noting: "We understand you meet together in part for social intercourse, but chiefly in the interest and honor of the profession and art you honor and adorn."[19] At that same convention, charter Missouri Press Association member and future

17. Barrett, *History and Transactions*, Preface, i.
18. John S. Marmaduke, "May 27, 1872 Annual Missouri Press Association Address," in *History and Transactions*, 68.
19. John Reid, "May 20, 1874 Welcome Address for the Missouri Press Association," in *History and Transactions*, 78.

association president Milo Blair expanded on the meaning of professionalization to journalism, discussing education and comparing it to traditional
professions. Blair stated:

> Journalism is a profession different from any other, and a man must be
> well adapted in it to be successful. This is a reef on which so many wreck.
> Men mistake their calling. A lawyer or doctor quite clever with the pen
> [*sic*], but a failure in his own profession, resorts to journalism, squibs a
> few weeks, but soon discovers that he is utterly unfitted for the business.[20]

Blair stated six times in his address that journalism was a profession. This
culminated in a call to action: "To unsullied journalism shall our land look,
and, to its trumpet tones march with the noble and fair, in the van of civilization. Then brethren of the pen, in your loved and noble profession,
'Press on!'"[21]

The Missouri Press Association's annual address the next year included
more references to journalism as a profession and Missouri Press Association members as professionals. Missouri Press Association member Mark
DeMotte explained why he felt it was important to discuss the philosophy
of journalism, that year's oration topic:

> Journals and journalists are often accused by those of other *professions* of
> talking too much about themselves. There is a maxim, I believe, to the
> effect that men talk best about that in which they are the most interested.
> We are most interested in ourselves and our *profession*, therefore, to talk
> best, we must talk about ourselves and our *profession* [author's italics].[22]

In 1867, William F. Switzler commented on the annual orations that discussed professionalism. Switzler suggested:

> About the responsibilities and labors and sacrifices and difficulties of the
> editorial *profession*. . . . They have tended to elevate the character of the edi-
> torial *profession*. . . . They have inspired us with new and loftier ambition,
> and quickened the dormant energies and flagging activities of *professional*
> life. . . . I shall present only a few thoughts, and in a plain, practical way,

20. Milo Blair, "May 20, 1874 Annual Missouri Press Association Address," in *History and Transactions*, 84.

21. Ibid., 86–87.

22. DeMotte, "May 26, 1875 Annual Missouri Press Association Address," in *History and Transactions*, 93.

with the hope of at least benefiting the younger members of the *profession* [author's italics].[23]

One way to define a concept is to provide a contrast. Switzler does this by comparing journalists to the public in saying: "The *unprofessional* public believe, but the *unprofessional* public do not understand the subject, that writing editorials comprises the chief labor of the editor's life [author's italics]."[24] Switzler explained that investigation was the most important aspect of the editor's job. Three years later Switzler again discussed the professionalization of journalism, claiming he had long believed journalism was a profession:

> I think that there are many cogent reasons in support of this conviction, long entertained and often propounded by myself, that editing newspapers is as much a profession as practicing law or medicine, and that a department of journalism ought to be established, and I have no doubt at no distant day will be established, in our own and other Universities.[25]

Switzler's statement on journalistic education may have been associated with an event at the University of Missouri that same year. In 1879, Professor David McAnally, Jr., offered the first journalism course at the University of Missouri. The class was called "History of Journalism—Lectures with Practical Explanations of Daily Newspaper Life."[26] It is not known if Switzler's comments preceded the formation of this course or had any connection with it. We do know Switzler was a strong supporter of education and lived not far from the university in Columbia, where he was editor of the *Columbia Statesman*.

Other notables had an interest in journalism professionalism after the Civil War. General Robert E. Lee attempted to establish editorial education at Washington College (now Washington and Lee University) in 1869 after seeing the excesses of Civil War correspondents. Norman J. Colman spoke of "professional" editorial education to the Missouri Press Association that same year. Colman explained:

23. William F. Switzler, "June 6, 1876 Annual Missouri Press Association Address," in *History and Transactions*, 124.

24. Ibid., 132.

25. William F. Switzler, "May 27, 1879 Annual Missouri Press Association Address," in *The Proceedings*, compiled by M. B. Chapman (Columbia: Missouri Statesman Book and Job Print, 1879), 5.

26. Sara Lockwood Williams, *Twenty Years of Education for Journalism*, 3, 13.

The Teacher, the Physician, the Lawyer, and the Divine, must each undergo a thorough prefatory course, before being permitted to enter his chosen career. . . . That institutions of this kind could be established [for publishers], and would be attended with the most beneficial results, can scarcely be doubted. Each member of the profession has now to learn for himself all the duties devolving upon him.[27]

Lee's efforts could have had an influence on the Missouri Press Association members because records indicate they greatly respected him. William Switzler gave a eulogy for General Lee upon Lee's death in 1870, and Missouri Press Association member Stilson Hutchins, the eventual founder of the *Washington Post*, named his son after Lee. As mentioned previously, influential Missouri Press Association members John Marmaduke and J. C. Moore were officers in the Confederate Army and would have been more familiar than most with Lee. Unfortunately, Lee's experiment was not to last. The training program dissolved in less than a decade, and no notable editors or publishers claimed it as their alma mater.

Other training centers emerged, including one for women in Detroit, but few people took the concept of any kind of formal journalism training seriously, believing instead that on-the-job training was sufficient. *New York Tribune* editor Whitelaw Reid noted in 1873:

Such an establishment as the *New York Herald*, or *Tribune*, or *Times* is the true college for newspaper students. Professor James Gordon Bennett or Professor Horace Greeley would turn out more real genuine journalists in one year than the Harvards, the Yales and the Dartmouths could produce in a generation. . . . The genius for the work is in them. It is not acquired at a college in Virginia or Massachusetts.[28]

It should be noted that the institutional training that did go on at this time was formal, not professional, in nature. Although students received instruction in printing and editing, aspects of training that would be considered professional were not covered, such as principles and societal connections. In contrast, the idea of professional university training was a continual topic of discussion at Missouri Press Association meetings.

Other state press organizations also had an interest in professionalization during the latter part of the mid-nineteenth century. A number of them congregated to form an umbrella organization called the National Editorial Asso-

27. Colman, "May 1869 Annual Missouri Press Association Address," 21.
28. Quoted in Hudson, *Journalism in the United States*, 714.

ciation. Such organizational efforts had implications for professionalization according to sociologist A. M. Carr-Saunders, who saw it as inevitable that regional professional associations would eventually merge into an umbrella association during the professionalization process. He noted in 1928,

> Moreover, the tendency is towards the dominance of a single professional association in each profession. Some professions have never been troubled by the rivalry of associations. Where rivalry formerly existed, it is generally found either that one association has grown to overshadow all the others, or that amalgamation has taken place.[29]

In fact the Missouri Press Association became a strong supporter of the National Editorial Association, which formed in 1886. The Missouri Press Association minutes note in 1886: "During the New Orleans Exposition last year, the idea of forming a National Editorial Association culminated in a preliminary organization.... This call constituted the presidents of the State Associations' members." The minutes went on to discuss how the MPA constitution had been a model for the National Editorial Association's constitution, stating, "When the [National Editorial Association] Constitution and By-Laws were adopted, we found that Missouri had been heard from and our own code largely drawn upon in preparing the various sections."[30]

When Missouri Press Association member E. W. Stephens became the first president of the National Editorial Association in 1891, he continued to stress the importance of professionalization. In one speech, Stephens twelve times told members of the National Editorial Association that journalism was a profession. Stephens admonished, "The journalist must realize that something more than natural and acquired qualifications for the technical duties of his profession is essential.... A disciplined mind is as essential to the editor as the lawyer, doctor or the college professor.... Journalism is a profession—just as much as law, medicine or theology."[31]

In attempting to professionalize, the Missouri Press Association members stressed two of the main criteria for professionalization: codes of ethics and university education. They *did not* stress getting a license. This was significant because traditional professions require not only education but also

29. A. M. Carr-Saunders, *Professions: Their Organization and Place in Society* (Oxford, Eng.: Clarendon Press, 1928), 15.

30. J. W. Jacks, "May 11, 1886 Annual Missouri Press Association Discussion," in *Proceedings* (n.p., 1891), 10, 11.

31. E. W. Stephens, "The Newspaper and Relations to the Public," in Jno. W. Jacks, comp., *Proceedings of the Missouri Press Association: 1891 Winter Meeting* (Columbia, Mo.: Herald Publishing House, Printers and Binders, 1891), 30–31.

a license to prove that training has been absorbed and that the student passes the muster of professional standards. A license would require approval, which would infringe on freedom of the press as a form of censorship by prior restraint. Yet, the MPA was an organization that wanted legitimization for its field.

The Missouri Press Association never suggested journalists should have a license, and perhaps this is because professionalization was new. Perhaps they did not see licensing as vital, and with their annual addresses on journalism history it is possible they too thought of licensing as repugnant, reflecting the British controls of the early American colonial press: "Published by Authority."

Rather, the Missouri Press Association members stressed ethical standards at their annual meetings; such efforts culminated in a loose code of ethics in 1876, just nine years after they formed as an organization.[32] William Switzler outlined the rules of conduct expected of Missouri Press Association members:

> *First:* Allow no temptation to secure your consent to the publication of articles long or short, in prose or poetry, original or selected, which are demoralizing in their character. . . .
> *Second:* . . . Give the substance. Omit the useless details. . . .
> *Third:* . . . As preliminary to profitable writing, and as a preparation for it, much reading and study is essential.
> *Fourth:* Let us illustrate a royal virtue by resisting them [bitter words and partisan excesses]. . . . While we are sometimes *partisans* we are always *patriots*—above all, that we are not only *editors*—but *gentlemen.*[33]

The specific points addressed grew into subsequent press codes, such as that expressed by the Society of Professional Journalists, Sigma Delta Chi, in 1926, exactly half a century later.[34] Similar to the Missouri Press Association, Sigma Delta Chi was founded in 1909 as a professional organization at DePauw University and as their manual notes, "Sigma Delta Chi, Professional Journalistic Fraternity is a professional society for men engaged in journalism, dedicated to the highest ideals in journalism, and is comparable to those professional organizations serving the professions of medicine

32. Stephen A. Banning, "Truth Is Our Ultimate Goal," *American Journalism* 16, no. 1 (Winter 1999): 17.

33. William Switzler, "June 6, 1876 Annual Missouri Press Association Address," in *History and Transactions*, 131–33.

34. Bert Bostrom, *Talent, Truth and Energy: Society of Professional Journalists Sigma Delta Chi* (Chicago: Society of Professional Journalists, 1984), 177.

and the law. In this unique role, Sigma Delta Chi constantly endeavors to raise the standards of competence of its members, to recognize outstanding achievement by journalists and to promote recognition of the fact that journalism is a true profession."[35]

By the turn of the twentieth century, journalists nationally had become more interested in the trappings of professionalism, if not professionalization itself. Following the excesses of yellow journalism and a perceived need by journalists to salvage themselves before loss of credibility damaged the bottom line, it was a time for reform in all areas. Muckrakers raised awareness of problems in fields ranging from meatpacking to medicine to journalism. Interest in professionalization of journalism made a quantum leap as the first school of journalism was founded at the University of Missouri in 1908. The first dean, former MPA President Walter Williams, began what became his well-known *Journalist's Creed* with the statement, "I believe in the Profession of Journalism," which reflected the "standards for the profession to aim at," later wrote the *New York Times* upon Williams's death in 1935.[36] The press associations had played a role in the idea of professionalization of journalism, with an aim of professional education for journalists and the establishment of professional standards through codes of conduct and ethics.

35. Victor E. Bluedorn, *Sigma Delta Chi Manual* (n.p., 1959), 7.
36. *New York Times*, 8 August 1935.

CHAPTER 5

Philosophy at Work

Ideas Made a Difference

Hans Ibold and Lee Wilkins

I believe in the profession of journalism. I believe that the public journal is a public trust; that all connected with it are, to the full measure of their responsibility, trustees for the public; that acceptance of lesser service than the public service is a betrayal of this trust.

—Walter Williams, *The Journalist's Creed,* 1914

Journalists at the turn of the twentieth century needed to believe in their field. Theirs was a profession in the making, with no certain identity. Through the early 1900s, Walter Williams would develop his now renowned *Journalist's Creed,* an attempt to enact principles for America's journalists. Williams took much of his inspiration for the creed from courses he taught on the campus of the University of Missouri, just blocks from the Presbyterian church where he was also a celebrated Sunday school teacher known for his thoughts on morality and rural Missouri life. To win believers in the profession of journalism at the turn of the century, figures like

Williams linked the craft to a higher calling, to standards and ethics. These early notions about journalism and the service it should perform, its "peculiar responsibility," as Williams put it,[1] coincided with the emergence of journalism education in universities. In this chapter, we explore how the work in higher education connected journalistic ethics or standards with embedded philosophical tenets.

Between Craft-Based Thinking and a Philosophical View

At the outset of this chapter, it is important to review some fundamental historical understandings that helped define practical journalism ethics in 1908. In the post–Civil War decades, journalists and press critics discussed the notion of journalistic standards.[2] These discussions focused on two levels: the relationship of the press to the larger society and, less frequently, individual decisions by journalists. As Dicken-Garcia notes, there was relatively little discussion of the press-society relationship until the 1880s, in large part because society itself was changing as rapidly as the institution of the press. During this time, marketing was being born and, with it, national advertising. Too, there was little time for reflection within the craft of news reporting, and the complexities, though acknowledged, were far less the subject of analysis than is the case today. In addition, the press itself was engaged in some definitional work. The most important of these engagements was reconceptualizing the construct of news, as the genre moved away from the political broadsheet of the revolutionary era and incorporated certain technologies, the most significant being the telegraph. These in turn influenced news routines and hence the content. By the 1880s, journalists were defining news as something that would appeal to a mass audience. The press was now financially supported through advertising as opposed to primarily subscriptions and funding through political parties, and news was separated from opinion and analysis. A subset of questions arose around particular categories of news; for example, whether sometimes-sensational crime reports were really appropriate subject matter for the media of the day, in almost all cases, the newspaper.

Few press critics during the last decades of the nineteenth century made the sophisticated connections between the press of the day and the role of

1. "Professional Education for Journalism," Sara Lockwood Williams Papers (Western Historical Manuscripts Collection, University of Missouri, Columbia), f. 922.
2. Hazel Dicken-Garcia, *Journalistic Standards in Nineteenth Century America* (Madison: University of Wisconsin Press, 1989).

newspapers in society that were the subject of Alexis de Tocqueville's obser-vations in the 1830s in *Democracy in America*.[3] For example, Tocqueville con-nected the existence of a local press to the development and maintenance of community, to the notion of an informed citizenry, and to the development of culture in a sophisticated way: "Newspapers therefore become more nec-essary in proportion as men become more equal, and individualism more to be feared. To suppose that they only serve to protect freedom would be to diminish their importance; they maintain civilization."[4] Tocqueville's sociological approach to press criticism seems to have made little impact on late nineteenth-century press critics, who focused most often on issues of craft or, less frequently, on applied standards. In sum, at the turn of the twentieth century, the discussion of journalistic performance was both broad, focusing on the press-society connection, and particular, with, for example, essays and columns focusing on the impact of the profit motive on news; on whether journalists could be educated in any place other than the newspaper newsroom; and on sensationalism, particularly in connection with news coverage of criminal trials or crime itself.[5]

What was missing from almost all of this discussion was an analytic phi-losophy as it was understood at the beginning of the twentieth century. Dis-cussion of journalistic standards, for example, did not reference either the work of Aristotle or Kant, both of whom were well known in Western intel-lectual circles. Writing about the relationship between the newspaper and society appears to have made some philosophical assumptions in common with utilitarian theory, but these were not enunciated in any formal way. Press critics did worry about morality, by which they meant the impact of newspaper content on public morals.[6] The word "ethics" and the applica-tion of ethical principles to journalistic decision-making were infrequent in nineteenth-century discussions of journalism. To be sure, there were lists of appropriate journalistic behaviors, some beginning as early as the 1870s with Horace Greeley of the *New York Tribune* and George Childs of the *Philadelphia Public Ledger*, and about a decade later by Melville Stone of the *Chicago Daily News*. Dicken-Garcia writes, "The word ethics appeared in discussions by 1850, but it remained rare through the 1880s. Writers gener-ally used the word moral when referring to desired journalistic conduct. Nevertheless, a trend toward formulating some guidelines was clear."[7]

3. Alexis de Tocqueville, *Democracy in America*, translated by Henry Reeve, 2 vols. (New York: Bantam, 2002 [1835]).
4. Ibid., 636.
5. Dicken-Garcia, *Journalistic Standards*, 171–73, 228–32.
6. Ibid., 138.
7. Ibid., 156.

That trend, however, was dichotomous. On the one hand, James Gordon Bennett, Jr., son of the founder of the *New York Herald*, emphasized the money-making and business-oriented drive of journalism. On the other hand, Joseph Pulitzer's newly formed *Post and Dispatch* in St. Louis made a kind of ethical statement upon publication in 1878, one that the newspaper would strive to live up to in the late 1800s:

> The *Post and Dispatch* will serve no party but the people; it will be no organ of Republicanism, but the organ of truth; it will follow no causes but its conclusions; will not support the "Administration," but criticize it; will oppose all frauds and shams wherever and whatever they are; will advocate principles and ideas rather than prejudices and partisanship. These ideas and principles are precisely the same as those upon which our Government was originally founded . . . They are the ideas of a true, genuine, real Democracy.[8]

However, Pulitzer's statement and others like it were not in any formal way connected with a particular moral or ethical theory. As Dicken-Garcia notes, by 1890, press critics were "still groping with what had become an immense social institution of overwhelming capabilities."[9]

An Unsung Role for Philosophy

But even though analytic philosophy may not have been acknowledged, that does not mean that it was not at work. Indeed, one of the real contributions of Walter Williams's creed to the profession was his ability to tie professional practice to statements with a clear claim in the realm of philosophy that could be enriched by ethical theory as it was developing and could then be applied. "We need such in our profession," Williams said in a speech to American newspaper editors in 1903, a year before the gathering of world journalists that Williams would orchestrate at the Louisiana Purchase Exposition in St. Louis. In the speech, Williams envisions a kind of moral transformation of journalism:

> We hear so much of type and presses, of advertising rates and subscription receipts. We are told again and again . . . of what we must do to bring business into our coffers as if mere business was the end and object of

---

8. Silas Bent, *Newspaper Crusaders: A Neglected Story* (Westport, Conn.: Greenwood Press, 1939).

9. Dicken-Garcia, *Journalistic Standards*, 219.

human life. We need to have our ideals raised. We need to have the vision splendid hung up before our eyes continually. The messenger is more than the types and presses with which he sends his message. We need such inspiration all the while. And if my wish comes true, this gathering of the world's journalists will strengthen the arm of him who strikes at iniquity entrenched. It will teach the editor how to resist the pleadings of the briber and the more dangerous, more subtle pleadings of bribery by his pocketbook as well.[10]

Thus, the vision, the inspiration, of a connection between the rise of professionalism and a kind of moral philosophy was a purposeful one. The founding of the Missouri School of Journalism in 1908 represented a convergence of intellectual and philosophic currents with history and craft, which presented the field with two choices.

The first choice was whether to remain a trade or to seek admission to the learned professions. As noted in previous chapters, Williams clearly sought to place journalism on an equal intellectual footing in a university setting with the traditional learned professions: law, medicine, and theology. This choice itself was controversial, for many publishers believed that early twentieth-century journalistic training could be accomplished only in newspaper newsrooms and that a university education would not provide young men with the necessary training to become journalists.[11]

The second choice was whether to become a profession that emphasized public service, similar to the three learned professions, or to be a profession that emphasized client-centered, industry-based relationships, similar to the professions of accounting and engineering. The call to public service was embedded in Williams's written creed, which he did not enunciate formally until six years after the Missouri school was founded. Williams provided an answer: academic journalism would seek to train professionals who had the ethically based goals of public service and the buttressing of democratic institutions. Williams was unequivocal about linking journalism to the higher calling of public service. In a speech made to a gathering of editors early in his deanship entitled "Professional Education for Journalists," he sought to elevate journalism above trade or mere business:

There is no surer test of the earning capacity of a newspaper than the measure of its public service. There is more in journalism than bread and but-

10. "The World's Press and the World's Fair," Sara Lockwood Williams Papers (Western Historical Manuscripts Collection, University of Missouri, Columbia), f. 581.
11. Dicken-Garcia, *Journalistic Standards*, 218–20.

The Journalist's Creed

I believe in the profession of journalism.

I believe that the public journal is a public trust; that all connected with it are, to the full measure of their responsibility, trustees for the public; that acceptance of a lesser service than the public service is betrayal of this trust.

I believe that clear thinking and clear statement, accuracy and fairness are fundamental to good journalism.

I believe that a journalist should write only what he holds in his heart to be true.

I believe that suppression of the news, for any consideration other than the welfare of society, is indefensible.

I believe that no one should write as a journalist what he would not say as a gentleman; that bribery by one's own pocketbook is as much to be avoided as bribery by the pocketbook of another; that individual responsibility may not be escaped by pleading another's instructions or another's dividends.

I believe that advertising, news and editorial columns should alike serve the best interests of readers; that a single standard of helpful truth and cleanness should prevail for all; that the supreme test of good journalism is the measure of its public service.

I believe that the journalism which succeeds best—and best deserves success—fears God and honors Man; is stoutly independent, unmoved by pride of opinion or greed of power, constructive, tolerant but never careless, self-controlled, patient, always respectful of its readers but always unafraid; is quickly indignant at injustice; is unswayed by the appeal of privilege or the clamor of the mob; seeks to give every man a chance and, as far as law and honest wage and recognition of human brotherhood can make it so, an equal chance; is profoundly patriotic while sincerely promoting international good will and cementing world-comradeship; is a journalism of humanity, of and for today's world.

As one of the earliest codes of ethics, *The Journalist's Creed* emphasizes a belief in the profession of journalism and states the profession's standards.

ter—necessary as that is—or than dividends upon shares of stock. Journalism has a nobler mission. It is preeminently the profession of public service. The newspaper small or large is the greatest public utility institution. While all other public utility institutions have been regulated by law, the newspaper is, in a special sense, its own regulator. It voices, even when it does not create, the public opinion to which itself must answer. Peculiar responsibility, therefore, rests upon journalism to recognize its mission as a public servant.[12]

This focus on public service, which Williams emphasized tirelessly, provided the school with a necessary toehold in the academy; it served both a philosophic and a political rationale for the nascent professional program and its acceptance at the university level. The decision made to found the school and to found it at a university required a philosophical rationale even though it was couched in some informal and unwritten understandings.

However, there remained a tension between public service and the more industry-based model that was reflected in the school's early curriculum.[13] Williams's vision for a required course that he taught, "History and Principles of Journalism," was clearly lodged in the realm of philosophy, even though the class itself included a fair amount of industry-promotion. Although Williams lacked formal education, he was well read in the roots of philosophy. He had a minimal knowledge of Latin and Greek as well as some other disciplines, having read "most of the books in the substantial collection of his cousin, James Muir, who was said to have the largest private library in the state" of Missouri.[14]

An essay written in 1898 and entitled "What an Editor Should Read, and Why?" suggests how Williams might have navigated Muir's collection. In the essay, Williams listed twelve books "for any editor's library."[15] It is revealing that Williams placed the Bible at the top of the list and devoted a substantive passage to comment on the book. The Bible topped a list that included various works of Shakespeare, histories of Missouri and the United States, Francis Amasa Walker's *Political Economy*, various journalist biographies, James Bryce's *The American Commonwealth*, Arlo Bates's *Talks on Writing English*, Nathaniel Hawthorne's *The Scarlet Letter*, and Victor Hugo's *Les Miserables*. Williams wrote of the Bible:

12. As found in folder, "Professional Education for Journalism," Sara Lockwood Williams Papers, f. 922.

13. Ronald T. Farrar, *A Creed for My Profession: Walter Williams, Journalist to the World*.

14. Ibid., 28–29.

15. "What an Editor Should Read, and Why?" Sara Lockwood Williams Papers, f. 751.

Whatever we may think of the faith taught by this book of books, whatever we may believe as its inspiration, no one can be a well educated man, no one can attain the highest usefulness as an editor, who is unfamiliar with the Scriptures . . . There has been no advancement in ethics, nothing new in education or morals or in teaching since the Great Teacher along the roads and paths of Judea, Samaria and beyond spake as never man.[16]

There is no doubt that Williams carried an emphasis on ethical principles to the School of Journalism. As Williams's wife, Sara Lockwood Williams, wrote of Missouri's nascent program:

The aim from the first has been to give the student high ideals and standards of ethics, and at the same time to put him in the "newspaper office" or laboratory to prove for himself that these standards may be successfully applied. The School paid heed to the old contention that the best place to study newspaper work is in the newspaper office. It recognized, however, that the drawback there was that the newspaper makers have their hands full without stopping to explain what they are doing and why.[17]

In 1908 Walter Williams and his small faculty would make this dual ethical/practical mission clear in the inaugural issue of the student-run, faculty-supervised *University Missourian* newspaper. It ran the following statement:

The University Missourian will accomplish its purpose well if the men and women trained by work upon its staff are, by such training, better furnished for public service; if they shall go forth into the world of journalism better equipped to know and print the news of the day; the unbiased news, attractively, accurately, helpfully; if they shall be better enabled to make comment on this news fairly, intelligently and with high ideals; if they shall learn that American journalism is, in its highest realization, schoolhouse and forum, teacher and tribune, a foe to wrong doing, an aid to education, a force for moral progress, an exponent of true Americanism.[18]

From the onset Williams made it clear that these "high ideals" were areas of interest and expertise. For example, when asked as dean to name the

16. Ibid.
17. Sara Lockwood Williams, *Twenty Years of Education for Journalism: A History of the School of Journalism of the University of Missouri Columbia, Missouri* (Columbia, Mo.: E. W. Stephens Publishing Company, 1929), 54.
18. *University Missourian*, 14 September 1908.

most important book for journalists, Williams again pointed his audience to the Bible. "Journalism attains its highest development in intelligent democracy," he explained in an essay entitled "The Bible: A Text-Book for Journalists." "The Bible promotes an intelligent democracy, which seeks to give every man a chance and, as far as law and honest wage and aggressive brotherhood can make so, an equal chance. . . . The whole Bible is a model of good journalism . . . The Book teaches the fundamental principle of good journalism, the principle of right selection."[19]

Of course, the philosophical influences on Williams's thinking about journalism ranged wider than the Scriptures, though this Christian influence was indeed formidable. The remainder of this chapter will point out the philosophical influences on the 1908 culture and explore the reasons for placing the school at a university. The decisions made that year had continuing ramifications for the vibrancy of journalism within the academy while providing a vision for journalism at its best: as a servant for democracy and the collected and collective insights of the citizenry.

The Philosophical Base at the Birth of the School

Canadian philosopher and historian Stephen Ward posits that the notion of a public ethic and its connection with the journalism of that day was essentially an eighteenth-century English invention.[20] The notion of a public, let alone one with an opinion, could not emerge until the monarchical authoritarianism in Britain and elsewhere subsided. In its place, at least in British intellectual life, arose the concept of the autonomous, rational citizen, capable of thinking and acting in his own best interests. Ward links these developments with what he characterizes as the commercialization of culture,[21] where the contents of the press ranged from the arts to the sciences and beyond. Indeed, the notion of the "public intellectual" dates to this day; some of Britain's best thinkers published their ideas not in academic journals but in the journals (newspapers) of the day. This public sphere was less subject to both internal pressures and external politics that were far more rough-and-tumble than their contemporary American counterparts.[22] Ward lodges

19. "The Bible: A Text-Book for Journalists," Sara Lockwood Williams Papers.

20. Stephen J. A. Ward, *The Invention of Journalism Ethics: The Path to Objectivity and Beyond* (Montreal and Kingston: McGill-Queen's University Press, 2004).

21. Ibid., 130.

22. For a full explanation of Habermas's concept, see Jurgen Habermas, *The Theory of Communicative Action,* 2 vols., translated by Thomas McCarthy (Boston: Beacon Press, 1984, 1987).

the beginnings of these developments in the eighteenth century, although it is worth noting that one of these public intellectuals was John Stuart Mill,[23] who wrote about one hundred years later when historic experience, particularly in England, impacted his discussion of liberty, of democracy, and of the public good. His underpinnings of utilitarianism, as well as a vehicle for getting it noticed in the press, were based on the era's potent political and cultural mixture.

At the beginning of the eighteenth century, a journalist had one of three roles: partisan, spectator, or reporter of events.[24] The polemical essay, still a staple of European elite journalism, was the focal point of much newspaper content and represented the partisan role. Essays, which melded analysis, fiction, and fact, "blurred the line between fact and interpretation."[25] Daniel Defoe's work provides an excellent example of the genre. His book written nearly sixty years later, *A Journal of the Plague Year,* is a fictional, imaginative reconstruction of the plague in London based on true accounts and became what some literary critics give as one reason why Defoe may be considered the first English novelist.[26]

By mid-century, Samuel Johnson was practicing much the same craft, but the ratio of fact to fiction in his work verged more toward fact: "Johnson wrote elevated journalism adorned by wit, handsome phrases, and wide learning."[27] Johnson became regarded as one of the most acute observers and spectators of English society.

Journalists could also act as reporters, a role that initially was perceived as less prestigious than either the partisan or the spectator. Nonetheless, Ward notes that the greatest stimuli to the reporting role "were the opening of the House of Commons to reporters in 1771, and of the House of Lords in 1775, although reporters were not allowed to take notes during debate for another 12 years."[28]

All three approaches, partisan, spectator, and reporter, justified their actions in terms of benefits to the public. The contribution of the reportorial role most obviously hinged on the provision of accurate and timely facts to the commonweal, something that as the century progressed became increasingly linked to a kind of facticity. On American shores, Thomas Paine,

23. Two works cover much of John Stuart Mill's thought: *On Liberty* (1859) and *On Utilitarianism* (1836).

24. Ward, *The Invention of Journalism Ethics,* 139.

25. Ibid., 141.

26. Daniel Defoe, *A Journal of the Plague Year* (New York: Penguin Books, 1966 [1722]); Lennard Davis, *Factual Fictions: The Origins of the English Novel* (New York: Columbia University Press, 1983).

27. Ward, *The Invention of Journalism Ethics,* 142.

28. Ibid., 144.

also a journalist, became what Ward characterizes as a "Tribune for the people,"[29] a role that again emphasizes the public service connection of journalism to political discussion and debate. But whether it was in France, England, or the colonies, the connection between journalism and democracy clearly solidified during the eighteenth century, despite intense government pressure on particular writers and sometimes on those who published them. Ward notes that toward the end of the century, British political philosopher Edmund Burke coined the term "the fourth estate" to characterize the press's relationship to government. Ward quotes Burke as follows:

> Whoever can speak, speaking not to the whole nation, becomes a power; a branch of government, with inalienable weight in lawmaking, in all acts of authority. It matters not what rank he has, what revenues or garnitures: nothing more is requisite. The nation is governed by all that has tongue in the nation. Democracy is virtually there.[30]

Whether Burke meant the phrase "the fourth estate" to be an entirely laudatory one is still difficult to discern. Burke's skepticism about the impact of public opinion on legislative decision-making was the focus of his now-famous analysis that the role of the legislator can also be inferred from the linking of democracy to a nation governed entirely by its tongue.[31] Nonetheless, the notion of the press as the fourth branch of government readily skipped across the pond, even though the upstart Americans had exchanged parliamentary for republican rule.

It is important to note that the eighteenth century also represents the building blocks of Enlightenment thinking. The notion of autonomous actors who can provide a public with facts that can be rationally evaluated became broadly accepted only in this century. The modern notion of fact also owes a debt to this historical era, for it comes about one hundred years after the beginnings of the scientific revolution in Europe. This construction of intellectual reality spelled doom for the divine right of kings and eroded the moral rule of a centralized church tied directly to political power. Facts became discoverable and knowable by the average person, a true revolution in thinking from the world of Saint Augustine or even Thomas Aquinas. Concomitantly, this foundation provided those who could speak to "the people," such as autonomous citizens, with clout, and with an emerging political and cultural role that could be summarized as an (independent)

29. Ibid., 162–64.
30. Ibid., 170.
31. Edmund Burke, *Reflections on the Revolution in France* (Stanford, Calif.: Stanford University Press, 2001).

fourth estate that served the public interest through publicity and that stimulated nonpolitical conversation.[32]

This remarkable shift in worldview, of course, was couched most often in the language of politics and power rather than of ethics. But, with exemplars such as Defoe, Johnson, and Paine, it was possible to discern how people of practical wisdom could use journalism for the public good.[33] The concepts of the good and the right, central to the realm of moral philosophy, could now enter professional debate, education, and aspiration. The notion of a public, of a community, equal in power and influence to that of any monarch funds much of later utilitarianism thinking. And, humankind, the rational actor, is a precursor to ethical reasoning in both nineteenth-century philosophical giants, John Stuart Mill and Immanuel Kant.

Thus, when Walter Williams, writing about two hundred years later, connected the profession of journalism to a duty to public service in a democracy, he summoned some of the best examples of political and ethical thinking in the then recent Western history. He tied them firmly to a journalism connected to political behavior in a way central to the maintenance of democratic governance. He also turned for sustenance and guidance to Christian-derived principles, and he made it clear that he wanted other journalists to do the same. "Journalism, in the final analysis, is a profession of public service, not a business or trade," Williams said, as he often would, in a speech entitled "Journalism as Light Unto a New World."[34] "The right practice of the best journalism, its use as a weapon for democracy, will come through the exercise of a wholesome, enlightened public opinion." And to cultivate that wholesomeness, Williams wrote, journalists would do well to acquaint themselves with Christian principles:

> We have been thrust as a nation from a secluded place into a central position among the peoples of the world. We have become a world's spokesman . . . We need to know ourselves and other peoples. This means study; it means an open mind and a sympathetic heart, and above all, unflinching faith . . . World leadership is spiritual. It is not a matter of faith in food, or in fuel, but faith in man and in God."[35]

Williams also wrote that his fellow journalists should share the commitment to Christian-derived principles:

32. Ward, *The Invention of Journalism Ethics*, 171–72.
33. The concept of a phrenesis, or practical wisdom, is best explained in Aristotle's *Nichomachean Ethics*.
34. "Journalism as Light Unto a New World," Sara Lockwood Williams Papers.
35. "The Bible: Text-Book for Journalists," Sara Lockwood Williams Papers.

From an intimate acquaintanceship with newspaper men, I can say with confidence there are few, if any, men who have not an abiding faith in the Fatherhood of God. They may not attend your churches as they should; they may sometimes speak lightly of ceremonials and creeds; they may appear affected with modern indifference; they may criticize the sermons of the yellow pulpit. But you will find, if you know newspaper men as I know them, that they have the highest reverence for holy things, the most sincere faith in a personal God, not a mere absentee First Cause.[36]

Thus, Williams viewed the profession of journalism as performing an essential public service in a democracy, and he connected this service role to ethics rooted in Christianity. In 1908, approaches to such ethical principles were often polarized. The muckraking period dichotomized thinking about these principles, casting journalists' professional values on one side and the nation's religious heritage on the other. "The muckrakers recognized that their investigative zeal was rooted, as Lincoln Steffens said, in the prophetic tradition of the Bible, and both he and Upton Sinclair urged journalists to look to Jesus and the prophets of the Hebrew Scriptures as the model for their reform campaigns." The muckrakers were, however, generally critical of Christian influences and tended to view organized religion as hypocritically indifferent to social issues.[37]

Williams subscribed to the aspirational element of a Christian ethic, the connection between "I" and "Thou" that would characterize the thought, decades later, of theologians such as Reinhold Neibuhr. Neibuhr, a member of the Hutchins Commission on Freedom of the Press, wrote in 1947 what has come to be known as the social responsibility theory of the press. Although Williams's practical theology was not as well developed as Neibuhr's, it is possible to see in both the same central organizing principle: an empathetic connection between the "I" of journalism and the "Thou" of community.[38]

Making Journalism an Ethical Profession

The concept of a profession lodged in Christian-driven public service in support of a democracy carries within it a contradiction, as William M. Sul-

36. Ibid.
37. Doug Underwood, "Secularists or Modern Day Prophets? Journalists' Ethics and the Judeo-Christian Tradition," *Journal of Mass Media Ethics* 16, no. 1 (2001): 33–47.
38. John P. Ferre, "A Short History of Ethics in the United States" in Lee Wilkins and Clifford Christians, eds., *Handbook of Mass Media Ethics* (New York: Lawrence Erlbaum and Associates, in press).

livan wrote: "Professionals take part in commercial society as the owners of a special type of wealth—producing property or 'capital' of a peculiarly intellectual sort: the skills and knowledge acquired through their specialized training and experience."[39] Such capital is at core a social and political good. This much the United States acquired from Europe. What was different was the American emphasis on egalitarianism. Professions in the United States had to reconcile their expertise and social standing, most often acquired through education and the sort of class-based wealth that makes attaining an education possible, with the political claims of equality that were the fabric of American culture in the 1830s and 1840s. As Sullivan explained, "During this time, the learned professions of law, medicine, and the ministry (largely including education) were forced to seek a new institutional form,"[40] a process that was far more difficult in the United States than it had been in Europe.

As usual, Tocqueville's analysis captured the roots of the problem. In the Jacksonian era, democracy meant a thoroughgoing commitment to individual liberty and equality. Yet Tocqueville assessed that such freedom was a collective achievement; it could be maintained only within a community in which individuals understood that their well-being was dependent on that of others. Tocqueville, like Burke, was concerned with the impact of an unthinking and reflexive drive for equality in the new republic. "Unless the democratic individuals were to understand that real fulfillment came not in comfort alone but through engagement with things of intrinsic significance and high value," Sullivan writes, "democracy would slump into a dull materialism without spirit."[41] For Tocqueville, that slump would begin with the pursuit of wealth, largely through the institution of private property that the founders, citing Locke, had elevated to constitutional status about fifty years earlier. Egalitarianism also meant that standards of excellence, themselves the subject of an egalitarian ethic, would be difficult to develop and maintain. Because of that difficulty, Tocqueville saw that Americans would be likely to substitute amassing wealth as a counterfeit measure of attaining excellence. He wrote that this would be a particular problem for the arts because, in an egalitarian society, every art was open to all, making for little stability in any craft community. The social connections between members of the community are "broken, and each, left to himself, only tries to make as much money as easily as possible."[42]

39. William M. Sullivan, *Work and Integrity: The Crisis and Promise of Professionalism in America*, 2nd ed. (San Francisco: Jossey-Bass, 2005), 67.

40. Ibid., 72.

41. Ibid., 78.

42. De Tocqueville, *Democracy in America*, 465.

When Tocqueville was writing about the arts, he meant the fine arts. But in the late 1800s, journalism was essentially a writer's craft. The problem that Tocqueville foresaw for the arts also accurately described much of journalism at the turn of the twentieth century: it was an endeavor characterized by a zealous pursuit of money achieved by newspaper owners who supported publications with the "look of brilliance" that replaced high quality. The era of yellow journalism, which was at its height in major cities at the turn of the century, was foreshadowed by Tocqueville's concern for the arts.

There were few institutions that could counter the philosophical force of egalitarianism and the economic force of an emerging, strong middle class in the American experiment, but as the professions writ large developed, they discovered their own way out of the morass. They would "establish and safeguard standards of practice that ensure public authority and confidence"[43] by linking those standards and expertise "to an ability to win support from outside their own membership, which will depend upon their fulfillment of tasks set by interests wider than their own."[44]

Professions tried to link their achievement with a better democratic future, something that Sullivan, a Carnegie scholar of professionalism, connected to the emergence of progressivism in American history. As noted in previous chapters, progressivism was at its height during the decade in which the School of Journalism was founded. The search for professional, political, and social legitimacy was acute. It was not surprising that journalism turned for succor to another institution that was also changing rapidly under the twin forces of democratic egalitarianism and an adolescent capitalism: the emerging research university.

Walter Williams's biographer, among others, linked Williams's establishment of the School of Journalism at the University of Missouri to an accident of geography: Williams began his journalistic career in Boonville, Missouri. Although there is some logic in this assertion, there were larger forces at work. While the elite universities such as Harvard and Yale functioned more as European, primarily British, academies and colleges, research universities began to emerge only at the turn of the century. The American prototype was Johns Hopkins University, whose trustees decided to model their approach on the greatest German universities, "places thick with men consumed with creating new knowledge, not simply teaching what was believed."[45] Johns Hopkins University, founded in 1873, built on this notion

43. Sullivan, *Work and Integrity*, 81.
44. K. Polanyi, *The Great Transformation: The Political and Economic Origins of Our Own Time* (Boston: Beacon Press, 1957), 52.
45. John M. Barry, *The Great Influenza: The Epic Story of the Deadliest Plague in History* (New York: Penguin, 2004), 33.

of creating new knowledge, and it was coupled with a professional school, in this case a school of medicine that opened its doors in 1893. The successful experiment at Hopkins linked a vision of the impact of science on knowledge creation and hence professional education.

The Hopkins approach spread. The University of Missouri, with its land-grant mission, was far more likely to be hospitable to professional education, in general, and a school of journalism, specifically, than were the traditional and prestigious institutions of American higher education. As Sullivan notes, "When all this changed around the turn of the century, it is not surprising that not just the new, aspiring fields such as management or engineering turned eagerly to appropriate the prestige of expertise for legitimacy; the older learned professions successfully did the same."[46] Professional schools became part of the university approach to education. The University of Missouri added journalism to the list.

The Professional Future

Journalism owes much to its cultural history. Media scholar James W. Carey explains:

> This is the point that I really want to hold on to—to enter any medium of communication is to enter a world of often predefined, but negotiable, identities, and, at the same time, in which a positive affirmation takes place. When Hegel writes, "The modern world begins with reading the newspapers," in some sense, that says it all. To get up and to make the choice to say that I'm going to enter the secular world, the political world in this case, the world of being a citizen or a subject. . . . Now, these are political acts.[47]

To paraphrase Carey, reporting news in the early part of the twentieth century was a political act. Training journalists to report news in a university setting implied a politics with an intellectual and philosophical foundation, full of the contradictions inherent in it.

Among the more difficult contradictions that Williams conjured is the source of ethical principles that he believed should guide journalism in a global context. By 1908, America was emerging in the world arena; international news was on the journalistic agenda as never before. Far ahead of

46. Sullivan, *Work and Integrity*, 93.
47. James Carey cited in *Thinking with James Carey: Essays on Communications, Transportation, History*, edited by J. Packer and C. Robertson (New York: Peter Lang, 2006), 203–4.

his time and unique in his thinking about journalism in the global context, Williams enjoined all journalists to form a universal brotherhood, as he would call it, and to conceive of their public service as a global enterprise, one that served humanity. As he championed journalistic freedom on his global travels and at home, much of it based in the rich history of political thought, so too did he advocate for a profound responsibility to Christian law and, unequivocally, to an American model of journalism that flowed from Christian-derived principles.

At various points in his career, Williams also advocated a rural Missourian model of journalism. He often proudly identified himself as a "country editor" and with "country journalism." Williams spelled out what this meant in an editorial he wrote in the late 1890s for the *Missouri Editor:*

> Gradually the truth is making itself felt that the journalistic power of this country lies largely with the country press. It not only, in the aggregate, reaches more readers but it wields more influence. It lives close to the people and is in touch with them. Its atmosphere is pure and removed from corrupting influence of demagoguery and money. This fact is recognized by no class more fully than public men who today stand more in awe of the country press by far than they do of the metropolitan dailies. They do so because they understand that public sentiment is controlled by the country press. In addition to its moral power, the country press is a money-making institution, if properly installed.[48]

This "country" bias would have been at odds with the wildly growing, immigrant-based cities of the United States in 1908. The time period saw a rapid and often turbulent transition moving from rural society to industrialized, multiethnic, urban life. It meant a dramatic shift in the demographics of the United States, as the rise of urban industry brought a wave of immigrants "whose religions, traditions, languages, and sheer numbers made easy assimilation impossible." America was certainly affected by this experience of the rural mind confronted with culturally diverse, urban life; for many who were "raised in respectable quietude and the high-toned moral imperatives of evangelical Protestantism, the city seemed not merely a new social form or way of life but a strange threat to civilization itself."[49]

48. Frank W. Rucker, *Walter Williams*, 61.
49. Richard Hofstadter, *The Age of Reform: From Bryan to F.D.R.* (New York: Knopf, 1965), quotes from pp. 8, 175.

The high ideals Williams had in mind were profoundly challenged by this chaotic, multicultural scene. A student once asked Williams what newspaper he would print if he was once again a newspaper editor. Decades after the school's founding, his response is telling:

> You have a better chance to put your individuality in [a country paper] than you would if tied up to a department in one of the city papers. In the small town the paper you run is yours. You can do what you want, say what you want . . . Liberty of the press means the right to express your honest opinion about things, and the small town is the garden wherein is developed the perfect flower.[50]

Contradictions between the individual and society make up ethical thinking. By making journalism responsible for and to a democratic public, the school welcomed a difficult discussion of duty and of loyalty. Kant, of course, had written about duty thirty years before the school was founded. America's most thoughtful analyst of loyalty, Josiah Royce,[51] was writing in the same year that the school's first class met for the first time. And Aristotle's presence could be felt, too, in the history and principles class, with its focus on role models such as Thomas Paine, John Peter Zenger, and Horace Greeley. Community, and whether it is ontologically prior to autonomous individuality or emerges only as a result of it, was present, as well. Politics does not happen to hermits. It takes one's fellow citizens, a community. And it is the impact of mass communication on people, as individuals and as members of local, national, and international groups, that has become the increasing focus of the university-housed school. Standards of performance, their long-term and short-range consequences, also became the subject of systematic study.

Among the many reasons for these developments is at the core the deep learning of philosophy and how that understanding, acknowledged or not, works itself out in everyday professional life. For journalism and the Missouri School of Journalism, ethics foreshadows much. There are still many contradictions that are being worked out, as media and technology are dynamic and change cultures while they disseminate information, and become the focus of much study. The impact of ownership on media content and the more traditional issues of deception, sensationalism, and the role of practitioners in larger organizations all have become the focus of systematic study. New questions are being asked, and yet ethics remains the cornerstone of the intellectual foundation that was laid in 1908.

---

50. Notes from conversation. Sara Lockwood Williams Papers, f. 279.
51. J. Royce, *The Philosophy of Loyalty* (New York: Macmillan Co., 1908).

PART III

Institutional Rumblings and Change

In 1908, cheap newsprint, faster presses, and something-for-everyone news offerings and advertising profits meant that newspaper entrepreneurs could make great fortunes in journalism. That year represented a rise in corporate journalism, with major owners from Hearst to Scripps and Pulitzer owning multiple newspapers. Mergers and consolidations of competing newspapers became common. New York City had as many as twenty-nine daily newspapers just nine years before state universities began schools of journalism.[1] One way to compete was through sensational coverage. Larger circulation figures meant more advertising dollars. In major American cities journalism had become a corporate business, but with questionable standards. The call for reform had become a national issue.

At the same time all newspapers, large and small, had to have financial support in order to survive. Circulation was not enough. Advertising would be the way. The new *University Missourian* was no exception to the need for economic support; even with university support, the laboratory newspaper had to be supplemented with advertising revenues. In its first issues, the *Missourian* had large paid advertisements for local groceries, men's wear, cleaning services, and drugstores. Too, the *Missourian* emphasized that subscriptions cost two dollars per school year, and two cents per

1. Maurine Beasley, "The Emergence of Modern Media, 1900–1945," chapter 15 in William David Sloan, ed., *The Media in America, A History*, 6th ed. (Northport, Ala.: Vision Press, 2005), 284.

daily copy. Promotion of the newspaper was important, since Columbia already had three other competing newspapers.

Walter Williams knew that there had to be both promotion and extra financial backing. During the fall of 1908 the school sent copies of the *Missourian* to the state's public schools and academies to alert interested parties about the newspaper's founding.[2] To advertise the new newspaper immediately, Williams brought in two St. Louis newsboys to hawk the newspaper up and down Broadway in downtown Columbia. The stunt was unusual; the *Missourian* had pictures of the "boys" with the caption, "Their chief asset is lungs."[3] The cry of the newsboys represented big-city journalism and also big business. Such an emphasis was part of the newspaper institution, even though there were plenty of critics of both the business side and the status of advertising.

The new school of journalism had classes on newspaper administration and publishing, which incorporated advertising and circulation. As more of a community newspaper than a campus paper, the *Missourian* would be a commercial operation that solicited subscriptions and advertisements to run with its news stories. It would compete with the other Columbia newspapers for not only news but also business, no matter what the reaction from the other papers.[4] Indeed, there were rumblings of complaint from the competition, especially about competing against a taxpayer-supported business for advertising dollars.

Within two weeks of the School of Journalism opening, the editor of the *Columbia Daily Tribune* fumed, not over the training of journalists, but over the competition for advertising. Editor Ed Watson asked, "in all fairness should the state go into the newspaper business against private individuals?"[5] This accusation resonated with other publishers in the state; it became a crisis. Walter Williams quickly reassured the next Missouri Press Association meeting about the newspaper, "It was not regarded as proper for the State in training for journalism to pay for the support of such a public enterprise. The competition was not large if it really was competition." When the *Tribune* and Columbia's two weeklies asked the Board of Curators to pull out of the local advertising field, the curators deferred. Next, the local newspapers tried through the state legislature to stop the new paper; the response was that a newly formed University of Missouri Publishing Asso-

---

2. "Thanks!" *University Missourian*, 14 October 1908, 2. This column had snippets of letters primarily from school superintendents thanking the journalism school for the *Missourian*.

3. *University Missourian*, 16 September 1908, 2.

4. Farrar, *A Creed for My Profession*, 144.

5. Edwin Moss as quoted in Farrar, *A Creed for My Profession*, 146.

ciation incorporated with an off-campus printing plant would take over the production of the newspaper. The *Missourian* survived.[6] A university-based competitive newspaper remained an issue, not for news so much as for advertising, and such rumblings continue today.

The following two chapters examine the institutional rumblings and change by 1908. The arguments, and their connections with journalism education, are found in Fred Blevens's chapter, "Power, Irony, and Contradictions: Education and the News Business." Caryl Cooper's chapter discusses the status of advertising and journalism education in 1908: "Profits versus Pedagogy: Advertising Education's First Battle."

6. Ibid., 149–51.

CHAPTER 6

Power, Irony, and Contradictions

Education and the News Business

Fred Blevens

The persistent debate about whether journalism was trade or profession continued well into the twentieth century, fueled in part by an industry that had evolved rapidly into a remarkably sophisticated form of mass communication. Much had happened. By 1908, the U.S. newspaper business had survived a tumultuous revolution, a partisan era, the Industrial Revolution, the radical adjustments of the Penny Press, and a Civil War to find itself positioned as a powerful social, political, cultural, and economic force in the wake of the Gilded Age and in the midst of the nation's shift from producerism to consumerism. This chapter will examine the connections between industry and the rise of journalism education, the status of the journalism business, the industry's contradictions in its political role, three 1908 events involving major publishers, and the industry's role in the journalism education curriculum.

In two regions of the country, the East and the Midwest, the past combined with explosive industry growth and emerging contemporary issues to create environments hospitable for the development of journalism education. In New York City and Columbia, Missouri, the approaches, philosophical to practical, mirrored the country's definitive urban-rural split. As the urban newspapers moved rapidly toward consolidation, merger, and combination, rural papers actively participated in the industry's battles against monopolization of the newsprint paper industry. The urban press, especially in New York, tried to shed its guilt from yellow journalism; rural newspaper owners and editors continued to lead local and state political campaigns, sometimes putting themselves on the ballot for public office. As urban editors and publishers sought strength through circulation and advertising sales numbers, rural newspapers focused most on community collaboration in business and public life.

For the newspaper industry, the effort to establish journalism education was a study of chaos and contrast, one that sprang from a need for maturity and order in structure, behavior, and, most important, economics. As a business starting to professionalize, a particular maturation required a collegiate discipline. Journalism schools would help.

A Boom on the Landscape

By 1908, the number of daily newspapers in the United States had peaked at twenty-six hundred, with the majority of those publishing during the evening cycle in urban areas. Before the Civil War, there were few evening papers, even in the largest urban areas, but the rapid development of telegraphic communication and the expansion of pre-press and press automation helped to reduce the morning share of the national market to less than 30 percent during the early twentieth century.[1] In the cities, every thriving newspaper had reduced its newsstand price to a penny or two cents, sometimes sacrificing circulation revenue to build advertising. The *New York Times*, for example, had reluctantly entered the penny field in 1898 with a daily circulation of 25,726. In 1908, the *Times* was selling 172,880 copies without engaging in sensationalism. *Times* editors, on the day of change, pledged that "no reader of the *Times* in the past need scan the columns of this morning's issue, or any subsequent issue, with the least misgiving or apprehension lest the reduction in price may be concurrent with a lowering in tone and quality."[2]

Many papers of the period entered the penny market to appeal to a burgeoning population of immigrants and lower social classes. The focus of attention in the New York circulation wars was on Joseph Pulitzer's *World*,

1. Alfred McClung Lee, *The Daily Newspaper in America*, 66–69; Willard Grosvenor Bleyer, *Main Currents in the History of American Journalism* (Cambridge, Mass.: Riverside Press, 1927), 393–97.
2. "ONE CENT!" *New York Times*, 10 October 1898, 1.

James Gordon Bennett, Jr.'s *Herald,* and William Randolph Hearst's *Journal.* The race for readers and profits was so intense that the papers advertised in trade publications to tout their advantages over one another. In one ad placed in *Editor and Publisher* during 1908, Pulitzer bragged that in the previous year, his paper had recorded a daily circulation gain of 84,083 and that it had printed 1,405,032 "separate advertisements—the largest number ever printed in any newspaper anywhere." The ad claimed that the *World's* ads in 1907 outnumbered the *Herald's* by 292,747, that no other paper deserved comparison, and that "every other newspaper shows a LOSS compared with its own record of that year," an obvious insult to Hearst.[3]

For nearly three-quarters of a century, publishers, reluctant to challenge observance of the Christian Sabbath, had ceded the Sunday field primarily to freestanding urban weeklies that featured sensational fare and sports coverage. However, by 1908, most successful daily publishers, morning and evening, were printing seven-day papers with impunity. Challenges to Sunday publication were based primarily on state blue laws, designed to prohibit the sale of products that were not necessities on the Christian Sabbath. Judges across the land, as well as clergy, had become convinced that Sunday editions of daily newspapers were, in fact, essential.

Hearst and Pulitzer are credited with discovering the commercial potential of distributing a distinct Sunday morning edition to an audience that exceeded their daily edition numbers and geographic zone. Between 1880 and 1900, the number of dailies publishing Sunday editions increased from 113 to more than 567, co-opting nearly 80 percent of the freestanding Sunday papers that once dominated the market.[4] In December 1908, Frank Munsey successfully launched Sunday *afternoon* editions in his papers in Boston, Philadelphia, and Washington, triumphantly declaring this effort "the newest thing, the boldest thing and the biggest thing . . . since journalism emerged from the order of things to its present position of tremendous power."[5]

Munsey's move into Sunday afternoons required some employees to staff the paper during at least the early hours of the customary day of rest. Munsey's boldness was the tipping point in the ongoing challenge to tradition for profit. The trade paper *Editor and Publisher,* in an editorial prior to the launches, questioned whether it was "morally right to print and sell a Sunday afternoon paper." Too, the editorial asked why Munsey, who would not dare "offend the moral convictions of dogmatic church members," was "pandering to impulses that seek to break away from strong, clear solid

3. "The *New York World's* growth in 1907," *Editor and Publisher,* 28 March 1908, 7.
4. Lee, *The Daily Newspaper in America,* 393–400.
5. "Sunday Afternoon," *Editor and Publisher,* 12 December 1908, 1.

Businessman Frank Munsey adopted the profit-maximizing ways of early twentieth-century entrepreneurs for his eighteen newspapers and his flagship magazine, *Munsey's Magazine*. Library of Congress.

principles and policies which were ingrained in the founders of the nation and are today a vital element of our national life."[6]

The sharp increase in the number of daily and Sunday editions, however, was not as impressive as the growth in the number of subscribers. Driven by rapidly increasing literacy levels, improved distribution networks, and new printing technologies, urban publishers boosted readership from about 750,000 in 1850 (3.2 percent of the population as newspaper readers) to 24.2 million in 1909 (about 27.5 percent of population as readers), according to newspaper sociologist Alfred McClung Lee.[7]

The phenomenal growth in the industry also prompted an emphasis on market consolidation and chain ownership. That trend, which continues

6. "Sunday Evening Newspapers," *Editor and Publisher*, 5 December 1908, 8.
7. Lee, *The Daily Newspaper in America*, 65.

today, benefited the legendary empires of Hearst, Pulitzer, Munsey, and E. W. Scripps. Lee noted that publishers and observers claimed that such "cleaning up" maneuvers in the industry constituted a market realignment to maintain stability and to maximize profits. By 1910, there were at least 13 chains operating 62 newspapers, establishing a trend that would result in 59 chains owning 329 dailies during the next quarter of a century.[8]

The Final Stages of Political Partisanship

In a May 16, 1908, editorial, *Editor and Publisher* trumpeted what it called the "decline in the influence of the party newspaper," reporting that "the growth of the independent press is certain proof that the hidebound party newspaper is losing its hold on the public . . ." The editorial said the history of the party newspapers was easily explained as a "legacy of the Civil War," a time when "fists and clubs" often settled disputes among political opponents. Conceding that many "independent newspapers" still carried party affiliations, the editorial claimed that those allegiances "do not interfere with their editorial freedom."[9]

To many readers of the day, the editorial did not ring true because as campaigns went into full swing a few months later, newspaper publishers and editors were still greatly involved. In its August 1 edition, the trade paper carried the main front-page headline "Newspaper Men to Run Campaign" in reference to the 1908 presidential campaign between William Jennings Bryan (Democrat) and William Howard Taft (Republican). The lead paragraph said, "More newspaper men are to be engaged in the active management of the political campaigns this year than ever before in the history of the great parties. In fact, the most important work—the planning and carrying on of the fight for victory of both the Democrat and Republican organizations—is in their hands."[10]

Leading the Democratic charge for Bryan was Henry Watterson, publisher of the *Louisville Courier-Journal,* who was appointed chairman of the press committee of the Democratic National Committee, and Norman E. Mack, editor of the *Buffalo Times,* who was selected DNC chairman. *Editor and Publisher* described Mack as "the kingpin, the man at the throttle, the commanding general of the Democratic forces." Selected as assistant secretary

8. Ibid., 210–15; Bleyer, *Main Currents,* 410–17.

9. "Decline in the Influence of the Party Newspaper," *Editor and Publisher,* 16 May 1908, 4.

10. "Newspaper Men to Run Campaigns," *Editor and Publisher,* 1 August 1908, 1.

of the committee was newspaperman John R. Burton, and Herman Ridder, publisher of the German-language *Staats-Zeitung* in New York, was made an adviser to the Democratic press bureau. Josephus Daniels, editor of the *Charlotte Observer*, and Willis J. Abbot of the *New York Journal* ran the "executive press bureau." This massive effort was designed "to meet the Republicans on their own battle ground, and will engage the services of all the newspaper men that they can secure to scatter the doctrines of the Democracy."[11]

Frank H. Hitchcock, a postmaster and future newspaper publisher in Tucson, Arizona, headed up the Republican National Committee. *Editor and Publisher* reported, "Experienced, diplomatic newspaper men will be sent out in all directions, under the instruction of Hitchcock. They will not only see that Taft news gets into the various newspapers, but they will act as a secret service force to report the doings of the enemy to their chieftain."[12] The GOP selected Representative Albert Foster Dawson, a former newsman in Iowa, to be chairman of the Republican Congressional Committee. The Independence Party nominated John Temple Graves of the *New York American* as vice presidential candidate and William Randolph Hearst was selected as party chairman.

On smaller stages all across the country, journalists were enmeshed in the electoral process. Two editors in New Hampshire sought the GOP nomination for governor; the editor of the Huntsville, Alabama, paper ran for mayor; and a number of editors and publishers stood for election to statehouses in at least a half dozen states.[13] William J. Conners, owner of several Buffalo newspapers, was chosen to head the New York Democratic State Committee. In September, he addressed Democratic editors at a meeting in Rochester, saying, "Whatever is done in this campaign will be done by newspapers. If there is any reward if we win, I promise to you gentlemen you'll get your reward."[14]

The Newspaper Owners' Campaign to Bust the Paper Trust

Despite their pervasive efforts in party politics in 1908, newspaper publishers could not persuade Congress to reduce tariffs on foreign newsprint

11. "Newspaper Men in Politics," *Editor and Publisher*, 5 September 1908, 4.
12. Ibid.
13. Ibid.
14. "Rewards for Party Service by Newspapers," *Editor and Publisher*, 26 September 1908, 4.

to challenge an evolving domestic paper trust that was controlled by a few powerful timber combinations. The fight, brewing since the late 1890s, was officially engaged in 1906, when the American Newspaper Publishers Association (ANPA) instigated antitrust action against the giant General Paper Company. That effort resulted in the dissolution of the firm under the Sherman Anti-Trust Act.[15] In late 1907, ANPA had petitioned the Justice Department again to investigate the paper companies, charging that the industry had added an average of $10 to each ton, resulting in a windfall profit of nearly $2 million per year. Twenty-two companies pleaded guilty and were fined a mere $48,000, prompting ANPA President Herman Ridder to ask President Roosevelt for an investigation of "a travesty upon government."[16]

By early February 1908, the executive committee of the National Editorial Association appealed to Congress to remove the tariff on paper and wood pulp, claiming that a "tax upon newsprint, or material entering into manufacture of the same, is a tax upon knowledge and upon the education of the people."[17] A few weeks later, Ridder alleged that the large paper companies, specifically the International Paper Company, had reduced productivity to 60–65 percent of capacity in an effort to sell off their full warehouse inventories at inflated prices. Prices had escalated so much, he said, that the Canadian mills, facing a $6 per ton tariff, were starting to undercut American mills operating without the tax.[18]

The debate simmered through the spring and into May, when a special congressional committee reported that the publishers had failed to prove a trust existed or that tariffs influenced the price of paper. In its May 30 edition, *Editor and Publisher* chastised Congress for refusing to provide relief to the nation's publishers; the executive branch for failing to enforce portions of the Sherman Anti-Trust Act; the ANPA for not properly prosecuting the case; and publishers across the country for failing to "back up those who were conducting the fight."[19]

The Trends of Prosperity

The crisis over the price of newsprint notwithstanding, the newspaper publishers in 1908 were building empires that produced desirable financial returns and more opportunity for growth. Three major 1908 examples are

15. Lee, *The Daily Newspaper in America,* 108.
16. "Asks President's Aid," *Editor and Publisher,* 18 July 1908, 1.
17. "Editors Seek Help," *Editor and Publisher,* 8 February 1908, 1.
18. "Paper Business Bad," *Editor and Publisher,* 29 February 1908, 1.
19. "Paper Trust Wins," *Editor and Publisher,* 30 May 1908, 8.

offered here. Joseph Pulitzer marked the twenty-fifth anniversary of his purchase of the *New York World,* treating the city to a party that made as much history as it celebrated. Frank Munsey, with the purchase of the *Baltimore News,* became the most vocal proponent of conglomeration and consolidation, calling it "the ultimate destiny of American journalism." The Christian Science Publishing Society announced the launch of its daily *Christian Science Monitor,* vowing to fill the paper with "healing, purifying thought."

Pulitzer, an immigrant, had entered the New York field against all odds, purchasing the *World* in 1883 at its lowest ebb. On May 9, 1908, the *World* opened a new building addition that doubled the size of the facility on Park Row. To commemorate the event the next day, Pulitzer published the largest Sunday edition in world history, a two-hundred-page issue that cost $100,000, took nearly a year of preparation, and carried separate color sections on cars, music, real estate, national affairs, and the city. On the Saturday evening of the anniversary celebration, the *World* sponsored a banquet for invited guests in the newspaper's new library and biographical room. Afterward, pyro-technicians used the roof of the new building addition to launch a fireworks display that could be seen by more than a million people in the city and surrounding area.[20] *Editor and Publisher* declared "that no newspaper in America, if in the whole world, possesses such a large and well equipped plant as Mr. Pulitzer's paper."[21]

Pulitzer, who was overseas during the party, sent a lengthy cablegram stating he had dedicated his paper to democratic ideas, which he defined as "popular government by the best, by the wisest, by the most virtuous." He added, "They [democratic ideas] are the permanent protest against privilege; they are the eternal vigilance over public liberty; they are the inherent impulse for progress and reform, against injustice."[22] With effusive praise, *Editor and Publisher* credited Pulitzer with curing the "dry rot of conservatism" in the city's newspapers, developing the use of illustrations and pictures, ferreting out municipal corruption, establishing playgrounds for inner-city youths, cracking down on corrupt landlords, and promoting state legislation to advance public interests.[23]

If Pulitzer's party in New York was 1908's end-all celebration of the past, Munsey's 1908 purchase of the *Baltimore News* provided plenty to predict the future of corporate newspaper structure. In his statement at purchase, Mun-

20. "World Anniversary," *Editor and Publisher,* 9 May 1908, 1.
21. "Joseph Pulitzer and the New York World," *Editor and Publisher,* 9 May 1908, 8.
22. "The World Jubilee," *Editor and Publisher,* 16 May 1908, 1–2.
23. "Joseph Pulitzer and the New York World," *Editor and Publisher,* 9 May 1908, 8.

sey blamed "unhealthy competition" for forcing newspapers, along with other industries, into market conglomeration. He was quoted as saying,

> There is no form of industry that lends itself to combination more naturally and readily than newspaper publication. Through combination the iron and steel interests have been enabled to have the advantage of the best administrative genius at the helm, regardless of the cost of such a man's services.[24]

Munsey envisioned a collection of talent bigger than a university faculty, performing journalism in a central location, and transmitting work to hundreds or thousands of points of distribution. At the helm of these massive corporate enterprises would be "geniuses" who could justifiably command salaries of $150,000 to $200,000 per year, more than double the salary of Arthur Brisbane, whose $72,000 in 1908 to run Hearst Newspapers was the highest in the nation.[25] Editorial pages, he said, would be relatively uniform, with on-site proprietors furnishing their own local material. With an organization supplying its own paper, ink, and machinery, there would be no threat of "extortion at the hands of the white paper trust or any other monopoly." In essence, Munsey saw the future of the industry becoming a monopoly to protect itself from monopolies.[26]

While Munsey and Pulitzer dominated industry developments in 1908, the Christian Science Publishing Company quietly charted plans to create a national, and, in some respects, an international newspaper that would provide news for Christian Scientists and "the better class of people everywhere." The irony was that Pulitzer himself furnished some of the motivation for the founding of the paper. Pulitzer and other publishers repeatedly portrayed the founder of the Christian Science Church, Mary Baker Eddy, as a self-absorbed religious zealot. At one point, the *World*'s news reporting helped provoke a lawsuit intended to have Eddy declared mentally incompetent in a fight over control of her substantial estate.[27] Spun from a weekly, the *Christian Science Monitor* has outlived by a large margin almost all the papers that once were Eddy's harshest critics. Doubling the irony, the *Monitor* has won seven Pulitzer Prizes in its history.[28]

24. "Baltimore News Sold," *Editor and Publisher,* 7 March 1908, 4.

25. "Our Best Paid Editor," *Editor and Publisher,* 27 June 1908, 4.

26. "Baltimore News Sold," 4.

27. B. O. Flower, "The Recent Reckless and Irresponsible Attacks on Christian Science and Its Founder, with a Survey of the Christian-Science Movement," *Arena,* January 1907, 47; Georgine Milmine, "Mary Baker G. Eddy: The Story of Her Life and the History of Christian Science," *McClure's Magazine* 31, no. 1 (May 1908): 16–30.

28. www.pulitzer.org. Accessed 27 January 2006.

Optimism and Reform Leadership

The ironies and contradictions of 1908 were the result of an industry undergoing unprecedented growth while trying to find a moral and professional compass, a combination that produced angst over credibility, integrity, factual reportage, boosterism, sensationalism, conglomeration, and the characteristics of a good newspaper. The conversation of the period, in fact, cast the die for discussions about what role commercialization, and the business of newspapers, should play in journalism education.

In its October 1908 issue, the *Atlantic Monthly* carried a critique of the New York news press written by an unnamed "New York Editor" whose study posed a single question: "Can a newspaper tell its readers the plain unflattering truth and pay its way?" The study sample was a group of papers, "the half-dozen with any pretense to wide popular appeal," and the "indispensable" variables it measured were popularity and authority.[29]

Each of the unnamed New York dailies in the study failed to unite popularity with authority. As the author said, "Here we have heard at least one voice crying in the wilderness, one smothered under a blanket of self-conscious rectitude, one choked with childish spite and petulance, one crying out an old man's perversity, and two crying a message from the devil or no message at all."[30]

The anonymous author said newspapers, by failing to unite popularity and authority, could not provide strong, factual content without "putting certain axiomatic principles of economics and morals as assumed and sealed, written forever on two tables of stone." In the end, he wrote, the public wants "a newspaper that treats its readers not as a child or sage, neither as a hero nor as a fool, but as a person of natural good instincts and average intelligence, amenable to reason, and one to be taught tactfully to stand upon his own feet, rather than to take his principles ready-made from his teacher . . . A paper which gives the senator and the shop-girl what they both want to read and are the better for reading."[31]

Editor and Publisher earlier disputed such ideas and stated that readers only want facts and "real news" without interpretation. *Editor and Publisher* said the public did not need lessons in economics or morals, doubting with some sarcasm "that the public is longing very hard for a great 'authoritative' newspaper to teach the people." Throwing more bait, the anonymous editor challenged the idea, put forth earlier in the year by *Editor and Publisher*,

29. "Is an Honest Newspaper Possible?" *Atlantic Monthly*, October 1908, 441–47.
30. Ibid, 442.
31. Ibid, 446.

that a newspaper must take the lead in restoring community faith and optimism while downplaying rumors, disasters, and "sensational flub-dub." In the throes of the economic downturn of 1907–1908, editors were admonished to "whoop it up for prosperity."[32] The *Atlantic* critic had disagreed, saying "the newspaper, indeed, should be critical rather than constructive" because it has a duty under constitutional mandate and the inherited British concept of a "fourth necessity" to critique the executive, legislative, and judicial branches of government.[33] The author, in effect, was extolling the press's "watchdog" role, which primarily meant guarding against corrupt legislation and corrupt public officials.

Transition and Consolidation

The broad backdrop of the debate on the press's role for the individual or community was outlined by Louisville editor Henry Watterson, who labeled the first decade of the century as one of transition, one in which personal journalism had ceded to "counting-room journalism," a developing trend that eventually would bring the profession into comfortable harmony with a populace that rapidly was becoming more literate, astute, and discriminating in taste.[34] It was a trend that also was at the heart of the continuing debates over whether journalism education should be focused on professionalization of the practice or the development of journalists steeped in a nonprofessional, liberally based curriculum.

The essential component to survival in the transition was the "well-ordered newspaper office," one that paid as much attention to the business details as to the journalism details. Even though the industry had passed from when "an editor, a printer, and a printer's devil were all-sufficient," Watterson insisted that a newspaper had to behave like an autocracy. He wrote, ". . . when at midnight wires are flashing and feet are hurrying, and to the onlooking stranger chaos seems to reign, the directing mind and hand have their firm grip upon the tiller-ropes, which extend from the editorial room to the composing-room, from the composing-room to the press-room, and from the press-room to the breakfast-table."[35]

Watterson viewed the transition as one of natural evolution, providing more stability, respectability, and responsibility because "it would establish

32. "Preach Optimism," *Editor and Publisher,* 22 February 1908, 4.

33. "Is an Honest Newspaper Possible?" 446.

34. Henry Watterson, "The Personal Equation in Journalism," *Atlantic Monthly,* July 1910, 40–47.

35. Ibid., 41.

a more immediate relation with the community." Newspaper management should resemble management of banks or railroads, every bit a "common carrier."[36] The "common carrier" analogy, which resounds even today in the discourse on media management, was as bold as it was prescient. It put Watterson in a position of challenging the very foundations of the popular newspaper press of the day and in very specific ways portended the management structure that developed through the century.

But the essay also had another purpose: to join the public dialogue about the press and why it was so important to professionalize the newspaper workforce. It was, in part, a response to famed sociologist Edward Alsworth Ross, who had written a previous *Atlantic* essay titled, "The suppression of important news." Ross, who had developed the theory of social control, was the subject of a celebrated firing at Stanford that provoked a national debate on and redefinition of academic freedom and tenure protection. He also was a cofounder of the American Association of University Professors. His essay, following his economic application of social control, challenged the wisdom of comparing newspapers to railroads, hotels, banks, amusement parks, and vaudeville shows. Ross argued that putting business before news compromised the integrity of the product and jeopardized the role of journalism in a democracy.[37] In 1908, Ross had just published *Social Psychology,* that discipline's first textbook, which examined social stability in the frameworks of customs and public opinion.

"The editors are hired men, and they may put into the paper no more of their conscience and ideals than comports with getting the biggest return from the investment," Ross wrote. A newspaper is nothing more than "a factory where ink and brains are so applied to white paper as to turn out the largest possible marketable product." He continued, "The capitalist-owner means no harm, but he is not bothered by the standards that hamper the editor-owner. He follows a few simple maxims that work out well enough in selling shoes or cigars or sheet-music."[38]

Watterson took great offense at Ross's assessment of the contemporary transition from personal to "counting-room" journalism. The editor said, "leading dailies everywhere are rarely without aspiration," noting that except for rare occasions, newspapers without tone and character do not survive in the marketplace. More newspapers fail due to "ignorance and indolence" than to suppressing news under the influence of big advertisers

36. Ibid., 43.
37. Edward Alsworth Ross, "The Suppression of Important News," *Atlantic Monthly,* March 1910, 303–11.
38. Ibid., 305.

or wealthy interests in the community. Watterson said Ross's description of suppression actually was editorial judgment, the industry's efforts to "guard equally against exaggeration and pruriency," combined with its willingness to hold out "that which may be too vile to tell."[39] Ross suggested there be endowed newspapers, removing some of the editorial values of profit, sensationalism, prurience, and titillation and putting newspapers and journalists in a better position to assess facts and present stories closer to the truth.[40]

Watterson heatedly dismissed Ross's ideas and strongly asserted that "disinterestedness," "unselfish devotion to the public interest," was "the soul of true journalism." He said there was no reason such journalism could not emerge from the counting room as long as the business manager also was a journalist.[41] Watterson hinted that building the character of a newspaper editor in the face of the realities of the counting room might lend itself to some practical application in ethics training as the basis for experiments being conducted in journalism education.[42] Conceding that the new counting room approach had created chaos and some bad effects in its infancy, Watterson said most of the problems could be attributed to "too many ill-trained, uneducated lads" rising to management posts too high for their capacity. He called the conditions "ephemeral," citing "a process of popular evolution which is steadily lifting the masses out of the slough of degeneracy and ignorance." He wrote, "The competition in sensationalism, to which we owe the yellow press, as it is called, will become a competition in cleanliness and accuracy. The counting-room, which is next to the people and carries the purse, will see that decency pays, that good sense and good faith are good investments."[43]

Watterson bade farewell to Horace Greeley, Henry Raymond, and Charles Dana, the "star" personal editors who exploited and glorified themselves through their papers. All were superior newspapermen, Watterson said, but their brand of journalism was limited by their personal tastes, habits, and prejudices. He welcomed counting-room executives as better qualified to "render a yet better account to God and the people in unselfish devotion to the common interest."[44] Watterson's views were consistent with Munsey's perceived orderliness of monopoly and reflected the values of the evolving corporate America.

39. Watterson, "The Personal Equation in Journalism," 44–45.
40. Ross, "The Suppression of Important News," 308.
41. Watterson, "The Personal Equation in Journalism," 46.
42. Ibid., 46–47.
43. Ibid., 47.
44. Ibid.

Origins of the Debate:
Chi-Squares versus Green Eyeshades

By 1908, the consolidating newspaper industry, the transition from personal to corporate newspapering, and the concurrent focus on professional reform had pushed a decades-long debate over the propriety of journalism education to the point of *when,* and not *if,* the phenomenon would occur. The idea had emerged numerous times only to be put asunder by working editors who thought the task impossible or ridiculous. In every decade after the Civil War, editors put forth "plans" for journalism education, from simple apprentice-style extracurricular activities such as General Robert E. Lee's at Washington College, to elective-style cognates, to full-blown coursework in writing, editing, management, and ethics. The discussions, conducted largely in the best journals of the day, amounted to a progressive debate over what part of journalism education belonged in the newsroom and what part in the classroom, or, in essence, whether it would be taught by commercial or noncommercial methods.

The earliest conversations focused on whether journalists needed college at all. Some editors argued that only a newsroom offered a full curriculum, that time spent studying the liberal arts was time better spent at the feet of master editors, most of whom never went to college and some of whom never finished formal public education. In 1880, Harvard statistics showed that journalism was all but absent from its annual lists of graduate placements, indicating that the profession was perhaps the only one without a recognized gateway. At the time, some of the most successful editors of the day were not college graduates. Horace Greeley, for example, came through the ranks from a typesetter; James Gordon Bennett was a proof-reader. Scores of editors or proprietors never attended college and for some that was a source of pride, one that guided their hiring practices.[45]

Though in 1880 newsroom professionals without college degrees far outnumbered those with a degree, college graduates were beginning to populate the newspaper management landscape, a trend that by 1908 would lead to a more rational and productive debate on the value of a college education and a full curriculum in journalism. Indeed, the list of college-educated editors in late century should have been enough to convince even the hardliners. College grads included Whitelaw Reid, Charles Dana, William Henry Hurlburt, John Foord, Henry Raymond, William Cullen Bryant, and Nathan Hale, some of the era's best-known and most respected editors and publishers.[46]

45. George F. Babbitt, "The College Graduate in Journalism," *Harvard Register,* April 1881, 210–17.
46. Ibid, 211.

Resistance in the early stages of the trend came from some editors and publishers who claimed that a college degree created a new level of newsroom elites who did not appreciate the meager pay or rudiments associated with apprenticeship. In a prescient essay published in 1881, George F. Babbitt made a strong case for a college education, balanced with an appropriately thorough newsroom apprenticeship, "the lower down in the scale in the beginning . . . the better." In a cautious endorsement of the concept of schools of journalism, Babbitt warned, "Unless the routine of the department bears a close resemblance to that of a well-regulated newspaper office, it will probably confer no more practical benefits upon the profession than some of our agricultural colleges have conferred upon the farming interests of the country."[47]

In other words, without a college curriculum that could teach the practice and business of journalism, Watterson's hopes of a counting-room approach would be mired in a hopeless cycle of newsroom personnel who could not adapt to the modern profit-centered approach to newspapering.

The Emergence of a Journalism Curriculum

Whitelaw Reid has been credited with inspiring Joseph Pulitzer in 1903 to announce the endowment of a School of Journalism at Columbia University. Thirty years earlier, Reid had proposed such an academic unit "to be appended to the regular college course, as one of the additional features of university instruction, like the School of Mines, or Medicine, or Law." His plan would have students taking courses in history, law, business, philosophy, arts and sciences, literature, and modern languages. He doubted the feasibility of such a program for that time (1872), but his idea would foment and inform the debate for several decades.[48]

The push for the education of journalists was not exclusive to the United States. In February 1893, M. de Blowitz, the Paris correspondent for the *London Times*, advocated the establishment of a journalism curriculum that would require two additional languages; a command of the history of Europe; the study of the leaders, budgets, climatology, geography, and ethnology of all countries; and instruction in boxing, sketching, horseback riding, and use of a revolver. Upon completion of that curriculum in the first two years, the student would rotate among foreign journalism programs

47. Ibid., 217.
48. James Boylan, *Pulitzer's School: Columbia University School of Journalism* (New York: Columbia University Press, 2003), 7.

organized in a confederation of learning.[49] In April the same year, Albert F. Matthews, writing in the *Chautauquan*, proposed setting up in the United States a university program in which aspiring journalists would report stories not for publication but for daily comparison to professionals' published work, covering the same stories.[50]

Ten years later, after having invited interest from Harvard and Columbia, Pulitzer announced that he was giving a $2 million gift to Columbia to start a school. If Reid's suggestion three decades before was the challenge, Pulitzer's stake was a gauntlet, one that sparked a steady stream of debate, and which provoked an institutional conflict that, despite groundbreaking on a $500,000 building, delayed the actual start of the program by about eight years.

Lincoln Steffens, the celebrated muckraker of the Progressive Era, wrote that Pulitzer was investing in "what he could not do: teach journalism and, perhaps, make journalists," as well as offering to others the opportunity to earn a degree that he, Pulitzer, never pursued. Steffens also speculated that the endowment to Columbia was Pulitzer's crowning reparation to ameliorate his actions in perpetrating and stoking the era of yellow journalism. Even so, Steffens applauded Pulitzer for filling a void created by severe deficiencies in both higher education and the newspaper industry. In a popular theme of the day, however, Steffens warned against a curriculum laden with the rudiments of formulaic writing and the "business and mechanism of newspapers." Instead, he urged Pulitzer to fill the curriculum with Latin and Greek, philosophy, literature, traditional English, ethics, sciences, what he described as "knowledge so understood by men so intelligent that they can tell it so that all men may read as they run."[51]

In an essay published in the *North American Review* a few months later, Horace White, a college graduate who had gone on to become a top editor in Chicago and New York, responded to Pulitzer's challenge to explain his concerns about the conceptual framework of a school of journalism. The university, he wrote, "has nothing to teach journalists in the special sense that it has to teach lawyers, physicians, architects and engineers." Those, he said, can teach *technique*, but journalism schools cannot, unless they commit to "publishing a newspaper in competition with other newspapers in the same town," a suggestion that would play a big role later in the founding

49. "Blowitz's School of Journalism," *Current Literature*, March 1893, 341; "The Training of Journalists," *Congregationalist*, 23 February 1893, 304.

50. Albert F. Matthews, "Can Practical Newspaper Work Be Taught in College?" *Chautauquan*, April 1893, 48–51.

51. Lincoln Steffens, "The News School of Journalism," *Bookman*, October 1903, 173–80.

Publisher of the *New York Tribune* Whitelaw Reid formulated an early plan
for journalism education and inspired Pulitzer's endowment at Columbia
University. Undated portrait from Bain News Service.

of the Missouri School of Journalism. White cynically doubted the feasibility of such a clinical component, asserting that "Pulitzer's money would
probably be spent in less time than he took to earn it."[52]

Unlike Steffens, who only hinted at the enduring criticism of corporate
journalism, White disputed Pulitzer's stated dream of producing journalists
capable of breaking the cycle of sensationalism. Borrowing philosophically
from Ross and literally (and liberally) from E. L. Shuman's *Practical Journalism* book of 1903, he indicted the industry for creating a profit-centered purpose that left young college-educated journalists with no choice but to
compromise their own work to sell more newspapers and generate more
advertising. White said the newspaper industry had become so profit-corrupt

52. Horace White, "The School of Journalism," *North American Review,* January 1904,
25–31.

that fewer and fewer college graduates saw it as noble or financially benefi-cial. In White's mind, newspapers were redistributing resources toward "pic-tures, head-lines, color scheme, job type, sports, gossip." The best journalists, he charged, were driven to magazines, the primary purveyors of real pro-gressive journalism, because those publications rewarded the best writers for reporting and writing substantive stories that challenged the business and political establishment. White's brutal critique finished with a plea for jour-nalism education that featured "a field of labor worthy of noble minds."[53]

White's essay pushed Pulitzer directly into the debate, provoking the publisher to write a response in hopes of addressing the mounting critiques. In thirty-nine pages in the *North American Review* in 1904, Pulitzer expressed his dream mostly in grand strokes, positioning the modern journalist as "the lookout on the bridge of the ship of state." Pulitzer agreed with Stef-fens, envisioning a "journalism-specific" curriculum designed to "divert, deflect, extract, concentrate, specialize" in subjects such as law, economics, history, science, and sociology. He adamantly rejected White's suggestion, and one fundamentally supported in a competing bid by Harvard Presi-dent Charles William Eliot, of providing commercial training through clin-ical newsroom practice. Instead, Pulitzer said ethics and public service should be the foundations for preventing a journalism dictated by the "counting room." He wrote, "The knowledge that a reputable journalist would refuse to edit any paper that represented private interest against the public good would be enough of itself to discourage such an enterprise."[54] He continued, "The school of journalism is to be, in my conception, not only not commercial, but anti-commercial."[55]

By 1907, Pulitzer's health was in serious decline. Citing a desire to see his school founded without influence, he announced plans to delay its opening until after his death, which he and most observers expected to come sooner rather than later. In effect, wrote school historian James Boylan, Pulitzer "transformed the birth of the school of journalism into a death watch," which ended October 1911, when Pulitzer died on his yacht in Charleston, South Carolina. The next year, Columbia took its first class of journalism students.[56]

Pulitzer's powerful essay probably was the breakpoint in the public dis-course over journalism education. Debate would continue, but at this moment, his words portended the next step, a step that would have to be taken out West, far from the bustling East Coast newspaper empires.

---

53. Ibid., 31.
54. Joseph Pulitzer, "The College of Journalism," *North American Review,* May 1904, 676.
55. Ibid., 680.
56. Boylan, *Pulitzer's School,* 23–24.

Newsboys gather on Frankfort Street near Joseph Pulitzer's World Building in February 1908. Photo by Lewis W. Hine.

Missouri Takes the Commercial Route

When Walter Williams conceived the Missouri School of Journalism, he developed a curriculum inadvisable to Reid, Pulitzer, White, and Steffens. He envisioned a program more in line with Watterson's ideas, linked inextricably to industry practice and the business side through a clinical newspaper, a paper that, as White suggested facetiously four years before, would compete on a daily basis with commercial newspapers. The *University Missourian* published its first issue on the first day of classes in fall 1908. Williams, the founding dean who had been an editor in Columbia and Boonville, Missouri, assembled a group of three seasoned journalists to form the staff backbone for instruction and newsroom management. Williams hired Silas Bent from the *St. Louis Post-Dispatch* and Charles Ross from the *St. Louis Republic*. As part of the first curriculum, Williams had courses titled "Newspaper Administration," concerning editorial direction and control, and "Newspaper Publishing," for the business side of journalism, including advertising and circulation.[57]

Some three months before the school opened in fall 1908, Williams boldly reiterated his intent to base the Missouri curriculum on a laboratory experience from the business side. He straight-on challenged criticisms that journalism could only be taught in a newsroom. "So be it," Williams told the Missouri Press Association, "but if the school of journalism is also a newspaper office, then this objection is without weight."[58] In January 1909, with one semester gone in the history of the school, Williams adapted his speech as a bylined article in *Editor and Publisher*. The article was not filled with the soaring rhetoric of Pulitzer's thirty-nine-page opus, but it was a manifesto on the merger of theory and practice.

"Such training means the dignifying of journalism," Williams wrote, "the strengthening of the arms of those in the profession who would strike at inequity entrenched, the furnishing of young journalists with equipment for the largest service of the State." Williams used the dreaded phrase "vocational education" to describe a professionally based curriculum that would put journalism on the same footing as the other academic units. He clearly defended the clinical approach, and forcefully rejected arguments that it would be geared like a factory stamping out consumable goods. Williams wrote, "It is absurd to suppose that an untrained, uneducated, unequipped man can be as successful in journalism as one whose training is broad, whose knowledge is large, whose clearness of vision has been increased, and whose equipment in general has been increased by training in a school." The Missouri program, Williams said, was "a real school for real newspaper men."[59]

Promoting the Experiment

In its first months of publication, the *Columbia Missourian* would become the hymn book for Williams's passionate and fervent religion of clinical

57. Farrar, *A Creed for My Profession*, 142.
58. Walter Williams, "The State University School of Journalism: Why and What," speech to the Missouri Press Association, Excelsior Springs, Missouri, 29 May 1908.
59. Walter Williams, "Journalism Schools," *Editor and Publisher*, 2 January 1909, 5.

At the Missouri School of Journalism, Walter Williams taught the newspaper management class in 1912 in Switzler Hall. Courtesy of the University of Missouri Archives.

training. Nearly every week through the first semester, the paper carried testimonials, endorsements, and congratulations. The journalism school brought in prominent journalists to speak: Arthur Brisbane, Norman Hapgood, and Jacob Riis, for instance. Students aggressively covered them and prominently displayed news about their visits. Frequently, the paper carried a column titled "About Journalism Schools" on its editorial page, usually an aggregated and glowing collection of stories on the subject from other papers and congratulations to the school. The editorial-page articles often extolled Missouri's efforts, sometimes showing the divide between the eastern noncommercial approach and Williams's commercial and clinical approach. For example, the cited *Columbia Herald* column said that "despite the boasted worth of other states," it was Missouri that took the lead.[60] On September 22, 1908, letters of congratulations were published from the World Press Association in Paris, the *Hallsville News*, the *Rolla Herald Democrat*, and the *Lebanon Journal* in Illinois.[61]

Even so, there were times when the column published protestations. One paper, the *Centralia Courier*, wrote that the school of journalism was another

60. "About Schools of Journalism," *Columbia Missourian*, 15 September 1908, 2.
61. "About Schools of Journalism," *Columbia Missourian*, 22 September 1908, 2.

burden on taxpayers and "will not make a successful journalist in 100 years." In the same column, editors of the nearby *Boonville Democrat* bemoaned the state becoming involved in the newspaper business and having a newspaper with a state subsidy in direct competition with other local papers.[62] Other critics admonished the school to avoid producing an elite class of educated journalists who saw no need to take rudimentary jobs early in their careers.

What Set Missouri Apart?

The irony of Walter Williams's Midwest experiment raises important questions about why first success at professional training emerged so far from the dominant and thriving newspaper industry in eastern urban centers. The East Coast, specifically New York City, had skyrocketing circulations, phenomenal new buildings, and industry combination and consolidation. It was the place where a wealthy publisher could dedicate a million dollars to an anniversary celebration and another two million to a city university to endow a new school. National newspapers could be started from scratch with resources large enough for staff and multiple editions seven days a week, 365 days a year. Only a look at how industry players approached the phenomenon can offer a basis for reasoned speculation. The differences between the two efforts led by Pulitzer in the East and Williams in the Midwest are as dramatic as they are instructive.

Pulitzer, racked by a lengthy list of lifelong physical maladies, was faced with the potential legacy of yellow journalism, a very real stain on an immigrant bootstraps career that separated him from a field full of brilliant publishers and editors. He intended to put his name on a cornerstone of university respectability. But, like the celebration of his twenty-fifth year as publisher of the *World*, his solution was to invest personal wealth in the statement, to try to go alone in a higher education system that works best when private and public sources join in an objective. Had he not viewed his endowment as personal amelioration, he could have avoided the necessity of dying first to avoid any conflict of interest. Like Watterson and Dana and Greeley, he was among the vanishing personal journalists who saw themselves holding the reins that linked to readers in a herd growing daily in number and loyalty. Pulitzer, with an extremely favorable fate, did not build the kind of network necessary for a partnership in higher education, preferring instead to work from the outside and finding himself in potential financial conflicts on the inside.

62. "About Schools of Journalism," *Columbia Missourian,* 30 September 1908, 2.

Williams, a country newsman in Missouri, had neither the resources nor the daily reins to throw such weight and he had no reason to take on a mission to restore personal rectitude. As a result, he had to assume a posture of collaboration, one that would bring powerful industry forces into the fight for public funding. Like Pulitzer in the later years of his short life, Williams accumulated capital from respect. Williams, unlike Pulitzer, earned his from rural readers, country editors, politicians, and the university's highest administrators. His persistence in building institutional support at every level, and in generating outside influence from the Missouri newspaper industry, displayed a homegrown savvy and sophistication learned only through the press association network in Missouri. His stake, perhaps by necessity, started in relationships, not in cash. Financially, though, the aim was the same: a viable journalism business.

CHAPTER 7

The Age of "Glory and Risk"

The Advertising Industry Finds Its Worth

Caryl Cooper

By 1908, New York City advertising agencies were referred to as "places of temperament, disorder, and imagination," and the advertising world was said to be "seething with glory and risk."[1] Much of the industry was homogeneous in gender and race. Although white Protestant men dominated the industry, a few women, only 3 percent of the workforce, used copywriting and clerical work as an entry into the field.[2] Historian Stephen Fox writes that as the twentieth century began, the total volume of advertising had reached $500 million with several companies enjoying the fruits of advertising on a national scale.[3] For example, in 1908, Royal Baking Powder, headed by Joseph C. Hoagland, wrote its own copy and placed advertising in women's and religious journals. Enoch Morgan's Sons produced

1. Helen Woodward, *Through Many Windows* (New York: Harper and Brothers Publishers, 1926), 99, 108.
2. Jackson Lears, *Fables of Abundance: A Cultural History of Advertising in America* (New York: HarperCollins, 1994), 154.
3. Stephen Fox, *The Mirror Makers: A History of American Advertising and Its Creators* (Chicago: University of Illinois Press, 1984), 39.

and advertised Sapolio, a popular soap. Harley T. Procter, who had begun marketing Ivory Soap in 1882, still pushed this popular item in 1908. In fact, more than one hundred years later, Ivory Soap uses the same slogan: "99 44/100 pure." Department stores, such as Marshall Field's and Wanamaker's, also relied on advertising, primarily in newspapers. In fact, department store advertising contributed greatly to the development of copywriting as a profession.[4]

Although New York City was the center for advertising, educators began incorporating advertising into the business curriculum in the 1890s. In 1893, the Wharton School of Business added to the first journalism curriculum by covering aspects of advertising in a course that included discussions of libel and business management. This type of inclusion was the norm until 1905 when New York University offered the first stand-alone advertising course, which was taught by W. R. Hotchkiss, the advertising manager for the John Wanamaker Company. Short-lived, the course was dropped from the curriculum in 1909. Northwestern University offered a course called "Psychology of Business, Advertising, and Salesmanship" in 1908.[5]

When the Missouri School of Journalism was formed in 1908, one of the courses offered that first year was "Newspaper Publishing," which focused on the "business side of journalism, including discussion of advertising and circulation."[6] Charles G. Ross, later to be known as President Harry S. Truman's press secretary, taught the course.[7] Advertising, and its relationship to publishing, proved to be important to the new school in more ways than one. It was opposition to the *University Missourian*'s pursuit of advertising revenue that created one of the first hurdles Williams had to overcome.

Originally, Williams conceived of the *Missourian* as a journalism laboratory, a teaching newspaper that would operate like a daily newspaper serving the city of Columbia, Missouri, rather than as a campus newspaper. Operating like a daily newspaper meant that students would be engaged in the "practical work of soliciting and writing advertisements for the paper."[8] Although initially enthusiastic about the School of Journalism, Edwin Moss Watson, the publisher of a local newspaper, the *Columbia Daily Tribune*, changed his tune when he realized that the *Missourian* would compete for local advertising. After a flurry of *Tribune* editorials claiming that the

4. Ibid., 24–25.
5. Billy I. Ross, Anne C. Osborne, and Jeff I. Richards, *Advertising Education: Yesterday—Today—Tomorrow* (Lubbock, Tex.: Advertising Education Publications, 2006), 10–13.
6. Farrar, *A Creed for My Profession*, 142.
7. Ross et al., *Advertising Education*, 13.
8. Sara Lockwood Williams, *Twenty Years of Education*, 30.

Missourian, as the product of a tax-supported institution, competed unfairly with a tax-paying private enterprise, the Missouri legislature passed a measure stipulating that no state funds could be used to support newspapers. In response, Williams created the Missourian Publishing Association during the summer of 1909 to handle the production of the newspaper. After a short hiatus, the *Missourian* resumed publication in the fall of that year.[9] Watson's efforts to end competition, and Williams's response to this challenge, demonstrate how important advertising revenues had become to a newspaper's survival. This case also illustrates how important advertising education was as an integral part of a school's journalism education.

This chapter reviews advertising's history with an eye on how it developed into a profession. At the turn of the century, advertising practitioners worked in cities far away from the industry's heart, New York City. In 1908, eighty-five advertising agents and agencies were operating in St. Louis.[10] It is within this environment of growth, professionalization, and challenge that advertising education emerged.

Advertising and Promotion: 1800–1850

Historians date the beginning of the penny press to 1833, when Benjamin Day began publishing the *New York Sun.* In addition to selling newspapers for pennies, Day included advertising in the paper. Other penny press newspaper publishers, such as James Gordon Bennett of the *New York Herald,* followed suit and included classified-style advertising. Most ads were separated by lines but contained few illustrations. However, in 1836, two-column advertisements containing illustrations began appearing in Bennett's *Herald.* Businesses using smaller ads with no illustrations began to complain about the larger ads.

By the 1840s, the relationship between local business and newspapers had matured from the depression during the 1830s. The environment was right for a new type of business to emerge: an intermediary. In Philadelphia in 1843, Volney Palmer, son of a newspaper publishing family, declared himself an agent for several newspapers in the area.[11] As a newspaper agent, Palmer focused on securing subscriptions and advertising. Although subscriptions were important to most newspapers, Palmer is known for his innovative strategy in bringing the print media and advertising together.

9. Farrar, *A Creed for My Profession,* 151–54.
10. *Gould's St. Louis Directory: 1908* (Gould Directory Co.), 2061–65.
11. Fox, *The Mirror Makers,* 14.

Palmer sold newspaper space to advertisers and, in return, kept a 25 percent commission for services rendered before paying the newspaper. He also advised businesses to use advertising, use it frequently, and use newspapers in other parts of the nation to reach regional markets. Palmer did not use the term "advertising agency" to describe his company until 1849. Less than ten years after opening his agency, Palmer had opened offices in Boston, New York, and Baltimore. In the late 1850s, he formed a partnership with three other men, John E. Joy, J. E. Coe, and W. W. Sharpe.[12]

Unlike more recent advertising agencies that represent businesses, Palmer's agencies represented newspapers. Historian Stephen Fox describes the relationship between agents and newspapers as contentious: the agent would buy the space from the newspapers at a discount, sell it to an advertiser at a higher cost, and keep the difference as a commission, a system that often led to abuses and feelings of ill will for the advertiser and the newspaper.[13] However, historian Bonnie Vannatta colors Palmer with a more ethical paintbrush. In addition to providing information about the newspapers he represented, Palmer offered copywriting and layout services. This "system of advertising," as he called it, brought together production, marketing, distribution, sales, and transportation. His sales pitch to potential clients included the success stories of other clients, cost estimates, and a list of suggested newspapers.[14]

Despite the liberties some agents took, the success of Palmer's advertising agency demonstrates how newspapers and advertising evolved into a symbiotic relationship during a time when the general economy and the political landscape of publishing were changing. These changes also gave birth to another type of advertising, that of promotion.

One of the most famous nineteenth-century advertisers was Phineas T. Barnum, best known for his company, The Barnum and Bailey Greatest Show On Earth. Barnum began his business of promoting oddities to a "fickle, and ofttimes, perverse" public in the 1830s.[15] For example, in 1834 Barnum promoted Joice Heth, an elderly African American woman, as the 161-year-old former nursemaid of George Washington. He also used special promotional tours to introduce Tom Thumb in the 1840s and opera singer Jenny Lind in the 1850s. Barnum used a variety of promotional techniques,

12. Bonnie Vannatta, "Volney B. Palmer (1799–July 29, 1864)," in Edd Applegate, ed., *The Ad Men and Women: A Biographical Dictionary of Advertising* (Westport, Conn.: Greenwood Press, 1994), 248, 250.

13. Fox, *The Mirror Makers,* 14.

14. Vannatta, "Palmer," 249–50.

15. Phineas T. Barnum, *Struggles and Triumph* (New York: Viking Penguin, 1869), 171.

including advertising, posters, playbills, and releases for newspapers. Moreover, he understood the need to use different methods and messages to attract different audiences, mostly the middle class and immigrants.[16]

Barnum recognized that different audiences extended beyond the middle-class white audience. Although he followed the laws regulating segregation during the 1840s, Barnum permitted African Americans to visit his American Museum in New York City during specific times of the day. Historian James W. Cook found two newspaper articles inviting "persons of color" in the *New York Atlas* and the *New York Tribune* in February 1849.[17] In addition, African Americans appeared in several lithographs produced for Barnum by Nathaniel Currier and James Merritt Ives in the 1860s: two lithographs featuring "The What Is It? Or, Man-Monkey,"[18] described by Barnum as "[the combination of] the native African and of the Orang Outang" and "playful as a [k]itten," which may demonstrate how Barnum used racial caricatures and different appeals to attract audiences. In another lithograph, a black woman was billed as the mother of albino and black children. Such techniques were ethnocentric and relied on stereotypes that subordinated other races and reinforced the notion of the superiority of the Anglo-Saxon culture.[19]

Barnum's use of tours, advertising, posters, and different appeals demonstrates how different communication tactics could be used to make an impact. Such tactics, however, were not always appreciated. Early advertising agents sought legitimacy, preferring to disassociate from the peddler class and "carnivalesque frivolity" that Barnum represented.[20] This desire for legitimacy, as well as other social and economic factors, contributed to the development of advertising as a profession from 1850 to 1900.

Mass Production and Advertising Growth

In the 1850s, several industries connected to the rise of advertising were growing. The transportation industries, including railroads, waterways, and roads, were gaining prominence. As historian Juliann Silvulka points out, these industries opened new markets and distribution points for local

16. "Phineas T. Barnum" in James W. Cook, ed., *The Colossal P. T. Barnum Reader: Nothing Else Like It in the Universe* (Chicago: University of Illinois Press, 2005), 6.
17. Ibid., 243.
18. The Man-Monkey was a short African American man dressed as a savage. Ibid., 170.
19. Ibid., 134, 175, 173.
20. Ibid., 89.

companies. The Civil War changed the way people bought and sold products. Prior to the Civil War, many staples, including flour and sugar, were shipped and sold in bulk. The division of labor in farming families left women to preserve foods and make clothing for the family while men did the heavy lifting and managed the household income. The war created a demand for innovations in food preparation and storage. Instead of making goods such as soaps and other household items, women began to buy ready-made, prepackaged items that were mass-produced.[21]

Consumer demand for prepackaged items continued after the Civil War ended. As more families moved from rural to urban areas in search of factory jobs, the desire for prepackaged, inexpensive items increased. The producers of these goods used decorative bottles, labels, and pre-made boxes to distinguish their products from others. Companies such as Proctor and Gamble, Pillsbury, and Levi Strauss began using brand names, symbols, trademarks, and graphics as identifiers and indicators of quality.[22]

The consumer demand for prepackaged items extended to medicines. Patent medicine advertising flourished from the Civil War until the turn of the century. The producers of these medicines, many of which contained excessive amounts of alcohol and other narcotics, used advertising messages designed to appeal to the psyche. Sales were sparked by soldiers needing to self-medicate while in battle. Historian Stephen Fox says that many soldiers became addicted to these medications. Drake's Plantation Bitters, St. Jacob's Oil, and Lydia Pinkham's Vegetable Compound were some of the most heavily advertised products in the 1880s.[23] Although many of the claims made about the products were fraudulent and the products were sometimes dangerous, the relationship between advertising and sales did not go unnoticed. Advertising, even for disreputable products, seemed to work.

The Making of the Advertising Profession: 1850–1900

Marketers began to understand the importance of using advertising to stimulate consumer demand and using the media to reach mass markets. The relationship between media and advertising agents, as well as the relationship between ad agents and advertisers, was tenuous at best. Trust was

21. Juliann Silvulka, "History: 19th Century," in John McDonough and Karen Egolf, eds., *The Advertising Age Encyclopedia of Advertising, Volume 2* (New York: Fitzroy Dearborn, 2003), 752–53.

22. Ibid., 755.

23. Fox, *The Mirror Makers*, 16–19.

the major issue. Some advertisers believed that ad agents overcharged for prepurchased newspaper space. In addition, many advertisers suspected that agents did not know the value of advertising or how and why it worked. During this time, some of the founders of advertising agencies and publishers sought ways to demystify the process.[24]

In addition to the controversy surrounding patent medicines, other issues plagued the advertising industry. When advertisers wanted to place advertising in newspapers, they had to rely on incomplete or inaccurate information. Newspaper publishing was not always profitable, especially in smaller towns. Some advertisers ordered space from advertising agents only to find that the newspaper no longer existed. In the absence of any other data, advertisers relied on circulation data provided by the newspaper or the agent. This information was either unknown or inflated. Because no standardized rate structure existed, newspapers were evaluated on newsprint quality and the amount and type of advertising they carried. For advertising to increase its legitimacy, the system needed to change.

In 1869, George Rowell, a broker for advertising space, published the *American Newspaper Directory,* a listing of five thousand American and Canadian newspaper titles and circulation estimates. Rowell would ask newspapers to supply circulation data. If no data were provided, he would make his own estimate. Moreover, he charged newspapers to be included in the directory. For a fee of five dollars, advertisers could get fairly accurate circulation figures.[25] Although Rowell's directory was a welcome change, advertisers continued to push for accurate information on newspaper circulation.

Rowell's *American Newspaper Directory* was not the only innovation that helped to standardize the advertising industry. That same year, Francis Wayland Ayer opened N. W. Ayer and Son. Ayer created several institutions that helped ground the advertising industry. He created the open contract that provided financial terms for the agent and the advertiser and set up a commission for fees. This arrangement severed the ties between the newspaper and the agent.[26] Such an arrangement eventually became the model adopted by most advertising agencies because the advertiser could see the ad in print before it was sent to the publishers. With content provided by the advertiser, Ayer established an in-house printing department, another innovation that helped build trust. In the 1880s, Henry McKinney, one of Ayer's partners, conducted the first marketing study and developed an advertising proposal for a potential client. McKinney's success led to the establish-

24. Lears, *Fables of Abundance,* 88–92.
25. Fox, *The Mirror Makers,* 21.
26. Ibid.

Students in Charlie Ross's editing class learned copyediting as well as how to write advertisements. Courtesy of the University of Missouri Archives.

ment of a department devoted to such studies. Although the advertiser was responsible for writing and illustrating ads, Ayer's agency began writing copy for its clients. This arrangement was successful, but the first copy-writer was not hired until 1894. Historians note that Ayer's commission structure, market analysis, and copy services made N. W. Ayer the nation's first full-service advertising agency.[27] By the turn of the century, Ayer's clients included American Tobacco, National Biscuit Company (Nabisco), H. J. Heinz Foods, and American Sugar Refining. After a scandal threatened the future of American Telephone and Telegraph, the agency created a campaign for the company and Western Union to restore consumer confidence, the first institutional advertising campaign.[28]

Similar to Rowell, Ayer established his own publications for the growing industry. In 1874, Ayers began publishing the *Manual for Advertisers,* a journal that listed the periodicals with which the agency did business. In 1880,

27. John Vivian, "Francis Wayland Ayer (February 4, 1848–March 5, 1923)," in Applegate, ed., *The Ad Men and Women,* 5–6.
28. Ibid., 9.

Ayer began publishing the *American Newspaper Annual* and, later, the *N. W. Ayer and Son's Directory of Newspapers and Periodicals,* a standard reference for advertisers that lasted for many years. *The Advertisers Guide,* established in 1876, contained information as well as articles claiming advertising's effectiveness and propounding social benefits.[29]

Other advertising agencies opened during the 1890s. For example, in 1891 George Batton, a former employee of N. W. Ayer's office in Philadelphia, opened the George Batton Newspaper Advertising Agency, which emphasized hard work, honesty, and good writing as the keys to good advertising. That same year, Daniel Lord and Ambrose Thomas founded what was to become another prominent advertising agency, Lord and Thomas, in Chicago.

The Quest for Professional Legitimacy

The emergence of the modern advertising agency, changes in advertising images and copy, and advertising's quest for legitimacy as a profession are best understood within the economic and social environment of the early 1900s. Fueled by consumer demands created by the Civil War and the rise of mass production following the war, the consumer economy, along with consumer wealth, blossomed. Historian Juliann Silvulka writes that Americans spent millions of dollars on prepackaged consumer goods, including cereals, soaps, and ready-made clothes. The rise in consumption fueled the emergence of corporate "trusts," corporations that controlled utilities and smaller companies that produced basic goods, such as sugar and tobacco.[30] Historian Frank Presbrey writes that many feared that trusts would be the demise of advertising because having fewer corporations would "eliminate competition and set up a belief that advertising was unnecessary."[31] Rather than eliminate it, the mergers increased the need for advertising because corporations needed to sell more products in order to remain viable enterprises. Corporations also needed specialists, a need that contributed to the increasing number of advertising agencies.

The growth of the industry was not limited to large cities such as New York and Boston; the advertising industry grew in the Midwest as well. Although St. Louis's business directory did not contain a large amount of

29. Ibid.
30. Silvulka, "History: 1900–1920," 758–859.
31. Frank Spencer Presbrey, *The History and Development of Advertising* (Garden City, N.Y.: Doubleday, Doran and Company, Inc., 1929), 437.

display advertisements, several companies used this type of advertising to describe the services they offered. For example, Lesan-Gould Advertising and Publishing Company offered "Advertising Plans Prepared and Advertisements Written and Placed in Newspapers, Magazines, Street Cars and Bill Boards."[32] In addition to designing, writing, illustrating, and giving estimates for advertising campaigns, Chesman Nelson and Company gave "expert counsel to those contemplating publicity of any kind."[33] Herbert S. Gardner opened Gardner Advertising Company in 1908.[34] Gardner, born in Warsaw, Missouri, and a resident of St. Louis since 1888, started in the advertising industry when he partnered with Harry Lesan in 1902. The company quickly expanded and established an office in New York. In 1908, the two separated, with Lesan taking over the New York office. Gardner remained in St. Louis and ran the company for many years.[35]

The rising number of advertising agencies reflected the increase in advertising expenditures, which, in turn, reflected the increase in industrial productivity. Silvulka writes that "the annual volume of advertising surged nearly six-fold in the 20-year period following 1900, from $540 million to just less than $3 billion." Several industries emerged and quickly became leaders in consumption and advertising expenditures. As immigrant labor contributed to America's growth and to a rising middle class, Henry Ford's automobile increased the population's mobility and advertisers such as U.S. Rubber, Firestone Tire, and Goodyear used billboard advertising to reach this moving target. Due, in part, to advertising's impact on consumer demand, Coca Cola, Kellogg's, and Welch's Grape Juice became household names.[36]

The increasing number of advertising agencies and advertising's obvious, though not scientifically proven, impact on sales motivated practitioners to question the nature of advertising. As indicated earlier, even for successful practitioners, advertising was difficult to define. Advertisers wanted advertising to shed the association with the carnivalesque and the hawkers of patent medicines and be considered an honorable profession, such as law or medicine.[37] Rather than belabor the issue, practitioners began analyzing and determining what constituted excellence in the field, and

32. *Gould's Directory*, 2062.

33. Ibid.

34. Henry Assael and C. Samuel Craig, eds., *Printer's Ink Fifty Years: 1888–1938* (New York: Garland Publishing, Inc., 1986), 222; "H. S. Gardner Marking 50th Year in Advertising," *St. Louis Globe-Democrat*, 26 September 1952, 88.

35. "H. S. Gardner Marking 50th Year in Advertising"; Assael and Craig, *Printer's Ink*, 222.

36. Silvulka, "History: 1900–1920," 758, 759.

37. Lears, *Fables of Abundance*, 155.

sought to cultivate a sense of professionalism based on values such as commitment to the client and established measures of accountability.

In 1905, in what has become known as one of the first advertising textbooks, *Modern Advertising,* authors Earnest Elmo Calkins and Ralph Holden struggled to define advertising. No strangers to the evolving industry, Calkins had written advertising copy at the Bates Agency for more than five years before he and Holden, his associate at Bates, opened their own agency in 1902.[38] "No definition of advertising is here possible," they explained, "except as this entire book may be accepted as a definition."[39] Calkins and Holden, however, looked at the effects of advertising, rather than the process. "Advertising," they posited, "is that subtle, indefinable, but powerful force whereby the advertiser creates a demand for a given article in the minds of a great many people or arouses the demand that is already there in latent form."[40] This search for meaning and professionalism was one of the driving forces in the development of the industry and a byproduct of its sometimes checkered past.

As stated earlier, advertising practitioners began as agents for newspapers, buying space from the publications in bulk and selling it, frequently at greatly inflated prices, to advertisers. With the growth of advertising agencies, practitioners had to consider their loyalties. Was it to the publication in which they placed advertising or to the advertiser who paid for the advertising? The rise of the modern advertising agency, with its wide range of clients willing to spend millions of dollars on advertising, helped define the nature of the relationship between the advertiser and the agency. "The modern advertising agent," Calkins and Holden surmised, ". . . is the employee of the advertiser, but his relation to the advertiser is more like that of a lawyer to his client . . . a confidential one." Yet practitioners still struggled with the nature of the accountability to the client and measurements for success. Calkins and Holden suggested that advertising's success be "measured by the amount of actual business brought in by it," rather than by the agate line. Other standards of professionalism included not letting the advertiser overspend or waste money.[41]

Calkins and Holden also developed a kind of job description for those engaged in advertising. The practitioner planning to increase a company's business should "utilize every form of publicity, and every method of mak-

38. Arthur Kaul, "Earnest Elmo Calkins," in Applegate, ed., *The Ad Men and Women,* 96.

39. Earnest Elmo Calkins and Ralph Holden, *Modern Advertising* (New York: D. Appleton and Company, 1905), 1.

40. Ibid., 4.

41. Ibid., 165, 58, 60.

ing an impression upon the public . . . keeps a constant and thoughtful hand on the pulse of the market, knows exactly what his advertising is accomplishing [or] failing to accomplish . . . [and] adapts his advertising to each locality." This laundry list of responsibilities reflected Holden's specialty, the business side of advertising. However, Calkins, a copywriter, reflected on the purpose of this position. According to the authors, the practitioner must know "something of salesmanship, something of the law of supply and demand, a great deal of human nature and the best methods of appealing to it."[42]

The question of human nature and ways to appeal to it spoke to the role and purpose of copywriting and the copywriter, Calkins's specialty. What makes good advertising? By the early 1900s, most agreed that advertising was an art rather than a science. In order to be considered a profession with professional standards, practitioners realized that there needed to be a way to know how and why advertising worked. Although Calkins and Holden did not specifically use the word "psychology," they recognized that persuasive tactics in copy were important to advertising's success. "All the great forces that have moved the race, the eloquence of the orator, the fervor of the religious enthusiast, superstition, terror, panic, hypnotism—all these things are utilized in advertising."[43] These "things," as the authors put it, were elements of psychology, a topic of investigation and discussion among advertising practitioners that began as early as 1895.[44]

Many ads produced during the late 1800s featured images of robust women with major parts of their torsos displayed, a characteristic of abundance imagery that projected the feminine as the source of wealth and prosperity. These images had proved to be successful. Advertisements created during the early years of the century gradually moved away from these types of images, replacing them with representations of the modern woman, frequently disembodied and disempowered, and male-operated machines.[45] The new imagery was complemented by a change in copy, fueled, in part, by manufacturing's growing interest in trademarks, those designs and slogans that differentiated one product from another.[46]

Early advertising copy focused primarily on the product's availability and characteristics. Calkins, however, had a different vision of advertising that he defined as "that combination of text with design which produces a

---

42. Ibid., 6.
43. Ibid., 61.
44. Presbrey, *The History and Development of Advertising*, 441.
45. Lears, *Fables of Abundance*, 117–22.
46. Presbrey, *The History and Development of Advertising*, 524.

complete advertisement."[47] Rather than using a simple illustration of a product, Calkins artfully illustrated the product in a setting containing cultural items that signified prestige. This became known as the "soft-sell" approach.[48] Another of Calkins's techniques was the use of the trademark, which was complemented by a poem or catchy jingle. For example, one of Calkins and Holden's early accounts was Force breakfast cereal, whose advertising included poems such as the following:

> Jim Dump's half-sister, pale and slight,
> Had very little appetite.
> She said: "such dainty-looking food
> Will please the most capricious mood.
> So crisp and light—it takes my whim!"
> "It takes with all," quoth Sunny Jim.[49]

Although these soft-sell ads were extremely popular with the public, Calkins and others realized that a popular ad did not always translate into sales. This observation kept advertising practitioners debating what types of appeals would be successful. Historian Steven Fox writes that Albert Lasker, who joined Lord and Thomas in 1898 and became the agency's owner in 1910, frequently pondered the purpose and meaning of advertising. One man he hired, John E. Kennedy, gave him the answer. Influenced by his experiences while working in a Canadian department store and at the Bates Agency, Kennedy defined advertising as "salesmanship on paper."[50] Advertising did not have to be fancy or aesthetically pleasing. Trademarks, jingles, and basic information could not do the job thoroughly. Rather, advertising should give the customer a reason why the product should be purchased. Consumers should be told, in very basic and unadorned terms, why they needed to buy the product.

Kennedy did not stay with Lasker long, but in his relatively short tenure, he helped develop the tools for diffusion and influence of the "reason-why" approach. Lasker and Kennedy developed an in-house school where future copywriters learned "the gospel of reason-why and salesmanship on paper." As these copywriters moved on to other agencies, they took the rea-

47. Fox, *The Mirror Makers*, 43.
48. Ibid., 44.
49. Kaul, "Earnest Elmo Calkins," 95. Fox notes that the first jingles were written by Minnie Maude Hanff, and the image of Sunny Jim was created by high school student Dorothy Ficken. When Calkins and Holden assumed the account, they expanded on the strategy. Fox, *The Mirror Makers*, 46–47.
50. Fox, *The Mirror Makers*, 50.

son-why approach with them. In 1906, Claude Hopkins replaced Kennedy and continued to create copy using the reason-why technique. Lasker's career is noted for his dedication to this principle and his influence on advertising copywriting.[51]

Advertising's quest for professionalism was not limited to perfecting business practices or improving copywriting. As indicated earlier, advertising agencies compared their relationship with advertisers to that of lawyers with their clients. Advertisers sought the same prestige as that of the legal field, which had an educational component. In fact, a distinguishing professional characteristic was education. And, as advertising began to rise in prominence within the publishing and manufacturing industries, advertising education became increasingly important to the professionalization of the field.

Advertising Education at the Missouri School of Journalism

The Missouri School of Journalism offered its first advertising course during the 1908–1909 academic year, three years after New York University offered its first advertising course in a business school. The course at Missouri, "Advertising and Publishing," was described as "a study of newspaper and magazine advertising, preparation of advertising copy, display and a consideration of the business side of journalism including circulation." The course was primarily composed of lectures by an "experienced advertising man in the faculty,"[52] followed by the application of skills required to fulfill the advertising needs of the *Missourian*. Lectures included discussions of the local business environment and an analysis of national advertising campaigns. Students were expected to solicit and produce ads for the *Missourian* and later for the *Missourian Magazine*. Although several books had been published about advertising, including Calkins and Holden's *Modern Advertising* and Dr. Walter Dill Scott's *The Psychology of Advertising*, textbooks were not required for the course.

During these first courses, the types of advertising were part of the national debates on whether the "salesmanship on paper" approach to writing copy was more effective than the "soft-sell" approach that used text and design. In addition, advertisers considered what elements were important for creating effective advertising. For example, an article published in the

51. Ibid., 49–51.
52. Lockwood Williams, *Twenty Years of Education*, 78.

May 1908 issue of *Bankers' Magazine* remarked, "Bare statements, cold figures and even logical argument, alone, are not the best means to use to get people to do as you would like to have them do."[53] That national debate was not evident in the advertising that appeared in the *Missourian*.

Most of the initial *Missourian* ads published during the early months of 1908 through 1909 were small, classified advertisements of local businesses. The display ads, however, usually contained an illustration and a reminder that items were available or on sale. An overwhelming majority of the ads in the *Missourian* were for products consumed by men, such as men's clothing. No advertising directed at women appeared in the newspaper. Perhaps the lack of creativity exhibited in the *Missourian's* early ads is a reflection of the instructor's journalistic, rather than copywriting, background. Ross had come out of the editorial side of newspaper work, and when he resigned from the faculty in 1918 he became a Washington correspondent for the *St. Louis Post-Dispatch*.[54]

Conclusion

By 1908, with national manufacturing increasing, with a population moving toward an urban culture, and with the product results of an industrial country, the United States was well on its way to becoming a consumer society. The boom in manufacturing, population, and innovation in transportation made it easier for products to be mass-produced and prepackaged. The rise in production of similar goods led manufacturers to look for ways to differentiate and sell their products. At the turn of the century, many companies looked to the mass media, primarily newspapers and magazines, to create demand and expand into new markets. This drive for differentiation and sales created the need for a service that mediated the relationship between the media and the manufacturer. The advertising agency filled that void.

In the early 1900s, the advertising industry, similar to the publishing industry, was evolving and finding its soul. An industry that began with simple listings similar to classified ads had, by the turn of the century, become an important revenue stream for the publishing industry. This was especially true for magazines, a medium that, with advertising revenues and content, influenced the development of a mass culture. The road that advertising traveled, however, was not without its bumps. The advertising industry struggled with its image, as personified by P. T. Barnum's huckster

53. "Advertising to Real People," *Bankers' Magazine* 76, no. 5, APS Online, 754.
54. Lockwood Williams, *Twenty Years of Education*, 32.

practices and the manufacturers of patent medicines. Although the advertising industry worked to separate itself from a shady past, patent medicine advertising continued to appear in publications long after the Pure Food and Drug Act was passed in 1906 to control it.

Within the milieu of growth and a burgeoning recognition of its influence, advertising sought to define itself, rather than be defined by others. The founders of some of the most famous advertising agencies questioned the meaning of advertising as a profession and what made it work. The questions "What is advertising?" "Why does it work?" and "How does advertising best serve the advertiser?" were more than mere intellectual ruminations of self-absorbed practitioners. At the same time, advertising sought professional status and respect. Practitioners wanted those engaged inside and outside of the business to know that advertising was indeed a noble profession, one that brought art and science together in a way not seen before. By including advertising in the first journalism school's curriculum, Walter Williams and the Missouri School of Journalism gave the industry a measure of the credibility and respect it sought.

PART IV

Journalism's Extended Family

All kinds of specialized journalism existed in 1908, such as the labor press and women's newspapers and magazines. Their focus was on a particular interest, even while their issues and topics were part of the mainstream mass media.

Labor, its rise, its conflicts, and its issues over boycotts, strikes, hours, pay, child labor, general conditions, and power were all issues in 1908. Strikes and boycotts were controversial and not easily supported outside the unions. That year the U.S. Supreme Court ruled that a labor union's boycott of industry restricted trade and was illegal under the Sherman Anti-Trust Act. Yet, the Supreme Court did rule that an Oregon law limiting women's working hours in industry was indeed constitutional. Also, in 1908 Congress passed a bill to regulate child labor in the nation's capital, hoping that the states would do the same.[1]

In 1908 the working men and women within newspapers and other journalism enterprises, who were an early part of the labor movement, had problems too with low pay and long hours. Yet, there were no guilds then, and little public and no industry support for the labor issues of journalists, no matter what their gender or race or positions in the production of newspapers.

Even though the Progressive movement related to labor issues and unions, the press coverage of labor was primarily invisible in 1908, with the

1. Laurence Urdang, ed., *Timetables of American History*, 276–77.

exceptions of covering conflict, discord, and union organizing. There were indeed labor issues concerning media jobs other than reporting: workforces involved in typing, editing, graphic design, and overseeing were all on the fringes of the era's central labor issues. Circulation and hawking and selling newspapers were expensive too. Pay and work-hour issues were to be remedied by professionalism.

In 1908, unionization of any kind was often perceived as conflict. For example, a front-page *Missourian* story was about the governor of Oklahoma's controversial letter to the Muskogee Business Men's Alliance that cited a labor union as a threat to employers' rights to conduct their own business. "Muskogee should induce non-union laborers to move there," he was quoted as saying.[2]

At the same time, the labor force was changing. There were more and more women journalists: not just the well-known late nineteenth-century sob sisters such as Nellie Bly, but more ordinary reporters and writers, as well as editors. Women wanted to enter not only journalism but also many other professions through university education. The issue about higher education for women was such that a September 1908 *Missourian* ran a gender-related feature on higher education for women, matrimony, and motherhood, asking "Should a Girl Have Brains?" in an editorial.[3] This major societal issue reflected the question about taking women seriously.

The Missouri School of Journalism must have thought that women had brains. When it opened in 1908, the school's first class had six women among its sixty-four inaugural students.[4] The *Missourian* coverage included women, primarily as consumers, for those 1908 "society" sections, usually on page 2.[5]

The next two chapters look at journalism's extended family through labor and the inclusion of women in the field as well as through news coverage thereof. Bonnie Brennen examines the connections in "Work in Progress: Labor and the Press." Maurine Beasley looks not only at how women were represented in the news but also at their role in the journalism field in "Good Women and Bad Girls: Women and Journalism in 1908."

2. "Controversial Letter from Gov. Haskell of Oklahoma," *University Missourian*, 25 September 1908, 1.

3. "Do Girls Have Brains?" *University Missourian*, 15 September 1908, 2.

4. Farrar, *A Creed for My Profession*, 143.

5. "Society," "Women Exchange Plans, Tea Room," *University Missourian*, 17 September 1908, 2.

CHAPTER 8

Work in Progress

Labor and the Press in 1908

Bonnie Brennen

The Progressives Rally

Seen within the context of the Progressive Era, this chapter frames the year 1908 through a focus on the rise of labor and the coverage of labor-related issues by muckraking reporters in the United States. The Progressive Era of American history is an era of reform that began with the ascension of Theodore Roosevelt to president after William McKinley was assassinated in September 1901 and lasted until the beginning of American involvement in World War I in 1917. The stage was set, however, in April 1901, when United States Steel became the first American business incorporated with more than $1 billion in capital stock. This incorporation of U.S. Steel had been preceded by the unprecedented growth of giant industries at the end of the nineteenth century.[1] In response to record-breaking industrial growth and to the

---

1. For further discussion of the press and the Progressive movement see William David Sloan and James D. Startt, *The Media in America: A History,* 3rd ed. (Northport, Ala.: Vision Press, 1996), 365–82.

concentration of wealth and power in a small percentage of the population, the Progressive movement became, in the words of social historians Keith Bryant, Jr., and Kate Barnard, a "heterogeneous mass reform movement without geographical or class boundaries" that fought to reduce the political power of corporate interests through government regulation.[2]

Progressives incorporated some elements of the earlier Populist movement, which radical historian Howard Zinn notes had sparked "the greatest movement of agrarian rebellion" and created an independent radicalized culture for U.S. farmers in the 1890s that questioned dominant power relations.[3] Yet Progressives primarily focused on urban problems and issues challenging the prevailing capitalist structure and order.[4] Concerned that business interests were corrupting the political process, Progressives fought to reduce the political power wielded by special interests by making the government more responsive to U.S. citizens.

The Growth of Labor

By the turn of the twentieth century, industrialization, urbanization, immigration, and the resulting growth of corporations and mass-produced goods fueled the development of modern cities throughout the United States. Scientific and engineering developments aided the growth of machines that mass-produced goods rapidly, cheaply, and uniformly, sparking a revolution in industry that greatly changed the work process as well as the relationship between individuals and their work.

In his research on the origins of working-class radicalism, historian Melvin Dubofsky found that "Technological innovations increased productivity, but in so doing diluted labor skills and disrupted traditional patterns of work."[5] Whereas earlier a craftsperson would construct an entire product, with the age of industrialization came the division of the production process into a series of small steps aided by a variety of machines. People became appendages to machines, working at the machines' pace, and increasingly they felt alienated not only from their work but also from others and even from themselves. As psychoanalytic theorist Eric Fromm

2. Keith L. Bryant, Jr., "Kate Barnard, Organized Labor, and Social Justice in Oklahoma during the Progressive Era," *Journal of Southern History* 35, no. 2 (May 1969): 164.

3. Howard Zinn, *A People's History of the United States* (New York: Harper Perennial, 1990), 275–76.

4. Melvin Dubofsky, "The Origins of Western Working-Class Radicalism, 1890–1905," in Daniel J. Leab, ed., *The Labor History Reader* (Urbana: University of Illinois Press, 1985), 230–53.

5. Ibid., 236–37.

explains, although individuals developed a variety of technological machines and products, they stood apart from these creations, feeling powerless and estranged, and in a sense becoming slaves to the very machines that their own hands had built.[6]

Urbanization was also a significant trend in the development of modern society. In 1880, the United States was still an agrarian society with less than one-fourth of the population living in cities of 2,500 inhabitants or more. By 1908, nearly half of the population lived in cities, many of which now had in excess of 100,000 inhabitants. In his book *Discovering the News: A Social History of American Newspapers*, sociologist Michael Schudson notes that as cities grew and individuals went from "self-sufficient family economies to market-based commercial and manufacturing economies, people came unstuck from the cake of custom" and felt free to challenge existing social relationships and traditions. Individuals began to question core values, take issue with the existing social order, and envision society as having a material existence apart from their own lives. Urban life quickly became detached, "a spectacle of watching strangers in the streets, reading about them in newspapers, dealing with them in shops and factories and offices."[7]

Immigration was an additional labor-related factor in the transition to modern American society. Nearly ten million Europeans emigrated to the United States during the 1880s and 1890s, providing a glut of cheap labor for factories and corporations. As Zinn maintains in his book *A People's History of the United States*, the culturally displaced immigrants increased competition for jobs, and employers often opted to use immigrant labor because they considered the newcomers "more controllable, more helpless than native workers."[8]

Coupled with industrialization, immigration, and urbanization was the development of the mass media. Media critic Alfred McClung Lee found that as cities continued to grow, individuals faced a sense of "urban anonymity and craved news and information about their communities";[9] small-town gossip evolved into sensational news stories, feature articles, and gossip columns that could be found increasingly in newspapers and magazines. The media also provided urban dwellers with useful information on political, economic, religious, and educational matters, which sometimes called into question traditional ways of thinking about family and lifestyle choices, ethical values, and cultural norms.

6. For further discussion on the issues of technology and alienation, see Eric Fromm, *Man for Himself: An Inquiry into the Psychology of Ethics* (New York: Holt, Rinehart, and Winston, 1947), and Eric Fromm, *The Sane Society* (New York: Henry Holt, 1955).

7. Michael Schudson, *Discovering the News: A Social History of American Newspapers* (New York: Basic Books, 1978), 59, 60.

8. Zinn, *A People's History*, 261.

9. Alfred McClung Lee, *The Daily Newspaper in America*, 82.

In response to the challenges of industrialization, immigration, and urbanization, workers began strengthening existing national labor unions, including the American Federation of Labor (AFL) and the Knights of Labor, and started organizing local unions, political parties, and labor organizations throughout the country. By the turn of the twentieth century, two million Americans were members of labor unions; about 80 percent of unionized workers were members of the AFL, a union composed primarily of white, male, skilled workers. A "Protest Conference" was organized by the AFL and held on March 18, 1908, in response to the Supreme Court's ruling in the Danbury Hatter's case in which the court ruled that the union's boycott of industry restricted trade and was illegal under the 1890 Sherman Anti-Trust Act. Although the act had first been used by the U.S. government to quash the 1894 Pullman strike, the decision was unexpected and set off fears that labor unions would soon be bankrupted due to lawsuits challenging violations under the Sherman act.[10]

In 1908 there were more than half a million female office workers, and women represented nearly one-fifth of the labor force, but only one in a hundred women were members of a labor union.[11] The founding, in 1900, of the International Ladies' Garment Workers Union, and of the Women's Trade Union League in 1904, were particularly significant to the women's labor movement, especially as they began their sustained campaigns for better working conditions and higher wages for women working in sweatshops. As the labor movement continued to grow, hundreds of daily and weekly newspapers were published in a variety of languages. In working-class communities, these newspapers not only covered local news and labor activities but also provided editorial space for readers to debate contemporary economic, political, and social issues.[12]

Labor and Journalism

At the turn of the twentieth century, reporters provided an important link between the coverage of business and economic news and the creation of public information on labor issues. Reporters worked long hours for low

10. Russell O. Wright, *Chronology of Labor in the United States* (London: McFarland, 2003), 42.

11. Ibid., 320.

12. For further discussion of the labor press during this era, see Jon Bekken, "The Working-Class Press at the Turn of the Century," in William S. Solomon and Robert W. McChesney, eds., *Ruthless Criticism: New Perspectives in U.S. Communication History* (Minneapolis: University of Minnesota Press, 1993), 151–75.

wages, and their positions were often tenuous. While top-paid New York reporters earned from $40 to $60 each week, in many cities with fewer than a hundred thousand people, reporters received only $5 to $20 per week.[13] Journalists were often conflicted by the disparity between the mythology of journalism and the material realities of urban reporting. The myth stressed the romance of journalism, with its rugged individualism and supposition that the excitement of journalism more than compensated for the low pay and poor working conditions.[14] On the other hand, reporters from this era confronted the reality of long hours, poor wages, and limited job security. Despite these harsh truths, most journalists remained wary of organized labor and did not wish to affiliate with mechanical workers, preferring instead to identify with management's perspectives.[15]

Journalists' romantic vision of journalism also conflicted with the influence of new technologies on their own work in the newsroom. In her study of editorial workers, media historian Marianne Salcetti found that the mechanization of the news process created a division of labor that devalued the work of reporters though "it produced commercial credibility as part of a newspaper's selling point."[16] The use of these new technologies also encouraged notions of progress that created conditions for newsworkers which communication theorist Hanno Hardt suggests "defined their role as producers of specific images and appeals rather than as independent sources of cultural and political enlightenment."[17]

By the turn of the twentieth century, issues of consolidation became key in the newspaper industry. As newspapers grew into, in Lee's words, "large and complicated segments in a vast communication system,"[18] they began to feel financial pressures similar to other businesses; concerns regarding increased costs, improved efficiency, and greater market shares resulted in

13. Frank Luther Mott, *American Journalism*, 3rd ed., 603.

14. See, for example, Ted Smythe, "The Reporter, 1880–1900: Working Conditions and Their Influence on the News," in Jean Folkerts, ed., *Media Voices, an Historical Perspective*, 214–31.

15. For further discussion of the romance of journalism and how it affected the development of labor in newsrooms, see Bonnie Brennen, "The Emergence of Class Consciousness in the American Newspaper Guild," in Don Heider, ed., *Class and News* (Boulder: Rowman and Littlefield, 2004), 233–47.

16. Marianne Salcetti, "The Emergence of the Reporter: Mechanization and the Devaluation of Editorial Workers," in Hanno Hardt and Bonnie Brennen, eds., *Newsworkers: Toward a History of the Rank and File* (Minneapolis: University of Minnesota Press, 1995), 59.

17. Hanno Hardt, *Interactions: Critical Studies in Communication, Media, and Journalism* (Boulder: Rowman and Littlefield, 1998), 178.

18. Lee, *The Daily Newspaper in America*, 74.

newspaper consolidations throughout the United States. Although advertisers found the larger-circulation newspapers a more efficient way to reach potential customers, critics warned that newspaper mergers fueled the standardization of the news and resulted in the decreased availability of space to express conflicting viewpoints.[19] During this era, Frank A. Munsey's treatment of newspapers as mere business commodities was the target of lively editorial attacks by newspaper editors and served as a cautionary tale for the newspaper industry. Extending to newspapers the same economic principles that he used on his other commercial endeavors, Munsey considered multiple competitors inefficient, and he began to reduce the number of urban newspapers. With his purchase of the *Philadelphia Times* and the *Baltimore News*, Munsey, dubbed the Grand Executioner of Newspapers, was by 1908 well on his way of buying, reorganizing, and consolidating newspapers and then killing them.[20]

At the beginning of the twentieth century, the newspaper industry, which previously had been aligned with readers' interests, underwent major social changes. As Lee explains:

> The huge newspaper units, once subject to popular whims, reared higher and higher above the tides of mass fancies and needs. Readers began to learn that newspaper publishers mostly aligned themselves with other large employers of labor and capital. They found that mounting costs led publishers to adopt the methods of "big business" to maintain profits: monopolies, horizontal expansions of holdings into chains, vertical expansions to include papermills and power plants, lockouts, shipments of "scabs" to open closed shops, strike injunctions, high pressure deals with labor unions, lobbying for special privileges, and many more.[21]

In 1891, the International Typographical Union (ITU) began to authorize local charters for editors' and reporters' unions; by 1893, the ITU began exempting reporters from its four-year apprenticeship rule; and between the years 1891 and 1908, thirty-five charters had been granted to journalists' unions. Certainly, Henry Clay Frick's brutal handling of the July 1892

---

19. See, for example, the discussion of consolidation in Oswald Garrison Villard, "Press Tendencies and Dangers," in Willard Grosvenor Bleyer, ed., *The Profession of Journalism: A Collection of Articles on Newspaper Editing and Publishing, Taken from the Atlantic Monthly* (Boston: Atlantic Monthly, 1918), 20–29. In the same edited volume, Edward Alsworth Ross discusses issues of news judgment in large daily newspapers, in "The Suppression of Important News," 79–96.

20. Bleyer, *Main Currents in the History of American Journalism*, 413.

21. Lee, *The Daily Newspaper in America*, 162.

Homestead Steel Strike, which ultimately resulted in thirty-one deaths, may have provided an impetus for the early development of reporters' unions.[22]

However, only five of the unions established in this era remained in existence for more than five years, and most of the newsworkers' unions had a limited number of members and lasted only a year or two.[23] The ITU's authorization of reporters' unions may be seen primarily as an act of self-preservation. During labor disputes between publishers and printers, reporters had routinely acted as strikebreakers, working in backshops with editors to make sure that the newspapers were published on time.[24] In addition, ITU leaders may have hoped to garner more positive publicity from unionized reporters, and they also considered journalists yet another profession to organize.[25] By 1908, the majority of the efforts to organize newspaper reporters and editors on the local, state, and national levels were not successful, in part due to the lack of interest of newsworkers but also because newspaper publishers were hostile to journalists' unions. As journalism historian Willard Grosvenor Bleyer wrote in his 1927 book, *Main Currents in the History of American Journalism*: "In an era when organizations of all sorts flourished as never before, it seemed remarkable that the rank and file of the news and editorial staffs of daily papers remained unorganized."[26] In part one of his fourteen-part series "The American Newspaper," which ran in *Collier's Magazine* from January through July 1911, muckraker Will Irwin described how *Los Angeles Times* publisher Harrison Gray Otis ran news that was intended to injure unions and suppressed necessary information integral to labor. Irwin determined that Otis, like other U.S. newspaper publishers at the beginning of the twentieth century, "created in the minds of readers originally unbiased a picture of a labor union as a grotesque, unfair tyrant."[27]

One notable exception was the creation of the Scranton Newswriters' Union Number Three, chartered by the ITU on March 11, 1907, after an earlier attempt to unionize in 1904 had failed. The Scranton Newswriters' Union was composed of reporters, city editors, copy editors, and telegraph

22. For further discussion on H. C. Frick's War at Homestead, Pennsylvania, see Les Standiford, *Meet You in Hell: Andrew Carnegie, Henry Clay Frick, and the Bitter Partnership That Transformed America* (New York: Crown, 2005).

23. Lee, *The Daily Newspaper in America,* 145, 751–52.

24. Salcetti, "The Emergence of the Reporter," 71.

25. Daniel Leab, *A Union of Individuals: the Formation of the American Newspaper Guild 1933–1936* (New York: Columbia University Press, 1970).

26. Bleyer, *Main Currents,* 415.

27. Will Irwin, "The American Newspaper: A Study of Journalism in its Relation to the Public. Part 1: The Power of the Press," *Collier's Magazine* 46, no. 18 (January 21, 1911): 18.

and correspondence editors who worked on the four Scranton newspapers. The Scranton Newswriters' Union successfully negotiated with the local publishers and set minimum wages and top salaries for its members, as well as negotiating paid vacations and remuneration for overtime work.[28]

Although sustained efforts to organize reporters were mostly unsuccessful until the 1930s, the charter of the National Press Club in 1908 marked the development of a national social institution that was recognized and respected by journalists, editors, and publishers alike, and that catered to the specific needs of working journalists. The prototype for the National Press Club was the New York Press Club, which had begun on December 4, 1872, according to Lee, as "an organization for mutual help, sympathy and culture" for professional journalists of "good moral character."[29] With an initial membership of two hundred, the National Press Club reinforced the romanticism of journalism while providing correspondents, reporters, and visiting editors with club rooms that served as their own social headquarters. Missourians would have to wait until 1915 for the development of the Missouri Writers' Guild. Sara Lockwood wrote in her history of the Missouri School of Journalism that Walter Williams, with the support of faculty and alumni, instigated the Missouri Writers' Guild during Journalism Week in 1915. Lockwood noted, "Pride in the literary history of a state that produced Mark Twain and Eugene Field and scores of other well-known writers, an ambition to perpetuate the tradition of the present and future, and a desire for inspirational and social intercourse were the motives back of the organization."[30]

Muckraking Reporters

Although the mythology of journalism kept most newsworkers from envisioning themselves as workers, at the beginning of the twentieth century, reporters wrote extensively on labor and class issues within American society. Muckraking reporters who sought to educate and inform the public about important social issues penned some of the most important labor investigations at this time. President Theodore Roosevelt initially used "muckraker" as a pejorative term to demean journalists who he felt lacked optimism about the United States. Yet reporters embraced the name. "Muckraker" soon became the preferred title of investigative journalists working on popular newspapers and magazines during the Progressive

28. Lee, *The Daily Newspaper in America*, 670–71.
29. Ibid., 666–67, 669.
30. Sara Lockwood Williams, *Twenty Years of Education*, 284.

Despite reporters' long hours for low wages and limited job security among other pressures, they identified with the management perspective. Cartoon from the 1914 *Savitar*, courtesy of the University of Missouri Archives.

Era. Muckrakers focused on sensitive social, political, and economic issues that evoked strong, even visceral, reactions from the public. Their words and images reached about three million urban, middle-class readers, targeted public ignorance and apathy, and were intended to rouse citizens to speak out against abuses of power in American society. In his study of the muckrakers, historian Richard Brown found that through books, inexpensive large-circulation magazines, and newspapers, muckrakers presented their investigations "as verifiable facts, usually based on months of their own painstaking investigations."[31]

31. Richard C. Brown, "The Muckrakers: Honest Craftsmen," *History Teacher* 2, no. 2 (January 1969): 52.

Inexpensive large-circulation national magazines provided an excellent venue for the muckrakers' investigations. The magazines encouraged a more fully developed presentation of material than was often possible on daily newspapers. Many of the muckraking articles focused on broad social patterns transcending a single city or state or on national institutions and problems that required extensive documentation. In addition, it was easier to break local scandals in national publications rather than in individual communities where special-interest groups might pressure local newspapers to remain silent. Muckraking journalists were often college educated, and their expertise lent "taste and talent to the mass circulation magazines."[32]

The development of general-audience magazines was tied to manufacturing and distribution changes within the U.S. economy. In *The Commercialization of News in the Nineteenth Century*, media historian Gerald Baldasty writes that by the turn of the twentieth century, "the main attributes of an industrialized economy were in place: large scale factory production, an urban workforce, strategic centers of investment capital, and expensive marketing of standardized products."[33] The rise of mass-produced and mass-marketed goods depended upon advertising for the large volume of sales needed to sustain significant capital investments. By the end of the nineteenth century, advertisers were seeking out national markets for their goods, and general-circulation magazines were an inexpensive vehicle to carry their advertisements. In 1890, advertisers spent $360 million to advertise their products. In 1900, that figure increased to $542 million, and by 1910, more than $1 billion was being spent on advertising each year.[34] Journalism historians William David Sloan and James D. Startt in *The Media in America: A History* explain that:

> Ironically, this economic transformation produced both the social problems that the muckrakers critiqued as well as the means for the investigative reporters to investigate them. In a further irony, the muckrakers' exposés often appeared alongside the advertisements for products created by the very system they were attacking.[35]

During the first part of the twentieth century, approximately two thousand investigative reports, based on the careful examination of public documents, informed readers of strong alliances between business and

32. Ibid., 54.
33. Gerald J. Baldasty, *The Commercialization of News in the Nineteenth Century* (Madison: University of Wisconsin Press, 1992), 52.
34. Brown, "The Muckrakers," 54.
35. Sloan and Startt, *The Media in America*, 368–69.

government, provided evidence of deception and corruption, and exposed economic inequities between the wealthy elite and the working class. Although muckrakers considered the corruption of politicians and business leaders a major problem in American society, they maintained that members of the middle class, if educated about the current inequities, had the power to force change in social, economic, and political relationships between capitalists and workers.

In one sense, the muckrakers may be seen as press agents for the Progressive movement, spotlighting social and economic problems and, in Arthur and Lila Weinberg's words, "arousing a lethargic public to righteous indignation."[36] As a result of their investigations, the public was awakened to social, economic, and political abuses, and legislative reforms at the local, state, and federal levels were enacted. Early muckraking investigations primarily focused on powerful trusts, questionable business practices, and political corruption. For example, Ida Tarbell's eighteen-part history of the Standard Oil Company relied on public documents and congressional investigations to uncover illegal practices used by the corporation to destroy its competitors. Lincoln Steffens's series "The Shame of the Cities" investigated corruption in the Minneapolis city government and placed corrupt city politics on the national agenda, while David Graham Phillips's article "The Treason of the Senate" exposed the influence of special interests on the U.S. Senate.

Labor and Class Issues

Upton Sinclair's 1904 muckraking novel on the meat-packing industry, *The Jungle,* alerted citizens to the plight of exploited workers and helped bring issues of labor to the forefront of the American social agenda. The book, first serialized in several urban newspapers, provided the impetus for the passage of the Meat Inspection Act of 1906. By 1908, several key muckraking investigations addressed issues of race, class, and labor.

Historian Herbert Shapiro, in his article "The Muckrakers and Negroes," maintains that though some historians have considered muckraking "a journalism of white experts writing for an overwhelmingly white audience,"[37] William English Walling's investigation into the Springfield, Illinois, race riot in the summer of 1908 is an important example of the

36. Arthur Weinberg and Lila Weinberg, eds., *The Muckrakers: The Era in Journalism That Moved America to Reform—The Most Significant Magazine Articles of 1902–1912,* xviii.
37. Herbert Shapiro, "The Muckrakers and Negroes," *Phylon* 31, no. 1 (1970): 77.

muckrakers' examination of labor and race relations in the United States. In "The Race War in the North," published in the September 1908 edition of the *Independent,* Walling chronicled the two-day riot in which several thousand white citizens destroyed African American stores and houses; wounded black men, women, and children; lynched and killed black workers; and ultimately forced six thousand African Americans to leave Springfield.

In his analysis of the riot, Walling found "race hatred" at the center of the "fanatical, blind and almost insane hatred" illustrated by the mob during the conflict.[38] Shocked that such hatred and violence was alive and well in Abraham Lincoln's hometown, where African Americans constituted merely one-tenth of the city's population, Walling called for the revival of "the spirit of the abolitionists, of Lincoln and of Lovejoy" to extend social and political equality to all African Americans.[39] He warned that if white public opinion continued to insist on its need for "supremacy" and continued to treat blacks as second-class citizens, the race war would soon be transferred to the North. As a result of Walling's article and his call for absolute social and political equality, the National Association for the Advancement of Colored People (NAACP) was born. In his eulogy of Walling, fellow muckraker Charles Edward Russell referred to him as the creator of the NAACP and said, "It was Walling that saw what shape such a movement might take and called it into being and motion."[40]

In "The Tenements of Trinity Church," which ran in the July 1908 edition of *Everybody's* magazine, Charles Edward Russell described the terrible conditions of tenements owned by Trinity Church and questioned if the good brought by the church's charitable and philanthropic activities justified the squalor and filth of the tenements, housing thousands of workers, that financed their charities. Generally considered the worst housing units in New York, the Trinity tenements were little more than disease-ridden sheds. As Russell observed:

> The halls are narrow, dark, dirty, and smell abominably. The stairs are narrow, wooden and insecure. On the second and third floors are interior bedrooms that have no natural light or ventilation, and must therefore, according to the Board of Health, be a prolific breeding place for the germs of tuberculosis. A horrible, mephitic odor and the dampness that clings

38. William English Walling, "The Race War in the North," in Weinberg and Weinberg, eds., *The Muckrakers,* 234.

39. Ibid., 238–39.

40. Russell, quoted in Jack Stuart, "A Note on William English Walling and his 'Cousin,' W. E. B. DuBois," *Journal of Negro History* 82, no. 2 (Spring 1997): 272.

about old cellars and sunless courts seem to strike against you with a physical impact. You know that in this heavy and sickly air is no place to rear men and women.

The only sanitation for the families dwelling in this dreadful house is to be found in wooden sheds in the back yard . . . The back yard is a horror into which you set your foot with an uncontrollable physical revulsion against the loathsome contamination. It has much rubbish, it is vilely unkempt, it seems to exude vileness.[41]

This 1908 article was one in a series penned by Russell regarding tenements owned by Trinity Church, which Weinberg and Weinberg named the wealthiest church corporation in the country.[42] As a result of his investigations, Trinity Church first criticized Russell and *Everybody's* magazine for the sensational coverage of its tenements and attempted to sway public opinion on the matter.[43] Later, the church tore down approximately four blocks of its New York City tenements and began improving the other tenement properties that they owned.

Russell also focused on unfair labor conditions in his June 1908 article in *Everybody's*, "A Burglar in the Making." Russell detailed the inhumane prison conditions and the state of Georgia's policy of "leasing" prisoners to contractors to serve on chain gangs. In response to an increase in crime and inadequate penitentiary facilities to house convicted felons, in 1879 Georgia began a convict-leasing program. Contractors paid a minimum of one hundred dollars per year for desirable convicts who had been given sentences in excess of five years, while less-desirable convicts went to the highest bidder.[44] Russell determined that for the year ending May 31, 1907, Georgia had leased 1,890 convicts to contractors, resulting in state revenues of $353,455.55 "from a system that multiplies criminals, breeds brutality, encourages crime, and puts upon one of the fairest states in the Union a hideous blot."[45]

Russell's investigation found deplorable living conditions for leased convicts and contractors who treated the inmates as slaves. Three times each day, the inmates received a maggot-infested piece of boiled salt pork and a piece of greasy cornbread. There was disease throughout the work camps,

41. Charles Edward Russell, "The Tenements of Trinity Church," in Weinberg and Weinberg, eds., *The Muckrakers*, 314.
42. Ibid., 310.
43. Sloan and Startt, *The Media in America*, 374.
44. Charles Edward Russell, "A Burglar in the Making," in Weinberg and Weinberg, eds., *The Muckrakers*, 323.
45. Ibid., 337.

and inmates were routinely whipped if their work pace slowed. As Russell writes:

> Some of the men got pneumonia and died of it. Sometimes they stood for hours to their knees in icy water while they worked in the swamp. Always they were ill clad, ill nourished, and in no state to withstand the cold. The contractor furnished shoes as well as clothes, and the shoes were rotten and worthless even when they were new, and went quickly to pieces, so that in winter men with bare protruding toes walked in the slush. Some had no underclothes, some had no socks.[46]

Response to Russell's article was immediate. The Georgia legislature held hearings that quickly became front-page news. Newspapers throughout the state editorialized against the convict-leasing program. The *Atlanta Constitution* warned that the state should immediately end the "iniquitous and barbaric lease system," while the *Americus Times Recorder* opined that Georgia's reputation was being sullied because of this barbaric practice. The *Cordele Rambler* noted that the state has "been advertised to the world as allowing all kinds of cruelty, graft and corruption, and nothing short of an investigation will place us in good standing again."[47] On March 3, 1909, the Georgia legislature passed a convict bill that was signed by the governor, which began to rectify the situation.

By the beginning of the twentieth century, approximately one million children worked in factories, mines, tenement workshops, and textile mills. According to historians Keith Bryant, Jr., and Kate Barnard, Progressives who wanted "to save the children from neglect, overwork, and ignorance" made ending child labor one of their primary social platforms.[48] Labor unions also supported limiting child labor because low-paid children were competition to their workers, expanding the labor force and contributing to the increasing problem of joblessness.[49] William Hard's article "De Kid Wot Works at Night," published in the January 1908 issue of *Everybody's*, detailed the plight of newsboys selling papers on the street each night. In his muckraking investigation, Hard explains the pay structure for newsboys:

> The newsboy deals, generally speaking, with the corner-man. The corner-man pays the *Daily News* sixty cents for every hundred copies. He then hands out these hundred copies in "bunches" of, say, ten or fifteen or

46. Ibid.
47. Ibid., 323.
48. Bryant, Jr., "Kate Barnard," 150.
49. Zinn, *A People's History,* 261.

twenty to the newsboys who come to him for supplies. Each newsboy receives, as a commission, a certain number of cents for every hundred copies he can manage to sell. This commission varies from five to twenty cents. The profit of the corner-man varies therefore with the commission that he pays the newsboy. The public pays one hundred cents for one hundred copies of the *News*. The *News* itself gets sixty cents; the newsboy gets from five to twenty cents; the corner-man gets what is left, namely, from thirty-five down to twenty cents in net profit.[50]

The issue with such a pay structure, according to Hard, was that because newsboys bought their papers from "corner men" and then resold the papers on the street, newspapers considered them merchants rather than employees. As merchants, they had the status of independent contractors, and therefore child-labor laws did not apply to them. Although the Illinois legislature had previously rejected child-labor laws because many employers had labeled them "socialism,"[51] in response to Hard's article, new child-labor legislation was successfully passed in Illinois.

As the range of previous examples illustrates, within the Progressive Era, issues of race, class, and labor were a part of muckraking reporters' national agenda. Journalists covered all types of labor issues, including management and labor conflicts, child-labor issues, racial discrimination, and unfair labor practices. Although in 1908 newsworkers had yet to forge a collective identity as a group of workers with common interests and needs, in their reportage of labor issues and conflicts, journalists began to create a sense of class consciousness that by the 1930s would result in the development of the American Newspaper Guild.[52]

50. William Hard, "De Kid Wot Works at Night," in Weinberg and Weinberg, eds., *The Muckrakers*, 372.

51. Ibid., 360.

52. Brennen, "The Emergence of Class Consciousness," 233–47.

CHAPTER 9

Good Women and Bad Girls

Women and Journalism in 1908

Maurine H. Beasley

In 1908 women were no strangers to journalism on either the national or local level. They were subjects of news articles, contributors to publications, social writers, assistants to editors, and sometimes even editors and publishers themselves. A few bold individuals had attained fame as reporters for feats of derring-do, but journalism was considered a somewhat questionable occupation for a respectable female, unless she worked alongside her husband. Nevertheless, in spite of its reputation for dealing with the seamy side of life, or perhaps because of it, journalism presented itself as a more stimulating option for women seeking a career than teaching school, nursing, or being a "typewriter," the early name given to typists. It also provided an outlet for the display of women as satellites of the male power structure or representatives of what was billed as the eternal battle of the sexes, as well as offering some latitude for women to record their own activities and organizations.

When the world's first school of journalism opened in 1908 at the University of Missouri in Columbia, journalism in Missouri was already a thriving institution, which covered women as part of the social scene. Four years earlier Walter Williams, the founder of the new school, had written in *The State of Missouri: An Autobiography,* prepared for the World's Fair in St. Louis: "Missouri newspapers are well-edited, widely-circulated and influential. There is no county without a daily or weekly newspaper. Every shade of political, social, and religious thought is represented."[1] Williams, then editor of the *Columbia* [Mo.] *Herald,* known as "The Model American Weekly," might have added that women were among the various "shades" portrayed. True, journalism was a predominantly male domain centered on politics, which excluded women, who did not attain full voting rights until 1920. Nevertheless, in 1908 the role of women brought them into the orbit of news.

Newspapers frequently presented women as symbols of male achievement. Wives of important men were leaders of society with a capital S, purveyors of a public morality that served to keep in check women who transgressed conventional boundaries. Other women showed up as advocates for social reform, fighting for causes like Prohibition and woman suffrage. Treated as the quintessential "other," as opposed to dominant white males, women sometimes served as comic relief, used to lighten staid news columns. In an era of widening opportunities for higher education, women also appeared as the topic of editorial comment on what their role really ought to be in American life.

Most news of women, however, was confined to society columns replete with lists of names of middle- and upper-class women. Realizing that women represented a major source of buying power, advertisers expected news that would attract them. Editors routinely included notices of weddings, births, visiting friends and relatives, as well as announcements of women's organizations and religious activities. General-circulation newspapers depended on news of this nature to make their contents interesting and relevant to their readers. Williams's own writing and editing illustrated these points.

Newspaper Portrayals of Women

In his book on the state of Missouri, Williams, for example, used an illustration of the front page of the *St. Louis Republic* for November 16, 1903. It featured a three-column headline, "Mrs. D. R. Francis Succeeds Mrs. J. F. Blair as President of the St. Louis Women's Club," above a two-column

---

1. Walter Williams, *The State of Missouri: An Autobiography* (Columbia, Mo.: Stephens Publishing Co., 1904), 220.

headshot of Mrs. Francis beside a one-column, full-length photograph of Mrs. Blair in a floor-sweeping skirt and form-fitting jacket topped by a high ruffled collar.[2] Mrs. Francis's presidency received more play on the page than any other story, including one on U.S. military actions related to construction of the Panama Canal and another on a grand jury investigation of "boodle," or bribe money. It was obvious that women's clubs testified to the prominence of local elites and that Williams endorsed coverage of them. When he first had assumed editorship of the *Columbia Herald* in 1889, Williams had redesigned the eight-page weekly, making page three a repository for news of special interest to women.[3]

Not all coverage of women depicted them positively. In the 1880s as a youthful correspondent from Boonville, Missouri, for the *Sedalia* [Mo.] *Bazoo,* one of the most highly regarded weekly newspapers in the state, Williams must have become well aware of that publication's view of women during a formative period of his journalistic development.[4] Like other newspapers in Sedalia, a wide-open railroad town sixty miles southwest of the education center of Columbia, the *Bazoo* carried article after article on Sedalia's prostitutes, generally in reference to their repeated convictions for running "bawdy houses."[5] The colorful *Bazoo*, which sometimes expressed sympathy for the prostitutes in the face of middle-class hypocrisy, delighted in describing the stylish dress of the women who were hauled into court.[6] Another Sedalia newspaper summed up the situation, simply saying, "The Girls Must Pay."[7]

Females who were good were "women"; those who were bad were "girls." By 1908 the reading public had become accustomed to women as stereotypical objects of news articles. As might be expected, Williams included news of women in the five-day-a week community newspaper, the *University Missourian,* which he set up as the pivotal element of the curriculum when the Missouri School of Journalism opened its doors in 1908.[8] The *Missourian* was a laboratory for the school's first students, which included six women among an initial class of sixty-four, who came from

2. Ibid., 569.

3. Frank W. Rucker, *Walter Williams*, 54.

4. Ronald T. Farrar, *A Creed for My Profession: Walter Williams, Journalist to the World*, 40.

5. Rhonda Chalfant, "Sedalia's Ladies of the Evening: Prostitution and Class in a Nineteenth-Century Railroad Town," in LeeAnn Whites, Mary C. Neth, and Gary R. Kremer, eds., *Women in Missouri History: In Search of Power and Influence* (Columbia: University of Missouri Press, 2004), 154.

6. Chalfant, "Sedalia's Ladies," 166.

7. *Sedalia Capital*, 6 May 1899, as cited in Chalfant, "Sedalia's Ladies, 155n5.

8. Farrar, *A Creed for My Profession*, 144.

seventeen states and Canada.[9] No African Americans were among the group; the University of Missouri was racially segregated. In keeping with journalistic conventions, the *Missourian* routinely ran items on brides and respectable matrons along with other stories that provided juicier fare on gender-related topics. African American women were excluded from this coverage, even though Boone County, where Columbia was located, had some forty-five hundred African American residents in 1900.

No doubt Williams practiced journalism that expressed community values. As one authority on small-town journalism put it, "A community's future is [was] represented, symbolically and literally, by its women and children."[10] Therefore, news items made relatively frequent references to family life. Yet, women sometimes were portrayed in an amorphous state that fell between the extremes of "good" women and "bad" girls, making them the subject of human interest stories that served mainly to entertain readers. These news items often raised questions of gender relationships, consciously or unconsciously. Various illustrations can be drawn from the initial week's publication of the four-page *Missourian*.

A prime example was the lead story in the first issue, which appeared on Monday, September 14, 1908. Under the headline, "Says Leap Year Caused Suit for Failure to Wed," it gave a lengthy account of a five-thousand-dollar damage suit charging breach of promise. The story detailed efforts by two widows who purportedly solicited marriage proposals from Max Eisele, a fifty-eight-year-old widower described as a "substantial farmer" with "240 opulent acres." Decks under the main head gave the highlights: "Mrs. Catherine Clemens Was One to Propose, Declares Eisele, Not He— Bliss of Honeymoon Disturbed. Present Bride Also Popped Question to Aged Farmer." The story jumped to page three where pictures of Eisele and his wife were enclosed in a heart drawn by an artist and decorated with two cupids. The headline over the picture invited readers to look at the "Man Who Says Two Proposed to Him, and the One He Chose." Readers learned that "Mrs. Eisele is 45 and blond," while "her former rival . . . is 50 and brunette . . . thin and slightly stooped." Presumably the fifty-six hundred residents of Columbia wagged their tongues over the odd affair, ridiculing the seriousness of the widows' efforts to cement a legal relationship with a male provider in spite of Eisele's quoted desire that his main interest was obtaining "a housekeeper."[11]

9. Ibid., 143.
10. Sally Foreman Griffith, *Home Town News: William Allen White and the* Emporia Gazette (New York: Oxford University Press, 1989), 168.
11. *University Missourian*, 14 September 1908, 1.

MAN WHO SAYS TWO PROPOSED
TO HIM, AND THE ONE HE CHOSE

MAX EISELE   MRS. MAX EISELE

Farmer Max Eisele chose one woman over another while trying to avoid a lawsuit from the rejected suitor. *University Missourian*, September 14, 1908, courtesy of the State Historical Society of Missouri Newspaper Collection.

A briefer story centered on amorous attractions in a local church. Under the heading "C.C. Girls to Come Down," the two-paragraph item reported on a decision at the First Christian Church to move young women attending Christian College, a finishing school in Columbia, from the balcony to the main auditorium. The pastor was quoted as noting "a marked falling off in the number of conversions among the Christian College girls since they began sitting in the balcony two years ago." He said he had reseated the girls because of the "element" of men "with whom the seats next [to] the roof had grown into great favor."[12]

12. Ibid.

Women also appeared on page four, most of which was devoted to local advertising. A drawing of a schoolteacher ornamented an advertisement for Lowney's Chocolates with the heading "We Wish We Could Teach. . . . the harm that impure candy does."[13] Nearby was a typical announcement of a wedding, informing readers that R. H. Pinkly and his bride, "who until last Thursday evening was Miss Mabel Duncan of Columbia," would live in Milwaukee.[14]

The next day a major page one news article concerned women in society far distant from Columbia. Datelined New York, the story appeared to be a rewrite from an interview in a current magazine with Mrs. William Astor decrying the low state of "recent entertainments given by women in society."[15] Mrs. Astor, described as "for many years a recognized leader of New York society," claimed these unspecified entertainments belonged "under a circus tent, rather than in a gentlewoman's house."[16]

More relevant to local readers, considering the fact that the University of Missouri was a coeducational institution, was the editorial on page two titled "Should a Girl Have Brains?"[17] Fortunately for women students, publicly called "girls," including the six who had enrolled in the new school of journalism, the editorial rang out affirmatively. It concluded that "brains are no bar for matrimony and attractiveness in girls. They are the reverse."[18] In testimony to the charms and capabilities of Columbia women, page two also included the "Society" column, which contained news of weddings, sorority gatherings, and women's organizations, such as the state conference of the Daughters of the American Revolution. Since all journalism students had to gain practical experience on the *Missourian*, the six women very likely had been put to work preparing these items, which were more mundane than references to women in the rest of the newspaper.

For instance, on its third day of publication the *Missourian* featured women in the top left-hand corner of page one. The story was headlined "Y.W.C.A. Girls as Men in Play," and described plans by members of the Young Women's Christian Association to mimic university faculty, all of whom were male, in a comedy. To forestall accusations of impropriety, the subhead assured readers: "Women Only to Be Present When the Play Is Produced."[19]

13. Long and Heiberger Advertisement, ibid., 4.
14. "Graduates Marry Here," ibid., 4.
15. *University Missourian*, 15 September 1908, 1.
16. Ibid.
17. Ibid., 2.
18. Ibid.
19. "Y.W.C.A. Girls as Men in Play," *University Missourian*, 16 September 1908, 1.

On page two appeared another news article about women breaking conventional bounds. Its biblical interpretation seemed likely to have engendered considerable comment in Columbia and surrounding Boone County, with its total of more than seventy churches. "Commandments Only For Men," read the headline atop a report on an article by Colonel George Harvey, editor of *Harper's Weekly*.[20] Harvey was quoted as saying, "Women are not only not bound by, but are barred, at least by inference, from any obligation to observe the requirement of our fundamental religious laws. The Ten Commandments were written by men and apply to men exclusively."[21]

Whether women should or should not be obligated to follow laws made by men, other news articles made it plain that those who did not meet male expectations could expect unhappy consequences. A page one story on September 17 called attention to the death of a New York philanthropist, Giovanni P. Morosini, whose daughter Victoria had ended up in a convent after running off with the family coachman. "He Never Forgave Girl Who Eloped," the headline read, followed by a subhead, "Daughter Who Eloped with Coachman Won't Attend Funeral." At that Victoria seemed more fortunate than her sister Amelia, who "was never permitted to speak to a man," the news story said, "after being attacked and terribly lacerated by a tame bear that roamed within the [family estate] grounds."[22] This bizarre tale overshadowed a page three story on plans for the local Women's Exchange to open a tea room.

On the last day of the first week of the *University Missourian*, two stories on women represented prevailing, and conflicting, ideas about their social roles. One placed women on a pedestal; the other portrayed them as objects in a comic opera. Under the heading "Stephens College Begins New Year," the first article reported on an address given by Dr. W. J. Shamon, a Bible College dean, who "spoke in a cheerful and encouraging manner" to the students of Stephens, another Columbia finishing school. "You young women . . . are to be the queens of the schoolroom now, and you will be the queens in the various offices to which women are called, of which there are some thousand. You will bring queenliness into your homes, as God intended women should."[23]

By contrast page four offered a view of women as court jesters capable of driving men mad. "Loses His Mind Hunting Bargains," the headline began; "Shopping All Day with Daughter Drives Man Crazy." With a St. Louis

20. "Commandments Only for Men," *University Missourian*, 16 September 1908, 1.
21. Ibid, 2.
22. "He Never Forgave Girl Who Eloped," *University Missourian*, 17 September 1908, 1.
23. "Stephens College Begins New Year," *University Missourian*, 18 September 1908, 1.

dateline, the story told of Hubert Kunister, seventy-nine, of Waterloo, Illinois, who "suddenly became insane . . . In the observation ward of the City Hospital he imagines that he is still shopping and he argues with imaginary clerks."[24]

In short, without the presence of women, journalism would have been remarkably different than it actually was in the year 1908. The misogynistic cast of some news articles mirrored a social scene in which women tended to be considered objects of pity or scorn unless safely married. News stories about women may have been based on stereotypical biases, but at least they drew emotional responses and avoided being dull. In addition, women were important factors not only in terms of portrayal, but also participation, in the journalism of the day. College females were "girls," college males were "men."

Women Journalists in 1908

Lily Herald Frost, editor of the *Vandalia* [Mo.] *Leader,* a weekly newspaper, made history in state journalism circles in 1908 when she became the first woman officer of the Missouri Press Association, a group that had been founded half a century earlier in 1867.[25] She was elected third vice-president, a noteworthy achievement for a woman in an organization of male editors. Referred to as "Mrs.," she apparently was the wife or widow of an editor. Nine years later, in 1917, she addressed students during Journalism Week, an annual event at the School of Journalism featuring outstanding editors, on "Journalism as a Field for Women."[26]

Yet, Frost was far from being the first woman editor and publisher in Missouri. In 1876 Dora Sankey was listed as the first woman member of the press group, then called the Editors' and Publishers' Association of Missouri. Her husband, J. W. Sankey, owned the weekly *Holden* [Mo.] *Enterprise.* There was little doubt that she was a full partner in the operation. It was a common practice in weekly journalism for wives and other female family members to help produce newspapers. In the first fifteen years of the association, the names of some fifteen women "appeared in the association's printed minutes as taking part in programs or as members," according to a history of Missouri women journalists written by Sara Lockwood

24. "Loses His Mind Hunting Bargains," *University Missourian,* 18 September 1908, 4.
25. Sara Lockwood Williams, "The Editor's Rib," *The Matrix* 27 (December 1941): 10.
26. Sara Lockwood Williams, *Twenty Years of Education for Journalism,* 189.

Williams, the second wife of Walter Williams and herself one of the first women graduates of the Missouri School of Journalism (Class of 1913).[27]

In her history, prepared for the magazine of Theta Sigma Phi, a journalism sorority, Lockwood Williams drew on speeches by editors' wives at press association conventions. She pointed out the alluring picture of the possibilities awaiting editors' wives painted by Mrs. J. T. Bradshaw (identified only by her husband's initials) of the weekly *Lebanon* [Mo.] *Rustic* at a meeting of the Southwest Missouri Press Association in 1895:

> The editor's wife is generally capable of being his helpmate in the broadest sense. She can do more to promote moral growth in the community than anyone else if she uses her influence for good. In every department of country journalism the editor's wife can be at home. The local column is right in her line . . . the right kind of editor is glad to see his wife develop a money-making ability; it does not crowd him out or anybody else. He will have plenty to do to tend to the business part of the paper, and if his wife develops a taste for writing, he should encourage it. The general opinion prevails that the married woman has had her day and her chance. Not so with the editor's wife.[28]

Bradshaw's comments were similar to those of Mrs. R. M. White, the wife of the publisher of the *Mexico* [Mo.] *Ledger*. Also identified only with her husband's initials, she told the Northeast Missouri Press Association in 1891 that the editor's wife had the same opportunity to lead in her community as "her liege lord." Not that her life was easy, as White explained: "Of course, the editor's wife may have to take care of children, do her house work, cut the wood brought in by delinquent subscribers. . . . even get up on cold mornings and make fires, as I do. But, nevertheless, wife being the noblest sphere of women, it's better to be an editor's wife than nobody's wife at all."[29]

Marrying a small-town editor was one way for young women to pursue a journalistic career in 1908. Most of the young women who enrolled in the Missouri School of Journalism married soon after getting their degrees, although it is not clear how many used their journalism training as part of a marital partnership. Some undoubtedly did; for years Williams preserved a telegram from the editor of a small-town daily asking him to recommend a woman graduate for a job. After Williams sent him one graduate, he heard

27. Lockwood Williams, "The Editor's Rib," 10.
28. Lockwood Williams, "The Editor's Rib," *The Matrix* 27 (February 1942): 14.
29. Ibid.

from the same editor again: "Please send me another girl reporter. I married the other one."[30] In 1918 the school pointed out proudly that it had graduated 149 students, 29 women and 120 men, and that more than 85 percent remained engaged in journalistic pursuits. "Excluding the young women who have given up journalism for housekeeping, the percentage is more than 90 percent," the report continued.[31]

Even in 1908, however, it was possible for a growing number of enterprising women to have careers in journalism independent of family relationships. U.S. census figures in 1880 showed only 288 women out of a total of 12,308 persons, or about 2 percent, classified as journalists, but two decades later, in 1900, the number of women had increased to 2,193 out of 30,098, or about 7 percent.[32] Most of these wrote for women's and society columns. It is unlikely that census figures included women who assisted their husbands or fathers on small-town newspapers or sold written material to publications on a freelance basis. Writing in 1922 on editors in Mississippi since the Civil War, R. H. Henry called attention to the "large number of women editors and managers of newspapers . . . some succeeding their husbands, after they had been called hence, others assuming full responsibility of editorship while their husbands conducted other business, and in some instances, girls raised and brought up in the printing offices, [who] never left them, even to marry."[33] Unfortunately, he gave few names of these hardworking women.

A few bold women journalists had gained fame in the late nineteenth century by performing roles that set them apart from both male counterparts and society reporters. Fearless individuals known as "stunt girls" had donned disguises and performed feats of unbridled investigative reporting. Others, known as "sob sisters," turned out tear-jerking prose aimed at attracting readers during big-city circulation wars. The most notable woman journalist, Elizabeth Cochrane, writing as "Nellie Bly," raced around the world in fewer than eighty days in 1889 in a stunt that entranced the readers of Joseph Pulitzer's *New York World*. Previously, to persuade Pulitzer to hire her, she had faked insanity to be committed to a notorious asylum on New York's Blackwell Island so she could write an exposé of conditions there. Almost as well known was "Annie Laurie," Winifred Black

30. Rucker, *Walter Williams*, 176.

31. Lockwood Williams, *Twenty Years of Education*, 144.

32. U.S. Census Bureau figures, cited in Edith May Marken, "Women in American Journalism before 1900," master's thesis (University of Missouri, 1932), 129.

33. Carolyn Perry and Mary Louise Weaks, eds., *The History of Southern Women's Literature* (Baton Rouge: Louisiana State University Press, 2003), 172.

Bonfils, who worked for newspapers owned by William Randolph Hearst, Pulitzer's main rival. She specialized in covering sensational trials and writing stories with headlines such as "Strange Things Women Do for Love."[34]

It was Bonfils who played an influential role in the life of one of the women students who entered the Missouri School of Journalism in 1908, one who initially appeared less interested in marriage than in establishing herself as a journalist in her own right. She was Mary Paxton (later Keeley), the daughter of a leading family in Independence, Missouri, who received one of the first six bachelor's degrees awarded by the school in 1910. The only woman in the group, for many years Williams presented her at press meetings as "the first woman in all the world to hold a degree in journalism."[35]

Introduced to Bonfils, Paxton took her advice on having a career and became a reporter on the Hearst-influenced *Kansas City Post*. As one of the first, if not the first, women journalists in Kansas City, she gained celebrity status during her two years on the newspaper, writing first-person accounts about exploits such as a ride in a giant kite at the risk of losing her life, and a trip through the city's infamous red light district.[36] Paxton's enthusiasm for her job led to the cooling of her romance with Charles Ross, a young professor at the School of Journalism.

Although the two had been informally engaged, their paths diverged, in part because Ross's mother objected to Paxton's career as a journalist and Ross himself disapproved of her adventures.[37] Hurt by the breakup, Paxton suffered a physical and emotional collapse, finally deciding on the advice of Williams to obtain a master's degree in home economics, which she put to use as a home demonstration agent in Virginia.[38] Both she and Ross eventually married other people, but they continued to carry on a lengthy correspondence for years. Ross became a Pulitzer Prize–winning Washington correspondent for the *St. Louis Post-Dispatch* and eventually press secretary to President Harry S. Truman, his childhood friend from Independence.

Paxton went to France during World War I as a YMCA worker and on her return to New York made a sudden decision in 1919 to marry Edmund Keeley, a farm manager she had met in Virginia. Left a widow with a child to support, Keeley returned to Columbia where she taught journalism for a quarter of a century at Christian College. Living to the age of one hundred,

34. See section on "Stunt Reporters and Sob Sisters," in Maurine H. Beasley and Sheila J. Gibbons, *Taking Their Place: A Documentary History of Women and Journalism* (State College, Pa.: Strata Publishing, 2003), 64–73.

35. Rucker, *Walter Williams*, 172.

36. Farrar, *A Creed for My Profession*, 166.

37. Margaret Truman, *Bess W. Truman* (New York: Macmillan, 1986), 26–27.

38. Ibid., 53.

MISS IRENE SCRUTCHFIELD,
President Alpha Phi Sigma.

MISS MARY PAXTON,
President Junior Women.

Presidents University Women

MISS ALICE RICHARDSON,
President Sophomore Women.

MISS MARGARET ELSTON,
President Freshmen Women.

Mary Paxton, a 1908 transfer student, graduated in 1910 as the first woman graduate in journalism. She became the first female reporter for the *Kansas City Post* and later taught journalism at Christian College (later Columbia College). From the 1909 *Savitar*, courtesy of the University of Missouri Archives.

she was given the local title of "The First Lady of Journalism."[39] It seemed fitting for a path-breaking woman whose closest lifelong friend was Bess Wallace Truman, first lady of the United States from 1945 to 1953. Perhaps it was also belated compensation for what Margaret Truman, Bess's daughter, saw

39. Barbara Zang, "The First Lady of Journalism," *University of Missouri School of Journalism Alumni Magazine* (1987), 11, as cited in Farrar, *A Creed for My Profession*, 168.

as "more than a little ironic" that Paxton, "who had set out to conquer the newspaper world while Charlie Ross hesitated to leave his teaching job, [became] . . . the teacher while Charlie was a big-time reporter."[40]

Women and Newsroom Culture

As the story of Mary Paxton Keeley illustrated, journalism held a variety of obstacles for women. General news reporting itself, particularly on metropolitan dailies, was viewed as a male preserve. As Linda Steiner pointed out, vocational literature and editors' published remarks testified to the fact that "reporting is not woman's work," in the words of John Given, editor of the *New York Evening Sun,* in his 1907 book on newspapers.[41] Editors described reporting as a dangerous job with long hours that exposed journalists to the rougher elements of society. Most women were not thought to have either the stamina or the intellectual ability to chase down wayward facts and deal with uncouth elements in an effort to become what Ishbel Ross, the first historian of women journalists, called "a front-page girl."[42] Furthermore, those who engaged in journalism were seen as apt to lose their womanly sensibilities.

Although relatively few women actually worked in newspaper offices in comparison to those who submitted contributions written in their own homes, the presence of full-time female staff members on metropolitan newspaper staffs challenged cherished gender assumptions. The Victorian ideal, which carried over into the first decade of the twentieth century, held that middle- and upper-class women should exemplify the "cult of true womanhood" which was based on the four cardinal virtues of "piety, purity, submissiveness and domesticity."[43] Noisy, dirty, and situated in downtown locations, newspaper offices were polluted by tobacco smoke, foul language, and cheap whiskey.

One opponent of women's employment on newspapers was Edward Bok, editor of the *Ladies' Home Journal,* the leading women's magazine of the day. In 1908 he prepared an article, "Is the Newspaper Office the Place for a Girl?" that ran the following year. His answer: an unqualified "no." Bok reported that he had asked fifty newspaperwomen, "If you had a young

40. Truman, *Bess W. Truman,* 105.

41. As cited in Linda Steiner, "Stories of Quitting: Why Did Women Journalists Leave the Newsroom?" *American Journalism* 15 (Summer 1998): 91.

42. Ishbel Ross, *Ladies of the Press* (New York: Harper, 1936), 3.

43. Barbara Welter, "The Cult of True Womanhood: 1820–1860," *American Quarterly* 18 (Summer 1966): 151.

daughter, desirous or forced to go into the outer world, would you, from your experience as a newspaper woman, approve of her working in a daily newspaper office?" Only three of the forty-two women who responded to his query answered affirmatively, with mothers declining on both moral and ethical grounds to urge their daughters to follow their footsteps. He quoted one mother: "Women in absolutely every other line of work are not assailed to such an extent by individuals of the opposite sex as is the news-paperwoman."[44] Bok, however, did not ask why the women themselves stayed in the newspaper field if they found it so troubling.

Even the three newspaperwomen who answered Bok positively hedged their approval. They emphasized that only serious and high-minded women could survive the moral perils of newspaper offices. One explained to Bok: "She must expect from her men associates none of the courtesies of the drawing room, and she must make them understand from the first that they may expect from her only the perfectly cool, professional manner a business woman should wear."[45]

Bok ended his article with comments from thirty editors of "the most rep-utable" newspapers in the country who replied to the same question he had posed to the newspaperwomen. All thirty answered "no" most emphati-cally. One wrote, "No, a million times no, and no words I can command can make my objections appear strong enough."[46] Bok quoted another one:

> In my eighteen years of experience in this office I have never yet seen a girl enter the newspaper field but that I have noticed a steady decline in that innate sense of refinement, gentleness and womanliness with which she entered it, and we are extremely careful, too, in the surroundings of our women and their 'assignment.' Yet they lose something—what, I cannot express in words.[47]

As these comments reveal, prevailing ideas of gender roles made it almost impossible for women to succeed in daily journalism on an equal basis with men. Editors may have had good intentions in sheltering most women jour-nalists from harsh realities, but this protection meant that they were not given serious assignments. Confined for the most part to women's depart-ments, they received lower pay and less respect than their male counterparts.

---

44. Edward Bok, "Is the Newspaper Office the Place for a Girl?" *Ladies' Home Journal* (February 1909), 18.
45. Ibid.
46. Ibid.
47. Ibid.

Editors' apprehension about the presence of women was so intense that women's page writers routinely were separated from the rest of the staff at the start of the twentieth century. Marie Manning, who as "Beatrice Fairfax" originated a popular advice column for Hearst's [New York] *Evening Journal* in 1898, recalled in her autobiography that she and her coworkers were confined to what was called the "Hen Coop," a small room at the end of a corridor. There she and two other women "got out the woman's page of the *Evening Journal*, wrote book reviews, produced thrillers for the Sunday edition and added the 'woman's angle,' whatever this is, to murder trials."[48] Although the trio was summoned frequently to the city room to get assignments, Manning wrote:

> . . . No woman reporter had a desk in that inviolate masculine stronghold. . . . A feeling prevailed that skirted creatures were entitled to something vaguely known as chivalry. . . . With true feminine intuition, we realized that the borrowed knight-errantry awarded to us merely helped to rid the city room of something that might in the long run prove troublesome.[49]

Male journalists recognized the presence of women by such gestures "as hats off in the elevator . . . [but] they had a quaint way of showing us that, when all was said and done, we were practically supernumeraries," Manning concluded. When editors wanted to discipline a male, they sent him to the "Hen Coop," she added: "Forcing a man to work in the same room with us was the equivalent of sending a dog to the pound or standing a child in the corner."[50] By 1908 Manning had left New York for marriage to a Washington real estate dealer, quite aware that women journalists still were perceived as inferior to men.

Women's page writing itself abounded in clichés and flattery of those deemed important enough for its columns. As Anne O'Hagan, one of Manning's "Hen Coop" associates, wrote in 1898:

> No woman is ever mentioned on a "woman's page" who is not, if not transcendently beautiful, at least gifted with "a charm of manner all her own." No actress is there whose home life is not of a sort to gladden every mother's heart. No woman lawyer or doctor is anything but "deliciously

48. Beatrice Fairfax [Marie Manning], *Ladies Now and Then* (New York: Dutton, 1944), 23.
49. Ibid., 36.
50. Ibid., 126.

feminine." . . . There is no reformer harshly haranguing the world on unsavory subjects who is not herself a star of saintliness and a rose of sweetness. . . . No Congressman ever had a wife whose brilliancy as a hostess and whose personal fascination did not cause the enraptured woman's page editor and reporter to grovel before her.[51]

Formula writing of this type, which continued into the twentieth century, did little to elevate newspaperwomen in the eyes of their masculine colleagues, but it showed that women journalists were not grave threats to the male power structure. This point was borne home in 1889 when *The Journalist,* a weekly trade publication, devoted an entire twenty-four-page issue to women journalists, listing some one hundred women, ten of whom were African American. Allan Forman, the editor, said his intention was to "disabuse thousands of the case-hardened old fogies of the idea that a newspaper woman in any way interferes with the men, or that she is any less a woman became she earns her living by wielding a 'Dixon' [pencil] instead of sewing on buttons for the 'lords of creation.'" Forman expressed surprise at the large number of women connected with newspapers. When he started to work on the issue, he "did not know, as I do now, that I might publish a volume the size of Webster's Unabridged Dictionary and then not half cover the field."[52]

Conclusion

Forman may have overstated his case, perhaps in an effort to market his publication to women, but there was ample evidence that the number of women interested in newspaper work had increased exponentially in the years leading up to 1908 for a variety of reasons, some economic, such as the need for jobs, and others rooted in efforts to improve society. Women journalists were part of the Progressive Era's "municipal housekeeping" movement. A central tenet of the women's clubs that blossomed in the late nineteenth century was the concept of "municipal housekeeping," which called on women to take responsibility for improving their communities as well as their individual homes. According to Agnes Hooper Gottlieb, journalists affiliated with women's organizations reaffirmed "in print the belief that a woman's place was, indeed, the home, but that the home was a

51. Anne O'Hagan, "Women in Journalism," *Munsey's Magazine* 61 (July 1898): 612.
52. Allan Forman, "By the Bye," *The Journalist* 9 (January 26, 1889): 12.

'community' and it was woman's duty to clean up their communities to ensure the safety of their homes."[53]

The women's club movement included the formation of women's press clubs. Excluded from men's press clubs, women journalists formed some eighteen clubs of their own between the years 1885 and 1902. The clubs gave testimony to women journalists' need to form helpful alliances and socialize while they strove to legitimize their status in journalism.[54] Women's press clubs often published their own newsletters that advocated women's rights and suffrage. Many of the groups did not restrict membership to women employed on newspapers, but also accepted those who only occasionally published material or wished to do so. In doing so they helped to promote journalism as a suitable pursuit for women.

In a class by itself was a notable newspaper started in 1908 by an influential woman in religion. That year Mary Baker Eddy, founder of the Christian Science Church, began the well-respected *Christian Science Monitor*, known for its factual news coverage. Her motivation appeared mixed. She had long been a critic of yellow journalism as practiced by Hearst and Pulitzer with its concentration on crime and sensation. At the same time she probably sought to counteract the negative publicity that she had received from litigation involving herself and her church.[55] The *Monitor* was unusual in many ways. It was one of the nation's few newspapers, apart from club publications and some country weeklies, actually run by a woman.

Nevertheless, by 1908 it was apparent that the door to journalism as an occupation for women was definitely ajar, even though women were discriminated against and exploited in many situations, if they were able to get jobs at all in the metropolitan field. A few women journalists achieved celebrity status; others made a precarious living relegated to monotonous tasks on women's pages. In rural journalism most careers were based on family ties. Still, Walter Williams's new school helped push the door open further for women.

Malvina Lindsay, a 1913 graduate of the Missouri School of Journalism who became women's page editor of the *Washington Post*, said years later that women journalists owed a great deal to Williams:

53. Agnes Hooper Gottlieb, *Women Journalists and the Municipal Housekeeping Movement, 1868–1914* (Lewiston, N.Y.: Edwin Mellen Press, 2001), 3.

54. For a complete listing see Elizabeth V. Burt, ed., *Women's Press Organizations, 1881–1999* (Westport, Conn.: Greenwood, 2000), 321–23.

55. Sydney E. Ahlstrom, "Mary Baker Eddy," in Edward T. James, Janet Wilson James, and Paul S. Boyer, eds., *Notable American Women: 1607–1950*, vol. 2 (Cambridge, Mass.: Belknap Press of Harvard, 1971), 558.

Before the coming of schools of journalism, newspaper offices were largely closed to them [women] on the basis of any classified professional standards. . . . Their writing was expected to be flashy and maudlin. But through their training in schools of journalism and through Dr. Williams' personal sponsorship of them and belief in them, they were graduated into professional respectability and new fields of opportunity.[56]

The year 1908 marked the start of a new opportunity for women to learn journalistic skills. The new Missouri School of Journalism gave women more chances to show what they could do in journalism in spite of daunting prejudice against them.

56. Rucker, *Walter Williams*, 176.

PART V

General Assignment Plus

Much like apprenticeships at newspapers, early journalism education programs were structured to train journalists by having them practice general-assignment news coverage. The Missouri School of Journalism's first curriculum reflected that emphasis in its newspaper-making and news-gathering classes. The classes encompassed general-assignment practice in methods of getting the news, understanding news values, interviewing news sources, and then treating the news in the final accounts. The *University Missourian* served as a laboratory for putting the news process into the practice of journalistic work.[1]

But it soon became apparent that Walter Williams had more in mind for journalism students than general-assignment news reporting. The press in 1908 had a multitude of topics to cover, not just about local events, politics, and elections, but also in other newsworthy areas such as sports, the arts, and international news. And Williams also wanted to follow his record of mechanical graphic beauty from the *Columbia Herald*.[2] The physical appearance of newspapers was changing with the advent of better technologies for reproducing graphic art such as photos and illustrations, and Williams sought to add a class in illustrative art.

---

1. Ronald T. Farrar, *A Creed for My Profession: Walter Williams, Journalist to the World*, 142. Farrar cites the University of Missouri School of Journalism *Announcement of Courses in Journalism*, 1908–1909, 4–5.
2. Frank W. Rucker, *Walter Williams*, 58, 144.

There were the Olympic Games in London in the summer of 1908. It was also the year that "Take Me Out to the Ballgame" became popular. And, taking someone out to a ballgame also coincided with newspaper columns about sports, from local high school games to collegiate contests, with coverage of the athletes, the coaches, upcoming sporting events, and game results. For example, a fall *Missourian* featured the University of Missouri's football coach, noted that two hundred students were trying out for the team, and carried a picture of the team captain.[3] Leisure sports were part of the nation's culture, with tennis, golf, and cycling parts of a national sports craze.

Too, there were arts and cultural events in the news, as noted by community announcements of both visiting performers and local productions, reviews of theatrical, artistic, and musical performances, and literary examples of readings and lectures. Press coverage of the arts was a part of the *Missourian*'s pages. The first issue of the *Missourian* included a front-page story of a Columbia theater in financial trouble,[4] and subsequent issues featured writers, poets, artists, and musicians. One such article was on a law student poet, and included one of his poems.[5]

National and international cultural happenings were newsworthy, too. In 1908, D. W. Griffith directed his first film, *The Adventures of Dollie,* while notable books by both well-known and new writers were published, such as O. Henry's *Gentle Grafter* and Kenneth Grahame's *Wind in the Willows.* Nickelodeons, then numbering about eight thousand in the United States with two in Columbia, Missouri, showed continuous movies with piano accompaniment for an admission price of five cents. Music was in the news: Arturo Toscanini became the director of the Metropolitan Opera in New York, Oscar Straus completed the operetta, *The Chocolate Soldier,* and Arnold Schoenberg began his modernist experimentation with the atonal Second String Quartet.[6]

Certainly, by 1908 American journalism was not confined to focusing on the United States, but had correspondents all over the world, covering primarily wars and explorations. Cable and wire services transmitted the stories to magazines and local newspapers. Yet, journalism, American style, was also part of the cultural and commercial colonialism of American hegemony. Walter Williams's international interests prevailed in the new school. Before he was dean, Williams had promoted the St. Louis World's Fair and

3. "Coach of the Football Team," *University Missourian,* 15 September 1908, 4; "200 Try Out for Football," 21 September 1908, 1; "Athletics," 17 September 1908, 4.
4. "Two Suits Keep Playhouse Dark," *University Missourian,* 14 September 1908, 1.
5. "Law Student Poet," *University Missourian,* 16 September 1908, 2.
6. Laurence Urdang, ed., *The Timetables of American History,* 278–79.

held an international journalism conference there. The School of Journalism enrolled a Canadian in its inaugural 1908 admissions and let Chinese visitors audit those early journalism classes. Williams made sure that the first curriculum included his course, "Comparative Journalism," for studying journalism conditions both within and outside the United States.[7] The journalism school's library carried international newspapers, which became the text for the course. The 1908 *Missourian* included international coverage, such as "Reporting No Snap in Russia,"[8] "Poor Persia! Newspapers There Unknown . . . ,"[9] and "Failed Attempt to Assassinate President of Guatemala."[10] Too, the dean must have alerted international journalists about the opening of the school as the *Missourian* printed their endorsements and similar efforts.[11]

In 1908, there was much to cover internationally, via correspondents and the newsgathering of the Associated Press and the United Press. Readers learned of political upheavals such as the assassination of King Carlos I in Lisbon; revolutionary uprisings in Persia, Bali, and the Ottoman Empire; the deaths of China's emperor and the dowager empress; and the new leaders such as Ferdinand I, who proclaimed Bulgaria independent and himself czar, and Juan Vicente Gomez, who became the dictator of Venezuela. In 1908, the boundaries of nations changed: Austria annexed Bosnia and Herzegovina; Crete declared union with Greece. That year had newsworthy disasters: earthquakes in Calabria and Sicily killed 150,000 people, while the Japanese steamer *Matsu Maru* sank after a collision, killing some three hundred people.[12]

After his first few years as dean, Williams traveled extensively, wrote about world journalism, became director of the International Press Congress in San Francisco (1915), and was the first president of the Press Congress of the World (1916–1926).[13]

The visual capabilities of newspapers and magazines were impacted by the then existing technology for images in the midst of the legal parameters for the final journalism product. Jacob Riis had published *How the Other Half Lives*, a documentary about New York's slums that included halftones and drawings of his photographs, in 1890 as an effort for reform. A revolution

7. Farrar, *A Creed for My Profession*, 142.
8. *University Missourian*, 23 September 1908, 3.
9. Ibid., 24 September 1908, 3.
10. Ibid., 16 September 1908, 1.
11. See for example "In Journalism Abroad," *University Missourian*, 14 September 1908, 2; "British Journalists Indorse U. of M. Idea," *University Missourian*, 14 October 1908, 2. Both articles discussed university education for journalists.
12. Erdang, ed., *Timetables of American History*, 277–79.
13. Sara Lockwood Williams, *20 Years of Education in Journalism*, 31.

in graphic arts followed, affecting all printed media. By 1908, the field had an ability to print photography via halftones in major city newspapers; graphics were found in small-town weeklies as drawings in the advertisements and stories and portrait plates of notables. For small newspapers, the visual images were primarily headshot plates, graphics, drawings and cartoons, and graphic layouts.

The first issue of the *Missourian* carried a locally drawn cartoon on its front page: "Our Six Columns Will Help." In the foreground a seated baby is wrapped in a newspaper next to a tiger with a banner labeled "University Missourian"; in the background are six university columns, a reference to the landmark columns left standing in the quadrangle after Academic Hall burned to the ground, each representing an academic unit: Law, Teachers, Agriculture, Arts and Sciences, Medicine, and Engineering. Journalism as the newest unit would join the other six units. (See chapter 13 for the illustration and a discussion.)

Visually, that same issue had two headshots for news articles and illustrations in the advertisements for clothing and candy. The newspaper repeated this visual pattern of cartoons, drawings primarily in the advertisements, headshots from photographic plates, and graphics as to layout and design. The earliest classes in newspaper illustration, taught by an Art Department professor, gave students both lectures and laboratory practice in pen-and-ink technique. More advanced courses followed to where a student could specialize in design and illustration. By 1914 photoengraving was offered when the university equipped a photo-engraving laboratory to make halftone plates for use in the *Missourian*.[14]

The following four chapters look at news beyond general-assignment reporting to highlight the coverage of sports, the arts, international news, and newspaper design. Tracy Everbach places the emphasis on sports reporting within the national cultural fascination with sports in her chapter, "Sports Journalism and the New American Character of Energy and Leisure." Scott Fosdick contrasts the arts coverage with the national arts coverage and art criticism in major American cities in his chapter, "Enter, Stage Right; Critics Flex Their Muscles in the Heyday of Live Performances." John Merrill and Hans Ibold point to the status of international news in 1908 in their chapter, "1908: The Beginnings of Globalization of Journalism." And, Lora England examines and compares newspaper design and use of illustration in her chapter, "The Look of 1908: Newspaper Design Status at a Turning Point in Journalism."

14. Ibid., 81–82.

CHAPTER 10

Sports Journalism and the New American Character of Energy and Leisure

Tracy Everbach

A s the nineteenth century turned to the twentieth, newspaper coverage of sports reflected a new era in which American successes in athletics came to represent American ideals and America's national character. Flamboyant sports writing in the era of yellow journalism attracted newspaper readers and contributed to building a worldwide image of the United States as an economic, political, and athletic power.

A social movement toward sports and recreation had begun in the late nineteenth century as the nation became more urban and industrialized and people sought outlets to expend energy and enjoy leisure time. Team sports, including college athletics, also provided people with a social outlet in the form of both participatory and spectator sports. An organized movement for outdoor recreation was progressing as local and state officials increased the number of parks, athletic fields, swimming pools, beaches, tennis courts, golf courses, and other sports facilities across the nation.[1]

It was an era during which Americans felt a strong nationalism, represented on the playing field with pageantry and patriotism, including rallies,

1. Foster Rhea Dulles, *America Learns to Play: A History of Popular Recreation 1607–1940* (New York and London: D. Appleton-Century Company, 1940), 198–99, 348–49.

flag displays, and band performances that allowed Americans to show their loyalties to teams and to the nation.[2] The robust image of President Theodore Roosevelt, a vigorous outdoorsman, embodied the boom in recreation. He and other athletic figures came to represent the impending strength of America as an international power. They were to be emulated.[3]

As part of the sports movement, youth sport and women's sport activities expanded in both watching from grandstands and participation. Bicycling became a trend, college football grew in popularity, professional baseball drew larger audiences and became known as the "national pastime," and boxing garnered attention from the public and the press.[4] Athletes began to receive print media coverage that elevated them into national figures and heroes, playing into America's new sporting image.[5]

The rise in yellow journalism, as exemplified by Joseph Pulitzer's *New York World* and William Randolph Hearst's *New York Journal* newspaper coverage, contributed to the national interest in sports in the late 1800s and early 1900s. This splashy form of journalism featured sensational headlines, speedy news delivery, bigger newspapers, color printing, photos and graphics, comics, gossip, exaggerated reporting, and self-promotion to spur circulation. In the 1880s Pulitzer's *World* was the first newspaper to feature specific sports coverage with a sports department run by its own editor. That editor, H. G. Crickmore, turned his paper's spotlight on baseball and boxing and discovered those sports drew devoted readers. Pulitzer recognized the public's new hunger for information on sports and observed that sports news appealed to the "everyman." The innovative sports coverage complemented Pulitzer's credo that the *World* should reach as many readers as possible.[6]

In 1895, Hearst, who had purchased the *New York Journal,* copied Pulitzer's sports journalism prototype. Hearst not only beefed up sports

2. Steven W. Pope, "Negotiating the 'Folk Highway' of the Nation: Sport, Public Culture and American Identity, 1870–1940," *Journal of Social History* 27, no. 2 (1993): 183–85.

3. Bruce Evensen, "The Media and the American Character," in James D. Startt and Wm. David Sloan, eds., *The Significance of the Media in American History* (Northport, Ala.: Vision Press, 1994), 274; Pope, "Negotiating the 'Folk Highway,'" 183–85; Benjamin Rader, *American Sports: From the Age of Folk Games to the Age of Spectators* (Englewood Cliffs, N.J.: Prentice Hall, Inc., 1983), 146.

4. Rader, *American Sports,* 146.

5. Evensen, "The Media and the American Character," 274.

6. W. Joseph Campbell, *Yellow Journalism: Puncturing the Myths, Defining the Legacies* (Westport, Conn.: Praeger, 2001), 7–8; Will Irwin, *The American Newspaper: A Series First Appearing in* Collier's, *January–July, 1911* (Ames: Iowa State University Press, 1969), 18–19; Jon Enriquez, "Coverage of Sports," in W. David Sloan and Lisa Mullikin Parcell, eds., *American Journalism: History, Principles, Practices* (Jefferson, N.C., and London: McFarland and Company, Inc., 2002), 200; Denis Brian, *Pulitzer: A Life* (New York: John Wiley and Sons Inc., 2001), 72–73; George Juergens, *Joseph Pulitzer and the* New York World (Princeton, N.J.: Princeton University Press, 1966), 118–21, 131.

coverage in the *Journal* but also emulated other elements from the *World,* such as coverage of crime, sex, and scandals. The newspaper war between the *World* and the *Journal* became the pinnacle of yellow journalism, which drew its name from "The Yellow Kid," a cartoon character that the two papers battled back and forth to run as a comic.[7]

When Hearst ordered sports coverage increased and expanded, other newspapers followed suit, creating sports sections and covering sporting events around the nation. This widespread newspaper sports coverage "helped to establish sports as a respectable pastime for the middle classes" and set a precedent for the modern sports section, now featured in a majority of daily newspapers.[8]

The sportswriters of the time attracted audiences with a "flippant, humorous, slangy view of sport," wrote Will Irwin in 1911 in *Collier's.* These colorful and entertaining writers drew readers who bought newspapers to follow their favorite writers' bylines. Hearst assigned his best writers to the sports pages, including baseball writer Charles Dryden, who employed clever writing and jargon still used in today's sports reporting. Dryden used phrases like "the old horsehide" for a baseball and nicknamed Chicago White Sox owner Charles Comiskey "The Old Roman."[9]

Newspapers also employed new technology to enhance their sports coverage. For example, the *New York Sun* created a grid system for recording boxing results, and the *New York Herald* printed photographs through halftone photo engraving, enhancing the readers' experience.[10]

The *University Missourian* and Sports Coverage

When the Missouri School of Journalism opened in 1908, the curriculum included no specific courses in sportswriting and clearly shunned yellow journalism. In his fall 1908 convocation to the faculty, University of Missouri President Albert Ross Hill proclaimed: "I believe it is possible for this

7. Enriquez, "Coverage of Sports," 200; W. A. Swanberg, *Citizen Hearst* (New York: Charles Scribner's Sons, 1961), 80–81; John Tebbel, *The Life and Good Times of William Randolph Hearst* (New York: E. P. Dutton and Co., Inc., 1952), 120, 127; Brian, *Pulitzer: A Life,* 210–12.

8. Frederick W. Cozens and Florence Scovil Stumpf, "The Sports Page," in John T. Talamini and Charles H. Page, eds., *Sport and Society: An Anthology* (Boston and Toronto: Little, Brown and Company, 1973), 421–22; Enriquez, "Coverage of Sports," 200.

9. Irwin, *The American Newspaper,* 36; Cozens and Stumpf, "The Sports Page," 422; Enriquez, "Coverage of Sports," 200.

10. Peter R. Shergold, "The Growth of American Spectator Sport: A Technological Perspective," in Richard Cashman and Michael McKernan, eds., *Sport in History: The Making of Modern Sporting History* (St. Lucia: University of Queensland Press, 1979), 31–32.

School to give dignity to the profession of journalism, to anticipate to some extent the difficulties that journalism must meet and to prepare its graduates to overcome them" and "to give prospective journalists a professional spirit and high ideals of service."[11]

Walter Williams, a founder and the school's first dean, embraced high ethical standards and brought them to the *University Missourian* newspaper, the school's teaching laboratory. But one day a year, starting in 1909, the *Missourian* staff published a parody edition on "Yellow Day" featuring exaggerated and sensational stories.[12]

While sports reporting was not part of the new journalism school's curriculum, the first volume of the *Missourian* newspaper included comprehensive coverage of Missouri Tigers football. The team, its coach, W. J. Monilaw, and games were covered or mentioned in stories, photos, and cartoons in the majority of the fall 1908 semester's editions of the paper.

Football games, including game coverage and previews, received front-page attention in several editions. The biggest gridiron rival, the University of Kansas Jayhawks, played the Tigers in a ballyhooed Thanksgiving Day game. Unfortunately, Kansas won, as detailed in a page one *Missourian* story.[13]

Other sports coverage, mainly concentrating on Missouri football but also high school and professional sports, appeared that fall in several "Athletic News" or "News about Athletics" sections on pages three or four of the four-page newspaper.[14]

11. Ronald T. Farrar, *A Creed for My Profession: Walter Williams, Journalist to the World*, 140.

12. Ibid., 152–53; Frank W. Rucker, *Walter Williams*, 159–60, 162.

13. See "Fight before Football Game" and "Freshman War on Rollins Field," *University Missourian*, 5 October 1908, 1; "Ready for Rolla," cartoon of tiger dressed in football gear, *University Missourian*, 8 October 1908, 1; "Missouri Beats Rolla, 16 to 0, Despite Flukes," *University Missourian*, 12 October 1908, 1; "Hawkeyes Must Buck Missouri Weather as Well as Tiger Line," *University Missourian*, 16 October 1908, 1; "Outweighed, Tigers Defeat Iowa by 10 to 5 in Hard-Fought Game, Bluck and Alexander Score," *University Missourian*, 19 October 1908, 1; "Monilaw's Day Dream," cartoon depicting coach dreaming of Missouri football players stomping on "K.U." players, *University Missourian*, 22 October 1908, 1; "Tigers Wallop Westminster by 58 to 0 in Snow," *University Missourian*, 26 October 1908, 1; "Ames Plays Rings Round Missouri, Score 16 to 0," *University Missourian*, 2 November 1908, 1; "Tigers Whip Drake University Team by a Score of 11 to 8, Coming from Behind in Bitterly Contested Game," *University Missourian*, 9 November 1908, 1; "Tigers Defeat 'Scrubs' 25 to 14," *University Missourian*, 23 November 1908, 1; "Kansas Twists Tiger's Tail, 10–4," *University Missourian*, 30 November 1908, 1.

14. For example, the *Missourian's* October 8, 1908, edition included a page four section labeled "Athletics" that included a preview story of the Missouri-Rolla football game, "Tigers Need More Ginger in Play"; a story on intramural sports, "Class-Team Games Begin Tomorrow"; and a high school football game preview, "Columbia High to Play at Mexico," about a matchup with Missouri Military Academy. The October 9, 1908, *Mis-*

Only one story in the fall 1908 *University Missourian* addressed women's sports: an article about the "girls' trainer" criticizing the university's gymnasium equipment. The story's lead read: "The facilities for gymnasium work at the University of Missouri are not all they should be, in the opinion of Miss Frances Gardner, new head of the woman's department of physical training."[15]

Other fall 1908 *Missourian* sports stories addressed a new gymnastic society forming on campus, a Missouri Valley athletics conference organized to establish new sporting standards, a new university baseball team captain, and a preview of the Missouri Tigers basketball season.[16]

The sports coverage continued into winter and spring 1909, following the academic year. With the end of football season, sports coverage dropped off. Some basketball, baseball, and track coverage earned page one status, but the athletics stories that had appeared on pages three and four in fall 1908 virtually disappeared.[17]

By the School of Journalism's second year, beginning in fall 1909, the *Missourian* increased sports coverage by publishing a Sunday edition in response to the popularity of Tigers football. In the following decade, the paper published extra editions covering the university's homecoming football game and parade.[18]

America Strengthens Its Image at the 1908 Olympics

The Olympic Games, which had been revived as a modern competition in 1896, were the biggest worldwide sporting event of 1908. The 1908 Olympics are remembered for their controversy and rivalry between the United States and Great Britain, which at the time was the most powerful

---

sourian included "News About Athletics" on page four with a football story, "Tigers Present Battered Front," an item about Kansas football, and a story about the Chicago Cubs winning baseball's National League pennant headlined, "Victory of Cubs Pleases Columbia."

15. "'Gym' Inadequate, Girls' Trainer Says," *University Missourian*, 6 October 1908, 1.

16. "Gymnastic Society Soon to Be Formed," *University Missourian*, 6 October 1908, 1; "Athletics Benefited by New Conference," *University Missourian*, 12 October 1908, 2; "'Red' Morrow Is Baseball Captain," *University Missourian*, 13 October 1908, 3; "More Basketball Games Scheduled, *University Missourian*, 23 October 1908, 4.

17. For example, see "Basketball Five Off to St. Louis," *University Missourian*, 15 January 1909, 1; "K.U. Here Tonight," *University Missourian*, 12 February 1909, 1; "Now It's Baseball," *University Missourian*, 18 February 1909, 1; "Final Game Goes to Missouri Five," *University Missourian*, 19 February 1909, 1; "In Track Athletics," *University Missourian*, 26 February 1909, 1.

18. Farrar, *A Creed for My Profession*, 153; Rucker, *Walter Williams*, 162.

The Missouri Tigers' football rivalry with the University of Kansas is featured in this *Missourian* cartoon depicting Coach W. J. Monilaw imagining his Missouri team stomping the "K.U." players. *University Missourian*, October 22, 1908, courtesy of the State Historical Society of Missouri Newspaper Collection.

COLUMBIA, MISSOURI, TUESDAY, OCTOBER 20, 1908

*FRESHMEN GIRLS WHO PAINTED
BACKSTOP; SNAPSHOT OF SCENE*

Football was a popular spectator sport among women, and this issue of the Missourian featured two photographs of "freshman girls" who painted the backstop of Rollins Field. *University Missourian*, October 20, 1908, courtesy of the State Historical Society of Missouri Newspaper Collection.

nation in the world. By the end of the competition, America had sealed its dominance in athletics and the world political forum had come to embrace sports as an American standard.

The Games of the fourth Olympiad originally had been scheduled to take place in Rome, but in part because of the April 1906 eruption of Mount Vesuvius near Naples and also because the Italian government lacked funds to subsidize the games, they were moved to London.[19] England had not played a large role in any of the three previous Olympics, but it was eager to assert its power through athletic victories. The United States saw the competition as a chance to prove its athletic superiority to the world, and the press was ready and willing to assist.[20]

The 2,023 athletes who competed in the games hailed from twenty-three nations. Most were men, but forty-four women also competed. The games took place over several months, but the bulk of the competition occurred in July in London's Shepherd's Bush Stadium, a seventy-thousand-seat venue the British had built for the games. Even before the track and field competition began, American newspapers touted the U.S. team's ability to win. On the day before the opening ceremonies, the *New York Times*'s Sporting News section led with the headline, "American Athletes Sure of Success—Our Olympic Representatives Show Splendid Form on Track and Field." The next day, a headline in the *Times*'s news section read "Britishers Fear Yankee Athletes." The controversy began at the rainy July 13, 1908, opening ceremony when the Americans twice refused to dip their flag in front of King Edward VII as royal protocol required. U.S. shot-putter Ralph Rose was quoted as saying, "This flag dips for no earthly king." The British had neglected to or purposely did not fly the American flag, and the *Times* reported on "the failure of the Olympic Committee to have either the American or Swedish flags displayed in the Stadium." From then on, the games became a contest between British and American athletes. Great Britain, including England, Ireland, Scotland, and Wales, ended the games with a total of 146 medals, and the Americans concluded with 47. But the Americans won the bulk of the track and field competition, considered the heart of the games, dominating 15 of the 27 competitions.[21] Americans never before had shown such athletic success, and the British must have felt the competition.

19. Bill Mallon and Ian Buchanan, *The 1908 Olympic Games: Results for All Competitors in All Events, with Commentary* (Jefferson, N.C., and London: McFarland and Company, Inc., 2000), 3.

20. Mark Dyreson, *Making the American Team: Sport, Culture and the Olympic Experience* (Urbana and Chicago: University of Illinois Press, 1998), 127–28, 134, 135.

21. Mallon and Buchanan, *The 1908 Olympic Games*, 6, 8, 12, 18, 23, 37; Dyreson, *Making the American Team*, 125–26, 136, 137; Allen Guttmann, *The Olympics: A History of the*

During the games, American newspapers promoted the United States as having the world's superior athletes, citing a multicultural and multiracial society, an emphasis on athletic production and technology, and a vital and active populace.[22] The British scoffed, and relations with the Americans became tense after James Edward Sullivan, American secretary of the Olympic Committee, began filing daily protests on the way officials were treating American athletes. Sullivan, who had written a column for the *New York Journal*, was criticized in the British press as "a renegade Irishman, the purveyor of shameful and malicious falsehoods." Sullivan also encouraged sensational coverage of the games by American newspapers and failed to correct stories, even when they were not true. The coverage prompted Casper Whitney, president of the American Olympic Committee, to write in *Outing* magazine, of which he was editor: "I want to tell you that we Americans understand the highly colored and sensational newspaper stories that correspondents have been sending over. We have in America the same fault-finding, suspicious and bickering class that you have in England, but we know how much stock to take of the output; and I suppose you (i.e., your kind) in England also know."[23]

The British press offered its own assessment of the Americans' Olympic performance. The *Times* of London editorialized that the American team had "better athletes than sportsmen," and the English magazine *Academy* accused the Americans of cheating and commented that "the Americans behaved 'odiously' from first to last."[24]

Perhaps the most contentious event of the games was the July 24 marathon, in which British officials carried the first runner to enter the stadium, Italian Dorando Pietri, over the finish line after he had collapsed so that an American would not win. The next finisher was American Johnny Hayes, who eventually was proclaimed the winner. The *New York Times* described Pietri's dramatic finish: "Staggering like a drunken man, he slowly tottered down the home stretch. Three times he fell, struggled to his feet, and each time, aided by track officials, he fought his way toward the tape. This assistance by the officials of course put him out of the race, but his struggles were so pitiful that they continued to aid him until he was pushed across the line. Hayes, the American winner of the

Modern Games, 2nd ed. (Urbana and Chicago: University of Illinois Press, 2002), 29–31; "American Athletes Sure of Success," *New York Times*, 12 July 1908, Sporting News Section, 1; "Britishers Fear Yankee Athletes," *New York Times*, 13 July 1908, 5; "Two Americans Win at London," *New York Times*, 14 July 1908, 6.

22. Dyreson, *Making the American Team*, 127.
23. Mallon and Buchanan, *The 1908 Olympic Games*, 10.
24. Dyreson, *Making the American Team*, 138.

event, reached the Stadium while this scene was being enacted, and trotted across the line.[25]

Pietri received a trophy and officials raised the Italian flag, but the Americans appealed the decision, and the officials ruled Hayes the winner. Three of the top four finishers also were Americans, leaving the United States to dominate the race.[26] The *New York Times* proclaimed on its front page, "It was the most thrilling athletic event that has occurrend [*sic*] since that Marathon race in ancient Greece, where the victor fell at the goal and, with a wave of triumph, died."[27]

Most of the American press hailed the United States as Olympic victors, and even some of the British press acknowledged that Americans were strong athletes. The American press, on the other hand, criticized the British for being unfair throughout the Olympic Games. President Roosevelt told the American competitors to forget about the British: "We don't need to talk, we've won," said Roosevelt in the September 2, 1908, *New York Times*. Although the British won more medals, the Americans claimed victory based on their dominance in track and field and, with the help of the press, transformed the victories into an image of overall world dominance. The *New York Times* wrote on July 25 that the marathon "is not only a triumph for the United States, but in a larger sense for America," and the following day championed the "supremacy" of the American Olympic athletes. The *Times* also ran a cartoon on July 19 that left no doubt that Americans felt superior. The sketch featured a robust, muscular Teddy Roosevelt, smoking and carrying thousand-pound weights over his shoulder, facing a skinny, priggish Englishman wearing a top hat and monocle and carrying a pedometer. After the 1908 Olympics, the connection between sports and national power had "become a truism in popular culture and intellectual discourse," according to historian Mark Dyreson.[28]

Youth Sports and Women's Sports Rise in Acceptance

The early twentieth century also saw a growth in youth sports and a shift in societal perceptions of women's participation in sports.

25. "Hayes, American, Marathon Winner," *New York Times,* 25 July 1908, 1.

26. Dyreson, *Making the American Team,* 140; Guttmann, *The Olympics,* 30–31; Mallon and Buchanan, *The 1908 Olympic Games,* 10; "Hayes, American, Marathon Winner," *New York Times,* 25 July 1908, 1.

27. "Hayes, American, Marathon Winner," *New York Times,* 25 July 1908, 1.

28. Dyreson, *Making the American Team,* 143, 147, 151, 153; Pope, "Negotiating the 'Folk Highway,'" 147, 183–85; "Hayes, American, Marathon Winner"; "When Greek Meets Greek," *New York Times,* 19 July 1908, Magazine Section, 12.

A current evolutionary theory influenced the growth of organized youth sports, mainly for boys. Formulated by genetic researcher G. Stanley Hall of Clark University and Luther Halsey Gulick, Jr., an influential physical educator who worked with the YMCA and the New York City public schools, the theory asserted that humans had inherited through evolution the basic drive to play. The theory promoted the idea that children's physical activity developed not only their muscles but also their minds and helped shaped their character. Team sports, according to the theory, encouraged healthy development and taught young people about loyalty. Through team sports, young men could be averted from negative influences such as gang life and learn teamwork, self-control, morality, and altruism, according to Gulick. To become well-adjusted adults, boys needed regulated, supervised activity, and in response, Gulick and others formed the Public Schools Athletic League for school athletics, including track and field, basketball, baseball, marksmanship, and swimming. Gulick was savvy enough to realize that news coverage was important to spreading his message and persuaded several New York newspapers, including the *World, Herald, Times, Globe, Evening Post, Tribune, Sun, Brooklyn Citizen,* and *Brooklyn Eagle,* to support the league and give it coverage. Even President Roosevelt backed the league, serving as its vice president in 1905 and calling the group's efforts "patriotic" and necessary for "having the rising generation of Americans sound in body, mind and soul."[29]

While boys enjoyed a boom in sporting activities in the early twentieth century, girls also had outlets for sports, though their activities were segregated from the boys'. Gulick had theorized that boys were superior to girls and that girls should not be involved in strenuous activity because they were built to manage a home and bear children (his theory overlooked that housework and raising children were and are strenuous activities). In response to an increase in women's sporting activities, female educators began to formulate their own theories of how girls should participate in athletics. During Victorian times, most sports for women, such as croquet and golf, played along with that era's desired female traits of "passivity, delicacy and fragility." However, the new sport of basketball spurred some girls and women to buck this trend. In the early 1900s, basketball became the most popular sport of college women, though women's physical educators changed some of the rules from the men's game. For example, to avoid

29. J. Thomas Jable, "The Public Schools Athletic League of New York City: Organized Athletics for City Schoolchildren, 1903–1914," in Steven A. Reiss, *The American Sporting Experience: A Historical Anthology of Sport in America* (New York: Leisure Press, 1984), 214–15, 221–35; Rader, *American Sports,* 155, 156; "The Public Schools Athletic League of New York City," 222, 226, 228.

physical confrontation, women players could not knock or take the ball from other players. Such rules, formulated primarily at Smith College, set the precedent for others developed by college officials opposed to women playing men's "rough" games. The aim was to teach women teamwork and cooperation rather than competition, avoiding the win-at-all-cost mentality of men's sports. Several women's physical educators argued that only women could manage women's sports and socialize women athletes properly to maintain their femininity.[30]

However, in the 1908 Olympics, women competed in tennis, archery, figure skating, motor boating, and yachting and also participated in diving and gymnastics exhibitions. Although sporting women served as a minority during the era, they were able to transform the public press image of women as "swooning damsels" who remained indoors into women who enjoyed outdoor activities. Several magazines promoted the images of women who participated in and enjoyed sports as "an end in itself" rather than competition. For instance, *Godey's Lady's Book* encouraged its readers to swim and play golf and tennis, and *Ladies' Home Journal* ran articles on women's golf, tennis, and rowing. Physical fitness became more desirable and prominent than the inactivity of Victorian times. It should be noted, however, that these were activities mainly of the middle and upper classes. Working-class women labored most of the day and participated in other types of leisure activities such as dance halls, community social clubs, and amusement parks.[31]

Professional Sports Garner the Public's Attention

Spectator sports at the turn of the century helped instill a sense of community among Americans by providing social activities and entertainment and by drawing strangers together to embrace sports teams.

Baseball's immense popularity led the sport to become known as America's national game. The first World Series in 1903 helped solidify the concept

---

30. Rader, *American Sports*, 156–57, 164–68; Jable, "The Public Schools Athletic League of New York City," 231–32; Ronald A. Smith, "The Rise of Basketball for Women in Colleges," in Reiss, *The American Sporting Experience*, 241, 244–45; Donald J. Mrozek, *Sport and American Mentality, 1880–1910* (Knoxville: University of Tennessee Press, 1983), 152–53.

31. Guttmann, *The Olympics*, 31; Mallon and Buchanan, *The 1908 Olympic Games*, 34, 39–43, 141–46, 168–74, 180–88, 200–201, 256, 265–67, 294; Mrozek, *Sport and American Mentality*, 136–39, 143; Pamela J. Creedon, "From Whalebone to Spandex: Women and Sports Journalism in American Magazines, Photography and Broadcasting," in Pamela J. Creedon, ed., *Women, Media and Sport: Challenging Gender Values* (Thousand Oaks, London, New Delhi: Sage Publications, 1994), 112–14; Kathy Peiss, *Cheap Amusements: Working Women and Leisure in Turn-of-the-Century New York* (Philadelphia: Temple University Press, 1986), 163–88.

that professional baseball was "big business, entertainment for the masses."[32] People rooted for their home teams and followed the team's players and records through local newspaper coverage. However, it should be noted that professional baseball remained racially segregated for four more decades and the mainstream press covered primarily the organized white teams.[33]

The 1908 World Series between the Detroit Tigers and Chicago Cubs drew such a large audience that sportswriters were banished to the farthest seats from the field. Dismayed at the weather conditions, including rain and snow, and the bird's-eye seats they had to endure while covering the series, sportswriters from the ten major-league baseball cities met afterward to organize the Base Ball Writers Association. The group lobbied the presidents of the American and National Leagues to improve conditions in the press box and simplify the rules of scoring. The Cubs won that year and have not captured the World Series title since then. After the great popularity of the series, the Associated Press expanded its baseball coverage, recognizing the public's demand for sporting news. The year was topped off by Albert Von Tilzer's and Jack Norworth's penning of the signature baseball tune, "Take Me Out to the Ball Game," still sung in baseball parks today.[34]

Although not as exalted as baseball, football was evolving into a serious college sport, with large crowds of spectators. Newspaper coverage of college games helped elevate football's popularity. Michael Oriard, author and English scholar, noted that the "daily newspaper 'created' college football . . . transforming an extracurricular activity into a national spectacle." Pulitzer's *New York World* was integral in covering Ivy League football games, which led to other newspapers' coverage of college teams. The *World*'s attention to annual Yale-Princeton Thanksgiving Day football games helped make the holiday game a tradition for universities across the nation, including the University of Missouri. Both public and private colleges recognized that football drew students and fostered alumni loyalty and, in turn, donors, so they began to emphasize homecoming games as traditions.[35]

College football at the turn of the century became an acclaimed spectator sport among women, who were portrayed in the press as supportive cheer-

32. Dulles, *America Learns to Play,* 225.

33. Allen Guttmann, *A Whole New Ball Game: An Interpretation of American Sports* (Chapel Hill and London: University of North Carolina Press, 1988), 121–22; Rader, *American Sports,* 128.

34. Leonard Koppett, *The Rise and Fall of the Press Box* (Toronto: Sport Classic Books), 10, 11; John Rickards Betts, *America's Sporting Heritage* (Reading, Mass.: Addison-Wesley Publishing, 1974), 119, 245.

35. Rader, *American Sports,* 47, 75–77; Michael Oriard, *Reading Football: How the Popular Press Created an American Spectacle* (Chapel Hill and London: University of North Carolina Press, 1993), 57–58, 61–70, 121–23; "Kansas Twists Tiger's Tail, 10–4," *University Missourian,* 30 November 1908, 1.

leaders of the gridiron heroes. At Missouri, the *University Missourian* continued this image with coverage of "co-ed" football fans. A front-page story on October 19, 1908, featured a "girl reporter" who admired the Iowa Hawkeyes' football jerseys. "Blond Hawkeyes Especially Good Looking in Them, Girl Reporter Says," noted a sub-headline on the story. Another story that day reported seven freshman "co-eds" had painted the Rollins Field backstop to support the Tigers. Two photos of the women in their long, white dresses appeared the next day on page one.[36]

Hearst's *New York Journal* subverted the prevailing female image by sending a female reporter, Winifred Black, who also wrote under the name "Annie Laurie," in 1895 to cover the Yale football team. The *Philadelphia Inquirer* followed by sending "Diana" to write about football in 1899.[37] In following years, newspapers began to cover more women's athletic events, but few women earned positions as sports journalists.

One of the most covered sporting events of the late nineteenth and early twentieth centuries was boxing. Although Pulitzer personally rejected boxing as "barbaric" and wrote editorials criticizing it, his *New York World* sports pages at the same time glorified boxers such as heavyweight champion John L. Sullivan. Pulitzer recognized the crowd-pleasing aspects of boxing and knew his writers' boxing stories sold newspapers. Unlike baseball, boxing was not racially segregated, and several black boxers gained success in prizefighting. One was Jack Johnson, a bombastic, talented, controversial figure who in 1908 won the heavyweight championship. The victory spurred promoters and newspaper writers to look for a "Great White Hope" to retake the championship from Johnson. Much press coverage of Johnson, who dated and married white women, was infused with racially divisive and derogatory language. In 1910, former heavyweight champion James J. Jeffries came out of retirement to fight Johnson, who knocked him out in the fifteenth round. After Johnson's victory, race riots broke out in cities across the United States, and the controversies received nationwide press coverage.[38] Spectator sports and the crowd responses had become a nationwide phenomenon.

36. Oriard, *Reading Football*, 250–59; Rader, *American Sports*, 78; "Co-Ed Thinks Iowa Jerseys Becoming," *University Missourian*, 19 October 1908, 1; "Girls Have Final Word on Backstop," *University Missourian*, 19 October 1908, 1; *University Missourian*, 20 October 1908, 1.
37. Oriard, *Reading Football*, 260–78.
38. Brian, *Pulitzer: A Life*, 73; Rader, *American Sports*, 96, 104–5; Geoffrey C. Ward, *Unforgivable Blackness: The Rise and Fall of Jack Johnson* (New York: Alfred A. Knopf, 2004); Betts, *America's Sporting Heritage*, 168.

Conclusion

In the early twentieth century, American newspapers helped form a new national character based on sporting activities and achievements. After Pulitzer's *New York World* began the first sports section in the 1880s, other newspapers followed suit, glorifying the athletes and teams of the day as champions and heroes. The most convincing example of the press's influence on the American image came with coverage of America's victories in track and field at the 1908 Olympic Games, which helped seal the nation's image as a worldwide power in the political landscape. The perceived dominance of the U.S. athletes at the Olympics forced Great Britain to share its reign as an imperial world power.

At the same time, everyday Americans embraced sports and sporting activities as spectators and participants. Exercise and team sports became part of the youth experience in America and also gained acceptance among women, though they were cautioned against becoming too competitive. The press helped shape the image of baseball as America's national pastime and of football and boxing as popular spectator sports. The journalists of 1908 contributed to making sports part of America's national identity and forged an image of Americans as strong, adept, and athletic. This construct created by the press contributed to the growing worldwide perception that the United States had become a powerful world nation.

CHAPTER 11

Enter, Stage Right

Critics Flex Their Muscles in the Heyday of Live Performances

Scott Fosdick

To the extent that the first school of journalism set the tone and pattern for similar institutions nationwide, one must wonder at the impact of its location on the development of the field, especially for the coverage of the arts. As a university town, Columbia produced more art by students and faculty alike, as well as nonacademic artists catering to the university crowd, than one would find in other towns of a similar size. With a population of 12,151 by the time of the 1910 census,[1] this small town was nevertheless a limited market for the arts, far from the centers of production and entertainment business in the nation's major cities in 1908. The *University Missourian* noted local arts events, local exhibits and performances,[2] but

1. See www.census.gov/population.
2. See *University Missourian,* 14 September 1908: "Two Suits Keep Playhouse Dark," and "Lyon Back from Europe," 1; "Eugene Field Was First Editor Here," 4; *Missourian,* 16 September 1908: "YWCA Girls in Play," "Mayor [Chicago] Revoked License of Theater," 1; "Authority in England Who Praises Prose of the Bible," and "Law School Poet,"

Columbia's initial accident of geography, far from the metropolitan centers of the makers and purveyors of national culture, no doubt had an incalculable effect on the status of the arts beat in the young field of journalism. It could not hope to cover the major generative artists of the day nor the complex and rapidly changing business of creating, packaging, and shipping entertainment from cultural capital to hinterland. One can only speculate how that part of the business might have developed had our first school of journalism been located closer to the head of the production line.

Scanning the editorial and advertising columns of Boone County newspapers at the time, including the *University Missourian,* one finds evidence of an arts scene that mixed amateur and commercial efforts. There were occasional public lectures and student performances at the university, such as performances of the thirty-three-member "Glee and Mandolin Club." Sometimes performances were put on by civic organizations. For example, the YWCA presented a comedy that men were barred from viewing because it featured women dressed in trousers; the male reporter covering it for the *University Missourian* apparently got his information by interviewing women in attendance. Each August Columbia presented its own Chautauqua. The 1908 version was headlined by Billy Sunday. According to another item, the *Columbia Statesman* encouraged readers to try the latest form of entertainment, the two Nickelodeons in town.[3]

When it came to live, professional entertainment, the Columbia Theater rented itself to a variety of traveling companies, the majority of them offering melodramas or light musical comedies. One 1908 attraction is likely to be recognized by theater historians today: the black song-and-dance duo of Bert Williams and George W. Walker, who performed their musical *New Bandanna Land* on Monday, December 7. One might say that by attracting a national act such as this, Columbia was more than a backwater. The same show had run for three weeks in St. Louis after five months in New York.[4] Similarly, when Campbell's Circus came to town on October 9, it stayed just long enough to offer one parade followed by two shows.[5]

1; "Mrs. Belmont an Author," 4; *Missourian,* 17 September 1908: "Picture Shows Art Now Lost," 2; "Lillian Norica's Sister Loses Jewels," "Music Prevents a Panic," 3, and "Oratorio Artists" [advertisement], 4.

3. "Glee Club's First Concert Jan. 30," *University Missourian,* 14 January 1909, 3; "They Had 'Male' Characters in Y.W.C.A. Farce-Comedy," *University Missourian,* 21 September 1908, 1; "The Reign of 'The Nickel,'" *Columbia Statesman,* 11 December 1908, 1.

4. Advertisements, Williams and Walker, *Columbia Daily Tribune,* 2 December 1908, 4, and 3 December 1908, 1.

5. "Campbell's Circus Will Show in Columbia, Friday, October 9," *Columbia Daily Tribune,* 21 September 1908, 3.

Had Walter Williams founded his school of journalism in one of the nation's larger metropolises, his university newspaper would have functioned in a livelier cultural milieu and competed with daily newspapers that since the turn of the century had greatly increased coverage of the arts. Cities like Boston, Baltimore, Philadelphia, Chicago, Denver, San Francisco, and, of course, New York, were crammed with downtown palaces for the performance of classical music, opera, and the so-called legitimate theater, and every neighborhood featured less sumptuously appointed but no less functional stages for vaudeville, burlesque, ethnic theater, stock company melodramas—sometimes all of the above. Thus, it is the arts journalism of these major centers of population that is the main focus of this chapter.

Arts and entertainment were different in 1908. Film and phonograph reproduction of moving images and sound had been invented and were gaining attention. The *Missourian* that first month had an advertisement for the Elite Theater's "High Class Moving Picture Show Program Today," which included *Family Cats* and *Aeroplane Flights*.[6] Yet, in 1908 the great majority of arts production and consumption was live. The significance of this single fact cannot be overemphasized.

Live entertainment is, at any given moment, local. A theater company might be national in the sense that it begins in one city, gets on a train, and performs in other cities and towns across a variety of circuits. Indeed, the completion of the transcontinental railway system at the end of the nineteenth century transformed American culture. And reproduction of scripts can lead to multiple productions appearing more or less simultaneously across the country. But as long as the actors are live, the performance is unique to the venue. This favors local media. A national publication can discuss the script of *Hedda Gabler* and comment on how it was performed in New York or Oslo, but readers usually must turn to local media to discover how Ibsen's work played last night in their city. This makes local coverage of the arts important to both the producer and the consumer.

In 1908 the larger cities featured a profusion of morning and evening newspapers. For example, in the first decade of the twentieth century, Chicago offered as many as a dozen daily newspapers at any one time, most employing at least one drama critic.[7] New York had even more. "In 1900 there were twenty-five regular newspaper drama critics in New York City alone," noted Charles W. Meister in his history of drama criticism. "The newspaper drama critic in larger cities became a well-known personality.

6. "Elite Theater" advertisement, *University Missourian*, 30 September 1908, 4.
7. Scott Fosdick, "Chicago Newspaper Theater Critics of the Early 20th Century," *Journalism History* 27, no. 3 (Fall 2001): 122–28.

Frequently he was asked to write prefaces to books, and his picture appeared on billboards."[8]

The arts pages of city dailies across the country had similarities in the types of coverage given to arts and entertainment. The one truly national art form of the time was books, and most newspapers included weekly book sections that look remarkably similar to book supplements today, with drawn illustrations and a mix of news and reviews on contemporary books, authors, and publishers. There was greater emphasis on fiction, as well as on reprinting stories and poetry, often with a seasonal theme. It was a time of reading for pleasure and diversion. The *St. Louis Post-Dispatch* ran a story on January 10, 1908, under the headline, "Library Statistics Show Readers Prefer Fiction," with one philosophy book read for every one hundred books of fiction.[9] Graphic evidence of the prevailing reverence for books can be found in the illustration for a short story by Venita Seibert that appeared in the October 1908 issue of *American Magazine.* A pen-and-ink drawing showed a young girl, hand to chin, searching a shelf of books in a library. The caption read, "Books, things to be gazed at with profound respect and handled with reverence."[10]

The early *Missourian* offered a standing feature on books every Thursday. True, it only occupied columns five and six of a six-column format on page two, but that's a fair chunk of real estate in a newspaper that was only four pages long. Williams's love of reading appeared to inform his early coverage choices for the teaching newspaper.

Larger cities regularly published extensive weekly book sections, sections that grew at certain times of the year. On December 4, 1908, the *New York Times* ran on its front page a one-column house ad touting its special two-day holiday book section: "With this issue of The New York Times is published Part I of the Holiday Book Number—twenty-four pages of literary matter appropriate to the Christmas season. Part II, including a list of One Hundred Best Books of the season in all branches of literature, will be issued tomorrow, in conjunction with the regular number of the *New York Times.*"[11] The lead feature of this twenty-four-page section focused on the four hundredth birthday, five days hence, of John Milton. Page one reprinted his "Ode on the Morning of Christ's Nativity." Inside, on a page listed as 714,

8. Charles W. Meister, *Dramatic Criticism: A History* (Jefferson, N.C.: McFarland and Company, Inc., 1985), 111–12.

9. "Library Statistics Show Readers Prefer Fiction," *St. Louis Post Dispatch,* 10 January 1908, 7. Victor Hugo and Alexander Dumas were listed as popular authors.

10. Illustration by W. Benda appearing with a short story by Venita Seibert, "The Edge of the Fairy Ring," *American Magazine* 66, no. 6 (October 1908): 575.

11. House ad, no headline, *New York Times,* 4 December 1908, 1.

was a piece by William Aspenwall Bradley, titled, "Milton and His Mighty Music, An Appreciation of the Great English Poet on the Occasion of the Tercentenary of His Birth—Abiding Power of the Miltonic Measure."

The *Times*'s book section appeared to have a sense of itself as a purveyor and defender of history, including its own history: The following day's "Holiday Book Number, Part II" led with an article looking back on the Christmas Annual of 1847. The subheads to this story by Mary S. Watts read, "The Holiday Delight of Fifty Years Ago Reads Queerly Now—Highfalutin, Hysteria, and Bathos as Festal Food. Whoever liked such reading? Are We Less Ridiculous To-day?—Will Posterity Have the Laugh On Us?"[12] The article itself was more positive than these subheads imply toward the earlier volume, which Watts called "beautifully printed, beautifully illustrated, extremely well written . . ." She closed with a prediction of how well these things last: "In 1970 it will be a piece of antediluvian wreckage like 'The Amaranth.'" Grammatically, Watts appears to be writing about an 1847 volume, but the context suggests she really meant the current 1908 volume.

The *New York Times* was just one of hundreds of newspapers that regularly published extensive book sections in 1908. The *St. Louis Post-Dispatch* commissioned its own fiction, which it thought was enough of an attraction to promote. For example, on Friday, January 17, an item ran under the headline, "Clara Morris has written a novel, 'The New East Lynne' for the Post-Dispatch."[13] The first section of the novel was to run in the paper the following Monday.

The *San Francisco Chronicle* at this time included books in its Sunday arts section, excerpting, for example, *The Captain of Kansas,* a novel by Edward J. Cole, a couple chapters at a time. That paper also tended to integrate news of authors and artists into the main news section.[14]

One way for an artist to make the news pages nationwide was to commit a sensational crime. For example, when actor Chester Jordan killed his actress wife and was put in a Boston jail, halfway across the country the *St. Louis Post-Dispatch* ran an item on page two, "Actor Travels with His Wife's Body in Trunk."[15]

Magazines were a true national medium in 1908. When they were not investigating corporate and civic malfeasance, many magazines devoted a

12. Saturday, 5 December 1908, literary section.
13. "Clara Morris Has Written a Novel, 'The New East Lynne' for the Post-Dispatch," *St. Louis Post Dispatch,* 17 January 1908, 5.
14. Edward J. Cole, "The Captain of Kansas," *San Francisco Chronicle,* 26 January 1908, Sunday Supplement, 8.
15. "Actor Travels with His Wife's Body in Trunk," *St. Louis Post Dispatch,* 4 September 1908, 2.

good section to the arts. Again, since the book industry was national and performing arts were local, the arts coverage in national magazines concentrated on authors, book reviews, original fiction, poetry, and excerpts from novels. For example, in the 1908 index for the *American Magazine,* one finds no reviews or commentaries on the arts, but rather a great deal of poetry, short fiction, and articles under such bylines as O. Henry, Lincoln Steffens, and Ray Stannard Baker. The noted author and playwright William Dean Howells, the 1908 editor of *Harper's Monthly Magazine,* had regular commentary, often covering literary matters. *Harper's* also was more likely to run longer articles on other art forms than most magazines. For example, in June 1908, the magazine ran a nine-page critical appraisal of "The Art of Edmund C. Tarbell," complete with seven reproductions of his paintings.[16]

For more thorough coverage of performing arts, there were a number of dramatic magazines and two trade publications still in production today, *Billboard* and *Variety.* Begun just a couple of years earlier, *Variety* was devoted to the art and commerce of the popular stage, particularly the mixture of vaudeville and burlesque that at the time was known as "variety acts" in the United States and as "music hall" in London. Both New York and London abounded with magazines serving the show business trade. *Variety* survived both because of its location in a growing cultural empire and because, unlike its London counterparts, it adapted to new entertainment forms, giving positive ink to the young film industry in one column while it was inveighing against the intrusion of the celluloid upstart in the next.[17] Perhaps the best-known voice at *Variety* in its first years was Epes Winthrop Sargent, of whom theater historian Tice Miller wrote the following: "An astute observer of popular entertainment, Sargent was the first significant critic of vaudeville in America."[18]

The great bulk of arts coverage in 1908 was produced at local urban newspapers covering local live performances. The sheer number of newspapers in each major city, most featuring active critics of the legitimate theater, suggests

16. Charles H. Caffin, "The Art of Edmund C. Tarbell," *Harper's Monthly Magazine,* June 1908, 65–74.

17. Scott Fosdick, "Follow the Worker, Not the Work: Hard Lessons from Failed London Music Hall Magazines," *Journal of Magazine and New Media Research* 5, no. 2 (Fall 2003), available online: http://aejmcmagazine.bsu.edu/journal/archive/Fall_2003/Fosdick.htm. See also: Scott Fosdick and Sooyoung Cho, "No Business Like Show Business: Tracking Commodification over a Century of *Variety,*" *Journal of Magazine and New Media Research* 7, no. 1 (Spring 2005), available online: http://aejmcmagazine.bsu.edu/journal/archive/Spring_2005/Spindex.htm.

18. Tice L. Miller, "Epes Winthrop Sargent (1872–1938)," in Don B. Wilmeth and Tice L. Miller, eds., *Cambridge Guide to American Theatre* (Cambridge: Cambridge University Press, 1993), 412.

a dynamic interplay among critical voices. In research on Chicago critics in the new century's first decade, this writer found newspaper reviewers openly challenging each other's opinions in print. Rather than viewing the arts as a commodity to be consumed or avoided, depending on critical advice, readers at that time were encouraged by a multitude of critical voices to view the arts as open to interpretation and debate.[19]

Throughout this decade of rapid cultural change, drama critics took a stand on a variety of issues. Three controversies stand out that were debated in the press. First, technology impacted the theater. The completion of the transcontinental railroad enabled theatrical producers to transport companies, costumes, and scenery from one city to another, greatly increasing the return on investment. This dovetailed with the increasing popularity of machine-driven productions: heavenly ascensions, sea battles, et cetera.

At the same time, the theater industry came to be dominated by the Theatrical Syndicate, which owned dozens of theaters in New York and across the country and exerted monopolistic control over bookings and tours. Some critics supported the Syndicate, viewing it as simply a good business that employed and organized actors better than the more chaotic combination companies that preceded it. Other critics viewed the Syndicate as anticompetitive and bad for the theater as both a business and an art form. By 1908, the Syndicate found its greatest threat came not from the critics, however, but from the competing Shubert brothers, who eventually won the day and proceeded to establish their own near monopoly.

The commercial rise of the machine play led to a second debate among the nation's critics over the direction of the art form. The majority of the critics of the time concentrated their attention on the larger commercial stages. A few critics, however, supported the rise of the Little Theater movement, which championed serious drama performed in small venues by serious amateur actors.

The third major issue of the day involved the reaction of American critics to the influx of realistic drama from European playwrights, particularly Henrik Ibsen and George Bernard Shaw. In 1908, American criticism was just emerging from a long period in which it was dominated by a moralistic tradition. Critics at the turn of the century were likely to focus their comments on whether they considered a play to be morally uplifting, either leaving aside questions of artistic value or conflating morals and art. When the plays of Ibsen were performed with greater frequency in the 1890s and

19. Fosdick, "Chicago Newspaper Theater Critics of the Early 20th Century," 122–28; Scott Fosdick, "From Discussion Leader to Consumer Guide: A Century of Theater Criticism in Chicago Newspapers," *Journalism History* 30, no. 3 (Summer 2004): 91–97.

early 1900s, many critics saw their depictions of incest, suicide, and maternal abandonment as the apotheosis of depravity. Other critics welcomed the new plays, both for their aesthetic sophistication and for their courageous questioning of social values. This debate became quite heated on the drama pages of America's newspapers, and in its magazines. This was particularly important for women's issues: Long before women received the vote, and at a time when the news sections routinely ignored the suffrage movement, critics were forced to discuss the issues of male control and female rebellion personified by characters like Nora and Hedda.

By 1908, a new crop of critics was winning the battle against the moralistic tradition. A larger question that faces critics of any period: Were their opinions honestly arrived at? Walter Williams might have had little to say about arts journalism, but his pioneering efforts in establishing an ethical foundation were needed nowhere so much as in arts reviewing. In his book on American theater critics of the nineteenth century, Tice Miller detailed Walt Whitman's serious misgivings about critics at midcentury, misgivings America's greatest poet put in ink when he was editor of the *Brooklyn Daily Eagle*. Whitman demanded reforms in theatrical reviewing. He wrote in 1847:

> There is hardly anything more contemptible and indeed unprofitable in the long run, than this same plan of some paid personage writing laudatory notices of the establishment which pays him, and then sending them to the newspaper, to be printed as spontaneous opinions of the editors.

He accused all New York theaters of "keeping a 'puffer' who sends daily notices to the newspapers." The practice of puffing he found so widespread that he claimed five-sixths of the criticism was written before the performance.[20]

Theater historian Meister noted that early nineteenth-century critics had been catered to by theater owners, quite literally: "At the Bowery Theatre in 1826 a 'cold-cut room' offered the press food, beverages, and writing materials." By the turn of the century, the environment for critics was less than ideal, wrote Meister: "Their limitations were readily apparent. They were forced to write hurried reviews. Often they were reporters with little background in the theater. They generally followed the editor's (or publisher's) whims. Sometimes they reviewed only those plays that purchased advertising."[21]

20. Tice L. Miller, *Bohemians and Critics: American Theatre Criticism in the Nineteenth Century* (Metuchen, N.J., and London: Scarecrow Press, 1981), 8. Miller quoted in Cleveland Rodgers and John Black, eds., *The Gathering of the Forces* (New York: G. P. Putnam and Sons, 1920).

21. Meister, *Dramatic Criticism*, 99, 112.

The question of the independence of critics is bound to be raised whenever the publications they write for sell advertising to theater producers. A particularly complex case in point involves the celebrated, and vilified, critic William Winter, who in 1908 was in the final stages of an epic battle with Hart Lyman, who had replaced Whitelaw Reid as editor of the *New York Tribune* in 1905. Although Winter was, according to Meister, "probably the most influential nineteenth century drama critic in America,"[22] by 1908 his influence was waning, and Lyman began editing out Winter's most negative remarks. Winter appealed to managerial editor Roscoe Brown, who supported Lyman by saying that Winter's criticism hurt the paper's advertisers. The complexity of this case, from our modern perspective, comes from the fact that much of this editorial heavy-handedness involved Lyman's excision of remarks that now appear either priggish or anti-Semitic. There is evidence that the editors were doing the bidding of the advertisers, but there is also evidence that they were simply trying to limit the damage done by a critic whose old-fashioned ideas had become an embarrassment. In any case, by August of 1909, Winter had had enough, and resigned. The *Tribune* didn't even mention his departure, so Winter took out an advertisement in the paper announcing his retirement after fifty years of steady, unbending moralizing.[23]

Independence was not yet a well-established principle of arts criticism. The problem has always been this: The best informed and most passionately committed critic is the man or woman who has worked as an artist; but then, that critic will also be the one with the most friends and enemies in the business, if not lovers, debtors, and creditors.[24] By the end of the twentieth century, many American newspapers, most notably the *New York Times*, had developed strict rules against critics working as artists or socializing with artists. In theory, that policy would lead to independence and public trust. In practice, it meant the end of a tradition of great artist-critics that included George Bernard Shaw, Stark Young, Harold Clurman, and Walter Kerr.

Arts journalism has always been an untidy business, and it was particularly so in 1908, with underpaid reviewers crossing over the fence and back, striving to establish reputations covering a business that seemed to offer opportunities for personal fortune. The art itself was changing, both in theme and form, even more rapidly than the journalistic landscape. For all that, it was a yeasty situation for commentators.

22. Ibid., 104.
23. Miller, *Bohemians and Critics*, 100.
24. Perhaps the most cogent argument in favor of bringing to the table intimate knowledge of the art form can be found in Richard Wollheim's essay, "Criticism as Retrieval" in *Arts and its Objects*, 2nd ed. (Cambridge: Cambridge University Press, 1980), 185–204.

Perhaps the best example of an artist/critic in this period is Stephen Ryder Fiske, who for fifty-four years wrote and edited for a variety of newspapers and magazines in between writing plays, managing theaters, and guiding the career of his actress wife, Minnie Maddern Fiske, famed for her portrayal of Ibsen heroines. He eventually came to question whether a playwright can fairly judge the plays of others. Rather than blaming the critics, though, he blamed the publishers who hired them: "They profess to require intelligence and integrity, and they will not pay the salaries which these qualities are worth."[25]

Miller held that at the turn of the century the pressures of mass marketing struck the theater and newspaper worlds at the same time:

> Newspapers, now becoming Big Business, were intent on making a huge profit rather than serving traditional interests. Theatrical managers brought increased pressure to bear upon editors and critics, threatening to remove advertising if one of their productions was harshly reviewed. Since they also were expanding their empires—buying and leasing theatres from coast to coast—publishers listened to their threats. While much was written about the need for independent criticism—especially in relationship to advertising pressures—in practice money usually affected policy.[26]

The most flagrant case of quid pro quo reviewing occurred in 1908 and was painstakingly documented in Will Irwin's fourteen-part series on "The American Newspaper" that appeared in *Collier's* magazine in 1911. Originally from San Francisco, Irwin had worked as a newspaper reporter and magazine editor in New York and in the years after this series appeared he wrote seventeen books and two plays. The series' tenth installment, subtitled "The Unhealthy Alliance," was dominated by an investigation of Hearst's *New York Evening Journal.* Irwin provided convincing evidence that Arthur Brisbane's editorial page and two regular theatrical features of that newspaper were "for sale." Hearst is sometimes credited with spurring the increased use of non-news features in American newspapers in the early years of the twentieth century, a development that in turn led to increased coverage of the arts.[27] Prior to 1908, though, according to Irwin, the *Evening*

25. Written in the *Dramatic Mirror,* 1 March 1890, and quoted in Miller, *Bohemians and Critics,* 106–7.

26. Miller, *Bohemians and Critics,* 159.

27. American newspapers had always had at least some non-news features, if only for filler and levity. And a major increase in feature matter was begun by Pulitzer in the 1880s: "It was Pulitzer, on taking over the *World,* who discovered that readers wanted a richer diet than a daily dose of facts . . . They wanted useful information for coping with

Journal did not pay much attention to the theater. Early that year the paper began a new policy of "Constructive Criticism"; it would only mention shows worth seeing, and let those not worth seeing languish without mention. One feature that Irwin charged was for sale was C. F. Zittel's "Vaudeville Racing Chart," an item that reported on the various acts at a vaudeville theater by listing them in order of Zittel's preference, like horses on a racing form. The other feature in question was Nell Brinkley's illustrated column. This new coverage coincided with the hiring as critic of Ashton Stevens, who Irwin implies was charged with conducting "Constructive Criticism." Irwin found that only heavy advertisers would receive positive mention in a Brisbane editorial; and for a set price you could buy Brisbane and Brinkley in one transaction.[28]

Irwin did not charge that Stevens's reviews were for sale, and did not say whether Stevens wrote any negative reviews for the *Evening Journal*. But there is some evidence that Stevens developed the habit of writing gently. Later, he moved to Hearst's Chicago papers, where he was a celebrated critic for more than three decades. He was known as a mercy killer, because his negative reviews were so tactfully written. In the years prior to Claudia Cassidy's ascendance, Stevens became known as the dean of Chicago critics.[29]

With Irwin's careful reporting of the abuses at the *New York Evening Journal,* he leaves little doubt that the opinions of that newspaper were for sale. On the other hand, the *Evening Journal* was just one of many newspapers in New York. In the introduction to this particular article, Irwin took care to make clear that he felt most of the arts coverage in New York's papers was beyond reproach, although he dealt a glancing blow, without evidence, to journalism elsewhere in the country:

> From certain instances the public has gained the impression that the dailies of the metropolis are forced to trim their dramatic criticism to suit advertisers. That is not generally true of New York, although it is the case in some smaller American cities. Daily dramatic criticism in New York is shallow; but so, generally, is all American criticism, whether of the drama, literature, or art. That branch is the last to sprout on the tree of culture; it

---

modern life." George H. Douglas, *The Golden Age of the Newspaper* (Westport, Conn.: Greenwood Press, 1999), 131.

28. Will Irwin, "The American Newspaper," fourteen-part series appearing in *Collier's Magazine* (January to July, 1911). Reprinted in one bound volume with comments by Clifford F. Weigle and David G. Clark, eds. (Ames: Iowa State University Press, 1969).

29. Scott Fosdick, "Ashton Stevens," *American National Biography* (Oxford: Oxford University Press, 2005).

has hardly budded in America. But New York criticism is generally free from business control; most managers understand that their theatrical advertising will not buy favorable notices.[30]

Some indication that such practices were more widespread appeared a decade later, in 1922, when the critic George Jean Nathan published *The Critic and the Drama*. Nathan did not make specific charges of critics or editors selling their opinions to advertisers, but he did charge, without naming names, that critics had been fired for writing negative reviews of advertised plays, and that many more had been intimidated by editors who ruled by implication more often than by edict. For this, Nathan blamed the critic more than the editor: "The American critic . . . sedulously plays safe. A sheep, he seeks the comfortable support of other sheep."[31]

Irwin's other charge for the new century's first decade, perhaps the most damning part, was his assertion that most American criticism was shallow. That is a charge that could be best appraised by considering critics individually. Space and time do not permit a detailed analysis of every critic who received a byline in American publications in 1908. But several individuals wielded sufficient influence to demand mention here. It is the presence of such voices that, according to George H. Douglas in *The Golden Age of the Newspaper*, provides the best ammunition against ". . . the running stereotype of the newspaper reporter as the hard-drinking, foul-talking, free-living, cocked-hat vulgarian . . . In the early twentieth century, with metropolitan newspapers augmenting their feature and opinion sections, with the establishment of book reviews and other departments dealing with the arts and ideas, the newspaper also proved to be a major staging point for serious intellectual writers."[32]

Easily the most noted critic of 1908 was James Gibbons Huneker, a critic whose love of the arts led him to try his hand at nearly all of them, with limited success. "I have written of many things from architecture to zoology without grasping their inner substance," he wrote in *Steeplejack*, his autobiography. "I am Jack of the Seven Arts, master of none."[33] His name figures prominently in histories of the criticism of painting, music, and the drama. Born in Philadelphia in 1860 and educated at the Sorbonne, Huneker began

30. Irwin, "The American Newspaper," reprint, 57.

31. George Jean Nathan, *The Critic and the Drama* (Cranbury, N.J.: Associated University Presses, 1972), 146. Originally published in 1922 by Alfred A. Knopf.

32. Douglas, *The Golden Age of the Newspaper*, 169.

33. Quoted in Mark N. Grant, *Maestros of the Pen: A History of Classical Music Criticism in America* (Boston: Northeastern University Press, 1998), 112–13.

as a music critic in 1887, added drama in 1891, and eventually ranged over all the arts, in books, magazines, and for a variety of New York newspapers, particularly the *New York Sun*.[34] Alfred Kazin wrote of Huneker, "Almost singlehanded, he brought the new currents of European art and thought to America and made them fashionable."[35] Music historian Mark N. Grant wrote, "Huneker was doubtless the most influential and most widely read by other writers and intellectuals of all the music critics in our history."[36]

Huneker's biographer Arnold Schwab emphasized:

The first effective opponent of the "genteel tradition," he also encouraged the most daring and enduring *American* writers, composers, and painters of his day—a contribution that has never been adequately acknowledged. . . . Influence is difficult to measure, of course, but every person in this country who has any traffic with the arts might well be indebted in some way to Huneker for his incessant ridicule of the shoddy American fiction and drama of the 1890's and afterward; for his championing of adventuresome Continental novelists, dramatists, and poets; and for his support of neglected painters and composers.[37]

Huneker's books were largely out of print by the time of Schwab's biography, and his name is nearly forgotten today. Yet, in his own time, Huneker was known both for his prodigious writing and for his conversational powers, particularly when he was in his cups. He was both a model for and a colleague of H. L. Mencken, who wrote in 1909, as Mencken's career was getting started and Huneker's was heading into the home stretch, "If a merciful Providence had not sent James Gibbons Huneker into the world we Americans would still be shipping union suits to the heathen, reading Emerson, sweating at Chautauquas, and applauding the plays of Bronson Howard."[38] Of course, Mencken may have meant this ironically, since it appears that many Americans were still doing most of these things. In Columbia, Missouri, at any rate, they were still sweating at Chautauquas. But the fact remains that Huneker was quite influential in shifting America's artistic orientation from the moralistic to the aesthetic.

34. Montrose J. Moses and John Mason Brown, *The American Theatre as Seen by Its Critics, 1752–1934* (New York: W. W. Norton and Company, 1934), 381.

35. Quoted in Arnold T. Schwab, *James Gibbons Huneker: Critic of the Seven Arts* (Stanford, Calif.: Stanford University Press, 1963), vii.

36. Grant, *Maestros of the Pen*, 106.

37. Schwab, *James Gibbons Huneker*, vii, viii.

38. Quoted in Grant, *Maestros of the Pen*, 106.

In terms of the progress of American art and culture, Huneker's greatest single act may have occurred in 1908 on the occasion of the opening on February 3 of an exhibit of American artists at Macbeth's gallery in New York. Most critics at the time panned this collection of gloomy cityscapes, portraits of prizefighters, and barroom scenes. But just as he had led the charge a few years earlier in defense of the realistic European dramatists, Huneker championed the Ashcan School; known as "The Eight," they included John Sloan, Robert Henri, William Glackens, George Luks, and Everett Shinn. He wrote the first positive review Sloan had received; years later, when his fame was established, Sloan returned the compliment: "He's different from the average critic, in that they usually think they are sent by God to shield mankind from what they don't care for themselves."[39]

Huneker was also among the first to praise the photographs of Edward Steichen and Alfred Stieglitz. His views stand the test of time incredibly well, with the possible exception of his distaste for the young movie industry. He wrote the following in the *New York Times* on October 4, 1914:

> A monstrous olla-podrida of incidents, a jumble of movements, all without sense or relevance, nevertheless so filled with action that the eye is raped by the sheer velocity of the film. No story can ever be definitely related, for the essence of photography is the arrest of motion, and despite the ingenious mimicry of movement there is no narrative, only poses.[40]

While Huneker is primarily remembered, when remembered at all, for his praise of new art that endured, his protégé, H. L. Mencken, whose first love was also music, is remembered more for his vicious wit. Having rapidly worked his way up through various critical and editorial positions at Baltimore newspapers in the early twentieth century, Mencken became in 1908 the literary editor of *The Smart Set,* from which perch he began to gain national notice. Mencken ranged rather widely as well, covering music, then books, then finding the time and space to champion Shaw. His odious political ranting came later.

In 1909 Mencken was joined at *The Smart Set* by the young drama critic George Jean Nathan. Just a decade earlier, most criticism in American newspapers had been published without a byline. Yet, by 1908, that had changed, and we begin to see the dawn of an era of celebrity critics, some educated, like Huneker and Nathan, some working their way up through the ranks of

---

39. Quoted in Schwab, *James Gibbons Huneker,* 181.
40. Quoted in Grant, *Maestros of the Pen,* 129.

reporters and printer's assistants, and some moving in and out of the arts. Nathan edited *The Smart Set* and then the *American Mercury* with Mencken, wrote books and criticism, and left behind money that established the George Jean Nathan Award for Dramatic Criticism, still awarded annually.

Perhaps the most famous critic at the time was William Dean Howells, known first for his writing of novels and plays, second for his magazine editing, and finally for his criticism. Largely self-educated, Howells became editor of the *Atlantic Monthly* in 1871, then a columnist for *Harper's*, who befriended Mark Twain and Henry James and championed realism in his novels and his criticism. Among the most sophisticated and educated was Walter Prichard Eaton, who in 1908 left his position as drama critic of the *New York Sun* to work for the *American Magazine*. Eaton eventually became a professor of playwriting at Yale. Another academic critic of the period was Brander Mathews, who had been a critic for the *Nation* but by 1908 was writing books and teaching drama at Columbia.

Of the many drama critics who spent their careers at newspapers, three of the most prominent spent at least part of their careers in Chicago. Known for his dry wit, Percy Hammond moved from the *Chicago Evening Post* to the *Chicago Tribune* in 1908, and then to the *New York Tribune* in 1921. Others included Amy Leslie, a prominent socialite and a drama critic for the *Chicago Daily News,* and Burns Mantle, who began his career as a printer, became a critic in Denver in 1898, then covered theater for the *Chicago Inter-Ocean* (1901–1907) before moving to the *Chicago Tribune* to work first as a theater critic and then as its Sunday editor. By 1911, he moved to the *New York Evening Mail* as drama critic, and then, in 1922, began a twenty-year stint as drama critic at the *New York Daily News.* Mantle is famous today for his *Best Play* series of annual books, which he edited from 1919 until his death in 1948.

Conclusion

Critics in 1908 came to their jobs with wide backgrounds, from experience in the arts to college education to the university of hard knocks. There is some evidence of quid pro quo reviewing, but little that it was widespread. More prevalent was an unspoken attitude of writing gently about advertisers, at a time when the entertainment industry was indeed a major advertiser. There is some indication that the generally poor pay for reporters was not much better for arts writers and critics. According to his biographer, even the great Huneker had to pinch pennies: "In December 1907 the *Sun* raised Huneker's pay to $25 per column with the understanding that he was to turn in a total of four columns a week, including one special editorial in addition to his regular art criticism, and that he was not to write for any other daily newspaper on any subject or for magazines on the fine arts."[41]

For all that, 1908 offered a yeasty mix of plentiful newspapers, crusading magazines, and an art scene that was brimming with new ideas and movements. The critics that year were coming into their own as a force of culture, moving America from a Victorian conception of art as moral education into a Progressive Era climate of socially aware realism and aesthetic evaluation. Their bylines gave their criticism an identity. The arts pages were forced to deal with aspects of society that were still being ignored by the news pages. The seeds of a long-standing schism were planted then, a schism in both journalism and history between those who focus their gaze rigidly on the front-page world of wars and politics and those who would direct the public's attention to life as it is lived. In 1908, the feature and arts pages were in the ascendancy in the print media, although it would be a while before they impacted the curricula of journalism schools.

41. Schwab, *James Gibbons Huneker*, 193.

CHAPTER 12

1908

The Beginnings of Globalism
in Journalism Education

John C. Merrill and Hans Ibold

In the United States and Missouri, so far as the world of journalism was concerned, 1908 was a pivotal year, not only for journalism education generally but also for a heightened interest in the international press. Tucked midway between two wars, the Spanish-American War and World War I, 1908 ushered in a more transitional press system, merging the more sensational tone of the Joseph Pulitzer and William Randolph Hearst dailies of New York with the more subdued and thoughtful editorial demeanor of James Gordon Bennett, Jr., and Adolph Ochs.

American journalism had a strong injection of yellow journalism with the coming of the Spanish-American War and the competition between Hearst's *Journal* and Pulitzer's *World* in New York. This extremist journalism concerning an international war made an impact on the makeup and news content of many papers across the country, but not to all. In fact, it drew an opposite reaction from some publishers.

The best example of this was the *Christian Science Monitor,* also begun in 1908. Mary Baker Eddy founded the *Monitor* as a protest against yellow journalism. Consisting of ten pages, and sold for two cents, the 1908 *Monitor* focused probably more than any other American newspaper on international news and opinion. With its serious and conservative tone and a cosmopolitan focus, the *Monitor* prompted at least mild changes in many American papers, bringing a slow change toward more family oriented and civil reporting and commentary. Along with such stalwarts as Bennett's *Herald* and Ochs's *New York Times*, the *Monitor* from its inception provided a deeper, more news-oriented cast to American journalism. For example, on the *Monitor*'s pages in 1908, news about China was featured prominently; a December article led with a prescient view attributed to a British official: "China will be the strongest nation in the world within 100 years and will guarantee the peace of the world."[1]

A few years later international events brought back flashes of earlier sensationalism. Coverage of the sinking of the *Titanic* in 1912 and the civil disturbances in Europe and other parts of the world prior to World War I reflected press sensationalism, but the early twentieth-century world situation also stimulated a new interest in global news and views. This was truer in Europe, however, than in the United States and other parts of the world. American journalism was still largely provincial, with little attention being given to public events in the rest of the world.

Most "journalists" in the America of 1908 were newspaper reporters or editors, and there was no standard way to become a newspaperman (women reporters were rarities at the time). Foreign correspondents were stepping into the journalism picture, and such international correspondents as Richard Harding Davis were putting a spotlight on troubled parts of the globe. Most foreign news then, as it is now, was primarily negative and did little to provide real insight into the various cultures of the world.

In 1908, these diverse cultures were becoming a fixture in America's fast-growing cities. Immigration had peaked in 1907, when 1,285,000 immigrant entries were recorded. As historian Richard Hofstadter says, "the whole cast of American thinking in this period was deeply affected by the experience of the rural mind confronted with the phenomena of urban life, its crowding, poverty, crime, corruption, impersonality, and ethnic chaos."[2] Journalists, and particularly the reporting-reforming muckrakers, would become central figures in the effort to understand the abundant changes sweeping American cities.

Publishers initially had little real confidence in school-taught journalism, unless it was obtained in some kind of trade school and taught by actual practitioners. Listen to these words in an editorial in the *St. Louis Globe-Democrat*:

1. *Christian Science Monitor*, "China in 100 Years a Peacemaker?" 1 December 1908, 2.
2. Richard Hofstadter, *The Age of Reform: From Bryan to F.D.R.*, quote from p. 175.

"The country printing office is really our only school of journalism. . . . There is no other place where preparatory general training for the duties of the profession can be obtained, where a young man can learn to be an all-around journalist." These words were in response to a plea by E. W. Stephens, a Columbia journalist, urging that journalism be taught at the University of Missouri. Stephens was instrumental in the university's having the first journalism school but has not received very much credit for his work.[3] Outside the United States, however, little support for such university education could be found.

During the years surrounding 1908, the emphasis on international news grew steadily. The war fever at the end of the nineteenth century, largely stirred up by America's big newspapers, brought news of such places as Cuba, Spain, and the Philippines into America's homes. Various conferences, social, political, economic, religious, and newspaper, popped up in various countries and found their way into global headlines. World's Fairs expanded international interests, such as those in Chicago with the Columbian Exposition in 1892 and in St. Louis in 1904 with the Louisiana Purchase Exposition.

This latter event, it turned out, promoted international journalism like few efforts had before 1904. Walter Williams, the self-proclaimed "country editor" from Missouri, served the Exposition as the grandly titled Commissioner to the Foreign Press. Williams took a six-month travel leave in 1902 from his editor post at the *Columbia Herald* to travel and drum up publicity for the event among foreign journalists. On this trip, he met with the International Congress of Press Associations in Berne, Switzerland, and invited the group to convene its next meeting during the Exposition. Two years later, St. Louis hosted the country's first World Press Parliament, at which five thousand journalists representing more than thirty-seven nations were in attendance. In a speech to the Missouri Press Association prior to the Exposition, Williams envisioned journalism as a global force: "One touch of printers ink makes the whole world akin. There is a fraternity among newspaper workers everywhere, a free masonry which binds together German and French and British and Americans, toiling with pen and press and pencil, with type and typewriter."[4]

After visiting more than a thousand news offices in twenty-seven countries, a feat unprecedented among journalists at the time, Williams said that

3. Ronald Farrar, *A Creed for My Profession: Walter Williams, Journalist to the World*, 96–97.
4. "The American Editor and His Foreign Brother," Sara Lockwood Williams Papers (Western Historical Manuscripts Collection, University of Missouri), vol. 36.

there were of course differences among them, "but the baptism of printers ink makes them all members of the same family."[5] Building a fellowship among journalists across the world would become a persistent theme in Williams's future work as the founding dean of the Missouri School of Journalism.

While passionate about international journalism, Williams and other educators at Missouri could little know that they were sitting on the brink of international journalistic growth. In their classes, they had a variety of foreign newspapers to refer to and analyze. Williams wrote innumerable letters to editors of foreign newsrooms requesting lists of the latest papers of record. The journalism school's emphasis from the beginning was broad and cosmopolitan, not narrow and provincial as the typical stereotype presented it. Most of the foreign papers accessible to the faculty and students were serious, respectable journals, certainly reflecting the kind of journalism prized by Williams. He had met, or would meet, many of the editors and publishers of these papers.

In 1908, Williams taught two courses, "History and Principles of Journalism" and "Comparative Journalism." The latter course is described in the 1908–1909 catalog as "a study of journalistic conditions in all countries. Comparisons with conditions existing in the United States, and study of American newspapers."[6] A syllabus for the course reveals Williams's thinking about journalism in the global context. An objective, the syllabus reads, is to explore "traditions, customs, education and general background; a glimpse of how people live in these other countries; what their ideals, ambitions, resources, and religions are—so that from their manner of living, their background, you may be able better to evaluate, understand, and compare their various types of journalism." Later, the syllabus outlines an objective to understand "the progress of science, education, invention, discovery, exploration, which have brought the world into close relationship, which are standardizing not only the customs, manners, the arts and crafts, education, etc. of the world, but standardizing world journalism."[7]

With no texts focused specifically on comparative journalism, the 1908 course was surely informed by Williams's extensive international travel in Europe and Asia in the early 1900s. He would summarize his views of international journalism gleaned from these travels in "The World's Journalism," a manuscript intended as a book but only published as an essay in the *University Bulletin* in 1915. In it, Williams wrote, "Journalism, universal in

5. Ibid.
6. *General Catalog 1908–1909*, University of Missouri Archives, Series C:0/51/1, vol. 2.
7. Sara Lockwood Williams Papers, f. 1032.

Walter Williams meets with former students in Tokyo during his 1921 world travels to promote the field of journalism and the school at Missouri. Courtesy of the University of Missouri Archives.

its concern, existence and appeal, is a world profession . . . Its history may be observed unfolding itself from the veriest news summary of the less civilized countries to the all embracing newspaper of social service in nations we call more civilized."[8]

Weltnachriten, or world news, was getting a big boost in Germany during this period. Along the famous Kochstrasse in Berlin (the *Zeitungsviertel,* or newspaper quarter), the giant publishers such as Mosse and Ullstein and the serious *Berliner Tageblatt* were significantly adding to the global concern with the press. And the *Frankfurter Zeitung* had become a world-famous newspaper largely because of its international emphasis and careful reporting. In the early twentieth century, it joined the ranks of such elite dailies as Britain's *Times* and *Manchester Guardian* and France's *Le Temps,* prime examples of progressive and reliable journalism. A great example of

8. "The World's Journalism," *University of Missouri Bulletin* 3 (1915): 3–44.

a newspaper that provided high-quality literary content by leading writers and stressed the arts in general was *ABC* of Madrid. A few other papers, mainly in Europe, tried to imitate *ABC* but were less successful.

On the world newspaper scene, a handful of newspapers, demonstrating quality exemplified by such dailies as noted above, were rising above the mass-appeal, middle-level press to stand for serious and influential, progressive journalism. In 1908, there were probably no more than twenty-five or thirty such papers, found mainly in Europe and North America. These dailies can be referred to as the "elite" press or the "class" press as differentiated from the "mass" and the "crass" press.[9]

Among the best newspapers outside the United States during Williams's early days at Missouri would have been the *Times,* the *Manchester Guardian,* and the *Telegraph* in Britain; *Le Temps* and *Le Figaro* in France; *Svenska Dagbladet* in Sweden; *Berliner Tageblatt* and the *Frankfurter Zeitung* in Germany; *ABC* and *La Vanguardia* in Spain; *Neue Zuercher Zeitung* in Switzerland; *Berlingske Tidende* in Denmark; *Corriere della Sera* and *La Stampa* in Italy; and *Helsingen Sanomat* in Finland.

Beyond Europe was a smaller number of elite newspapers. Notable among them were the *Straits Times* in Singapore; the *Hindu,* the *Times of India,* and the *Statesman* in India; the *Rand Daily Mail* in South Africa; *O Estado d. Sao Paulo* and *Jornal do Brasil* in Brazil; *Diario de la Marina* in Cuba; *El Mercurio* in Chile; *La Prensa* and *La Nacion* in Argentina; the *Sydney Morning Herald* in Australia; and *Asahi Shimbun* in Japan.[10]

Globally, in the late nineteenth century journalism education was dismissed as unnecessary: an intelligent publisher, editor, or reporter would know instinctively what news is and how to present it most advantageously in the newspaper. What training was needed could be obtained on the job, from observing, and from talking with outstanding journalists. Especially in Europe, with its large number of serious, trendsetting newspapers, there was no desire to see journalism enter the university as a course of study. On-the-job training and maybe a trade school here and there; this was generally thought to be enough. And even years later, after World War II, the German tendency to call journalism-related courses in the university by the more scholarly title of *Pressewissenshaft,* or press science, was a typical way of referring to such study.

Europe had set the global pace for newspaper development. This was true, technologically and editorially. Britain, France, Germany, and Spain,

9. John C. Merrill, *The Elite Press: Great Newspapers of the World* (New York: Pitman, 1968).

10. Ibid.

for instance, saw their newspapers as exemplary, and they planted such papers in their colonies around the world. The *Times* of London, the *Manchester Guardian,* and the *Telegraph,* extremely popular, were trendsetters in many parts of the world. In France, there was the influential *Le Temps,* the forerunner of today's *Le Monde.* In Germany were a number of well-edited dailies such as the *Frankfurter Zeitung* that served as examples of quality journalism. And journalism, the European journalists were quick to point out, was surely *not* part of the university system in these countries.

There were some luminous names on the scene at the turn of the century in world journalism: men such as Alfred Harmsworth (Lord Northcliffe), who was the influential publisher of the *London Daily Mail* and who in 1908 purchased and rescued the *Times* from possible financial extinction. And there was in England the influential C. P. Scott, who bought the *Manchester Guardian* in 1907 and greatly enhanced its quality and reputation. In France, there were Francis Magnard and Hubert Beuve-Mery. And in Spain, at the literary-oriented *ABC,* there was Torquato Luca de Tena. In Argentina was the great Ezequiel Paz, director of *La Prensa,* who was a brilliant journalistic guru for the continent and fighter for press freedom, and closer to home, in Mexico, the influence of the versatile Felix Palavincini was being felt.[11] In the area of public relations, a questionable part of journalism, interest was mounting in a few countries, stimulated by the success of the amazing American Ivy Lee, who was prospering and pioneering as a press agent for the Pennsylvania Railroad and Bethlehem Steel.[12]

World news flow increased with the end of the Spanish-American War as foreign correspondents became a fixture in global journalism. Augmenting the correspondents from the giant newspapers during this period were the worldwide news agencies: the Associated Press, the United Press, and Hearst's International News Service (INS) of the United States; Reuters of Britain; Wolff of Germany; and Havas of France. In addition, many national news agencies, like Stefani of Italy, added to the world's flow of news.

On American soil in 1908, news flowed faster and more efficiently than ever before with technological advances. Indeed, the newspaper business was booming in the United States due, in part, to advances in typesetting and the availability of more affordable wood pulp. Between 1870 and 1900, the population of the United States had doubled and the number of newspapers had quadrupled. By 1915, in the United States there were more than

11. John C. Merrill, *A Handbook of the Foreign Press* (Baton Rouge: Louisiana State University Press, 1959). See also Merrill and Hal Fisher, *The World's Great Dailies* (New York: Hastings House, 1980).

12. Frank Luther Mott, *American Journalism,* 3rd ed., 597.

2,200 English-language papers, along with more than 160 foreign-language dailies.[13]

Most countries were very much underrepresented in the mainstream news, as they still are, but a certain cosmopolitanism was creeping slowly into the newspaper press of the time, to be greatly augmented in the 1920s with the coming of radio and in the 1950s with the explosion of television. But even soon after the turn of the century, a world-consciousness was developing, albeit slowly, in response to the elite global newspapers. It is true that most of this openness to world events was among the rich and aristocratic, for, by and large, the great readers, the masses wanted mainly local news. The war with Spain changed this provincial attitude to some degree, and the upcoming world war with Germany would change it more dramatically.

But still, localism and nationalism were the main newspaper emphases around the world in 1908. This was true even in Europe, where national newspapers, because of good transportation and small countries, were quite common. In the United States, local and regional papers supplied meager news and views to their audiences. In Africa, the darkest of continents so far as press enlightenment, the local sheets were the norm. This was true in spite of European colonialism's planting of some reputable papers in countries such as Rhodesia (today's Zimbabwe), Kenya, and South Africa.[14]

In Asia, with the help of British publishers, several influential English-language dailies were in operation, dailies like the *Statesman*, the *Hindu*, and the *Times of India*. In Japan, sizable circulations were being registered by the big nationals such as *Asahi* and *Yomiuri Shimbun*. The rest of Asia, in spite of very early type development and sophisticated calligraphy, was wrestling with all kinds of journalism problems, least among them governmental control.

Latin American newspapers were unexpectedly good in 1908. Maybe this came from a main common language, Spanish, and the cultured and literate tradition inherited from Spain and Portugal. At any rate, several dailies were well above average: *La Prensa* and *La Nacion* of Argentina; *El Diario de la Marina* of Cuba; *O Estado d. Sao Paulo* of Brazil; and two great family papers, *El Mercurio* of Chile and *El Comercio* of Peru.

Despite calls for it by U.S. state press associations, journalism professionalism was, for the most part, not a global issue in 1908. Individualism was rampant. Freedom was enshrined. Self-education was dominant. Many educators and journalists saw no need for regimentation, and they saw indoctrination as a probable result of journalism education. A person who

13. Mitchell Stephens, *A History of News* (New York: Oxford University Press, 2007).
14. Merrill, *Handbook of the Foreign Press.*

could write well, who could ask good questions, who could persist in getting a story—that was enough. The regular university course offerings could provide adequate additional education if it were needed. That was generally the world of journalism education in 1908.[15]

Very seldom in those years was the term "professionalization" used; the whole idea smacked too much of conformity, which most publishers abhorred. But that journalism was a "profession" or should be one was very much on the mind of Walter Williams. At the age of twenty-two, he even gave a speech before the Missouri Press Association in 1886 entitled "The Profession of Journalism from a Business, Moral and Social Standpoint."[16] His best-known writing, *The Journalist's Creed,* was probably the most talked about for its first line, in which Williams avowed journalism as a profession: "I believe in the profession of Journalism." After Williams's death in 1935, a column by Arthur Hays Sulzberger of the *New York Times* included a sentence he had uttered earlier at the University of Missouri's journalism week: "Walter Williams . . . found journalism a trade and helped make it a profession."[17]

One of the ways he did so, of course, was to affiliate journalism with the prestige and rigor of higher education. Beyond technical skills that could indeed be learned on the job in a newsroom, Williams envisioned a journalism education that would elevate the profession in intellectual stature and moral influence—and on an international scale: "Schools of journalism may accomplish other and larger things—things necessary for the practice of the profession," Williams said in a speech entitled "Professional Education of Journalists."[18] Chief among these were a sense of personal responsibility and a "professional spirit among journalists." Drawing on themes he would repeat often to American and foreign journalists, Williams emphasized a kind of nascent professionalism and social responsibility emerging from higher education:

> Journalism has as yet little or no literature and the schools from which the journalists of tomorrow are to come have just begun to be. From these schools it may be hoped will go out men who will not use journalism as a stepping-stone to something else and who will not permit themselves to be

15. To some degree this anti–journalism education position was still around in 2006; for example, see a highly critical article in the *Wall Street Journal,* "Schools for Scribblers," by Jonathan V. Last, May 19, 2006, W 19.

16. William H. Taft, *Missouri Newspapers and the Missouri Press Association: 125 Years of Service* (Columbia: Missouri Press Association, 1992), 7.

17. *New York Times,* 3 August 1935.

18. "The Professional Education of Journalists," speech found in folder, "Professional Education for Journalism," Sara Lockwood Williams Papers, f. 922.

used for low or wrong purpose. Each journalist will regard himself as holding a brief humanity and will accept no lesser client. With the development of a professional spirit will come higher ideals among all who practice this profession, a more determined insistence upon these ideals, and a more resolute adherence to them. We need to emphasize in journalism that professional spirit which makes for journalistic brotherhood, which upholds the dignity of the noblest profession, which declines to be employed for the base or unworthy purpose to satisfy passion, prejudice or greed."[19]

In his 1902 speech to the Ethical Society entitled "The Ideal Newspaper for the Future," Williams laid a foundation for thinking about such a school and why it should exist: "To have an ideal newspaper, we must have the ideal editor," he said. After extolling such editor qualities as "freedom," "sanity," and "fraternalism," Williams argued for journalism education: "There will some time be schools where such men are trained. The advocates of such an institution are now scoffed at, but so were those at the beginning who spoke out for medical schools."[20]

When he was not working at the newspaper office, Williams was hobnobbing with university people or talking with leaders in the capital, Jefferson City. And he was also traveling and writing about other cultures. During that six-month leave from the Columbia newspaper in 1902 when Williams drummed up international publicity for the World's Fair, he arguably became the most widely traveled journalist of his time.[21]

Williams sent back many articles, illustrated by Moss, that found publication in many newspapers. They were "informative and folksy"[22] and the *Herald* ran them under such headlines as "Switzerland, the Colorado of Europe"; "Jerusalem, City of the Great King"; "Seven Hills of Rome and Other Things"; "Three Days in Darkest Africa"; "Venice: Where Gondolas Take the Place of Cabs"; and "A Scamper through Scotland."[23] In several of those articles, he began by describing the region he was in and then wrote, rather idealistically, of journalism and its role internationally. For example, a 1903 article justified the upcoming gathering of journalists at the World's Fair:

We hope to hold a press parliament. Why? For educational purposes, for the teaching of peace and purity and prosperity among journalists of the world. The fair is itself an educational agency. It is itself a great moral and

19. Ibid.
20. "The Ideal Newspaper for the Future," Sara Lockwood Williams Papers, f. 245.
21. Ibid., 83.
22. Ibid.
23. Quoted in Frank Rucker, *Walter Williams*, 90.

civilizing force. It is no commercial enterprise. It is rather an enterprise, as every newspaper should be, that is above simply the bread and butter problems of life which allure us on in our baser moments from our highest ideals. It is an educational and inspirational force in this land of ours.[24]

After Williams was selected as the new dean for the new School of Journalism, he spent much of the summer of 1908 working on lectures for his "History and Principles of Journalism," a course that would review the history of journalism and emphasize ethics. It was the course, according to Williams, that should set the tone for the whole school, generating the spirit and energy for the other courses. In addition, Williams taught the international journalism course, "Comparative Journalism." The two would allow him to bring together his high ideals for fraternalism and public service. And it was from these courses that his widely known *Journalist's Creed* was inspired.[25]

In those early years, the list of books in Missouri's journalism library collection reflected Williams's international emphasis, as well as his interest in Christian moral principles. The library included a handful of international reference books (*Webster's New International Dictionary, World Almanac, Principles of International law, New International Encyclopedia, Epitome of Universal History*) as well as several Bibles and numerous Bible dictionaries and commentaries (*Dictionary of the Bible, History of the Christian Church, Church and the Changing Order, Commentary on the Holy Bible.*)[26]

In general, the Missouri journalism offerings in the new school were modest. There were eight courses, and astonishingly for this time in journalism-educational history, one of the courses was the international course.[27] This perhaps shows Williams's early interest in the global press and his strong belief in the increasing importance of cross-cultural communication. Such a course also dovetailed nicely with all of Williams's foreign travel, his interest in global newspaper conferences, and his love of Asia, where he later established exchange programs. As Williams put it in an introduction to the World Press Congress, "Travel alone is a great educator. Travel, with the alert eyes of the journalist, and with the purpose of seeing other places and peoples than those of one's own neighborhood, makes for better informed, more sympathetic and more tolerant journalists."[28] Later,

---

24. "The World's Press and the World's Fair," Sara Lockwood Williams Papers, f. 581.
25. Notes for biography on Walter Williams, Sara Lockwood Williams Papers, f. 171.
26. University of Missouri Archives, Series No. C:11/17/1, Box. No. 1.
27. MU Catalogue, 1908–1909.
28. Sara Lockwood Williams Papers, f. 283.

during World War I, Williams would speak more resoundingly about journalism's international influence: "Journalism . . . should be in this world's crisis a steadying influence; the prophet to the world chaotic, the pilot to a world at sea." In that same speech, he argued that "lack of acquaintanceship between peoples promotes misunderstandings among nations. Undue boastfulness leads to strife."[29]

Williams wanted the journalism student body to be international at the Missouri School of Journalism. A Canadian was in the first class and several Chinese students audited the first courses. By 1912 the class included two Chinese students: Hin Wong and Hollington Tong.[30]

An example of the international connections that Williams forged can be found in the relationship between the Missouri School of Journalism and China. Within a decade, several University of Missouri graduates established a newspaper in China, a country that, at the time, was in the midst of political agitation led by Sun Yat-sen and his partisans.[31] And a little later, University of Missouri alumni helped found journalism education in China and improve the Chinese press. Williams's trips to China helped publicize the need for such education.

Williams felt strongly that Asia needed to advance its journalism, and it could do so, he believed, by modeling the standard-setting journalism of America: "The journalism of China and Japan has been greatly hampered by restrictive laws," Williams wrote.[32] "Japan has made much progress toward freedom of expression and China's journalism is also moving forward. In both countries, particularly Japan, much is published which seems to the Westerner trivial and often, vulgar or worse."

Journalism educational reform was debated from 1912 until such training began in China. The first journalism course was started in 1921 at St. John's University in Shanghai, an old missionary university. The teacher, Don Patterson, a University of Missouri graduate, had been a newspaperman in Kansas City. Patterson's full-time successor at St. John's was Maurice E. Votaw, who had two degrees from the University of Missouri. He had been a reporter in Oklahoma and had taught at the universities of Arkansas and Colorado. Votaw was at St. John's until 1930 when he went to Chungking and Nanking with the Chinese ministry of information. On leaving China, Votaw joined the University of Missouri faculty and had a long association

29. "Democracy's Challenge to Journalism," Sara Lockwood Williams Papers, vol. 47.
30. Letter from Yong Z. Volz to Betty Winfield, April 12, 2004.
31. Wei San Lau, "University of Missouri and Journalism in China" (Master's thesis, University of Missouri, January 1949), 24.
32. "The World's Journalism," 44.

with the School of Journalism; he taught at the university until his death in the 1970s. Many Chinese students were lured into the Missouri journalism program by Votaw, who had many friends in Chiang Kai-shek's Nationalist government. Missouri's first exchange was with Yenching University in Peking, with Frank Martin in 1932 being the first exchange professor there.[33]

Williams laid the groundwork for such exchanges, and it was his missionary-like zeal for journalism as a world influence that spurred him on. "American influence is contributing largely toward the newer journalism in China," Williams wrote. American and Chinese graduates of Missouri, Williams said, are guiding the development of this new journalism. And standing in the way, as far as Williams was concerned, were oppressive governments. "The news agencies in foreign countries are, almost without exception, owned, controlled or inspired by the government. The result is that only such news is sent out as meets the government's approval . . . Much of the difficulty in promoting international amity has been caused by the existence of these government news agencies reflecting the jealousies existing between the governments rather than the friendships between peoples who are governed."[34]

Back in Missouri, the new journalism school was very soon receiving newspapers from other countries including Britain, France, Germany, Australia, Canada, the Philippines, and a few from Africa and South America. These were used extensively in the "Comparative Journalism" course, there being no textbook in the field of global journalism at the time.[35] Williams was his own textbook, drawing on his trips abroad. His interest in foreign-press matters would be carried on by deans Frank Martin and Jay Neff; and then much later, after World War II, by deans Frank Luther Mott, Earl English, and R. Dean Mills.

In the earliest days of the course on the global press at Missouri and subsequently at a few other universities, there were few textbooks. The faculty member teaching the international course had to scrounge around in the library and write to newspapers and embassies to get information. The first book that might have been a kind of common reader, helpful to the international-journalism course teacher, was not published until the late 1930s. It was *Press and World Affairs* by Dr. Robert Desmond of the University of California, a general and well-informed book that was his doctoral dissertation at the London School of Economics. A 1939 syllabus for the "Comparative Journalism" course described the text as "an excellently writ-

33. Wei San Lau, "University of Missouri and Journalism in China," 34, 38–40, 67.
34. "The World's Journalism," 35.
35. Sara Lockwood Williams, *Twenty Years of Journalism*, 61, 73.

ten, fascinating summarization of world journalism, particularly as it is handled through news agencies and foreign correspondents."[36]

A truly comparative book, however, did not appear until the 1950s when John Merrill's *A Handbook of the Foreign Press* was published. It was widely used in the late 1950s and 1960s and was followed from the 1970s on by a large number of books devoted to international communication and national press systems.

Williams, with his frequent traveling and wide interest in global associations and conferences, began a legacy at Missouri that stressed global journalism activities. For example, Williams as the president was instrumental in 1915 in the meeting in San Francisco of the Press Congress of the World as the Pan-Pacific International Exposition, which followed on his work for the St. Louis World's Fair.[37] He also helped reconvene the World Press Congress in Honolulu in 1921 during the backdrop of the Naval Disarmament Conference in Washington, D.C. These conferences and other similar international meetings got journalists from around the world talking about their common problems.[38] Williams was likely in his element at the congresses, for these gatherings symbolized journalism as a global force for good, a notion that Williams held sacred.

Although Williams and his colleagues participated in exchange programs with universities in other countries in the early twentieth century, such activities languished at the School of Journalism until about 1970, when Dean English got the idea of sending graduate students to Brussels to cover the Common Market. As a teacher of international journalism, Merrill encouraged and aided him and handled the program on the Columbia campus. English hired a seasoned journalist, Henri Schoup, a Dutchman who spoke several languages and had worked for newspapers, Dutch broadcasting, and the BBC in Europe, to take charge of the Missouri graduate students who went to Brussels. This reporting venture lasted for at least six years, then it was moved to London, and after a short stint there, died out. Dean English started another project in Taipei, Taiwan, but it was not as successful as the graduate reporting program in Europe. By the 1990s, Dean Mills pushed and expanded formal exchange programs for students and faculty to the University of Navarre in Pamplona, Spain, Central Asia, South Korea, Singapore, and Taiwan. By 2006, more than 15 percent of Missouri School of Journalism students had studied in these programs, and 70

36. Sara Lockwood Williams Papers, f. 1032.
37. Farrar, *A Creed for My Profession*, 198.
38. Walter Williams, ed., *The Press Congress of the World in Hawaii* (Columbia, Mo.: E. W. Stephens Publishing Co., 1922).

percent of the faculty had worked abroad. By 2008, the projections are that the foreign programs will grow by 20 percent.[39]

International journalism and communication courses are commonplace today throughout the world. Especially good programs are in Denmark, Finland, Sweden, France, Spain, Italy, Singapore, South Korea, Egypt, Kuwait, Russia, Jordan, China, India, and on the island of Taiwan. In most countries, however, journalism education programs are very small and poorly funded and are limited in most cases by tight curriculum controls by the government. However, faculty and student exchanges are common, and cultural press values are being spread everywhere. With so many academics communicating, there are few gaps in global journalism literature, unlike what Walter Williams found one hundred years ago.

Regardless of current assessments on global progress, press credibility, and general journalistic morality, the past century has made the earth smaller, and journalism can immediately respond to whatever happens anywhere. Williams's great love, newspapers, may not now be as important as in his day, but "journalism"—with a much broader definition—is perhaps the most potent force on the globe.

From the very beginning, the school shed all pretense of provincialism and tied the curriculum to a global concern. From 1908 until today, the school's thousands of graduates, many world-renowned, as well as its many faculty members who teach and act as media consultants around the world, are bringing about the international vision of Walter Williams.

39. Interview with Fritz Cropp, Director of International Journalism Programs, University of Missouri, May 18, 2006.

CHAPTER 13

The Look of 1908

Newspaper Design's Status at a Turning Point in Journalism Education

Lora England Wegman

The newspaper that reached the twentieth century was quite a different product from its earliest American form, centuries before. By 1908 illustrations and photographs were changing the face of newspaper design. In fact, the previous thirty years had seen the first newspaper printing of illustrations and the beginning of halftone photographs. The invention of the linotype had vastly improved printing with greater speed, lesser cost, and higher quality.[1] Large urban American newspapers had traditional layouts with lots of text and headlines and graphics and photographs that look tiny by today's standards. For most newspapers, banner headlines were a decade away; some papers still carried advertising on their covers.

By the new century, editors had begun to take notice of the importance of visual elements for attracting readers and communicating better.

1. Sally I. Morano, "Newspaper Design," in W. David Sloan and Lisa Mullikin Parcell, eds., *American Journalism: History, Principles, Practices* (Jefferson, N.C.: McFarland and Company, Inc., 2002), 320.

Competition, technology, and mass circulation all impacted the medium, as did a widening array of choices in regard to printing and visual elements. More generally, by the last years of the nineteenth century American readership was growing, newspaper costs were affordable, literacy had increased, and more and more children were being educated.[2] U.S. newspapers were creating their own visual identities apart from each other and apart from their counterparts in Europe.

This chapter examines front-page newspaper design in 1908 and asks how American newspaper design had developed and how it contrasted with that seen in Europe. Such a comparison indicates the status of design in 1908 during the founding of the first journalism school and also indicates design trends on more of a global scale.

Design and Walter Williams

By the time the world's first school of journalism opened, founding dean Walter Williams had a reputation for not only his talents as a newsman but also his attention to the form, or design, of news. Long before the Missouri School of Journalism opened, Williams, an accomplished professional journalist and editor of the weekly *Columbia Herald* since 1889, had emphasized newspaper design as an important service to readers.[3] His *Herald* became narrower in size and therefore easier to handle and was more clearly organized; attention was paid to the importance of advertising placement and general appearance. The *Herald* was six columns wide at a time when eight columns or more were typical.

The *Herald*'s attention to design did not go unnoticed in the newspaper world. The *St. Louis Times* wrote, "A prettier weekly newspaper than the *Columbia Herald* cannot be found west of the Mississippi. . . . It is a model of tasty typography, good press work and admirable arrangement."[4]

For a while, the *Herald* experimented with a tabloid format; in fact, it was one of the first small papers in the country to use halftone engravings. Williams's biographer Frank Rucker wrote, "it used them extensively and produced them excellently."[5] When Williams left the paper in 1908 to be the first dean of the newly formed School of Journalism, his experience influenced the campus laboratory paper, the *University Missourian*. At the time,

2. William David Sloan, ed., *The Media in America: A History*, 5th ed. (Northport, Ala.: Vision Press, 2002), 224.

3. Frank Rucker, *Walter Williams*, 53, 54.

4. Ibid., 54.

5. Ibid., 58.

New York Globe publisher Jason Rodgers is quoted as having hailed the new paper as "in a class far and away above the average small-town daily" in terms of its format and typography.[6] Such an emphasis was noteworthy.

Design's Historical Context and News Process

Design has long played a lesser role in newspapers. During the American colonial era, the relative rarity of printed news meant early American newspaper readers would pay attention to almost any content, no matter how dully presented.[7] It was unusual for any images to accompany the news articles.

The articles, often written in a coded fashion, required prior political knowledge that the casual reader would not have. The first colonial newspapers, strongly influenced by the British press in look and content, were understood to be a public institution, beholden to patronage and licensing. The first regularly published newspaper in North America, the *Boston News-Letter,* carried the notice "Published by Authority" in prominent type, letting readers know to expect government-approved news.[8] An American ideal of press freedom came from Britain, although such practice lagged in the colonies. These early colonial newspapers were also influenced in terms of the news they reported; that is, the content often was simply reprinted from foreign sources.[9] The early newspapers looked and read much like their European counterparts.

The appearance of the early American papers was also a result of technology. They looked more like books than modern newspapers, with only four pages of three columns each and no illustrations. The latest, biggest news would be not at the top of the front page but inside the paper. There was a reason for such a practice: the outside pages were printed first so that the surfaces handled most would have more time to dry.[10] But the ordering of items did not matter much. A printer expected each reader to read every item, regardless of which came up first.

Initially, nineteenth-century printers were not particularly concerned with making their papers more accessible to the masses. Instead, their goal

6. Frances Ethel Gleason, "Twenty-Three Years Development of the Columbia Missourian," Master's thesis (University of Missouri, 1931), 3–4.

7. Morano, "Newspaper Design," 318.

8. Sloan, ed., *The Media in America*, 40–41.

9. Ibid, 39–41.

10. Kevin G. Barnhurst and John Nerone, *The Form of News* (New York: Guilford Press, 2001), 39.

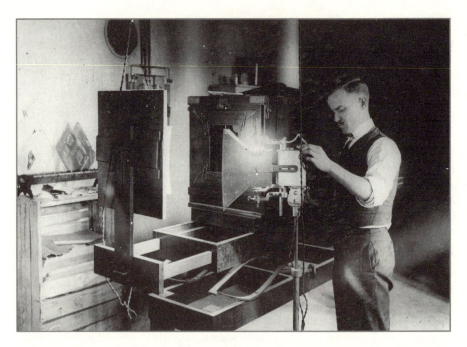

In 1913 Herbert Smith operated the photoengraving laboratory for teaching newspaper illustration and advertising at the Missouri School of Journalism. Courtesy of the University of Missouri Archives.

was intelligible public printing for educated insiders.[11] Newspapers changed around the time of the American Revolution. There was a shift to a larger newspaper format, which increased the capacity for news items. In fact, until then, print processes had changed little since the invention of Gutenberg's press in 1450; many American papers were more limited in the number of issues produced.[12] There were few layout or type innovations prior to the nineteenth century, except by masthead.

Some printers experimented with different nameplates; the formal black-letter nameplate was established as a lasting popular choice.[13] In general, for most of the nineteenth century except in the largest cities, most newspapers remained quite gray, more so than ever because of their larger size. Design, however, evolved into a Victorian style, which dominated into the early 1900s. This style was expressed through larger pages, more numerous

11. Ibid., 32–34.

12. Robert F. Karolevitz, *From Quill to Computer: The Story of America's Community Newspapers* (Freeman, S.D.: National Newspaper Foundation, 1985), 36.

13. Barnhurst and Nerone, *The Form of News,* 81.

columns, and tight typesetting, but with a growing variability in display typography and with illustrations providing some contrast.[14]

Several inventions soon revolutionized printing, journalism, and the design world. The development of the telegraph greatly sped up the transmission of information globally and created a pyramid reporting style, with the most important immediate news printed first. Previously, written news, written in an essay manner, often had been passed along through personal letters, a slow process.[15]

The late nineteenth-century yellow journalism led to design modernization as it emphasized circulation and competition for readers.[16] By 1908, according to the advertising trade publication *Printers' Ink,* the changes affected all newspaper content: "In both editorial and advertising and in circulation matters, the magazines and newspapers have been wide-awake, active and hopeful."[17]

Steam power had already sped up the printing process and paved the way for a cheaper newspaper since the penny press in the 1840s. The nineteenth century saw the invention of the cylinder and rotary presses and advances in papermaking and photography that led to increased prominence for news design. The first halftone photograph reproduction in a U.S. newspaper appeared in 1880.[18] This process reproduced images by rephotographing them through a screen that created a matrix of dots. The size and spacing of the dots resulted in the perception of different shades of gray. By the early 1900s, some large daily U.S. papers, realizing the appeal of photography, had begun publishing special photo sections on Sundays.[19] More than technology influenced the visual image.

The Influence of Society and Art

Like any artistic form, newspaper design was influenced by other aspects of culture, such as art and fashion. Most artistic movements originated in

14. Ibid., 82.

15. Betty Houchin Winfield, "The Press Response to the Corps of Discovery: The Making of Heroes in an Egalitarian Age," *Journalism and Mass Communication Quarterly* 80, no. 4 (Winter 2003): 866–83.

16. Morano, "Newspaper Design," 320.

17. "Looking Backward on 1908 and Forward to 1909," *Printers' Ink* 66, no. 3 (January 20, 1909): 3.

18. Susan Thompson, "Printing Technologies," in Sloan and Parcell, eds., *American Journalism: History, Principles, Practices,* 364–65.

19. Lisa Mullikin Parcell, "Newspaper Illustrations," in Sloan and Parcell, eds., *American Journalism: History, Principles, Practices,* 330–31.

Europe, and then filtered across the Atlantic to influence American style. Such influences resulted in a new visual image for the press.

In the mid–nineteenth century, Victorian style took hold, manifesting in newspaper form through bolder type, ornamentation, column rules, and engraved advertising images. The changes reflected an age of romanticism during which art and architecture were used to mask what scholars Barnhurst and Nerone called the Industrial Revolution's "unsightliness."[20] Display typography took on larger size and more contrast, while tighter spacing between lines of copy meant more text could fit on a page. The appearance became more dramatic and ordered, and newspapers used differing degrees of contrast that reflected style and personalities. On one end were the most reserved papers, such as the *Washington Post,* and on the other were Western papers such as the *Denver Post,* which used extreme contrasts.

Aspects of the Victorian style still dominated in 1908; the reserved and emphatic extremes were still evident. The European modern art movement had not yet arrived in the United States; the movement's new design ideas would not cross the Atlantic until the New York City Armory Show of 1913.[21] Other Europeans brought an artistic influence to the United States during and after World War I, leading to a transition to the modern design for newspapers.

The Status of Design in 1908

To reflect the progress of newspaper design in 1908, this chapter aims for three assessments and comparisons: the front pages of four metropolitan daily American newspapers; the design of selected newspaper covers on a global scale; and then the *University Missourian* covers, published at the Missouri School of Journalism.

The American papers are the *Washington Post* (Figure 1), the *Denver Post* (Figure 2), the *Chicago Daily Tribune* (Figure 3), and the *San Francisco Chronicle* (Figure 4). These publications represent different geographical areas and an array of design styles characteristic of the period. They show the beginning use of more illustrations and photographs, which spawned a greater variety in newspaper design with those disparities, as well as many standard design conventions.

This study looks at the front pages from the January to July 1908 editions. For a more representative sample, the issues studied include the first Monday

---

20. Barnhurst and Nerone, *The Form of News,* 55.
21. Ibid, 227.

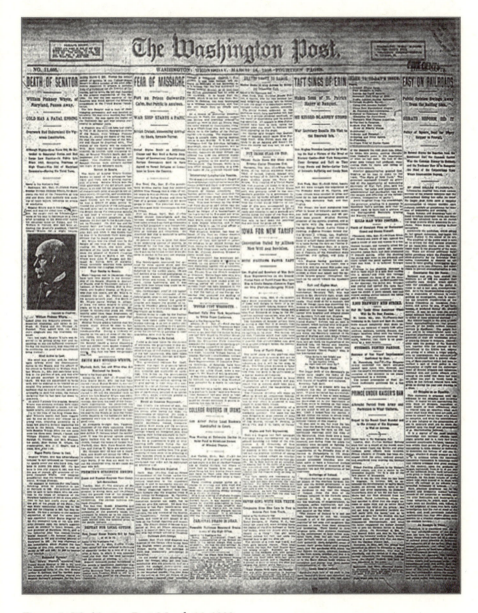

Figure 1. *Washington Post*, March 14, 1908.

of January, the second Tuesday in February, the third Wednesday in March, and so on through July, resulting in front pages from each day of the week.

The *New York Times*, typically regarded as the premier U.S. newspaper, was excluded from this study for design-related reasons. The *Times*, then as now, is not representative of a typical newspaper appearance. Yet New York City

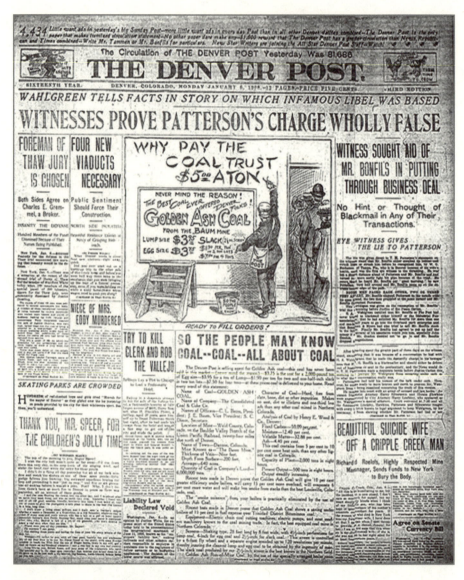

Figure 2. *Denver Post*, January 6, 1908.

was and is known as a hub for newspapers and publishing, so a brief look at the city's papers is in order. The *New York Times* of 1908 shows a close similarity to the *Washington Post*, which will be described in detail. Photographs and illustrations generally were not seen on the seven-column front page, and headlines were small with multiple decks. The *New York Tribune*, similar in look, had even less differentiation in headline sizes but had photographs

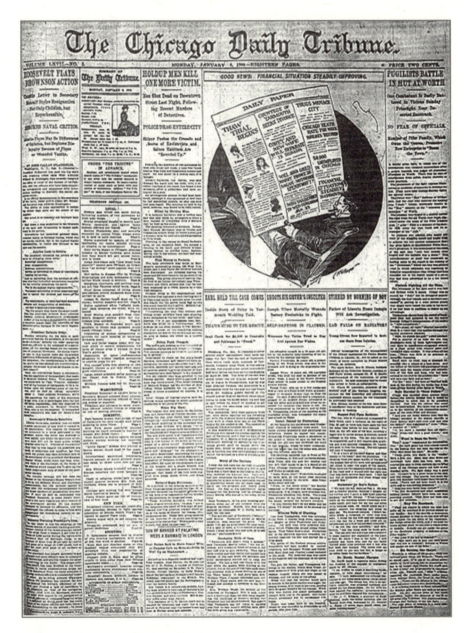

Figure 3. *Chicago Daily Tribune*, January 6, 1908.

Figure 4. *San Francisco Chronicle*, January 6, 1908.

on some covers. Both of these New York papers used a large number of short stories, as did the *Washington Post*.

The popularity of one-column headlines stemmed from the mechanics of the rotary press. The thin vertical rules between columns kept type in place. Thus, deck headlines became popular, allowing more display type within the confines of one column.[22]

The status of printing and photography in 1908 necessarily affected some aspects of design. Illustrations were widely used by this time, having been around since colonial newspapers. The most famous colonial-era illustration was Benjamin Franklin's "Join or Die" segmented snake cartoon promoting unity among the colonies.[23] In 1908, photographic images were growing in interest and importance, but they were still relatively new to the newspaper industry. The technology lagged for reproducing photographs for small dailies and community newspapers cheaply.

Too, information graphics had begun to appear in newspapers by the 1890s. Maps related to the Klondike gold rush, for instance, were popular in the American Northwest, and editors realized the value of illustrations and graphics for providing information as well as for selling newspapers.[24]

Most 1908 information graphics, albeit few in number, took the form of maps or charts. In this study the front pages yielded just one map: the *San Francisco Chronicle* used a one-column drawing in its March 18, 1908, edition to show where the steamer *Pomona* ran ashore and was destroyed in northern California. Simple in design, the map clearly marked the steamer's path from San Francisco to the point of impact along the coast. There is no scale and no directional marker.

The *Chicago Tribune* includes charts on occasion. The July 12, 1908, issue is most notable, with several simple one-column charts. One above the fold tracks the previous day's temperature by hour; the paper reports that heat caused five deaths that day. The others demonstrate electoral vote predictions for that year's presidential election and a company's dividend sales.

Some aspects of design were shared among the four papers. The front-page covers are divided into seven or eight columns, with most headlines confined to the width of one column. The page's lead headline may be wider, but almost all others are one column wide. The *Denver Post* had the most exceptions by spanning more than one column.

Many deck headlines conveyed details of each story. Only small stories had no decks; more important stories contained between one and five. In addition, the design remained nonmodular, meaning that each story is not

22. Morano, "Newspaper Design," 319.
23. Parcell, "Newspaper Illustrations," 325–26.
24. Ibid., 329–31.

contained within a rectangular shape but instead might be wrapped around other stories in a dogleg style. This results from stacking stories vertically rather than using horizontal story layouts.

Also, some newspapers used a variety of typefaces. The *Washington Post* shows the least variety, but it still uses a mix of serif type, which has small extra strokes on the ends of the letters and is sometimes seen as more formal, and sans serif type, which has no extra strokes. The *Denver Post*, the most eclectic, relied on at least five typefaces regularly. In each paper, the headlines are set in all capital letters. Bolding and italics provide emphasis and contrast. Editors appeared to recognize the effects of typography on readers' perceptions by the early twentieth century. In fact, articles in *Printers' Ink* discussed the importance of using appropriate, appealing type in conveying messages and attracting audiences.[25]

Moreover, these early twentieth-century newspapers used no color and little white space, as is obvious in these examples. Each front page also featured a centered flag bearing the paper's name at the top of the page, with the date beneath it surrounded by horizontal rules. The nameplate on three of the four newspapers is in a traditional blackletter style. The *Denver Post*, as an exception, relied on a more modern "fat-face" style, a serif font with bold strokes.

Few advertisements showed up on the front pages. The *San Francisco Chronicle* routinely includes a small ad in the right bottom corner, and the *Denver Post* occasionally includes an ad above the flag.

As was the practice of the day, stories had no reporters' bylines. Bylines were found more regularly in the 1920s and 1930s, as journalists touted their objectivity and accountability.[26]

All four newspapers had created some degree of hierarchy, or order of importance, in their design. Though the *Washington Post* appeared the least hierarchical, it is generally clear that the stories on top were of most importance. They had larger headlines and more decks underneath to flesh out details. The more important stories are also headlined in bold sans serif type, but less significant stories have smaller serif headlines and usually just one deck. There is a sense of order, though the top four stories generally are not differentiated visually in any way. More than hierarchy, perhaps, there is a sense of symmetry, with alternating headline styles atop each column. This symmetry often was seen in Victorian design.[27]

25. F. W. Williams, "How Advertising Type is Made to Talk," *Printers' Ink* 67, no. 11 (June 16, 1909): 16–17, and Russell B. Kingman, "Typography of an Ad Is Its Personality," *Printers' Ink* 68, no. 2 (July 14, 1909): 51–52.

26. Barnhurst and Nerone, *The Form of News*, 248.

27. Ibid., 222.

Hierarchy is more pronounced in the Western newspapers studied here. The *Denver Post* and *San Francisco Chronicle* each had a clear lead story each day, emphasized through the use of larger headlines that break the standard one-column layout of the rest of the stories. Often, the *Chronicle*'s lead story has an accompanying photo or illustration as the largest visual element on the page, another way of creating hierarchy.

In contrast, the *Denver Post* has lede headlines across four to six columns or more. The January 6, 1908, edition is notable in that it has a banner headline across the entire width, eight columns, for a story regarding developments in an important local trial. This headline treatment is unusual for the period, although it became much more common a decade later when World War I made large banner headlines a constant in most American papers.[28]

Variety in U.S. Design

As indicated here, newspapers began displaying unique individual design techniques by 1908, despite the many lingering conventions. As shown in these four U.S. examples, the newspapers did vary significantly in overall appearance, even if they were all relatively gray by today's standards.

One area of distinction is in the number of stories carried on the front page. Historically, the number of stories on front pages had begun to dwindle by the twentieth century. Barnhurst and Nerone's study of one hundred years of design trends reported an average of twenty-five front-page stories in 1885, but fewer than six stories in 1985.[29] Their average for 1905, the year nearest to 1908, was 21.5 stories. Of the papers examined here, only the *Washington Post* regularly had that high a number. One likely explanation the others did not is that they used more visual elements; thus, less room for text.

The *Washington Post* covers contained the greatest number of stories, despite its being the only one of the four papers that does not jump articles to inside pages. The *Post*'s headlined stories ranged from sixteen to twenty-four per issue. Many of these stories are quite short, seventy-five words or fewer, but they all had headlines and sometimes decks.

The *Washington Post* also carried no illustrations and few photographs on its front pages, so more space was available for stories. In fact, when the *Post* used photographs, they were almost never from staff photographers,

---

28. Morano, "Newspaper Design," 321.

29. Kevin G. Barnhurst and John C. Nerone, "Design Changes in U.S. Front Pages, 1885–1985," *Journalism Quarterly* 68 (Winter 1991): 796–804.

but instead from photo organizations,[30] a cooperative feature standard. In this newspaper sample, the *Post*'s appearance stood out with small headlines and a conservative use of decks. The headlines appear to range from fourteen to twenty-four points in size, about the size of a news-brief headline in today's papers. Only in one instance in a June issue does the *Post* deviate from this practice, with two headlines of approximately thirty-six points; the stories treated this way covered the awarding of contested votes to William Howard Taft and a fatal train collision. The size is a big move for the *Post,* but would hardly have registered at the other three newspapers.

The *Chicago Tribune,* while traditional in style, still had more visual elements and featured just six to ten stories on its covers, the lowest average count among the four papers. One obvious style reason is the *Tribune*'s daily use of a three-column cartoon. Yet, a closer look reveals other explanations for the low story count. The *Tribune*'s news index takes up an entire column of front-page space every day, summarizing what else is in the paper. This leaves six columns for newspaper stories, many of which are long and run the full column length but are still jumped inside the paper. Also, while the *Tribune* had few brief stories here—not nearly as many as those in the *Washington Post*—their overall story count remained relatively low.

The *Denver Post* and *San Francisco Chronicle* remained in the middle regarding story count, fluctuating considerably by issue. Denver totals ranged from five to thirteen stories and San Francisco from eight to twenty-one. Considering the trends, these counts are on the low side for the era, but they are relatively high considering the number of visual elements available. Similar to the *Chicago Tribune,* the *Denver Post* generally uses one cartoon daily, but the cartoon is large, usually spanning four or five of the eight columns. The *Chronicle,* however, used both photos and illustrations on its front pages, up to five in one day. In both newspapers, the highest story counts come from issues that include many short stories. Both continue front-page stories inside the paper, though Denver tends to jump stories more.

In overall appearance, the *Washington Post* can be seen as the most traditional. Stoic and unchanging, the *Post* had little diversity in headline sizes and typefaces and no variety in layout. With a strictly vertical eight-column grid and rare use of front-page photographs, the *Post* generally stuck to a one-column rule. The only breaking of this grid occurs in the June 6, 1908, edition, which features two important news stories that each run two columns wide, the previously mentioned Taft and train collision stories.

30. Chalmers M. Roberts, *The Washington Post: The First 100 Years* (Boston: Houghton Mifflin Co., 1977), 90.

In many ways, the *Denver Post* is in a class of its own. Its history may explain why. In 1908, the newspaper was still young; the *Post* was founded in 1892 and then shut down for two years before resuming printing.[31] The *Post* had a recognizable image tradition. In some ways its appearance was more modern than these other American papers, and reflects Western sensibilities. The design is generally bolder, livelier, and less serious than that of its counterparts. More banner headlines are used. Also, headlines and illustrations are larger than in the other papers, and the flag bearing the paper's name uses a modern typeface, whereas the others are in a traditional, old-style type. A large mix of typefaces is used in all kinds of styles, bold, light, italic, and condensed, in serif and sans serif varieties.

The diversity of design differences can also be seen in the way visuals are used. The *San Francisco Chronicle* often used a photograph or illustration with its lead news story, adding emphasis and visual content. However, the *Chronicle* is the only paper out of the four to regularly use visuals in this way. Like many small community newspapers, the *Washington Post* uses almost no front-page visuals, the exceptions being three one-column portrait photographs in the March and April editions. The March example was of Senator William Pinkney White, who had died; the April pages featured photographs of prominent Chicago businessman Joseph Leiter and the woman he was engaged to marry, Juliette Williams.

The Chicago and Denver papers always featured a political cartoon as the main front-page visual, which was not directly tied to any news story. As a vestige of the Victorian era, the use of cartoons on the front page remained until the 1930s.[32]

The *Chronicle* also is unique among the four papers for its use of ornamentation. Nearly all the front-page photographs and illustrations have decorative borders, ranging from simple swirls to ornate drawings. This traditional practice had gained popularity in the decades leading up to the U.S. Civil War, before news photography was introduced.[33] Such ornamentation was seen in type and borders, mostly in advertisements. The process of stereotyping, which created a replica of a typeset page and allowed advertising designs and type to be shared, had made it easy for papers to borrow type and border collections. Although these developments primarily affected advertising, the *Chronicle*'s use demonstrates the technique's spread as a design tool for news as well.

31. Robert F. Karolevitz, *Newspapering in the Old West* (New York: Bonanza Books, 1965), 63.
32. Barnhurst and Nerone, *The Form of News*, 232.
33. Ibid, 88–90.

Some newspapers, including the *New York Times*, ran daily indexes on their covers, a practice that became more useful as newspaper pages increased. News summaries or indexes are also on the covers of the Washington and Chicago newspapers. The Washington "Index to To-Day's Issue" included a short list of headlines and page numbers, perhaps two to three inches in length daily. The *Chicago Tribune* has a much more extensive index, occupying an entire column of space in every issue. It listed headlines and page numbers by category, grouping together news on Washington, international news, sports, and other topics.

Newspaper Design Globally

Four international newspapers will be examined here for their design practices in 1908. They include *Justice*, a partisan London weekly (Figure 5); the *Times*, a major London daily (Figure 6); *Le Temps*, a Paris daily (Figure 7); and the Russian daily *Russkiia Vedomosti* (Figure 8). Because of the historical influence of Britain on the American press, two British papers, a major daily and a smaller weekly, were chosen. The French and Russian papers were selected to provide a look at whether European societies with varied languages and cultures showed different development in terms of design. The issues are from the same dates or closest dates of the American newspapers examined, except for the weekly *Justice*.

While in 1908 the American papers examined had almost eliminated front-page advertisements, the British papers had not reached that point. The *Times* contained almost nothing but ads and public notices on its cover, a practice it would continue until the 1930s.[34] In fact, the *Times*'s news stories generally did not appear until page 3.

There are almost no illustrations accompanying these ads. Some are government notices; others announce concerts or other events. Notices of births, marriages, and deaths are featured daily in the far-left columns. For example, the June 6, 1908, edition included a note indicating that these announcements are also paid notices, six shillings for six lines.

Also, *Times* advertisements are stacked vertically with enlarged initial letters beginning each entry, much like the style common among U.S. newspapers during the 1820s to 1850s. This practice served to signal a classification for the ad: the first word represented the item for sale, with its initial letter emphasized. This style is associated with current classified

---

34. Barnhurst and Nerone, *The Form of News*, 225.

Figure 5. *London Justice*, February 8, 1908.

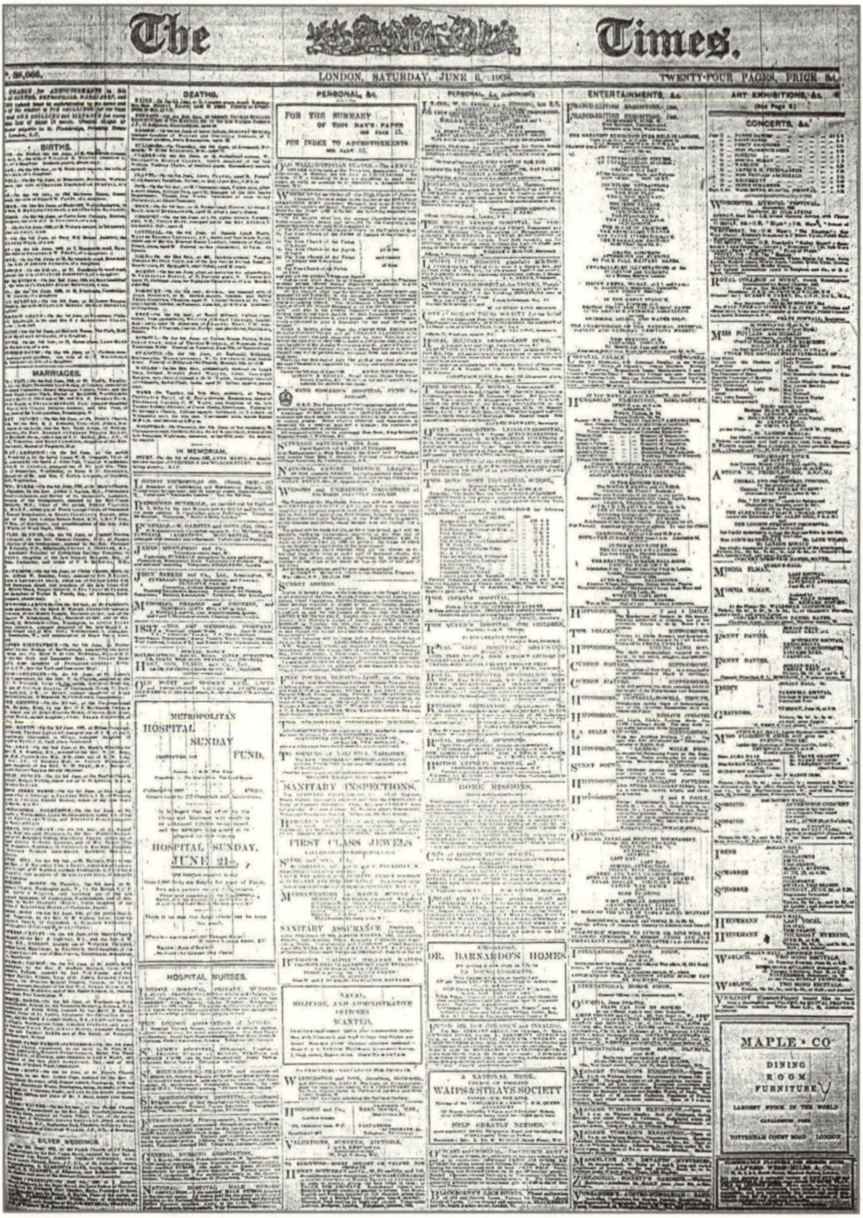

The Times.

LONDON, SATURDAY, JUNE 6, 1908. TWENTY-FOUR PAGES. PRICE 3d.

DEATHS.

BIRTHS.

MARRIAGES.

IN MEMORIAM.

PERSONAL, &c.

FOR THE SUMMARY OF THIS DAY'S PAPER SEE PAGE 13.

FOR INDEX TO ADVERTISEMENTS SEE PAGE 12.

ENTERTAINMENTS, &c.

ART EXHIBITIONS, &c.

CONCERTS, &c.

METROPOLITAN HOSPITAL SUNDAY FUND.

HOSPITAL SUNDAY, JUNE 21.

HOSPITAL NURSES.

SILVER WEDDINGS.

SANITARY INSPECTIONS.

FIRST CLASS JEWELS

SANITARY ASSURANCE

NAVAL, MILITARY, AND ADMINISTRATIVE OFFICERS WANTED.

DR. BARNARDO'S HOMES.

HOME MISSIONS.

WAIFS & STRAYS SOCIETY

HELP GREATLY NEEDED.

MAPLE & CO

DINING ROOM FURNITURE

TOTTENHAM COURT ROAD LONDON

Figure 6. *Times* of London, June 6, 1908.

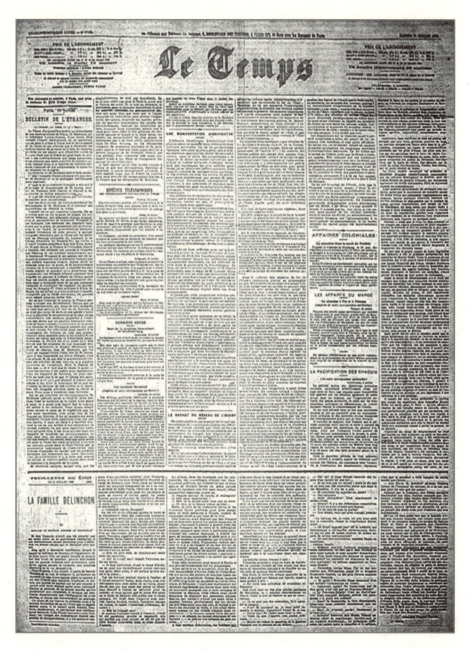

Figure 7. *Le Temps* of Paris, July 11, 1908.

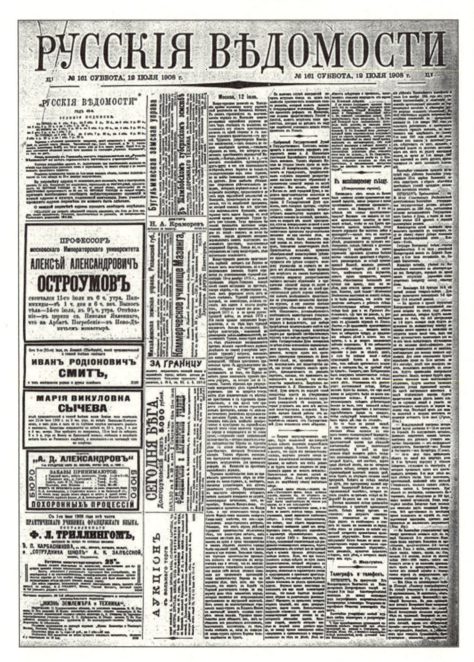

Figure 8. *Russkiia Vedomosti*, July 12, 1908.

advertising. At that time, however, the advertisements were for retailers or professional services.

On its news pages, the *Times* remains similarly gray, with small headlines and no illustrations or photography. The style is an exemplar of Victorian-era design reserve. "In the United States, imitation of the *Times* signaled a newspaper's seriousness, although no U.S. newspaper could quite match the *Times* in overall monochromatic reserve," summarized Barnhurst and Nerone.[35]

Both British papers do bear some similarities to their U.S. counterparts. Both feature vertical layouts in which items are confined to mostly one column in width. There are also column rules between each pair and a mix of typefaces. A major difference between the two is that *Justice* carries news articles and ads on its cover, while the *Times* has only ads. *Justice* also has a smaller format and is four columns wide. Advertisements usually occupy the left column, and stories with small one-line titles fill the other three. No visuals are used, but the nameplate at the top is sort of an illustration: a hand-drawn logo with ornamentation and the subtitle "The Organ of Social Democracy."

Of the four foreign papers, the French *Le Temps* looked the most like the American newspapers examined here, with five to nine articles on each cover, and no advertising. However, there also are no photographs or illustrations. The stories have relatively small headlines, probably fourteen to eighteen points in size, and some have one deck headline but no more. The page is strictly formatted: each of the seven pages included in this study has stories running vertically in six columns until about three-quarters of the way down, then a story is laid out in a horizontal format across the bottom of the page. This horizontal deviation from the standard vertical story layout seems to be unusual; it is the only occurrence of a six-column-wide story among all the papers studied. While some of the American front pages featured headlines that spanned several columns, none had stories that crossed more than a couple of columns.

The Russian newspaper, *Russkiia Vedomosti,* combined the styles seen in Britain and France but is not much like the American newspapers examined. Not consistent in design style, *Russkiia* sometimes contained only ads in its cover, and sometimes it combined ads and stories. Looking much like the British weekly *Justice* in terms of general layout, there are no photos or illustrations, and when there are both ads and stories, the ads occupy the left side of the page. The stories have the same style of small, one-column headlines as *Justice*.

35. Ibid., 222.

From these examples, it appears that by 1908, American papers had stepped away from the shadow of British influences and other international newspapers and had evolved into a uniquely American style. Moreover, as shown here, the American newspapers reflected regional personalities and stylistic differences.

The *Missourian* in 1908

On September 14, 1908, the first edition of the *University Missourian,* now known as the *Columbia Missourian,* was published. The paper, born along with the world's first School of Journalism, debuted on the first day of the fall semester classes. Students, under faculty supervision, did all the work on the paper except for the printing, which was done off site.[36] In the ten journalism classes offered that first year, students wrote newspaper stories and headlines and edited copy as part of their coursework. A course on office equipment taught students the mechanics of newspapers, such as type and presses.[37] For design, a newspaper-illustration class was added to the curriculum by 1909.[38]

In its first editions, the *Missourian* was just four pages long. On the front page of the debut edition, a cartoon depicts a baby with a "University Missourian" flag hugging a tiger in front of the university's landmark columns (Figure 9). Above the cartoon were the words, "OUR SIX COLUMNS WILL HELP," inferring readability. The front page also told its readers that it was "published on extra good quality of print paper."

The *University Missourian'*s eleven front-page articles carry a United Press byline, and the remaining twenty items are local stories, some no longer than a sentence or two. The layout, typical for the period with lines of body type, is spaced out generously, resulting in a less dense appearance than many other newspapers. The headlines are traditional, adhering to one column in width and keeping below thirty points in size.

Subsequent issues include other types of visuals, including head portrait photographs and information graphics. Some editions have no front-page visuals at all. The lede headlines sometimes spanned three columns.

One interesting design technique used frequently is a border of dots around certain items of text. It seems this is used to separate information

36. Sara Lockwood Williams, *Twenty Years of Education for Journalism,* 95.
37. Ronald T. Farrar, *A Creed for My Profession: Walter Williams, Journalist to the World,* 142.
38. Williams, *Twenty Years of Education,* 72–81.

Figure 9. *University Missourian*, September 14, 1908.

accompanying a story or to emphasize something short but important. Overall, the *Missourian* uses more decorative touches than some papers, including ornamentation, similar to that seen in the *San Francisco Chronicle*.

If the starting goal of the *Missourian* was to give students the experience of working at a real city newspaper, then it appears that was achieved well in the paper's appearance. Standard for its time, the layout appears professional and credible as well as innovative.

Designing the Big Story

Papers in 1908 might have featured little visual variety from day to day, but when a big news story broke, the design efforts tended to be taken up a notch. In 1908, the big story was an election of a new president and the congressional elections. This section will take a brief look at how the *Chicago Tribune* (Figure 10), the *Washington Post* (Figure 11), *San Francisco Chronicle* (Figure 12), *Denver Post* (Figure 13), and *University Missourian* (Figure 14) treated the election of William Howard Taft as president. The newspaper issues are examined from November 4, 1908, the day after the election.

All the newspaper covers have a significant deviance from their regular layouts. All the papers displayed unusually large headlines and visual elements, but to see these techniques in the particularly traditional-looking *Washington Post* and *Chicago Tribune* is most striking. The *Washington Post* and *San Francisco Chronicle* use banner headlines, and the *Tribune* uses no large headline at all, instead opting for a large box announcing the electoral vote count and information graphics to convey part of the story. First, a U.S. map shows how the states voted in terms of electoral votes, similar to the "red state/blue state" maps seen today. Also, there are two charts detailing votes by state and the Chicago city ward, as well as on congressional elections. The other papers all use a state electoral vote chart but no maps. On the other hand, the *Tribune* is the only paper without a photograph or illustration of the president-elect.

Keeping with its usual form, the *Denver Post* depicts Taft as a drawn cartoon figure. The *Chronicle* uses its ornamental style to decorate a three-column portrait of Taft, a huge photo by 1908 front-page standards. The *Washington Post* also uses an ornamental photo, while the *Missourian* carries a drawing as an illustration, probably due to the technology limits for photography there.

Another layout aspect that makes these front covers different from their ordinary front pages is their deviation from the one-column vertical layouts. All the newspapers have headlines or other items that occupy two or

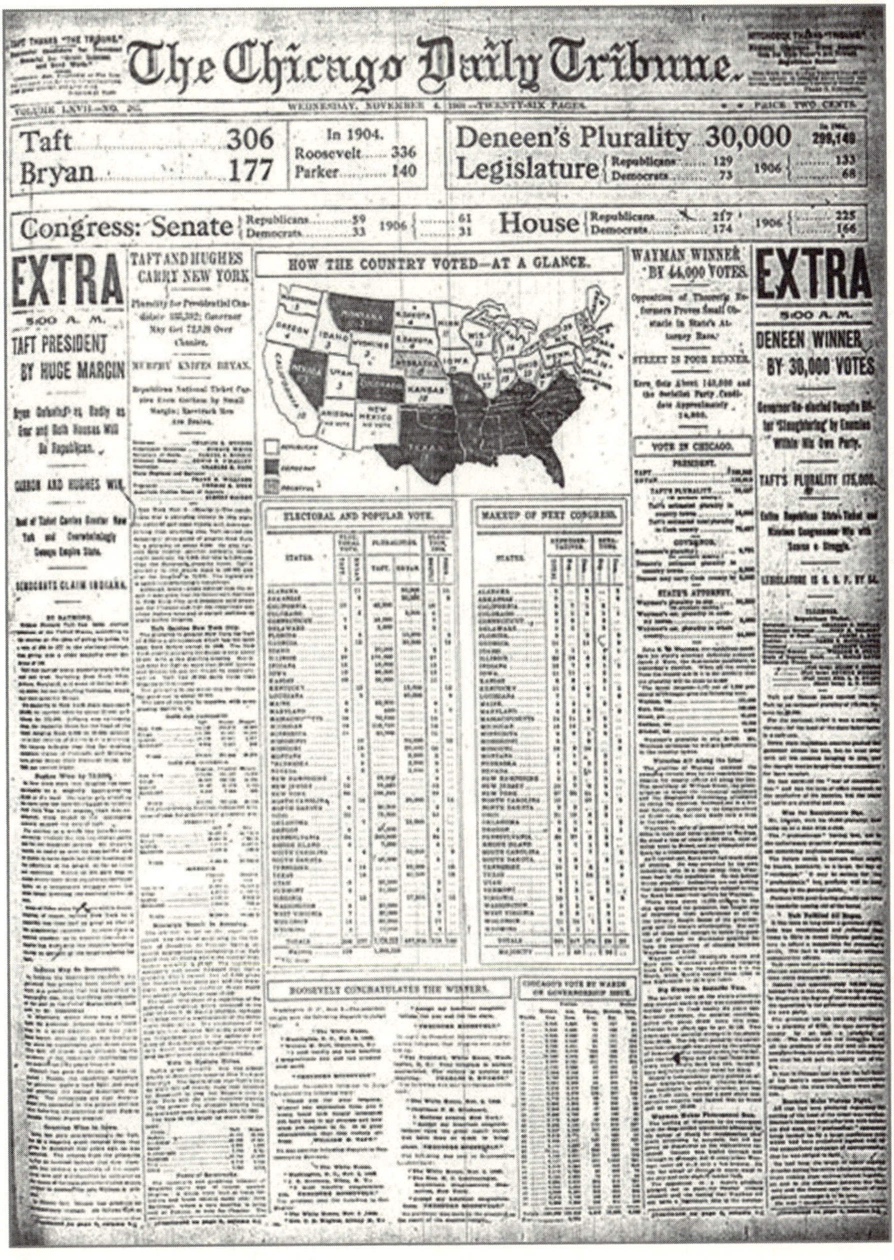

The Chicago Daily Tribune.

WEDNESDAY, NOVEMBER 4, 1908—TWENTY-SIX PAGES. PRICE TWO CENTS.

Taft	306	In 1904.	
Bryan	177	Roosevelt	336
		Parker	140

Deneen's Plurality 30,000

Legislature { Republicans 129, Democrats 73 } 1906 { 133, 68 }

Congress: Senate { Republicans 59, Democrats 33 } 1906 { 61, 31 } House { Republicans 217, Democrats 174 } 1906 { 225, 166 }

EXTRA

5:00 A. M.

TAFT PRESIDENT BY HUGE MARGIN

TAFT AND HUGHES CARRY NEW YORK

HOW THE COUNTRY VOTED—AT A GLANCE.

WAYMAN WINNER BY 44,000 VOTES.

EXTRA

5:00 A. M.

DENEEN WINNER BY 30,000 VOTES

ELECTORAL AND POPULAR VOTE.

MAKEUP OF NEXT CONGRESS.

VOTE IN CHICAGO.

ROOSEVELT CONGRATULATES THE WINNERS.

Figure 10. *Chicago Daily Tribune*, November 4, 1908.

Figure 11. *Washington Post*, November 4, 1908.

more columns in width, which was almost never seen in the *Washington Post* and the *Chicago Tribune*.

All of the papers dedicated their whole covers to election news, but layout lends prominence to different story angles. The *Post* heavily emphasizes Taft's victory nationwide, followed by elections in New York, Ohio, and

Figure 12. *San Francisco Chronicle*, November 4, 1908.

Figure 13. *Denver Post*, November 4, 1908.

Maryland, and then the results from across the country. This hierarchy is created through decreasing headline and story sizes, as well as placement on the page. The *Chicago Tribune* has a similar mix of stories, but the hierarchy is less clear. All of the stories start at the tops of the columns, but those about Taft and the Illinois governor are headed in bold, standing out in

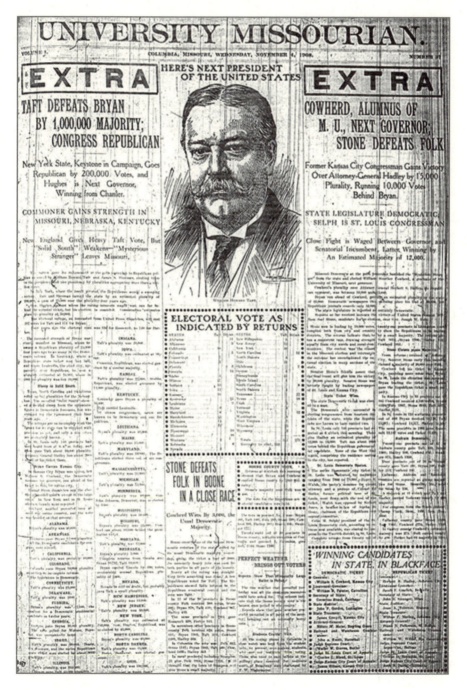

Figure 14. *University Missourian,* November 4, 1908.

emphasis. The *San Francisco Chronicle* has a banner headline about Taft, but also has a large banner deck underneath that emphasizes a local judicial election. The *Denver Post,* once again, keeps a unique design style: the lead headline covers Taft's win along with the other Colorado races, but the Taft story is actually relegated to the bottom half of the page, overshadowed by local election stories about the state's other races. Such a heavily local approach is important; the *Missourian* also takes that approach to some extent. The *Missourian* cover has a symmetrical layout, with two columns on the left dedicated to Taft and two on the right to the election of Missouri's governor and senator.

The treatment of layout on this big news day indicates that editors were aware of the role design plays in setting a tone that conveys importance and draws readers. On a day when many people would be likely to purchase a paper anyway, individual newspapers made an effort to convey the most important information quickly.

Conclusion

In 1908, front-page newspaper design was evolving in many ways. The comparison of the newspapers studied here shows many common practices, such as vertical layouts, varied typography, and text-heavy pages. But differences were also beginning to appear, both in the United States and worldwide. Photography and illustrations were growing in importance, and headlines were beginning to carry more dominance at some papers. The *University Missourian* took the styles of the era and created a new publication meant to inform future journalists on what the field demanded and, perhaps, to be on the cutting edge as much as a small-town newspaper could be.

Although advertising had nearly disappeared from U.S. front pages, the inclusion of front-page advertisements was still common overseas. Despite the historic influence drawn from European papers, especially British newspapers, the sample of issues examined in this chapter indicates that American journalism had developed its own practices and standards by the twentieth century. A range of design philosophies is shown across the country, from serious and muted layouts on the East Coast to more dynamic and sensational design in the West. The year 1908 indicates a turning point in front-page presentations and design.

PART VI

Journalism's Concurrent Voices

In the first decade of the twentieth century, American journalism thrived not only in the general newspapers but also in magazines. General-interest magazines, still in a golden age of popularity early in the twentieth century, reflected the rise of mass consumerism, with extensive advertising and promotion. Magazines were also part of the era of reform, publishing long pieces by muckrakers who investigated everything from city government administrations to the U.S. Senate, universities, patent medicines, and even the press.

Magazine journalism was important enough that the 1908–1909 University of Missouri course catalog listed "Magazine and Class Journalism" among the first journalism course offerings. This class covered the making of magazines, specialized magazines, and technical and trade publications.[1] While the School of Journalism did not initially publish a laboratory magazine, by 1924, the *Missourian Magazine* became a weekly supplement, originating from the *University Missourian*'s special pages and special features.[2]

The school's emphasis, primarily because of Dean Williams's World's Fair and World Congress experiences, may have been on international journalism in 1908, yet the program appeared to ignore the United States' own foreign-language press. By 1908 more than 81 percent of the immigrants

---

1. Ronald T. Farrar, *A Creed for My Profession,* 142. Farrar cites the University of Missouri School of Journalism, *Announcement of Courses in Journalism, 1908–09,* 4–5.
2. Sara Lockwood Williams, *20 Years of Education in Journalism,* 42, 66.

within the United States were from southern and eastern Europe—Poles, Russian Jews, Ukrainians, Slovaks, Hungarians, Romanians, Italians, and Greeks. These new arrivals, most of them poor and with little formal education, settled mainly in the large East Coast cities. They needed a press written in their own languages. Asian immigrants primarily settled on the West Coast. Fearing an Asian threat, nativists, including labor leaders, established an Asiatic Exclusion League in San Francisco. In 1906 the San Francisco School Board ordered Chinese, Japanese, and Korean children to attend a separate school. President Roosevelt intervened the next year and with a "gentleman's agreement" the school board reversed the segregation policy as the Japanese government agreed to stop the emigration of laborers.[3]

The country's own bustling foreign-language press, which included more than thirteen hundred newspapers by 1914, served millions of newly arrived immigrants by preparing them for American citizenship. As a unifying force, these primarily weekly publications were published in thirty-six different languages, with German being the most prevalent, and were found in a number of Missouri small towns as well as throughout the Midwest.

In 1908 not only was there overt nativism on the West Coast, but much of the country was overtly racist, by today's standards. African American boxer Jack Johnson may have indeed won the world heavyweight title, yet his reign pushed boxing fans to find a "white hope" to defeat him. While Chinese students were auditing the University of Missouri's first journalism classes and would be enrolled in the journalism school within a couple of years, no African Americans were in the first classes; the University of Missouri was closed to black students, and would remain so for more than forty more years. In the general press, African Americans were not seen as journalists, and were invisible in dailies, except for crime news, riots, or occasional unusual news stories. As an example of the unusual, a page one article in an early issue of the *Missourian* was headlined, "Negroes Want Black Doll Babies—So There" in reference to a resolution from the Colored National Baptist Association.[4] Conflict and riots made news in the dailies. The *Missourian* had in its first week a small United Press article about race riots in Springfield, Illinois.[5] Muckrakers covered that particular riot, as discussed in the Brennen chapter, "Work in Progress: Labor and the Press."

---

3. *The New York Public Library American History Desk Reference,* 2nd ed. (New York: Hyperion, 2003), 119.
    4. "Negroes Want Black Doll Babies—So There," *University Missourian,* 25 September 1908, 1.
    5. "Cause of Race Riot on Trial for Murder," UP, *University Missourian,* 15 September 1908, 1.

After the Civil War, hundreds of African American weekly and large-city daily newspapers began. These publications were aimed at African American communities, and they championed social justice and promoted better economic opportunities. The *Chicago Defender,* founded by Robert Abbott in 1905, was one of the more successful black newspapers, emphasizing coverage of race issues and mounting a militant attack against racism. Within ten years the *Defender* had a circulation of 230,000.[6]

The next three chapters look at journalism's concurrent voices. Janice Hume places magazines in 1908 within the reform era and consumer culture in her chapter, "Reform, Consume: Social Tumult on the Pages of Progressive Era Magazines." Berkley Hudson examines foreign-language newspapers in the United States in his chapter, "Foreign Voices Yearning to Breathe Free: The Early Twentieth-Century Immigrant Press in the United States." Earnest Perry and Aimee Edmondson discuss the African American press in their chapter, "Forced to the Margins: The Early Twentieth-Century African American Press."

6. Maurine Beasley, "Emergence of the Modern Media, 1900–1945," chapter 15, in William David Sloan, ed., *The Media in America, A History,* 6th ed. (Northport, Ala.: Vision Press, 2005), 296.

CHAPTER 14

Reform, Consume

Social Tumult on the Pages
of Progressive Era Magazines

Janice Hume

For better *and* worse, in 1908 American magazines were entrenched, successful, and influential, so it is not surprising that "Magazines and Class
Journalism" would be among the first courses offered at the new Missouri
School of Journalism. The sixty-four students in that first class had an
opportunity to study "the making of magazines of technical, trade and class
journalism."[1]

By 1912, Missouri graduate Lee Shippey had sold his first article to *Collier's*, the national consumer magazine that historian Frank Luther Mott
later called "a great force in public affairs" in the era.[2] Shippey's article,
illustrated with photographs, discussed ideas about national transportation.[3] *Collier's* numbered among the prominent muckraking publications of

1. Ronald T. Farrar, *A Creed for my Profession: Walter Williams, Journalist to the World*,
142–43.
2. Ibid., 169; Frank Luther Mott, *American Journalism, A History*, 3rd ed., 591.
3. Lee Shippey, "Building a National Turnpike," *Collier's* 48 (6 January 1912): 27–31.

the day, featured illustrations from renowned artists such as Frederic Rem-
ington and Charles Dana Gibson, and captured a good-sized share of
national advertising revenues.[4] Thus, newly minted Missouri alumnus
Shippey tied his journalistic fortunes to a magazine that reflected major
trends in American periodicals in the early twentieth century.

This chapter focuses on two important aspects of magazine journalism
prevalent in 1908. One was the rise in investigative reporting during the
Progressive Era, the era of the muckrakers, and the other was the magazine
industry's focused emphasis on selling audiences as consumers. In all, some
two thousand muckraking articles appeared between 1902 and 1917, mostly
in magazines, which had the format, the advertising structure, and the ability to focus on broad patterns that transcended cities and states.[5] These magazine journalists pioneered modern reporting techniques in stories
intended to serve the public good. Indeed, the muckrakers were credited,
at least in part, for inspiring reform in the food and drug industry, prisons,
and factories; for new regulations regarding child labor; and for hastening
the breakup of Standard Oil and major tobacco corporations. In his own
Creed for My Profession, the Missouri School of Journalism's first dean, Walter Williams, summed up this kind of journalistic commitment: "I believe
that advertising, news and editorial columns should alike serve the best
interest of the readers; that a single standard of helpful truth and cleanness
should prevail for all; that the supreme test of good journalism is the measure of its public service."[6] Muckraking was to provide that public service.

It is important to note that Williams emphasized both sides of the burgeoning news industry, editorial and advertising. The other significant and
longer-lasting trend prevalent in magazines of 1908 was their increasing
emphasis on readers as consumers, as targets for advertising. With both
advertisements and editorial content, inexpensive, mass-circulation magazines created a new class of American consumers and helped build "habit-
ual audiences, around common needs or interests . . . made for profit,"
according to Richard Ohmann.[7] American magazines fought for reform and
railed against the corruptions of an industrial society, but they also contributed to the kind of culture of consumption that fed that same insatiable
industrial society.

4. Theodore Peterson, *Magazines in the Twentieth Century* (Urbana: University of Illinois
Press, 1964), 83, 134.

5. For a synopsis of these arguments see James Aucoin, "The Media and Reform, 1900–
1917," in William David Sloan, ed., *The Media in America: A History,* 6th ed., 303–18.

6. Farrar, *A Creed for My Profession,* 203.

7. Richard Ohmann, *Selling Culture: Magazines, Markets and Class at the Turn of the Century* (London: Verso, 1996), 15–16.

Background

The American magazine initially did not have such clout. It, in fact, had a humble birth more than 150 years before 1908. Colonial-era printers and rivals Andrew Bradford and Benjamin Franklin introduced the first two indigenous magazines within days of each other in Philadelphia in 1741. Bradford's *American Magazine* lasted only three months, and Franklin's *General Magazine and Historical Chronicle* stopped publishing in six.[8] Titles appeared and disappeared for half a century until improved roads and printing technologies provided more opportunities for success. By 1900, the era of the national mass-circulating magazine had arrived. As Theodore Peterson explained in *Magazines in the Twentieth Century,* low prices had "put magazines within the reach of an increased proportion of the American people," and mass production and distribution had given them national circulations of unprecedented size. For example, Peterson noted that "before the last decade of the nineteenth century, publishers had been extremely proud of circulations between 100,000 and 200,000; but by 1900 . . . *Ladies' Home Journal* was moving rapidly toward a circulation of 1,000,000." Along with rising circulation and national audiences came lots of advertising and content geared toward "the large middle ground of public taste."[9] It was into this new era of affluence and mass audiences for magazines that the muckrakers began publishing their investigative reports and calls for political and social change.

The Muckrakers

Media history scholars have long heralded the muckrakers of the Progressive Era as the heroes of modern investigative reporting. Histories of American journalism note their efforts at reform. Emery, Emery, and Roberts wrote: "The crusading spirit is as old as journalism, but never in American history had there been more opportunities for 'the people's champions' than in the first years following 1900." Aucoin noted a change in style of reportage in these muckraking articles: "The better articles marshaled details unearthed in thorough investigations. Significantly, the exposés derived their power from well-selected facts, not the forceful polemics characteristic of earlier journalistic essays." Evensen wrote about

---

8. Sam Riley, "American Magazines, 1740–1900," in Sloan, ed., *The Media in America,* 249.

9. Peterson, *Magazines in the Twentieth Century,* 13, 14.

the journalists' "faith in the power of facts to move audiences to action when those facts were told in a compelling way." The muckrakers, mostly writing for mainstream mass-circulating magazines, relied on verified facts to expose social ills stemming from corruption and other problems in American politics and industry. They scoured public documents, pioneered the depth interview and social science reporting techniques, and wrote articles geared for a mass, rather than for an elite, audience. For example, muckraking periodicals *McClure's* and *Cosmopolitan,* according to Schneirov, "sought to assemble their stories and articles in a coherent and digestible package, no longer assuming an audience of cultural insiders." Their techniques worked. Walter M. Brasch said of the muckrakers: "Their names and stories about corruption and greed, monopolies, slumlords, and exploitation of the masses were known to every literate American."[10]

Legend has it that Theodore Roosevelt labeled the reformers "muckrakers" based on a character in John Bunyan's *The Pilgrim's Progress* who preferred to rake the muck at his feet rather than to look upward to the riches of heaven. But famous muckraker Upton Sinclair, writing for the *Independent* in 1908, disagreed with Roosevelt's pejorative assessment. He wrote that muckrakers did not love corruption but hated it "with an intensity that forbids them to think about anything else while corruption sits enthroned."[11] Whichever view was accurate, the nickname stuck, and as Ellen Fitzpatrick noted in her introduction to *Muckraking: Three Landmark Articles:*

> The work of talented writers and reckless hacks was lumped together from that time forward, obscuring in the haze of charges of sensationalism an important moment in the evolution of twentieth-century American life. The muckraking years represent a time when the writings of investigative journalists broke through the boundaries of literature and entered the arena of modern politics. They foreshadowed the complex and often contested relationship between journalists and public officials that exists today.[12]

10. Michael Emery, Edwin Emery, and Nancy Roberts, *The Press in America: An Interpretive History of the Mass Media,* 9th ed. (Boston: Allyn and Bacon, 2000), 213; Aucoin, "The Media and Reform," 303; Bruce J. Evensen, "Progressivism, Muckraking and Objectivity," in Steven R. Knowlton and Karen L. Freeman, eds., *Fair and Balanced: A History of Journalistic Objectivity* (Northport, Ala.: Vision Press, 2005), 136; Matthew Schneirov, *The Dream of a New Social Order: Popular Magazines in America, 1893–1914* (New York: Columbia University Press, 1994), 123; Walter W. Brasch, *Forerunners of the Revolution: Muckrakers and the American Social Conscience* (Lanham, Md.: University Press of America, 1990), ix.

11. Sinclair is quoted in Brasch, *Forerunners of the Revolution,* 130.

12. Ellen F. Fitzpatrick, ed., *Muckraking: Three Landmark Articles* (Boston: Bedford Books of St. Martin's Press, 1994), 2.

Thus, the muckrakers took their place in the lore of American politics and journalism. As Walter M. Brasch said in *Forerunners of the Revolution: Muckrakers and the American Social Conscience*, "they were the finest journalists of the era, well-educated writers who cared about the society and the people they wrote about. . . . They became a part of a social conscience of the people that would lead to sweeping state and federal reform."[13] Indeed they have been studied, discussed, and debated for the better part of a century. In 1979, Harry H. Stein evaluated studies about muckrakers in a bibliographic essay for *Journalism Quarterly* noting the "near wilderness of facts, notions, surmises, unknowns, instances and generalizations" that half a century of scholarship had sown.[14]

More recently, perspectives from different disciplines have added new layers of understanding of the activities and impact of the muckrakers. For example, film and literature expert Cecelia Tichi compares the crusading journalists of the early twentieth century to modern authors of book-length recent exposés and documentaries such as Barbara Ehrenreich's *Nickeled and Dimed: On (Not) Getting By in America* and Eric Schlosser's *Fast Food Nation: The Dark Side of the All American Meal*.[15] She argues that these modern muckrakers are operating in a new "gilded age," one of great wealth and corruption, just as were the muckrakers of the early twentieth century. Others have been critical of the muckraking movement, such as for what they ignored. Maurine Beasley, for example, pointed to one important crisis in American life that received scant attention: lynching and the plight of African Americans in the South.[16]

The phenomenon of muckraking in the years surrounding 1908 was possible thanks to what Tichi called the "standard textbook trio: urbanization, industrialization, and immigration."[17] America was dealing with all three in abundance. The United States, in the decades from 1860 to 1900, had experienced a crippling war and economic strife, followed by large-scale immigration. There were rapid technological advances in transportation and communication. The Industrial Revolution increasingly produced goods for national and regional markets.[18] New cities were formed and established

13. Brasch, *Forerunners of the Revolution*, ix.
14. Harry H. Stein, "American Muckrakers and Muckraking: The 50-Year Scholarship," *Journalism Quarterly* 56, no. 1 (1979): 9.
15. Cecelia Tichi, *Exposes and Excess: Muckraking in America, 1900/2000* (Philadelphia: University of Pennsylvania Press, 2004).
16. Maurine Beasley, "The Muckrakers and Lynching: A Case Study in Racism," *Journalism History* 9, no. 3 (Autumn–Winter 1982): 86–91.
17. Tichi, *Exposes and Excess*, 62.
18. Peterson, *Magazines in the Twentieth Century*, 4.

cities grew rapidly.[19] It was a time of great change, and so it follows that Americans would have been grappling with the increasing social pressures for decades. They were primed to be receptive to the investigative reporting soon to be done in record volume by an army of magazine and newspaper writers.

This new brand of investigative reporting was also born of changes in the news industry. Newspapers had become larger, cheaper, and more independent, and had long published stories about crime and politics. Yet, they were, according to Fitzpatrick,

> . . . inhibited by their format from presenting extensive and in-depth essays that probed current social issues in a thoughtful manner. They had large audiences but lacked the depth of coverage a magazine format could potentially provide. Magazines, however, often lacked a mass audience, an attention to human-interest stories, and the political sympathies that would appeal to a broad readership.[20]

This was about to change. At the end of the nineteenth century, improvements in printing and distribution technologies and the dropping cost of paper enabled magazines to reach larger and larger audiences. Rotary presses replaced flatbed presses at magazines such as *Harper's*, *Century Magazine*, *McCall's*, and *Munsey's*. A new "rotary art press" introduced in 1890 printed halftone illustrations from curved plates, and in 1908, the Curtis Publishing Company installed the "first Cottrell multicolor rotary press," just one of many innovations in magazine production. This meant that publishers no longer had to pay high prices for sketches engraved meticulously by hand. Photographs, too, were increasingly easier and cheaper to reproduce. All these new technologies made publishing handsome yet inexpensive magazines both possible and profitable. Peterson noted: "In such a setting the low-priced, mass-circulation magazine was born."[21] Circulations exploded. The *Saturday Evening Post*, for example, grew from 250,000 in 1900 to 886,000 in 1908, *Munsey's* from 590,000 to 618,000, and *McClure's* from 369,000 to 440,000.[22]

Editors and writers at some of these periodicals already had experimented with new kinds of stories before the turn of the century. Schneirov noted that "the social reform thrust of magazines was not entirely new. We can locate

19. Fitzpatrick, *Muckraking*, 4.
20. Ibid., 9.
21. Peterson, *Magazines in the Twentieth Century*, 5, 6.
22. Schneirov, *The Dream of a New Social Order*, 265.

elements of what has been called the new 'civic consciousness' during the years after the depression of 1893."[23] By the beginning of the 1900s, the press and its growing audiences were ready for the reformers. Indeed, reform movements in the Progressive Era touched many aspects of American society, not just the press. As one of the leading muckraking editors, S. S. McClure, said in his autobiography, the origin of the movement came not from a formulated plan "but was the result of merely taking up in the magazine some of the problems that were beginning to interest the people."[24]

Many scholars label his *McClure's* as being the leader in the movement.[25] Yet the muckraking trend touched many publications, including women's magazines such as *Woman's Home Companion, Good Housekeeping, Ladies' Home Journal, McCall's, Pictorial Review,* and *The Delineator*, according to Endres. These women's magazines, called the "big six," Endres noted, "tailored their muckraking journalism to the traditional roles and responsibilities of females and mothers and wives, as nurturers and homemakers. And women had a duty to carry their traditional roles and responsibilities into the 'larger household,' the community." These magazines, she argued:

> ... deserve a place in the history of muckraking. ... They offered practical solutions for eliminating some of the ills within the home and offered a blueprint for reform work outside it. ... Finally, these publications crafted an argument which would ring convincingly throughout the Progressive Movement: women had a right, indeed a duty, to correct the ills of society, the "larger household."[26]

It was *McClure's*, however, and other periodicals such as *Cosmopolitan*, the *Arena, Collier's, Everybody's, Hampton's,* and the *American* that achieved the most recognition for their investigative reporting.[27] Steve Weinberg noted: "Modern investigative journalism, based on high standards of evidence, had its birth in 1902, when Ida M. Tarbell began publishing her expose of the Standard Oil Company and John D. Rockefeller in *McClure's* magazine." Tarbell, he wrote, is remembered in the company of Lincoln Steffens, David Graham Phillips, Ray Stannard Baker, and Upton Sinclair:

---

23. Ibid., 203.

24. S. S. McClure, *My Autobiography,* 2nd ed. (New York: Frederick A. Stokes Company Publishers, 1914), 246.

25. See Stein, "American Muckrakers and Muckraking: The 50-Year Scholarship," 9–17.

26. Kathleen L. Endres, "Women and the 'Larger Household': The 'Big Six' and Muckraking," *American Journalism* 14, nos. 3–4 (Summer–Fall, 1997): 262, 263, 282.

27. Ibid., 263.

"It seemed as if their journalism of exposure was everywhere readers turned until about 1910, when the frequency decreased."[28]

Evensen has noted not only these muckrakers' calls for reform but also their faith in the power of facts. "Their determination to impose morality on the political and social landscape was grounded in the conviction that the truth was their weapon in uncovering wrongdoing and that the public, when made aware of what was wrong, would do the right thing."[29]

Tarbell was undaunted in her search for the truth. Research for "The History of the Standard Oil Company" took her five years and cost the magazine more than fifty thousand dollars. Fitzpatrick noted that:

> Tarbell's reliance on the public record was one of the most striking and persuasive aspects of her research. . . . Court records, the findings of state and federal investigative commissions, newspaper accounts from the oil regions, a large "pamphlet literature," and depositions from civil suits provided evidence of the methods Standard Oil had employed to amass its fortunes and of the ways in which it maintained its monopoly.

Tarbell was not only a meticulous researcher but also a talented writer who could provide "a powerful narrative structure that made a coherent whole of the company's history," he said. Her series included nineteen articles published over two years. Two years after that, the federal government under Theodore Roosevelt brought an antitrust suit against Standard Oil, precipitating the breakup of that company.[30]

Lincoln Steffens's series of six articles, later compiled into a book called *The Shame of the Cities*, told *McClure's* readers about corruption in the governments of St. Louis, Minneapolis, Pittsburgh, Philadelphia, Chicago, and New York. He, too, relied on facts to tell these stories, but he also believed his articles should have a point of view. Evensen noted that "While scientists might be neutral in their findings, Steffens and other muckraking journalists harnessed evidence—facts—to agitate for reform."[31] The fact that his series ran in a national magazine, rather than a newspaper, was important, according to Schneirov, who argued that "for the first time, a *national* medium of mass communication, the popular magazine, became a major political force, making

28. Steve Weinberg, "Avenging Angel or Deceitful Devil?: The Evolution of Drew Pearson, a New Kind of Investigative Journalist," *American Journalism* 14, nos. 3–4 (Summer–Fall 1997): 283.

29. Bruce J. Evensen, "Progressivism, Muckraking and Objectivity," in Knowlton and Freeman, eds., *Fair and Balanced*, 136.

30. Fitzpatrick, *Muckraking*, 25, 104.

31. Evensen, "Progressivism," 137–38.

news as well as reporting it." Steffens's series, he noted, was a sensation and helped to transform local reform movements into a national movement. Steffens himself is quoted as saying that magazines "could uncover patterns in local developments and provide readers with a deeper understanding of how corruption in their own city fit into this larger pattern."[32] After publication of his series, many states reformed their election and lobbying regulations.[33]

Ray Stannard Baker's "The Right to Work," another famous *McClure's* contribution, investigated unrest in the coal fields of Pennsylvania. Baker visited nonstriking miners "in their homes, in the fields and in union meetings," wrote Fitzpatrick, and found that labor racketeering and corruption left a trail leading back to business.[34] Articles from Baker, Tarbell, and Steffens were published in the January 1903 edition of *McClure's,* arguably the most famous issue of a magazine in American history. As Brasch argued, this national magazine took "muckraking farther than ever, pounding story after story of poverty, worker exploitation, corporate excesses, political corruption, and consumer abuse until the public demanded regulation and the federal government finally had to yield."[35]

As they considered their careers in retrospect, the muckrakers themselves began to recognize their contributions to the new standards of reporting. McClure, in his autobiography, claimed to have invented a whole new kind of journalism with his magazine's muckraking articles.

> These articles elicited an immediate response from the press, and undoubtedly had a strong influence upon the public mind. They were carefully and thoroughly worked out and were, in so far as things made with human instruments can be, accurate. In fact, they were the first accurate studies of this nature that had appeared in a magazine in America. To secure this accuracy, to make such studies of value, I had to invent a new method in magazine journalism.[36]

Whether McClure, writing more than a decade after publication of the famous January 1903 issue, was exaggerating the point or not, *McClure's* and many, many other magazines of the day set the bar for future investigative journalists. In her autobiography, Ida Tarbell wrote about the tensions between the serious investigative journalist and the sensationalist:

32. Schneirov, *The Dream of a New Social Order,* 203.
33. Fitzpatrick, *Muckraking,* 104.
34. Ibid., 33–34.
35. Brasch, *Forerunners of the Revolution,* 37.
36. McClure, *My Autobiography,* 243.

This classification of muckraker, which I did not like, helped fix my resolution to have done for good and all with the subject which had brought it on me. But events were stronger than I. All the radical reforming element, and I numbered many friends among them, were begging me to join their movements. I soon found that most of them wanted attacks. They had little interest in balanced findings. Now I was convinced that in the long run the public they were trying to stir would weary of vituperation, that if you were to secure permanent results the mind must be convinced.[37]

Even Theodore Roosevelt, who had labeled crusading journalists as "muckrakers," considered the positive contributions of a serious, conscientious periodical. He wrote for the *Outlook* in 1909, "It would be difficult to overestimate the amount of good which can be done by the men responsible for such a publication." Editors at the *Outlook*, he wrote, "hold as their first duty inflexible adherence to the elementary virtues of entire truth, entire courage, entire honesty."[38] Lincoln Steffens, in the second volume of his autobiography, wrote about his role as a reporter in his investigative series about corruption in state governments. That role, he wrote, was to "arrange the overwhelming mass of evidence, confessions, and underworld gossip so as to paint a picture of the government as it actually was . . . a writer's, not a detective's job: to select a few of the multitudinous facts to show the truth about any State in the United States."[39]

Indeed, "fact," as Tichi wrote nearly a century later, "was the muckrakers' antidote to rumor and to sensationalist yellow journalism."[40] Even the more sensationalist *Cosmopolitan*, which had published (to Roosevelt's dismay) its landmark series "The Treason of the Senate" in 1906, followed the trend. In 1908 and 1909, as the Missouri School of Journalism was opening its doors, the magazine published Alfred Henry Lewis's "The Owners of America," "a fact-based but still emotional series detailing the lives of America's corporate goliaths."[41] Missouri students such as Lee Shippey, learning both the skills and purpose of journalism, would likely be influenced by such exciting narratives, based in fact, which had real impact. For *Collier's*, a magazine distinguished for its coverage of current affairs and for

37. Ida M. Tarbell, *All in The Day's Work, an Autobiography* (New York: Macmillan Co., 1939), 242.

38. Theodore Roosevelt, "Why I Believe in the Kind of American Journalism for Which *The Outlook* Stands," *Outlook* 91 (6 March 1909): 510.

39. Lincoln Steffens, *The Autobiography of Lincoln Steffens*, vol. 2 (New York: Harcourt, Brace and Company, 1931), 444–45.

40. Tichi, *Exposes and Excess*, 69.

41. Brasch, *Forerunners of the Revolution*, 107.

its muckraking exposé of the patent-medicine business, "The Great American Fraud," Shippey contributed "Building a National Turnpike" and "Coast-to-Coast Highway."[42]

Consumer Culture

As the muckrakers called for reform, for dramatic change in American social, political, and economic life, the business of magazine publishing was also changing significantly. Peterson noted: "The new journalism, with its pressure for huge circulations, its pitching of content to mass audiences, its scramble for the advertising dollar, was well on its way. Editors . . . had found their market and had learned to give readers what they want." The reward for amassing huge subscription lists was advertising revenue and lots of it. The developments in and significant financial effects of advertising, he argued, "transformed the publisher from dealer in editorial wares to dealer in consumer groups as well."[43] Magazine editors of the era seemed stunned by their own successes. In May 1908, the *American Review of Reviews* marveled: "In a year the magazines of America devote over thirty times more space to advertising than is covered by Holy Writ and the dramas of Shakespeare combined."[44]

Scholars look to 1893 as a watershed year in magazine history. In that year, *Munsey's, McClure's,* and *Cosmopolitan* dropped their prices to a dime per copy and began relying more on advertising than circulation for revenues. "Readers who hadn't subscribed to the 'quality class' or elite publications" began flocking to these magazines, said Ellen Gruber Garvey in *The Adman in the Parlor: Magazines and the Gendering of Consumer Culture, 1880s to 1910s.* She wrote:

> The most crucial distinction between the new ten-cent magazine and the older elite magazines . . . was the reliance of the new magazines on advertising rather than sales, with advertising rates pegged to circulation figures. With this change, publishers made a definitive shift—from selling magazines directly to readers to selling their readership to advertisers.[45]

42. See Mott, *American Journalism,* 575, and Peterson, *Magazines in the Twentieth Century,* 134; Shippey, "Building a National Turnpike,"and "Coast to Coast Highway," *Collier's* 50 (11 January 1913), sup. 31.
43. Peterson, *The Birth of the Modern Magazine,* 17, 18.
44. "Reaching the Millions," *American Review of Reviews* 37 (May 1908): 608.
45. Ellen Gruber Garvey, *The Adman in the Parlor: Magazines and the Gendering of Consumer Culture, 1880s to 1910s* (New York: Oxford University Press, 1996), 9, 11.

These magazines, of course, did not publish in a cultural vacuum. They "existed in a symbiotic relationship with other aspects of mass culture," particularly with the huge corporations now part of the American economy, according to Carolyn Kitch. She noted: "When increasingly conglomerate corporations needed to launch major advertising campaigns in order to create demand for mass-produced goods, they found that magazines were the best way to reach a wide audience." Kitch examined the visual stereotypes in popular consumer magazines of the early twentieth century and argued that the combination of editorial and advertising content, fiction, and illustrations provided "an early example of the ways in which . . . mass culture would systematically blur the boundaries between 'high' and 'low' culture. It further instructed readers in upward mobility, showing them the lifestyles of the rich."[46]

What followed, according to Michael Schudson, was the creation of a society in which "people often satisfy or believe they can satisfy their socially constructed needs and desires by buying mass produced, standardized, nationally advertised consumer products." There are advantages and disadvantages to living in such a society. He wrote:

> The mass media help escort people into the wider world of choice, broadening horizons, blurring provincial demarcations. On the one hand, the media enlarge people's sense of their own and the world's possibilities; on the other hand, the media lead people to constantly compare themselves to others or to images of others.[47]

Tom Pendergast explored the effects of this phenomenon on the construction of gender in early twentieth-century America. Pendergast in *Creating the Modern Man: American Magazines and Consumer Culture, 1900–1950*, noted that magazines were "themselves a product of the forces that drove economic transformation" and that "those magazines that succeeded best at attracting advertising were those that promoted a consuming lifestyle." He argued that magazines presented "conflicting representations" of masculinity which "indicated a very real uncertainty about the meaning of manhood in a modern age." Of the editors, he wrote:

> There is no evidence to suggest that they were coerced into advancing the interests of advertisers and their corporate clients. In fact, the interests of

---

46. Carolyn Kitch, *The Girl on the Magazine Cover: The Origins of Visual Stereotypes in American Mass Media* (Chapel Hill: University of North Carolina Press, 2001), 4, 7.

47. Michael Schudson, *Advertising, The Uneasy Persuasion: Its Dubious Impact on American Society* (New York: Basic Books, 1984; paperback edition 1986), 147, 155.

the corporate class may well have been their interests. If selling out meant embracing the culture of consumption, then the big magazines incorporated selling out into the very fiber of their being. Selling things was why they existed.[48]

Garvey writes that the advertising-supported magazines of this era "constructed the reader, especially the female reader, as a consumer. Even as advertisements became touchstones of modernity and its fragmentations, ads came to seem natural and ordinary to readers."[49] This was especially true for women's magazines. Nancy A. Walker, in *Shaping Our Mothers' World: American Women's Magazines*, wrote of *McCall's*, which was founded to sell paper dress patterns, and *Woman's Home Companion* and *Good Housekeeping*, which had roots as mail-order catalogs:

> Their ties with the sale of products remained strong, and because they matured at the same time that the development of advertising for print and other media itself became a big business, much of what the magazines taught women was conveyed in ads.[50]

The magazines represented women of the middle classes who had "the potential for what was later termed upward mobility."[51] Helen Damon-Moore, who examined gender and commerce in *Ladies' Home Journal* and *Saturday Evening Post*, wrote that by 1910, "the gender norms themselves were convincingly commercialized, with women centrally defined as consumers and men centrally defined as breadwinners."[52]

The class distinctions were important, too. Richard Ohmann, in *Selling Culture: Magazines, Markets and Class at the Turn of the Century*, noted that manufacturers bought ads en masse when they "saw a chance to situate their products within a way of life that was becoming the norm for urban and suburban people, mainly of the professional and managerial class." These products altered the function of the home, moved it from a place of production to one of consumption and leisure, he wrote, adding, "National

48. Tom Pendergast, *Creating the Modern Man: American Magazines in Consumer Culture, 1900–1850* (Columbia: University of Missouri Press, 2000), 30, 63–64.

49. Garvey, *The Adman*, 4.

50. Nancy A. Walker, *Shaping Our Mothers' World: American Women's Magazines* (Jackson: University Press of Mississippi, 2000), 36.

51. Ibid., 37.

52. Helen Damon-Moore, *Magazines for the Millions: Gender and Commerce in the* Ladies Home Journal *and the* Saturday Evening Post, *1880–1910* (Albany: State University of New York Press, 1994), 187.

advertisers helped to create the new way of life, as well as seizing the opportunity it offered them." Ohmann further argued:

> The hegemony of the integrated corporation reached out *beyond* final sales of commodities, to a metamorphosis of aspirations and imaginations. In this, corporations were no less powerful because those who took up their messages *wanted* to be consumers.[53]

Ohmann examined thousands of advertisements in monthly magazines from 1890 to 1905, including *Atlantic Monthly, Harper's, McClure's, Munsey's,* and *Cosmopolitan,* and argued that the "saturation of public spaces with commercial messages and images" served as a "discourse of power," guided in large part by advertising agents, men who "needed a particular kind of social order, peopled by consumers rather than citizens or by workers." The result, he wrote, was "the establishment of mass culture in the United States." The mass-circulating magazines of the early twentieth century established what he calls a "new kind of cultural production—one of major historical consequence whether or not we call it mass culture."[54]

Even without the benefit of hindsight, magazine editors and writers of the era struggled with the social, cultural, and economic implications of the advertising phenomenon both to magazines and the nation. Some were optimistic. In 1908, the *American Review of Reviews,* for example, likened ads to business news. "New inventions, fabrics, articles of food and wear, and fads and fancies of fashion are communicated through advertisements, fields of thought and scenes of travel likewise. The comforts, conventions and conveniences of life are thus made known." The article opined about advertising's essential contributions to the American magazine, which it called "a national institution, progressive, alert, beautiful, enterprising, instructive, and entertaining. Without the advertising section to support it this triumph of thought and skill would be impossible."[55] Yet others were decidedly pessimistic. The *Arena* in 1909 warned readers, in an article titled "The Monthly Magazines in the Grip of Privileged Wealth," that the "bludgeon of power" of corporations and large stockholders was "at work to gain mastership of the opinion-forming magazines of the country."[56] The *Bookman* was critical of the kind of magazine that appealed to the lowest com-

---

53. Ohmann, *Selling Culture,* 91.
54. Ibid., 216, 361, 340.
55. "Reaching the Millions," 609.
56. "The Monthly Magazines in The Grip of Privileged Wealth," *Arena* 41 (January 1909): 106.

mon denominator to increase circulation and become more attractive to advertisers. "Journalism will, of course, deserve the title of profession only so long as there is an entire willingness on the part of editors that a certain and perhaps numerous class of readers should go hang themselves."[57]

Articles published in the *Nation* in 1907 and in *Living Age* in 1908 delved deeper into cultural implications of an America deluged with magazine advertising. In "What We Really Are," the *Nation* considered the "historian of the distant future who shall attempt to reconstruct the archaic civilization of America in the twentieth century." That historian would "resort to the advertising sections of our magazines . . . the spontaneous expression of a nation's universal needs and characteristics." This tongue-in-cheek article suggested the future history of America would reveal "the merits of various speaking machines, games, and literature for home reading" and would show "a circle of faces ranging from gray-haired age to early infancy, grouped about a phonograph." It would also show men and women engaged in different tasks—the men painting cottage roofs and the women varnishing furniture. "Contrary to what is usually believed, the Americans of that period builded [sic] for all time and with a sensitive eye for the beautiful. Else what is the significance of these various pigments and stains?"[58] The *Living Age* article, more serious in tone, warned, "the American genius for advertising is showing signs of degenerating." It said: "It is necessary for the ad-writer to-day to hammer hard at the people he desires to entangle in his net, and stun them into buying the wares he advertises, without their questioning the merits or the necessity that may exist for purchasing them." The author, Saint Nihal Sing, an Indian writing about how others around the world viewed Americans and their culture of advertising, said he was "coming into the belief that the aim of the ad-man is to fence in such a manner that the good sense and reasoning ability of the advertisement reader is successfully eluded, and then fire at him, in a hypnotic manner, a volley of syllogistic reasoning, calculated to touch his passion for greed, or appeal to his fear of death or appetite for sensation, or some such emotion, usually not of a very dignified order." Newspapers and magazines, he wrote, "are maintained in America for advancing the political interests of certain individuals . . . railroads and large manufacturing and commercial organizations control a number of publications."[59]

57. "'Happy Thought' Journalism," *Bookman* 28 (October 1908): 108.
58. "What We Really Are," *Nation* 84 (4 April 1907): 305.
59. Saint Nihal Sing, "As an Indian Sees America: The Yellow Ad-Man," *Living Age* 259 (28 November 1908): 521–22, 524.

Scholars might debate the consequences of a mass culture of consumption. Did magazines help raise the standard of living in the United States or help create a powerful hegemonic force that fostered consumer waste and corporate greed? Whatever the outcome, it is clear that magazines were changing at the turn of the century. In 1900, *Harper's* "carried a greater volume of advertising than in the entire preceding twenty-two years combined," according to Peterson, who wrote: "When a reader of 1908 picked up a copy of a monthly magazine favored by advertisers, he encountered an average of 137 pages of advertisements, about 54 percent of the total pages."[60]

Conclusion

Magazines in 1908 were experiencing a heyday in both the quality of news and the quantity of advertising, and both sides of the publishing industry had a real impact on American politics, business, and culture. *McClure's*, known for its muckraking exposés, was by 1900 a leading magazine in the nation with a circulation of 350,000. "It boasted," Theresa Luecke wrote in 2005, "a staff of excellent writers, the quality of which has not been equaled to this day."[61] The muckrakers at *McClure's* and many other magazines practiced a kind of reform journalism that "flourished as never before or since," according to Aucoin.[62] *McClure's*, of course, was dwarfed in circulation by *Ladies' Home Journal*, which in 1904 became the first magazine to reach a million readers. The weekly *Saturday Evening Post*, founded to "romanticize the accomplishments of American business," reached the million mark in 1908.[63] The danger of attracting such large audiences was that publishers would have to keep them, and as the muckraking era waned, magazines became more likely to include only what they thought the mainstream majority could stomach. "Minority views," Peterson wrote, "found little expression in the commercial magazine."[64]

Yet these mass-circulation consumer titles were not the only magazines published in 1908. African American magazines, all but extinct after the Civil War, experienced a small resurgence in the late nineteenth century. The *Colored American Magazine* lasted nearly a decade, at a peak circulation of 17,000, before it closed in 1909. These magazines struggled. For example, the popu-

60. Peterson, *Magazines in the Twentieth Century*, 443, 22–23.
61. Theresa L. Lueck, "The Age of Mass Magazines: 1900-Present," in Sloan, ed., *The Media in America*, 390.
62. Aucoin, "The Media and Reform," 303.
63. Lueck, "The Age of Mass Magazines," 391–92.
64. Peterson, *Magazines in the Twentieth Century*, 445.

lar (circulation 113,000) *Voice of the Negro* "was born in the midst of the Atlanta riots and fell victim to mob destruction," according to Armistead S. Pride and Clint C. Wilson II in *A History of the Black Press*. *Voice of the Negro* lasted only two years, from 1904 until 1906. Yet it was soon to be followed by the powerful and long-lasting *Crisis*, founded and edited by W. E. B. DuBois from 1910 to 1932. The *Crisis* was immediately successful, and DuBois's editorials "of force, beauty, cold irony and sharp thrust" had "no match anywhere in Negro magazine publication," wrote Pride and Wilson.[65]

Another movement in magazine publishing was gaining momentum in the early twentieth century, begun by editor Frank Munsey, who invented pulpwood fiction magazines, according to Ron Goulart in *Cheap Thrills: An Informal History of the Pulp Magazines*. Goulart noted: "If it had not been for him there might never have been pulps and, consequently, no Tarzan, no Sam Spade, no Dr. Kildare, no Doc Savage, no Zorro, no Shadow and no Tros of Samothrace."[66] Improvements in rural mail routes in the early part of the century inspired an impressive growth in the number of rural magazines in the West and Southwest.[67] Juvenile magazines such as *St. Nicholas* and *Youth Companion*, along with some of the general-interest titles, helped to create a public appetite for sports, particularly football, and paved the way for the sports pulp magazines of the 1920s to the 1950s.[68] There were religious publications, socialist publications, literary publications, and a variety of other kinds of magazines, most of which had, of course, a smaller reach than their mass-circulating contemporaries.[69]

Thus, as Lee Shippey and his classmates at the world's first school of journalism looked to their future, magazines held much promise for them and the other graduates at the new journalism schools. Such magazines were powerful, influential, and plentiful. Their crusading investigations were achieving desperately needed reform in government and business. They were packed with advertisements selling brands like Ivory Soap, Royal

65. Armistead S. Pride and Clint C. Wilson II, *A History of the Black Press* (Washington, D.C.: Howard University Press, 1997), 250–51.

66. Ron Goulart, *Cheap Thrills: An Informal History of the Pulp Magazines* (New Rochelle, N.Y.: Arlington House, 1972), 10.

67. Robert G. Hays, *Early Stories from the Land: Short-Story Fiction from American Rural Magazines, 1900–1925* (Ames: Iowa State University Press, 1995), xiii.

68. John Dinan, *Sports in the Pulp Magazines* (Jefferson, N.C.: McFarland and Co., 1998), 8.

69. See, for example, Donald E. Winters, Jr., *The Soul of the Wobblies: The I.W.W., Religion, and American Culture in the Progressive Era, 1905–1917* (Westport, Conn.: Greenwood Press, 1985) and Jayne E. Marek, *Women Editing Modernism: 'Little' Magazines and Literary History* (Lexington: University Press of Kentucky).

Baking Powder, and Gillette safety razors to a growing class of consumers. In decades to come, radio and television would compete for similar audiences and advertising dollars, but in 1908, magazines were America's only national medium. A career in magazines would give the first journalism alumni boundless opportunity, as their dean instructed, to promote truth and serve the public good.

CHAPTER 15

Foreign Voices Yearning to Breathe Free

The Early Twentieth-Century
Immigrant Press in the United States

Berkley Hudson

It was the fifth of October 1908. At the Columbia Theater in Washington, D.C., a play called *The Melting Pot* entertained an elite audience. Today, it provides a rich context to consider America's cultural consciousness at the turn of the century.

During that era, the foreign-language press flourished in the United States. Also, in the heartland and, intriguingly, with no focus on the immigrant press, the University of Missouri instituted the world's first full-scale undergraduate journalism program.

In Washington on that October night, two actors portrayed David and Vera, immigrants in love in New York City. Both born in Russia, he is Jewish, and she is Christian. Their families oppose their marriage. Another complication exists: his father was a colonel in the tsar's army and in 1903 authorized the killing of her relatives. At the performance's close, David and Vera held hands on the rooftop of her settlement house. In the distance, surrounded by the watery edge of Manhattan and with a brilliant sunset in the background, stands the Statue of Liberty.[1]

> DAVID: There she lies, the great Melting Pot—listen! Can't you hear the roaring and the bubbling? There, the gaps in her mouth.
> [He points east.]
> —the harbor where a thousand mammoth feeders come from the ends of the world to pour in their human freight. Ah, what a stirring and a seething! Celt and Latin, Slav and Teuton, Greek and Syrian,—black and yellow—
> VERA: [Softly, nestling to him]
> Jew and Gentile—
> DAVID: Yes, East and West, and North and South, the palm and the pine, the pole and the equator, the crescent and the cross—how the great Alchemist melts and fuses them with his purging flame! Here shall they all unite to build the Republic of Man and the Kingdom of God. Ah, Vera, what is the glory of Rome and Jerusalem where all nations and races come to worship and look back, compared with the glory of America, where all races and nations come to labor and look forward![2]

With the curtain's close, a chorus sang "My Country, 'tis of Thee." Then, as playwright Israel Zangwill, an English Jew, went on stage, someone shouted: "That's a great play, Mr. Zangwill." With that, President Theodore Roosevelt gave his approval.[3]

Zangwill's play sanctioned ethnic intermarriage. University of Chicago historian Arthur Mann interpreted Zangwill as "saying that the authentic . . . the real American ought to be an American of mixed ancestry. Zangwill made intermarriage a cause. Its success depended . . . on the disappearance of ethnic groups and their institutions."[4]

---

1. Arthur Mann, "The Melting Pot," in Richard Bushman et al., eds., *Uprooted Americans: Essays to Honor Oscar Handlin* (Boston: Little, Brown and Company, 1979), 292–95.

2. Israel Zangwill, *The Melting Pot: A Drama in Four Acts* (New York: Macmillan Company, 1909), 198–200.

3. A week after the play, the president permitted Zangwill to dedicate it to Roosevelt. He wrote Zangwill: "I do not know when I have seen a play that stirred me as much." See Mann, "The Melting Pot," 292–95.

4. Ibid., 294–95. It is unclear whether Zangwill coined the term "melting pot." Widely acclaimed, the play institutionalized the notion of America as an ethnic melting pot. As quoted in Mann, the *New York Herald Tribune* wrote: "Seldom has an author so molded thought by the instrumentality of a single phrase."

Foreign-Language Press Thrives in 1908

Yet as Zangwill popularized the notion of a melting pot, the foreign-language press thrived. It was to nativists a Tower of Babel in print in 1908, yet one that fostered assimilation. Another decade or two would pass before that press would peak. Targeted to the many languages of newcomers, foreign-language periodicals came from quarters that included religious, anti-religious, political, fraternal, and unionist viewpoints. By no means monolithic, these periodicals thrived in urban and rural settings. This press supplied the news, entertainment, and inspiration for millions. During the first decade of the twentieth century, more immigrants legally came to the United States than ever before, and such an influx would not be seen again until the end of the century.[5] One of the few media history scholars who refers to the foreign-language press, Lauren Kessler, in 1984 wrote: "Often these strangers would not read an English-language newspaper, and even if they could, they rarely found their concerns reflected in its pages. Ignored, stereotyped, sometimes ridiculed, these immigrants developed their own alternative press."[6]

This chapter focuses on the alternative press of Italians, Chinese, Latinos, Polish, Czech, Swedish, and Syrians, as well as Germans—then the dominant ethnic publishing force. Drawing from secondary sources and relying on English translations, this chapter is not comprehensive. Nor does it critique in detail scholarly failings of a marginalized sector of media history.[7] The chapter does capture flavors of the immigrant press as it blossomed, its history, and how it related to the creation of journalism education, in particular, the Missouri School of Journalism.[8]

In the 1920s, University of Chicago sociologist Robert Park analyzed the foreign-language press. Today that study remains a benchmark. Park compiled a quantitative list of newspapers from thirty-one language groups, reflecting their creation, longevity, and demise. From 1884 until 1920, these groups included Armenian, Bulgarian, Chinese, Croatian, French, Finnish,

---

5. From 1901 until 1910, 8 million immigrants were admitted to the United States. That represented a watershed number until the 1990s when more than 8.6 million arrived. See Web site for the Population Resource Center, http://www.prcdc.org/summaries/usimmighistory/usimmighistory.html. Accessed May 2, 2006.

6. Lauren Kessler, *The Dissident Press* (Beverly Hills, Calif.: Sage Publications, Inc., 1984), 18.

7. For an eloquent critique, see Hanno Hardt, "The Foreign-language Press in American Press History," *Journal of Communication* 39, no. 2 (Spring 1989): 114–31.

8. Although the Irish press was vibrant, it is excluded here because it was published in English. Neither does this study consider the ethnic press of African Americans or Native Americans.

German, Italian, Spanish, Slavic, Scandinavian, and Welsh newspapers. In that time, 3,444 such newspapers were established; a great majority, 3,186, stymied by wartime regulations, ceased by 1920. The year 1908 was emblematic; there were 1,183 foreign-language newspapers. More than half, 656, were published in German.[9]

Italian-language publications alone, from 1850 to 1930, accounted for one thousand titles. In 1910, forty Italian periodicals represented a circulation of 548,000. That year twenty-three Yiddish publications had a circulation of 808,000. Kessler wrote: "Print culture increasingly gained importance among . . . immigrants at the turn of the century, becoming . . . an instrument with which they fashioned ethnic identities and ethnic communities."[10]

Although discrepancies occurred with how to calculate foreign-press circulation, Park in 1920 estimated it at 10 million. That year, *Literary Digest*, according to Kessler, estimated 1,500 foreign-language publications with a circulation of 8 million and published in 33 languages in every state. The *American Newspaper Annual and Directory* estimated circulation at 7.6 million. Park cited a telling discrepancy: a Romanian newspaper, *Mare,* in New York, claimed 6,000 in circulation but was not in the newspaper directory. Yet Park quotes the July 15, 1920, issue declaring the newspaper as "the oldest and most popular Rumanian weekly in the United States. Reaches 50,000 peoples." Kessler quoted Park to say that in New York even the most insignificant language groups published periodicals. Park asserted: "There is . . . a definite relation between the foreign-language press and immigration."[11]

In 1883 Emma Lazarus wrote in "The New Colossus,"

Give me your tired, your poor,
Your huddled masses yearning to breathe free.[12]

As if in response, 1.3 million immigrants in 1907 legally came to America. Even into the twenty-first century, this was the largest number in a single year. The 1910 census indicated that immigration was at its highest: 15 percent of the population was born in a country other than the United States.[13]

9. See Robert E. Park, *The Immigrant Press and Its Control* (New York: Harper, 1922), table XVIII, between pp. 318 and 319.

10. Kessler, *The Dissident Press*, 17–19.

11. Park, *The Immigrant Press*, 296, 314; Kessler, *The Dissident Press*, 90.

12. Emma Lazarus, "The New Colossus," in Janet Gray, ed., *She Wields a Pen: American Women Poets of the Nineteenth Century* (Iowa City: University of Iowa Press, 1997), 215.

13. Lawrence H. Fuchs, "Immigration Reform in 1911 and 1981: The Role of Select Commission," *Journal of American Ethnic History* 3, no. 1 (Fall 1983): 69–70. See also annual listing of the U.S. Bureau of Citizenship and Immigration Services Web site at http://www.census.gov/statab/hist/HS-09.pdf.

Letters new immigrants wrote to Europe contributed to "endless chains" of migrations.[14] Kessler wrote: "Between 1901 and 1920, 3.25 million Italians, 1.5 million Poles, 1 million Germans, and hundreds of thousands of Greeks, Japanese, French, Scandinavians, Dutch, and Bohemians came. . . . Most arrived penniless, friendless, and unable to speak or read the language of their adopted homeland."[15] But they could read, or relatives or neighbors could read to them, from newspapers in their native tongue. In analyzing newspaper creation versus extinction, Park concluded, "The press of the earlier immigration is in general declining, that of the newer is increasing or holding its own."[16]

As immigration cycles have continued, so have those of the foreign-language press. For example, as Kessler wrote, a vibrant Vietnamese-language press developed in the 1970s when refugees fled Southeast Asia after the Vietnam War.[17] In Missouri, as Latino immigration increased in the late twentieth century, the Missouri School of Journalism worked with volunteers to create *Adelante,* a free Spanish-English paper. A typical story in the April 2006 issue was entitled "La nacion opina. Immigracion, en la mente de Estados Unidos y en la agenda politica." Translation: "The nation speaks. Immigration is on America's mind and the agenda of lawmakers."[18]

Similar to present-day arguments,[19] in the early twentieth century immigration "led to a fierce debate," Lawrence Fuchs wrote. This controversy, he said, centered on whether to limit immigration and how strict limits might be. As part of the debate, in 1907, the U.S. Congress instituted the Dillingham Commission, named after Vermont Republican Senator William Dillingham. Ten years earlier, President Grover Cleveland vetoed a literacy test that Congress had narrowly approved. The president said Congress was trying to exclude immigrants. Literacy tests posed complications for Republicans whose business constituency relied on immigrant labor. Likewise, Republican President Theodore Roosevelt feared that immigration restrictions

14. June Granatir Alexander, "Staying Together: Chain Migration and Patterns of Slovak Settlement in Pittsburgh Prior to World War I," *Journal of American Ethnic History* 1, no. 1 (Fall 1981): 56.

15. Kessler, *The Dissident Press,* 88.

16. Park, *The Immigrant Press,* 314.

17. Kessler, *The Dissident Press,* 109.

18. The monthly newsmagazine's purpose is "to serve the rapidly growing population of Spanish-speaking immigrants as they seek to bridge the cultural and language gaps they find here." See http://journalism.missouri.edu/about/media.html. Accessed May 2, 2006.

19. Randal C. Archibold, "Immigrants Take to U.S. Streets in Show of Strength. Planned Boycott Evolves into Protests," *New York Times,* 2 May 2006, A1; Greg Ip, "Trade and Immigration Battles of the Past Offer Lesson for U.S. In 1920s and 1980s, as Today, Political Response Is Key; Crackdown vs. Compromise," *Wall Street Journal,* 1 May 2006, A1.

would worsen his chances to negotiate with Japan at a time when "yellow peril fever" plagued the West Coast. Illegal immigration and asylum for refugees long would remain a hot topic, as would a key assumption: new immigrants likely would not become "good Americans." Three years later, the commission approved a literacy test that, in the context of World War I, became law in 1917, President Woodrow Wilson's veto notwithstanding.[20]

To glimpse America, and its foreign-language newspapers, of a century ago, one can walk through cemeteries where one will find the names of the kinds of people who read foreign-language newspapers, names similar to those now part of the patchwork quilt of the United States: Bast, Friedrichs, Hans, Kies, Perowicz, Zarnik, Hessoun, Koudelka, and Magnuson.

From Vermont to Wisconsin, Missouri and beyond, foreign-language newspapers told about precious moments of births in families; the tragedies of death and divorce; and the events from city halls, the governors' mansions, the White House, and capitals abroad. The papers reported news from foreign homelands and from the new homeland with its lodge meetings, robberies, or church socials.

In southeastern Missouri in 1908, the *Deutcher Volksfreund,* or *German Folk Friend,* reported the news for German-language readers of Cape Girardeau, Perry, and Scott counties. On January 2, 1908, if you read the front page with its old-style, German *fraktur* typeface, you would have learned that four rabbit hunters had an adventure when they shot an animal they could not identify at first but later realized was a bobcat. Blinded in one eye, the angry animal fled up a tree. The newspaper reported: "It got down out of the tree, seized the shooter's foot. The shooter was fruitlessly protecting himself with the unloaded rifle. Just then, the dogs pounced on the bobcat. It had no trouble defending itself against the dogs. But that gave the hunters another opportunity to shoot and kill the animal. The cat was 4 feet, 3 inches long."[21]

That same month in 1908, a Swedish newspaper in Missouri, the *Kansas City Tribunen,* reported on January 2 that a traveling library of Swedish books, a "Vandringsbibliotek," would visit Kansas City. Supported by Swedish King Oscar II, the project was designed to "create a link between Swedes in far-away countries." The following week the newspaper detailed the December 7 death of that king. Entitled "The Last Words of King Oscar," the article reported his dying words to his relatives and wife, the Queen of Sweden. The King told them: "God bless you all."[22]

20. Fuchs, "Immigration Reform in 1911 and 1981," 58.

21. "A Hunting Adventure. A Large Bobcat Is Killed Near Gordonville," *German Folk Friend,* 2 January 1908.

22. See *Kansas City Tribunen.* 2 January 1908 and 9 January 1908.

Who Were These Immigrant Readers?

In an age without radio or television, and with silent movies in their infancy, foreign-language periodicals served as critical communication outlets. Readers of these periodicals were like those people huddled together on shipboard and depicted in that famous photograph by Alfred Stieglitz in 1907, "The Steerage."[23] With words, Edward A. Steiner, in his 1906 book, *On the Trail of the Immigrant*, captured what Stieglitz did on film. In the chapter "At the Gateway," Steiner recounts the European immigrant view of the New York harbor and Ellis Island where federal officials determined who among the immigrants could remain:

> With tickets fastened to our caps and to the dresses of the women, and with our own bills of lading in our trembling hands, we pass between rows of uniformed attendants, and under the huge portal of the vast hall where the final judgment awaits us ... Mechanically ... we are examined for general physical defects and for the dreaded trachoma, an eye disease, the prevalence of which is greater in the imagination of some statisticians than it is on board immigrant vessels.[24]

As he made a reportorial journey through Manhattan's lower East Side, Steiner noted: "The two great social factors of the [New York Jewish] Ghetto are the Yiddish newspapers and the theatre, each of them in some degree entering into the life of every dweller of the Ghetto, as indeed each of them is a mixture of good and ill; a battlefield of past ideals and modern aspirations. The paper most in evidence on the street is the *Jewish Vorwaerts*, the Social Democratic organ."[25]

Definition of the Immigrant Press

Scholars debate what constituted the turn-of-the-century immigrant press. The terms themselves, "immigrant press," "foreign-language press," and "ethnic press," provoke controversy. Even identifying and counting the

23. See Sarah Greenough, *Alfred Stieglitz: The Key Set. Volume One 1886–1922* (New York: Harry N. Abrams, Inc., 2002), 190–94.

24. Edward A. Steiner, *On the Trail of the Immigrant* (New York: Fleming H. Revell Company, 1906), 64.

25. Ibid., 167.

ethnic groups is problematic, as Sally Miller has noted.[26] Park characterized the majority of the foreign-language press as commercial. To a lesser degree, he found fraternal organizations or institutions made up a second group, and a third group propagandized its readers. The earliest such press developed from religious organizations and those opposing them.

Critical Gap in Journalism Scholarship on the Immigrant Press

Contemporary scholars, such as Robert Harney and Hanno Hardt, have decried the lack of scrutiny of the foreign-language press. This oft-ignored press, Harney asserts, is filled with rich documents "through which we can reach some understanding of the mentalities and psychic maps of immigrants."[27] Complaining of an "ethnocentric bias" by media historians who eschewed researching the immigrant press with its "fugitive character," Hardt wrote that "the foreign-language press and other alternative or minority newspapers played a significant role in the strengthening and the defense of political freedom. . . . [T]his press continues to fulfill important cultural and political tasks in American society by occupying a different role in the minds of its readers than the English-language press."[28]

Scholar Sally Miller has complained, too. She wrote: "Given its importance in the various communities . . . and the vitality and growth of ethnic studies over the last two decades, the scant attention paid . . . is remarkable." Even as Miller wrote this in the 1980s, she argued that the predicted demise of the ethnic press was incorrect: "War displacement of hundreds of thousands of people and revised federal immigration policies have led to what may be a renaissance of the ethnic media."[29]

Making an additional critique, Rudolph J. Vecoli has pointed out that media historians have fixated on Robert Park's question: "Did the non-English-language press retard or facilitate the assimilation of the foreign born?" Cultural studies scholars have proposed alternative questions: How

---

26. Sally M. Miller, ed., *The Ethnic Press in the United States: A Historical Analysis and Handbook* (New York: Greenwood Press, 1987), xii-xiv. Stephan Thernstrom, ed., *The Harvard Encyclopedia of American Ethnic Groups* (Cambridge, Mass: Belknap Press of Harvard University, 1980) lists ninety groups.

27. Rudolph J. Vecoli, "The Italian Immigrant Press and the Construction of Social Reality, 1850–1920," in James P. Danky and Wayne A. Wiegand, eds., *Print Culture in a Diverse America* (Urbana and Chicago: University of Illinois Press, 1998), 18.

28. Hardt, "The Foreign-language Press in American Press History," 128.

29. Miller, *The Ethnic Press in the United States*, xi.

did the immigrant press construct "social reality and identity in the minds of the audiences" and how did the immigrant press embody "the site . . . of a struggle over meaning." Vecoli invoked theorists Stuart Hall and his "critical paradigm" and Antonio Gramsci and his idea of hegemony by a ruling elite.[30]

As an example, Vecoli cited factions in the Italian immigrant press vying "for hegemony over the immigrant masses." These contestants included "Italian nationalists, Americanizers, Roman Catholic clergy, the *prominenti* (the colonial elite), and the *sovversivi* (meaning radicals of various stripes). . . . Newspapers, magazines, and books took on an importance they lacked in the old country."[31]

Theories of the Role of the Immigrant Press

Scholars of the foreign-language press have offered competing visions for how it functioned: The immigrant press hastened acculturation. The immigrant press thwarted acculturation. It functioned as a "textbook" and "schoolroom" for immigrants, educating them about citizenship in an alien land. The newspapers provided news from motherlands and the new homeland. "The existing English-language press did not suit their need," Kessler wrote. "Even those few who could read English, or those who quickly learned, found the conventional press irrelevant. . . . Newspapers were written for the already acclimated 'older immigrants'—the American middle class—who had very different informational needs than the new immigrants. What these new immigrants needed, in addition to their religious organizations and self-help societies, was a press of their own."[32]

The creation and growth of the foreign-language press, Park argued, resulted from the suppression of a free press in the countries from whence the immigrants had come. Although Park said he could not supply the facts, "it seems probable that more foreign-language newspapers and periodicals are published and read in the United States, in proportion to the foreign-born population, than are published in the home countries in proportion to the native born." To illustrate, Kessler wrote: "By 1920 there were more Slovak papers in the United States than . . . in Hungary." This proliferation

---

30. Vecoli, "The Italian Immigrant Press and the Construction of Social Reality," 18–19.

31. Between 1900 and 1910, a huge range of literacy existed among immigrants—from as high as 99 percent among Scandinavians to as low as 35 percent among Portuguese. See Ibid., 17–19.

32. Kessler, *The Dissident Press*, 89.

stemmed, Park argued, from the immigrants' pressing need to know. "News is a kind of urgent information that men use in making adjustments to a new environment, in changing old habits, and in forming new opinions." Park said immigrants who passed through Ellis Island faced "the novelty of the American environment" and grappled with "lack of adjustment to it."[33]

Beyond that, Kessler has suggested the foreign-language press accomplished two things: "promoting Americanization while preserving feelings of ethnicity." These facets provoked controversy. "By publishing American news, the foreign press helped immigrants become familiar with U.S. events, ideas, and customs," Kessler wrote. Yet at the same time the press nurtured affections for the Old World, contributing to a self-imposed isolation.[34]

Beginning in the 1890s, immigrants had an incentive to learn to read, especially those fearing literacy admission tests. Vecoli advocated that viewpoint: "Contrary to the stereotype of . . . illiterate foreigners, immigrants did read and write. As evidence, they left an enormous library of publications that run the gamut from newspapers, periodicals, almanacs, books, pamphlets, and broadsides."[35]

The Missouri School of Journalism and the Immigrant Press

Although the Missouri School of Journalism had two students from China auditing its first class, in its early decades the school ignored the immigrant press.[36] This was not new. Even in 1880, when University of Missouri English professor David Russell McAnally taught a course called "History of Journalism," there was an international emphasis, but not an immigrant-press focus; the class examined the London *Times* but ignored the foreign-language press, including the vibrant ethnic press of Missouri and the surrounding region.[37]

33. Park, *The Immigrant Press*, 7–9; Kessler, *The Dissident Press*, 91.
34. Kessler, *The Dissident Press*, 91–92.
35. Vecoli, "The Italian Immigrant Press and the Construction of Social Reality," 18.
36. Thomas Benedict Hammond, "The Development of the Missouri Press," Master's thesis, University of Missouri, 1922, supervised by Walter Williams. "The Development of the Missouri Press" ignores the foreign-language press. An appendix of nineteenth- and twentieth-century Missouri newspapers does list immigrant newspapers. Most are German, including a St. Louis one that Joseph Pulitzer purchased, the *Staats Zeitung*, in 1874 (see pp. 155–56).
37. Ronald T. Farrar, *A Creed for My Profession: Walter Williams, Journalist to the World,* 89–90.

Mastheads of some foreign-language newspapers in the United States in 1908.

Walter Williams, the globe-traveling founder and first dean of the Missouri School of Journalism, focused outwardly, too. Six years before the school opened, he traveled to Switzerland. He persuaded the International Congress of Press Associations to hold its next gathering in St. Louis during the World's Fair and Louisiana Purchase Exposition. With five thousand journalists from thirty-seven countries and the United States, the group met in St. Louis and changed its name to the World Press Parliament.[38]

Despite Williams's global interests and although several Missouri journalism classes emphasized elements of the international press, documents from Missouri reveal an absence of the immigrant press in the curriculum. Neither did the ethnic press in general nor that in Missouri receive any noteworthy attention.[39] Course descriptions of two Williams classes, "History

38. See ibid., 84–86. Williams in 1904 again persuaded the organization to change its name, this time to the Press Congress of the World.

39. Author Steve Weinberg says that for research on a book on the centennial of the Missouri School of Journalism, *A Journalism of Humanity: A Candid History of the World's First Journalism School* (Columbia: University of Missouri Press, 2008), he learned that the school's documents from the early twentieth century contain no reference that links the school and the nation's foreign-language press. Conversations with Weinberg, Fall 2005.

and Principles of Journalism" and "Comparative Journalism," included no reference to it; neither did ones in advertising, publishing, reporting, writing, and editing. Williams's required history course, according to Sara Lockwood Williams, a Missouri journalism professor married to Williams, "considered briefly the history of printing of the earliest newspapers on the continent of Europe, in England, and in the United States . . . the effect of journalism as a social force." The "Comparative Journalism" course considered "types of newspapers throughout the world." Introduced in 1925, a course titled "International News Communications" focused on "cables, wireless, and news distribution" and did not in any way appear to address or explore the immigrant press.[40]

As stated above, in 1908, the first class at the Missouri School of Journalism did contain two students from China, Dong Xianguang (or Hollington Tong) and Huang Xianzhao (or Hong Hin). Chinese media historian Yong Volz notes: "By 1938, almost thirty Chinese students had studied at Missouri, accounting for ninety percent of those who studied journalism in America.[41] Upon returning to China, they became publishers or editors of leading newspapers in China and as a result, as Sun Jui-chin observed in 1935, these papers 'adopted the American way of presenting the news.'"[42]

German

The Missouri School of Journalism's lack of attention to the foreign-language press is puzzling given that the immigrant press, especially German-language newspapers, flourished throughout Missouri and gave a start to one of the world's foremost journalists, Joseph Pulitzer.

The Hungarian immigrant came to the United States as a potential soldier willing to serve as a Civil War draft replacement. Pulitzer arrived in New York near the war's end. After serving briefly, he was discharged. He was told, as a joke, that if he wanted a job, he should head to St. Louis, Missouri, the nation's fourth-largest city and a place where employment was not as plentiful as the jokesters implied.[43]

After three years of scrounging for jobs, Pulitzer landed on St. Louis's notable German-language newspaper, the *Westliche Post*, edited by Carl

40. Sara Lockwood Williams, *Twenty Years of Education for Journalism*, 73–89.

41. See Yong Volz, "Transplanting Modernity: Cross-Cultural Networks and the Rise of Modern Journalism in China, 1890s-1930s," Ph.D diss., University of Minnesota, 2006.

42. Jui-Chin Sun, "New Trends in the Chinese Press," *Pacific Affairs* 8 (March 1935): 56–65, 49.

43. Farrar, *A Creed for My Profession*, 126–27. See also Denis Brian, *Pulitzer: A Life*, 7–11.

Schurz. As President Abraham Lincoln's minister to Spain, Schurz was prominent in journalism and politics.[44]

For his part, in the mid-1870s, Pulitzer failed in an attempt to buy a weekly German-language newspaper in New York, the *Belletristische Journal*. A few years later, while writing for Charles Dana's *Sun* in New York, Pulitzer failed to persuade Dana that he should edit a German-language version of the *Sun*. Then, in 1878, Pulitzer did succeed in buying the run-down English-language *St. Louis Dispatch*. This set the stage for him to become one of the most significant journalists in the world.[45]

Although Pulitzer left behind the German-language press, it remained the main provider of news in a language other than English. To understand the German press, one must consider its origins and know that a German-language newspaper on July 5, 1776, scooped all other periodicals: it reported ratification of the Declaration of Independence.[46]

Cited as the earliest immigrant publication is *Philadelphische Zeitung*, which Benjamin Franklin first published on May 6, 1732. The German-language paper did not last long, perhaps two issues, and was aimed at some twenty thousand German immigrants in Pennsylvania. Readers likely did not respond well to translations made by Louis Timothee, the French Protestant printer Franklin had hired; Timothee misspelled German words, and non-German words peppered the paper. Despite the demise of *Philadelphische Zeitung*, for the next two hundred years the German-language press established itself as the dominant foreign-language voice. As soon as 1739, another German-language newspaper was born.[47]

By 1870, an estimated 1.6 million U.S. residents listed Germany as their birthplace. Five to six million Americans spoke German.[48] By the turn of the century, the numbers had grown larger: more than eight million residents said that Germany was their native land or that at least one parent was German-born.

Nonetheless, Edward Steiner criticized Germans in America for failing to sustain the vitality of their native culture. Steiner wrote in 1906: "With few exceptions the German stage nor the German newspaper has been able to keep alive that intellectual spirit.... [E]ditors ... were all intent upon telling

44. Brian, *Pulitzer*, 11–14. In 1869, Schurz had become a U.S. senator from Missouri, the first German-born U.S. citizen elected as a senator. Later Schurz was secretary of the interior in the cabinet of President Rutherford B. Hayes.

45. W. A. Swanberg, *Pulitzer* (New York: Scribner's Sons, 1967), 34–36, 27–37.

46. Kessler, *The Dissident Press*, 95–96.

47. Carl Wittke, *The German-Language Press in America* (Lexington: University of Kentucky Press, 1957), 10–15, 15–20.

48. Ibid., 201.

me how great their papers were and how many subscribers they had, and I could not go beyond the business point with any of them, although I wasted two hours upon one, trying to get a glimpse of his German soul; but if I saw it at all, it had the American dollar-mark written all over it."[49]

Italian

Between 1900 and 1915, about three million Italians left for the United States, contributing to the formation of "one of the most vibrant labor movements in North America." Italian-language newspapers in America reflected that vibrancy. From the late nineteenth century until 1910, ten Italian labor-movement newspapers, with longevity of at least fifteen years and some for decades, were established across the nation. These included *Mastro Paolo* in Philadelphia, *Il Proletario* in New York, *Critica* in San Francisco, and *Corriere di Chicago* in Chicago. The labor movement had an anarchistic bent that contributed to the periodicals' short life spans. The anarchistic newspapers were poorly funded. The workers themselves were isolated from the American labor movement. Dirk Hoerder wrote, "The only political and ideological common ground for Italian radicals was Italy. The Italian anarchist leaders . . . traveled extensively to the United States, starting journals, publishing pamphlets, traveling on propaganda tours, organizing debates."[50]

This ideological passion is reflected in the Barre, Vermont, Italian newspaper, *Cronaca Sovversiva,* or *Subversive Chronicle,* self-described as the "anarchical weekly magazine of revolutionary propaganda." Under the title, "Even Death Is Unfair," one 1908 article reported: "The average life of rich people exceeds 60 years, the average life of poor is between 20 and 30 years." Millions of people die in Europe, the article said, "because of their social conditions (lack of healthy air, decent hygiene or a harmonious job.)"[51] Prominent Italian-born anarchist Luigi Galleani edited the newspaper.

Besides this anarchistic press, newspapers flourished in Little Italys; some five hundred were started between 1900 and 1920. Ten Italian dailies were published, including ones in New York, San Francisco, and Boston. Often published by jack-of-all-trades operators who gathered news, sold

---

49. Steiner, *On the Trail of the Immigrant,* 100–101.

50. Dirk Hoerder and Christiane Harzig, eds., *The Immigrant Labor Press in North America, 1840s-1970s: An Annotated Bibliography,* vol. 3 (New York: Greenwood Press, 1987), 1, 20, 6–7, 20–21.

51. "Even Death Is Unfair," *Subversive Chronicle,* 4 January 1908.

subscriptions and ads, set type, and delivered papers, they sometimes sold political support "to the highest bidder."[52]

Robert Park reported on such corruption and economic vulnerability, including the case of Louis N. Hammerling. An immigrant from Poland, Hammerling blossomed from a Pennsylvania Polish newspaper worker into a Republican operative on a national scale. At the same time, he organized, in 1908, the American Association of Foreign Language Newspapers. Eventually, as many as eight hundred newspapers joined. Hammerling functioned as a public relations man, ad agent, and go-between for anyone wanting to get messages into foreign-language newspapers.[53]

Hammerling's influence and billings grew so much that a U.S. Senate committee called him to testify about propaganda for Germany and for the brewing and liquor industry. When asked if his organization exercised control over individual newspapers, Hammerling replied had he had no more power over newspapers than "the Pope has in a synagogue."[54]

Hammerling, who had obtained his immigration documents fraudulently and was in the United States illegally, was, Park concluded, "the first man who made any attempt to put advertising in the foreign-language papers on a sound business basis. But the opportunities for 'honest graft' were large."[55]

Spanish

For 1908, Robert Park recorded fifty-one Spanish-language newspapers in the United States. Within a decade, that number had doubled. Yet few scholars have addressed the Spanish-language press. Clint Wilson II and Félix Gutiérrez assert: "Journalism history is often told in terms that emphasize the English-speaking traditions of the media but ignore the historical past of other people. Although it may be useful to look to Europe to find some of the roots of media in the United States, a scholar looking there and nowhere else will get only a partial view of the media's rich history."[56]

As Wilson and Gutiérrez point out, the first chapter of Isaiah Thomas's *The History of Printing in America* in 1810 focused on the development of the

52. Vecoli, "The Italian Immigrant Press and the Construction of Social Reality," 20–21.
53. See generally Park, *The Immigrant Press,* 377–411.
54. Ibid., 382.
55. Ibid., 411.
56. Clint C. Wilson II and Félix Gutiérrez, *Race, Multiculturalism, and the Media: From Mass to Class Communication,* 2nd ed. (Thousand Oaks, Calif.: Sage Publications, 1995), 171.

Spanish-language press in the Americas in the sixteenth century in Mexico, a century before the development of the colonial press in New England. When the book was reprinted in 1864, that chapter was deleted. By 1941, a journalism textbook, written by the University of Missouri's Frank Luther Mott, gave a footnote to the thriving Spanish-language press in sixteenth-century Mexico. Wilson and Gutiérrez say Mott claimed that New England's newspapers were the first ones regularly published in North America.[57]

The first Spanish-language newspaper in the United States was published in New Orleans in 1808. While the Napoleonic Wars raged in Europe, Spanish-language readers benefited from the bilingual publication of *El Misisipí*. The pro-Spanish newspaper provided news from Europe and contained advertising, too.[58] Two other important Spanish-language newspapers of that era were *El Mexicano* in 1813 and *El Crepúsculo de Libertad* in 1834.[59]

Two scholars in the 1970s, Herminio Rios and Guadalupe Castillo, listed 372 Mexican-American newspapers dating before 1940. The establishment of 136 of those papers occurred in the nineteenth century. In that era, wrote Carlos E. Cortes, the newspapers "took strong editorial positions, ranging from criticism of societal discrimination to appeals for action and changes of behavior among Mexican Americans." By 1910, following the Mexican Revolution, what had been scant immigration when compared to the European immigration became major. Soon half a million Mexicans arrived. With them came Spanish-language newspapers, especially in the Southwest—some 203 papers existed between 1900 and 1930.[60]

Another development of the Spanish-language press sprang from tens of thousands of literate immigrants, most of them men and single, fleeing political turmoil in Spain. Some 105,000 came, mostly through New York, between 1890 and 1920 and often banded with Cuban, Puerto Rican, and Italian immigrants to fight for workers' rights.[61] Labor union newspapers, including ones for cigar factory workers in New York, resulted from this

57. Ibid., 174–76.
58. Ibid., 177. As with newspapers of that era, the news could be several months old and often came from abroad via ships' captains and sailors.
59. Hoerder and Harzig, *The Immigrant Labor Press in North America*, 154.
60. Carlos E. Cortés, "The Mexican-American Press," in Miller, ed., *The Ethnic Press in the United States*, 248–50. Lauren Kessler argues that the Mexican-American press of the Southwest is not an "immigrant" press and that "the Anglo pioneers who encroached . . . were the immigrants." See Kessler, *The Dissident Press*, 89.
61. Hoerder and Harzig, *The Immigrant Labor Press in North America*, 156.

cooperation. Among the newspapers were *El Despertar*, published from 1891 until 1912; *Cultura Proletaria*, published from 1910 until 1959; and *Brazo y Cerebro*, published in 1912.

The cigar industry of Florida also spawned a thriving press. Two anarchist newspapers were begun in Tampa and Ybor City: *El Esclavo* in 1894 and *La Voz del Esclavo* in 1900. In Tampa and Ybor City, beginning in 1906, immigrants provided the readership of *El Internacional*, the first labor newspaper for Florida cigar workers.[62]

Chinese

The first Asian-language newspapers appeared in the 1850s, shortly after the California Gold Rush of 1849 when Chinese immigrants answered the call for miners. *Kim-Shan Jit San-Luk* (*The Golden Hills' News*) was a combination of Chinese characters and English translation. A second Chinese-language newspaper, *The Oriental*, appeared in the early to mid-1850s. Both originated from Christian missions based in China and San Francisco where a Chinatown was developing. The publications advocated for immigrants who labored under arduous conditions and faced ethnic prejudice. The publications also had the motivation to convert Chinese readers to Christianity.[63]

By 1900, *Chung Sai Yat Po* was established in San Francisco. It lasted fifty years. The newspaper, historian Yumei Sun has argued, countered the conventional wisdom of the nineteenth and twentieth century that Chinese immigrants came with the single goal of making money that would allow them to return prosperous to China and support their families. Sun argues that *Chung Sai Yat Po* "helped the Chinese break through their social and cultural isolation and, in effect, become Americans." The newspaper was so much a part of everyday life that, according to one journalist in the early twentieth century, you could "hardly enter a Chinese home in California without seeing a copy. . . . Among the upper classes even the ladies read [it] as they sip their tea." The newspaper's founding editor, Ng Poon Chew, according to Sun, considered his periodical "a beacon of journalistic integrity in an age of yellow journalism and racism."[64]

62. Ibid., 155–57.

63. Wilson and Gutiérrez, *Race, Multiculturalism, and the Media*, 189–92.

64. Yumei Sun, "San Francisco's Chung Sai Yat Po and the Transformation of Chinese Consciousness, 1900–1920," in Danky and Wiegand, eds., *Print Culture in a Diverse America*, 85–97.

Arabic

Although Arabic-speaking immigrants were small in number, some one hundred thousand arrived between 1880 and World War I, and they created a vital foreign-language press. Twenty-one periodicals were published in Arabic, catering mostly to Syrian immigrants. The majority of the papers were in New York, but others were in cities such as Philadelphia and St. Louis. Scholar Alixa Naff has written that "the press brought elements of American life and values not experienced by Syrians themselves to the attention of the immigrants and provided guidance.... [I]t also idealized and oversimplified, presenting America, as a rule, in uncritical and glowing terms."[65]

The first Arabic-language paper, *Kawkab Amrika* (*Star of America*), was published in New York from 1892 until 1907. With local and foreign news, it was edited and published by two sons of an elite physician and educator. The newspaper gained permission from an Ottoman Empire sultan to introduce Arabic characters for typesetting in America. With an explicit political stance that backed the Ottoman Empire, *Kawkab Amrika* reflected a worldview that supported the Eastern Orthodox Christian Church.[66]

Polish and Czech

As with other foreign-language papers of the era, the January 1908 editions of a Polish newspaper in Stevens Point, Wisconsin, and a Czech newspaper in St. Louis function as a windows to the world of immigrants. Immigration is the subject in story after story, though a story, as was the custom then, may be only a sentence or two in length.

The January 3, 1908, issue of *Rolink,* or the *Farmer,* the Polish paper, reported this: In Canada, its minister of labor will travel to Japan to discourage further immigration. In Ogden, Utah, two hundred white men mobbed a neighborhood of Japanese immigrants, shouting: "Death to Asians. Hang Japanese." In Warsaw, officials warned Jewish immigrants about fraudulent immigration agents. Later, on January 31, 1908, *Rolink* reported under "News from USA" that a New York immigration inspector had traveled to North Carolina to investigate how six Russian immigrant families lost their money to dishonest realtors.[67]

---

65. Alixa Naff, "The Arabic-Language Press," in Miller, ed., *The Ethnic Press in the United States,* 2–4.

66. Ibid., 6–7.

67. See *The Farmer,* Stevens Point, Wisconsin, 3 January 1908, 24 January 1908.

In St. Louis, the Bohemian Literary Society published the biweekly *Hlas*, which means "voice." Its motto: "For the faith, for the language!" In 1908, the newspaper declared itself, after thirty-five years of publishing, as "the oldest newspaper of the Bohemian Catholics in America."

Datelined Vienna, a January 3, 1908, story, "Do Not Go to the United States!" reported that Austrian magazines warned against emigration to America. Many newcomers, after having difficulty finding employment because of a widespread financial crisis there, had returned to Europe. Under the headline "Mass Deportation of Immigrants," another story told of one hundred immigrants sent back to Europe because they suffered from trachoma, an eye disease. "Among these, Mrs. Lydia Ostermueller was extremely unlucky," the story said. "She arrived with her husband and small child. The child fell ill . . . had to be taken to a hospital. She and the child were forbidden to enter."[68]

Conclusion

After his study of the foreign-language press, sociologist Robert Park concluded that these periodicals illuminate "the inner life of immigrant peoples and their efforts to adjust themselves to a new cultural environment."[69] As Lauren Kessler has noted, though, Park neglected to mention that this press was not always welcomed in communities where it was published and read.[70]

Welcomed or not, the immigrant press thrived in the early twentieth century. For days, weeks, months, or years, in cities and villages, Chinese, Czechs, Germans, and Swedes established newspapers to serve communities in ways the English-language press could not or would not. By no means monolithic, the foreign-language press served as a "textbook" for homesick newcomers. Nonetheless, with an outlook that was at once local, regional, national, and international, the immigrant press was distinguished from many English-language newspapers that had narrow local interests. With its coverage, the immigrant press transcended geographical boundaries, functioning in many ways as the first global journalism.

The evolution of this press mirrored immigration patterns, when millions arrived; in some cases more in one year than ever before or since. Their arrival created political, social, and economic upheaval and opportunities that were reflected in the press itself.

68. See *The Voice*, St. Louis, Missouri, 3 January 1908.
69. Park, *The Immigrant Press*, xix.
70. Kessler, *The Dissident Press*, 91.

The lack of a connection between the Missouri School of Journalism in 1908 and the immigrant press points to potential gaps in pedagogy and scholarship today. As an indicator of how the United States continues to experience demographic change through immigration, and as an indicator of how the Missouri School of Journalism has adapted a century after its founding, the school publishes its own foreign-language periodical, *Adelante*. It serves a burgeoning population of Spanish-speaking immigrants in central Missouri, where a century and a half ago Germans first arrived.

Whether from the early twentieth century or today, Robert Park's findings hold true: "Foreign-language newspapers . . . are a power to be reckoned with in the Americanization of immigrants."[71]

In addition, significant is the clarion call by scholars who urge research of the foreign-language press. The lack of scholarship, according to Hanno Hardt, represents a "failure to overcome linguistic or cultural barriers." By correcting this, as Hardt makes clear, we could "enrich our understanding of American society through close analyses of foreign-language sources."[72]

71. Park, *The Immigrant Press*, 359.
72. Hardt, "The Foreign-language Press in American Press History," 128.

CHAPTER 16

Forced to the Margins

The Early Twentieth-Century African American Press

Earnest Perry and Aimee Edmondson

When Walter Williams founded the Missouri School of Journalism in 1908, the country's minorities were invisible in those first classes and for the most part in the pages of the *University Missourian*. African Americans were free from slavery thanks to the Civil War, but the failures of Reconstruction and the enactment of Jim Crow laws led to second-class citizenship and denial of admission to universities in former slave states. Too, at Missouri, there is no evidence that the classes, including Williams's "History and Principles of Journalism," mentioned African American journalists or their press, despite the fact that the black press by that time had existed for more than eighty years.[1] If the laboratory newspaper, the *University Missourian*, covered African Americans at all, it was about the unusual or as victims, such as the "Case of Race Riot on Trial for Murder,"[2] concerning the

---

1. Ronald T. Farrar, *A Creed for My Profession: Walter Williams, Journalists to the World*, 140–43; plus 160–61 and the Appendix, which had a copy of "The History Quiz," a Spring 1915 final examination, 239–42. *Freedom's Journal* was established in 1827 in New York City.
   2. "Case of Race Riot on Trial for Murder," *University Missourian*, 15 September 1908, 1. Also, that first week, "Night Riders in Illinois, Arola Farmers Guard Their Property,"

Springfield, Illinois, race riot in 1908, in which six thousand African Americans left Springfield.[3] This chapter will cover the status of the African American press in the midst of the nation's conflicting views about the status of African Americans as journalism education begins.

Equal education for African Americans was not part of the early professionalism of the founding of the first School of Journalism. In 1908 African Americans were denied access to the University of Missouri, and it would take forty-three years before that policy changed following a major failed discrimination lawsuit and desegregation at other universities. But the initial change in Missouri was only for courses not then offered at the state's historically black college, Lincoln University in Jefferson City.[4]

African American students in Missouri were to go to Lincoln Institute, founded in Jefferson City in 1866 by former Civil War soldiers of the 62nd Missouri Colored Volunteers, which had been recruited into the Union Army.[5] In 1921, the school's name changed to Lincoln University. In response to the University of Missouri's successful legal battle to keep out African Americans, Lincoln first offered journalism courses and a major in 1942 to accommodate Lucile Bluford's request for admission.[6] Bluford, then an editor at the African American *Kansas City Call*, had applied for graduate acceptance in 1940 to the Missouri School of Journalism's masters' program. During the court battle in 1942, administrators cancelled all graduate coursework in journalism, blaming World War II for declining enrollment. Bluford and others said officials shut down the graduate program in order to preserve segregation.[7]

---

16 September 1908, 1. See also previous chapters in this book by Bonnie Brennen on labor and Janice Hume on magazines.

3. William English Walling, "The Race War in the North," in Arthur Weinberg and Lila Weinberg, eds., *The Muckrakers: The Era in Journalism That Moved America to Reform — The Most Significant Magazine Articles of 1903–1912*, 234.

4. Several key U.S. Supreme Court rulings began eroding *Plessy v. Ferguson*'s application to higher education. In *Sipuel v. Oklahoma State Regents*, 332 U.S. 631 (1948), the court held that the state must offer college courses for blacks as soon as it did so for whites. In *McLaurin v. Oklahoma State Regents*, 339 U.S. 637 (1950), the court held that blacks must receive the same treatment as their white classmates in the university setting. In *Sweatt v. Painter*, 339 U.S. 629 (1950), the court ruled that the state must provide facilities of comparable quality for black and white students, holding that a black law school was not equal to that of the prestigious University of Texas program.

5. Albert P. Marshall, *Soldiers' Dream, A Centennial History of Lincoln University of Missouri* (Jefferson City: Lincoln University, 1966).

6. *State Ex. Rel. Bluford v. Canada*, 153 S.W. 2nd 12.

7. Diane E. Loupe, "Storming and Defending the Color Barrier at the University of Missouri School of Journalism: The Lucile Bluford Case," *Journalism History* 16 (Spring/Summer 1989): 26; Marshall, *Soldiers' Dream*, 24.

Bluford's case relied on an earlier Missouri case where the U.S. Supreme Court required that either the requested courses or majors be offered at Lincoln or the student be given admission to the University of Missouri. In 1935 a Lincoln graduate, Lloyd Gaines, had applied to Missouri's law school. In 1938, the U.S. Supreme Court struck down Missouri's law that paid African American students' tuition to schools outside the state, ruling that Missouri must admit Gaines or create a law school at Lincoln.[8] In 1939 Lincoln's law school opened with thirty students.[9]

Before the Civil War, there was no higher education system per se for any black students. Early schools, though called universities and institutes, primarily provided elementary and secondary education. The first was the Institute for Colored Youth, founded in Cheyney, Pennsylvania, in 1837, followed by Lincoln University in Pennsylvania in 1854 and Wilberforce University in Ohio in 1856. By the early 1900s, they began postsecondary training.[10]

Thus, African American journalists received their training on the job, some with the black national news service, before moving on to noteworthy careers with black newspapers.[11] Many of the news service reporters were actually volunteers. Anybody could file stories for the service.

Before the rise of the *Chicago Defender* in 1905, African Americans could not make a living as journalists, lamented Richard Thompson in 1902. "It is a stinging indictment of our much lauded race pride that the greatest proportion of our Negro journalists are compelled to depend for a living upon teaching, preaching, law, medicine, office holding or upon some other outside business investment."[12]

With the rise of historically black institutes, then colleges and universities, came more outlets for students to learn the craft. For example, Enoch Waters, a longtime reporter and editor at the *Chicago Defender,* got his start as a Hampton Institute undergraduate, where he covered intercollegiate sports for the student newspaper, the *Hampton Script.*[13] Hampton Institute, which began in 1868, did not have a journalism major until 1967.[14] Today, the *Script* goes to press once every two weeks.

8. *Gaines v. Canada,* 305 U.S. 337 (1938).

9. Marshall, *Soldiers' Dream,* 23.

10. U.S. Department of Education, Office of the Secretary, White House Initiative on Historically Black Colleges and Universities.

11. Lawrence D. Hogan, *A Black National News Service, The Associated Negro Press and Claude Barnett, 1919–1945* (London and Toronto: Associated University Presses, 1984).

12. As quoted in ibid., 26.

13. Enoch P. Waters, *American Diary: A Personal History of the Black Press* (Elizabeth, N.J.: Path Press, 1987).

14. U.S. Department of Education, Office of the Secretary, White House Initiative on Historically Black Colleges and Universities, Washington D.C.; http://www.hamptonu.edu/shsjc/aboutschool/, accessed November 29, 2007.

The oldest historically black journalism school, Howard University's John H. Johnson School of Communications, was founded in 1971. The student newspaper, *The Hilltop*, is distributed weekly during the semester.[15]

There were African American newspapers before 1908, the earliest being *Freedom's Journal*. Begun in 1827, the *Journal* opened the door for African Americans to tell their stories in their own words. In the eighty-one years between the first African American newspaper and the founding of the world's first school of journalism in 1908, the nation first fought its neighbor to the south and then its countrymen in the South. The War with Mexico secured Texas, a slave state, and increased the size of the country. It also increased tension between abolitionists, mainly found in the North, who sought an end to slavery, and Southerners, who wanted to maintain the practice that fueled their agricultural economy and was a large part of the regional culture.[16]

When the Civil War ended slavery, the black press shifted from seeking freedom from slavery to promoting the race. While the Reconstruction era offered more opportunities, the postwar decades also brought tremendous danger. As African Americans began to establish communities, set up businesses, and garner power, many whites grew angry over their inability to keep former slaves "in their place." In 1865, newly installed Southern state legislators enacted "black codes," a precursor to Jim Crow laws that hindered African Americans' economic and political progress. In response, Congress passed a Civil Rights Act in 1866 over President Andrew Johnson's veto that declared that anyone born in the United States is a citizen regardless of race, color, or previous condition of slavery. However, over the next century, various groups worked to undermine the law and deny African Americans equal rights.[17]

In the aftermath of the Civil War, the black press became more of a symbol of cooperation and community building when it came to dealing with the white establishment. The connection between the church and the black press began mainly as a major way to disseminate information: the minister would talk about the newspaper on Sunday, and the editor would write stories and publish announcements about upcoming church events.[18] That relationship continues today.

15. *Historically Black Colleges and Universities, Profiles of 91 Popular Schools* (New Orleans: Wintergreen/Orchard House Inc., 1995).

16. Armistead S. Pride and Clint C. Wilson III, *A History of the Black Press* (Washington, D.C.: Howard University Press, 1997), 115.

17. Ibid., 85–86.

18. Ibid., 88.

By the start of the twentieth century, there were about one hundred African American newspapers. Many of them started in the last decade of the nineteenth century in response to the end of Reconstruction and the 1896 "separate but equal" ruling in the Supreme Court's *Plessy v. Ferguson* decision. That court ruling gave constitutional weight to Southern Jim Crow laws that made it illegal for blacks to use the same public and private facilities and services as whites, including transportation, hotels, hospitals, recreation facilities, and schools. Some scholars suggest that the *Plessy v. Ferguson* decision also ushered in an era of violence, both sanctioned and vigilante, against African Americans.[19]

The *Plessy* decision also provided legal tools to disenfranchise African Americans in all aspects of American life. In response, African Americans were forced to create their own separate sphere. While some African Americans did not agree with the separation, the dominant voice within the race, Booker T. Washington, promoted the doctrine of accommodation in an 1895 speech. He said that if African Americans succeeded economically and socially, it would prove to whites that they were equal to them. The speech, referred to as the Atlanta Compromise, was well received by whites who heralded Washington as a leader who both African Americans and whites could support.[20] Washington, founder of the Tuskegee Institute in Alabama, received substantial financial support from many white philanthropic organizations. These organizations embraced Washington because his philosophy helped maintain white supremacy.[21]

An intraracial conflict grew, however, when other African Americans disagreed with Washington. This conflict ushered in an era of press partisanship that pitted the accommodationists, led by Washington, against militants, led by W. E. B. DuBois, the most dynamic, intellectual African American of the early twentieth century. DuBois, a Harvard-educated scholar, had been long involved in pushing for African American political involvement. As a professor at Fisk College in Nashville (1885–1888), where he had earned his first degree, DuBois began understanding the Southern African American disenfranchisement and racial violence. He disagreed with Washington's accommodationist stand; rather, DuBois saw that African Americans would be unable to gain equality without agitation.[22]

19. William G. Jordan, *Black Newspapers and America's War for Democracy, 1914–1920* (Chapel Hill: University of North Carolina Press, 2001), 16–17.

20. Ibid., 18.

21. Kevin K. Gaines, *Uplifting the Race: Black Leadership, Politics, and Culture in the Twentieth Century* (Chapel Hill: University of North Carolina Press, 1996), 36–38.

22. Jean Folkerts and Dwight L. Teeter, Jr., *Voices of a Nation: A History of Mass Media in the United States* (Boston: Allyn and Bacon), 294–95.

Before the Atlanta Compromise speech, DuBois had given Washington tacit support, but as Washington's stature and power grew, DuBois began to criticize "The Wizard."

Both Washington and DuBois used the African American press to further their own agendas, much like the nineteenth-century partisan press. The leading editors of the day were T. Thomas Fortune of the *New York Age,* a Washington supporter, and Monroe Trotter of the *Boston Guardian,* a Harvard friend of DuBois. Fortune began his newspaper career as a typesetter for the *Rumor,* the precursor to the *New York Age,* but as editor he changed the name to the *Globe* and began writing editorials that promoted civil rights. When the *Globe* folded, Fortune launched the *New York Freeman* in 1884 but left three years later for the white daily, the *New York Sun.* Fortune turned over the *Freeman* to his brother, Emmanuel Fortune, Jr., and his partner, Jerome B. Peterson. In the meantime Emmanuel Fortune and Peterson changed the name of the *Freeman* to the *New York Age* on October 15, 1887. After his brother Emmanuel's death in 1891, T. Thomas Fortune returned to the *Age* and remained for the next twenty years, while still continuing his relationship with Washington.[23]

In fact, the *Age* became Washington's vehicle to promote his conservative agenda. Washington supported the *Age* and other African American newspapers financially by giving money to them directly or steering advertising their way. In return, they carried stories and editorials generated by the Tuskegee news bureau run by Emmett J. Scott. The arrangement generated a great deal of publicity for Washington. His stature grew among white political leaders, which gave him enormous power. For example, an African American had to have Washington's endorsement before he or she could be hired for a government job or receive a government contract. A well-placed news article in a Washington-controlled newspaper could be the difference between success and failure for many African Americans in the late 1800s, according to media historian Charles Simmons.[24]

On the other side, the journalist Monroe Trotter, the first African American elected to Phi Beta Kappa at Harvard, despised Washington's accommodationist philosophy; the negative feeling was mutual. In 1901, Trotter, who had left the real estate and insurance business, started the *Boston Guardian* in the same building that had housed abolitionist William Lloyd Garrison's *Liberator.* Trotter's *Boston Guardian* carried news from all over the country. Yet, the big draw of the publication was the editorial page. Trotter

23. Pride and Wilson, *A History of the Black Press,* 121–22.
24. Charles A. Simmons, *The African American Press: With Special Reference to Four Newspapers, 1827–1965* (Jefferson, N.C.: McFarland and Co., 1998), 21–22.

argued against Washington's policies and the dangers of not pushing for racial equality in all areas, including politics and higher education.

In 1903, Trotter and his partner, George Forbes, challenged Washington as he gave a speech in Boston. A riot ensued, and Trotter and Forbes were arrested and sentenced to thirty days in jail. Washington retaliated by covertly starting newspapers in Boston. Each one of them failed, while the *Guardian* maintained its dominance among African Americans in the Northeast. DuBois agreed with Trotter's motives, but denounced his actions, according to historians Armistead S. Pride and Clint C. Wilson.[25]

In fact, DuBois went so far as to write a chapter about Washington and the evils of his accommodation philosophy in his 1903 groundbreaking book, *The Souls of Black Folk*. Washington stepped up his attack using Fortune's *New York Age* and other Tuskegee machine organs. However, with the founding of the Niagara Movement, precursor to the National Association for the Advancement of Colored People, Washington's loss of political influence signaled the end of his reign, according to DuBois's biographer.[26] When Washington died in 1915, the African American leadership, including those in the black press, had begun to take a more militant stand against Jim Crow. Northern black newspapers openly criticized white leadership policies.

After 1912, President Woodrow Wilson's failure to live up to his promise of curtailing discrimination in federal employment in return for African American votes had turned many African Americans against politicians from either party. The black press entered a new era. Gone were the days of partnership. There was no allegiance to Washington or DuBois. Each editor had to answer to his own paper's readers and the African American community at large. By then, the black press had moved from the era of the elites to the era of the masses.[27]

In order to reach the masses, the black press had had to change its philosophy. During Washington's accommodation era, a majority of the black newspapers, especially those in the South, were careful in condemning discrimination and racial violence for fear of being attacked. Probably the most famous African American journalist to be run out of the South for aggressively reporting and editorializing on violence against African Americans was Ida B. Wells. As editor of the *Memphis Free Press*, Wells fought racial injustice, especially the practice of lynching. In 1892, while she was in New York City, a group of whites, unhappy about the paper's coverage of the murder of three African American Memphis businessmen, burned down

25. Pride and Wilson, *A History of the Black Press*, 123–24.

26. David Levering Lewis, *W.E.B. DuBois: Biography of a Race* (New York: Henry Holt and Co., 1993), 286–87.

27. Jordan, *Black Newspapers and the American War for Democracy*, 10–11.

the *Free Press* offices. Wells remained in New York as a correspondent for Fortune's *New York Age,* but later she moved to Chicago, where she married the *Conservator* editor, Ferdinand L. Barnett.[28]

Wells-Barnett continued her fight for civil rights as a journalist for both the black press and the *Chicago Inter-Ocean,* a white publication. She also traveled the lecture circuit to speak on the evils of lynching.[29] Wells-Barnett, DuBois, Trotter, and others ushered in the era of a more militant African American press. Their press of the early 1900s attracted readers in large part because they challenged the status quo. However, most of the black press agitation occurred in the North; it was too dangerous to be a militant journalist in the South.

The black press in the South also faced the significant problems of a low literacy rate and poverty. Despite Washington's urging for African Americans to learn the basic skills of reading, writing, and simple math, many did not have the means to do so. Available schools were scarce, and it was more important to sustain the family than buy a newspaper. When there was time for a newspaper, it not only provided important news about employment but also kept African Americans abreast of the overall condition of the race, according to Pride and Wilson.[30]

As Washington's influence faded, DuBois and the NAACP replaced the philosophy of accommodation with a more aggressive approach to fighting for civil rights. For the next fifty years, the NAACP and the African American press would work together in the fight for equality and against racial violence. Some of those newspapers were in Missouri.

Missouri's first African American newspaper, *Negro World,* established in 1875 in St. Louis, was followed by eight other newspapers, mainly in Kansas City and St. Louis. Most of them died during the economic recession of 1907. Primarily family-run or connected to churches or fraternal organizations, they were mostly weeklies. The most famous Missouri African American newspapers, the *St. Louis Argus,* the *Kansas City Call,* and the *St. Louis American,* were started between 1912 and 1928. The *Argus* (1912), the oldest, championed equality and increased job opportunities for African Americans. The *American* took a similar stand but differed from the *Argus* by supporting the union formation of the Brotherhood of Sleeping Car Porters, which had its headquarters in St. Louis.[31]

---

28. Folkerts and Teeter, *Voices of a Nation,* 232–33.
29. Ibid., 233.
30. Pride and Wilson, *A History of the Black Press,* 129–30.
31. Vanessa Shelton, "Bennie Rodgers: Dean of the St. Louis Black Press," paper presented at the American Journalism Historians Association Convention, Portland, Oregon, 1999, 8–10.

In Kansas City, the African American newspapers followed a similar path. The *Call* was by far the most successful newspaper for publishing stories of African American achievement and pushing for civil rights in education and housing. Lucile Bluford, managing editor of the *Call* in 1932, became well known as an African American editor from Missouri because of her unsuccessful lawsuit against the University of Missouri for refusing admission to African Americans. The Missouri School of Journalism had accepted students from all over the world since its founding, but did not admit African Americans until 1950.[32]

Several newspapers epitomized the changing black press in the early 1900s. The *Chicago Defender*, founded in 1905 by Robert S. Abbott, was one of the first African American newspapers to cater to the masses. Abbott also published stories based on "race loyalty." Abbott's biographer, Roi Ottley, called it "racial propaganda" as there were no bylines or signed columns, nor stories that reflected negatively on the African American community.[33] There was little in the early editions about the discrimination and violence African Americans faced in Chicago and elsewhere; that type of journalism would come later and would position Abbott as a leader in the black press. Rather, Abbott had national news of the day on the front page, and devoted the rest of the paper to local news, mainly the activities of prominent people in Chicago's African American community.[34]

Advertisements in the early *Defender* were primarily for services, not products. The services ranged from barbers to lawyers to butchers to rooms for rent. Advertising was not a moneymaker for the *Defender* or any African American newspaper until after World War II. Major advertisers did not see the African American community as a viable market until the 1950s and 1960s.

Abbott and others in the black press made their money in circulation. In the early days, "Abbott was his own newsboy."[35] Along with reporting and writing and printing the paper, he was also responsible for folding and delivery. In delivering the paper, Abbott learned a lot about the community, making his newspaper coverage better.[36] He almost failed in the early days when he fell behind in his printing bills. He was forced to use the dining room table in the boardinghouse where he lived as an office for the next fifteen years. He

---

32. Ibid., 9.
33. Roi Ottley, *The Lonely Warrior: The Life and Times of Robert S. Abbott* (Chicago: Henry Regnery Co., 1955), 105.
34. Pride and Wilson, *A History of the Black Press*, 135–37.
35. Ottley, *The Lonely Warrior*, 96–99.
36. Pride and Wilson, *A History of the Black Press*, 137.

did not forget the generosity of his landlady. In 1916 he bought her an eight-room home in appreciation.

Abbott's growing success resulted in the hiring of J. Hockley Smiley as managing editor in 1910. Smiley transformed the bland pages of the *Defender* into a paper that resembled the white Chicago papers. Abbott still instilled his race propaganda into the headlines and stories, and the sensational era of *Defender* was born.[37]

In another part of the country around the turn of the twentieth century, the Murphys of Maryland built the *Afro-American*, which was an outgrowth of three small church papers: the *Ledger*, the *Sunday School Helper*, and the *Afro-American*. John S. Murphy, Sr., who owned the *Sunday School Helper*, had purchased the *Afro-American* at auction for two hundred dollars in 1892. The *Ledger*, run by Dr. George F. Bragg, pastor of St. James Episcopal Church in Baltimore, merged with the *Afro-American* a short time later.[38]

From its inception, the *Afro-American* was an independent newspaper from a political standpoint. Despite his religious roots, Murphy remained independent of churches and fraternal organizations. He also refused advertising from liquor distributors or their establishments. Just like Abbott and the *Defender*, Murphy promoted race propaganda. However, the *Afro-American* was not as sensational in its presentation as the *Defender*.[39]

Murphy used his newspaper to battle racial discrimination in education, employment, and transportation in the Baltimore-Washington, D.C., area. He financed the legal fight to end segregation of trains out of Washington to the South. Murphy also used his publishing and financial muscle to open the University of Maryland's law school, Maryland Art Institute, and other graduate programs to African Americans. He is known for promoting racial uplift and civic involvement, especially support for African American businesses and professionals.[40]

In the West, African Americans who had fled Jim Crow laws during reconstruction began establishing towns in states like Oklahoma, along with forming newspapers. Some supported the philosophy of Booker T. Washington, while other editors used their newspapers to agitate against the newly enacted segregation legislation passed by Oklahoma lawmakers. By the early 1900s, almost every African American newspaper in Oklahoma had begun to protest against the new disenfranchisement of African Americans. They also countered Washington's philosophy by encouraging

37. Ottley, *The Lonely Warrior*, 96–99.
38. Pride and Wilson, *A History of the Black Press*, 133.
39. Ibid., 134.
40. Ibid., 134–35.

African Americans to move to Oklahoma and not stay in the South, as Washington had begged. As the number of lynchings increased, these newspapers began to run the stories of violence prominently and published editorials against the practice.[41] Their press would become a political power.

Any history of the black press would be remiss if it did not address the issue of lynching, continuing in 1908. The period after Reconstruction saw a rash of violent acts committed against African Americans. Most of this was done in an effort to keep the former slaves fearful, docile, and subservient to whites. In the 1880s and 1890s, there was an average of two hundred lynchings a year. The effort by the black press to combat this practice was led by journalist Ida B. Wells. While on the staff of the *New York Age,* Wells wrote about racial justice and established anti-lynching societies around the country. Twice she toured Great Britain to lecture on the topic. During her second tour in 1894, American politicians reacted negatively to her speeches and articles, which were filled with statistics and other evidence.

In an effort to discount Wells's creditability, the president of the Missouri Press Association, John W. Jacks, wrote an incendiary letter to the secretary of the British Anti-Lynching Society, Florence Balgarnie, attacking Wells's character and morals in an effort to discredit her words, remove her British support, and stop her tour.[42] His efforts were for naught. Wells continued and used Jacks's message as a way to unite African American women in the First National Conference of Colored Women of America in July 1895. Later, after marrying and moving to Chicago, she also began to advocate for better treatment of African Americans in Chicago. Wells-Barnett, one of only two women to attend the Niagara Movement meeting in 1909, did not participate in the founding of the NAACP.[43]

Wells-Barnett was not the only African American journalist forced to flee the South after editorializing against lynching. Alex Manly, editor of the *Wilmington Daily Record* in North Carolina, left after commenting that white women accused African American men of rape to save their own reputations. The article, reprinted in the *Raleigh News and Observer,* set off mob violence that led to the murders of thirty African Americans and the burning of the *Daily Record* and other African American businesses. The attacks against militant African American editors in the South squelched protests in some areas, but in cities such as St. Louis, Dallas, Richmond, and

41. Henry Lewis Suggs, *The Black Press in the Middle West, 1865–1985* (Westport, Conn.: Greenwood Press, 1996), 267–95.

42. Jacqueline Jones Royster, "Introduction," *Southern Horrors and Other Writings, The Anti-Lynching Campaign of Ida B. Wells, 1892–1900* (Boston: Bedford Books, 1997), 37.

43. Pride and Wilson, *A History of the Black Press,* 94–95.

Nashville, African American editors continued to expose and editorialize against lynching.[44]

Mary Church Terrell, like Wells-Barnett, used the black press to battle racial injustice. Terrell, whose father was one of the richest African Americans in the South, worked closely with famed civil rights leader Frederick Douglass. She studied in Europe for two years and returned to teach and become a school administrator. After moving to Washington, D.C., she became the first African American woman appointed to a school board in the United States. With her family's wealth and her education, she could have lived a less stressful life than most African Americans, but she chose the path of an activist and a leader in the women's suffragist movement.[45]

Early in her journalism career, Terrell wrote for numerous publications, including the *Woman's Era*, the *Colored American*, and the *New York Age*. She focused on racial discrimination, especially in employment, education, and voting rights. She often challenged the white-owned press to stop its practice of misrepresenting African Americans. She complained that the white press referred to African Americans as inferior, lazy, or criminal. Broussard found that articles she submitted to white-owned publications which refuted the misrepresentations were not published.[46]

Just like Wells-Barnett, Terrell wrote extensively against lynching. She also criticized the South for perpetuating a paternalistic attitude toward African Americans. Terrell wrote that African Americans were capable of taking care of themselves if given the same rights and privileges as whites. While Terrell has received little recognition of her accomplishments as a journalist during her time, in recent years African American press scholars have begun to take a fresh look at her career.[47]

The African American press began to shift from the accommodationist views of Washington to take a more militant stand against disenfranchisement by 1908. The northern African American newspapers, particularly the *Chicago Defender*, championed African American migration away from the South. At the urging of Abbott's *Defender* and other newspapers, more than one million African Americans left the South. The *Defender* printed the train schedules and job information to people who fled north for a better life.[48]

Once they arrived in the North, Abbott published their letters to loved ones back in the South, letting them know that they made it safely. Pride and

44. Jordan, *Black Newspapers and America's War for Democracy*, 20–22.

45. Jinx C. Broussard, "Mary Church Terrell: A Black Woman Journalist and Activist Seeks to Elevate Her Race," *American Journalism* 19, no. 4 (Fall 2002): 13–36.

46. Ibid., 13–36.

47. Ibid., 13–36.

48. Suggs, *The Black Press in the Middle West*, 24–27.

Wilson wrote that the migration of African Americans to the North became such a concern to Southern businesses, especially those connected to agriculture, that circulation of the *Defender* was outlawed in certain areas. To get around the laws, the *Defender* used African American Pullman train porters to distribute the paper as they traveled through the South.[49]

In 1909, James H. Anderson started what would become one of the most influential African American newspapers on the East Coast. The *Amsterdam News*, based in Harlem, championed African American empowerment and union organization. During the 1930s and 1940s, the *News* would be one of the main supporters of Adam Clayton Powell, an influential African American congressman from New York City.[50]

On the West Coast during the first decade of the twentieth century, John Neimore, founder of the *California Owl*, later known as the *Eagle*, was building a great African American newspaper. After Charlotta Spears joined the staff in 1910 and then inherited the paper following Neimore's death, she purchased modern presses and helped African Americans moving west. She led the African American press's campaign against the pro–Ku Klux Klan film *Birth of a Nation*. In 1914, she married Joseph Bass, who took over as editor and publisher and continued the *Eagle's* tradition of championing the cause of the downtrodden into the 1930s. After his death, she led again for the next two decades.[51]

The early 1900s saw significant change for the African American press. As the conservative philosophy of Washington faded, it was replaced by a more militant tone espoused by DuBois. African American journalists, such as Robert Abbott, John Murphy, Ida B. Wells-Barnett, and others, ushered in an era of advocacy and racial uplift in their communities. In 1908, African Americans lived in a world separate from whites and those found in the faculty and student body at the University of Missouri's journalism school. No journalism school was available for African Americans during the next decade. Much like the nineteenth-century trade apprenticeships, the African American press provided not just their only journalism education but also the news and information of concern to those outside the mainstream in Missouri and elsewhere.

---

49. Pride and Wilson, *A History of the Black Press,* 136.
50. Jordan, *Black Newspapers and America's War for Democracy,* 34.
51. Ibid., 34–35.

CONCLUSION

1908:

The Aftermath

Betty Houchin Winfield

The year 1908 saw journalism at a watershed: the push for professionalization within the field had reached a point of critical mass, the extremism of yellow journalism had nearly run its course, and a vision of improving journalism through formalized education was gaining in appeal. Walter Williams was just one national visionary whose solution was academic training in a school of journalism.

The efforts of journalism leaders like Williams meant that the process of educating new journalists, which was on the cusp of change in 1908, would become less centered on individual apprenticeships at newspapers and other news media. The industry was growing too large for careful mentoring. There would be no returning to the craftsmanship days and solo apprenticeships of the Benjamin Franklin era. Increasingly, schools and departments of journalism within American universities and colleges would be the sources of journalism education in the twentieth century.

As academic departments and schools mushroomed, journalism leaders sought to establish an agreed-upon common curriculum and standards. Walter Williams surveyed some two hundred colleges and universities in

1912 to learn what journalism-related courses existed. He found that thirty-two higher-education institutions offered similar writing/reporting instruction in journalism, with three professional schools established and seven departments of journalism.[1] A century later, in 2008, there were more than four hundred schools and departments listed in the *Journalism and Mass Communication Directory.*

Those early journalism leaders would seek a consensus on a journalism curriculum. With the rise of the first professional organization for journalism educators in 1912, leaders such as Williams and Willard Bleyer at the University of Wisconsin would lead the way in establishing a broad-based liberal arts education as a knowledge foundation for journalists. In time, courses in social and natural sciences would join liberal arts classes as part of the degree requirements. The views of Williams and Bleyer were widely accepted, and a century later journalism undergraduate students were required to take, on average, some 73 percent of their courses outside of the journalism unit.

Employers of university graduates in journalism would know that their new hires not only had a broad-based education but also had been taught particular journalism courses ingrained with a particular school's methods. The mushrooming professional organizations would reinforce those values through membership requirements and with continuing education. Thus, the year 1908 became a critical point in the change and development of journalism's many educational dimensions. In the decades following 1908, people working full time in journalism would increasingly think of themselves as professionals.[2]

The power of professionalism through university education was bound to have an impact. With professionalism and advanced education would come agreed-upon standards. A school or department of journalism could define the terms, bring coherence to a fledgling field, establish unity, and indicate what was acceptable. University graduates would have not just the skills to be a journalist but also knowledge of the field's accepted values. Classes in journalistic principles and institutional courses described the acceptable and even laudatory behavior expected of professionals. Students would understand the larger reasons for their work and the public responsibility of journalism, and would be aware of the examples set by the field's past heroes, martyrs, and scoundrels. Extreme behavior could be condemned and sloppiness could be rooted out. With university education,

1. Tom Dickson, *Mass Media Education in Transition: Preparing for the 21st Century* (Mahwah, N.J.: Lawrence Erlbaum Associates, Publishers, 2000), 15.
2. See Burton J. Bledstein, *The Culture of Professionalism: The Middle Class and the Development of Higher Education in America*, 86–87, for a definition of professionalism.

journalism as a field grew in status and became recognized as a respectable calling, taking its rightful place among other professions.

A university education helped augment journalists' self-image and served journalism's professional rise by protecting and promoting professional standards. Having professional authority meant being certified as possessing superior knowledge about journalism skills and concepts. The university-based approach provided the credential of academic degrees and the advantage of alumni networks, as well as resources such as scholarly and professional journals, books, and research monographs.

The earliest journalism curriculum perpetuated the principle that American journalism was to be a watchdog over government, a critic and an agent for its citizenry. Courses would promote the examples set by Benjamin Harris, John Peter Zenger, Horace Greeley, Harry Croswell, and Thomas Nast, among others.[3] Journalism had a duty to discuss government affairs, report its malfeasances and errors, and warn of the dangers to the community. Williams and the Missouri School of Journalism practiced what they preached. The first issue of the *University Missourian* carried a top-front-page article on tainted food in the local jail. The watchdog role of the American press continued with the coverage of the Warren Harding administration scandals in the 1920s; by the 1950s it became a mantra of the "public's right to know," and it held fast through legal contests concerning institutional protections for the news media in the late 1970s.

The connections between journalism and politics remained strong, and not just as a result of news coverage. Possible conflicts of interest had to be sorted out when numerous journalists became officials or candidates. As one example, Walter Williams served on the University of Missouri Board of Curators, appointed by the governor, when the Missouri School of Journalism was being formed. Many other journalists served on commissions, boards, and agencies, or sought public office; a couple of prominent examples from the era surrounding 1908 included newspaper publisher William Randolph Hearst, who sought the Democratic Party nomination for president in 1904, and William Howard Taft, elected president in 1908, whose family owned the *Cincinnati Times-Star*.

The connections between the press and government had been strong prior to 1908 and remained strong a century later, but in different forms. Many newspapers kept vigorous editorial allegiances to a particular party until World War II, when a drop in competitive newspapers ended their partisanship, as noted by Betty Winfield's chapter on the press-government

3. Ronald Farrar, *A Creed for My Profession: Walter Williams, Journalist to the World*, 160–61.

relationship. A century later cable and radio networks, as well as Web sites such as Moveon.org and Townhall.com, have espoused particular ideological viewpoints and party identifications.

When the press was too aggressive, there has been recourse. For almost two-thirds of the twentieth century, officials, citizens, and even competing newspapers had a strong retaliation: libel suits, as noted by Sandy Davidson in her chapter on legal jurisprudence in 1908. Yet, a century later, prosecutions for seditious libel against public officials and public figures has all but ceased with the Supreme Court's decision in the famous *New York Times vs. Sullivan* case in 1964 and subsequent cases. Even falsehoods, as long as they were not proved to be malicious, had First Amendment protection, the Court said. Legal issues involving the press continue into the twenty-first century in other areas, such as privacy, particularly Internet privacy.

From a legal standpoint, the Supreme Court recognized journalism's connection to free expression through its rulings in post–World War I cases. Such recognition and even protection under the First Amendment at first concerned mainly newspapers, pamphlets, and magazines, but subsequently was extended to speech, books, film, radio, wire services, television, cable, and more recently the Internet.

The practice of journalism was to a follow a code of ethics. Walter Williams gave his own beliefs in the classroom before writing down *The Journalist's Creed* as a working code for all journalists. Besides acknowledging a belief in journalism as a profession, Williams emphasized a public journal's role as a public trust, with responsibilities for accuracy, fairness, and truth. Those standards, as recognized by Williams and his successors, included other aspects of journalism besides news coverage, as noted in the chapter on ethics in 1908 by Hans Ibold and Lee Wilkins. Williams had said that advertising, news, and editorial columns should alike serve the best interests of readers. In fact, the earliest advertising classes emphasized how to avoid hucksterism in the midst of the reform era of the pure food and drugs legislation, as noted by Caryl Cooper in her chapter on advertising in 1908.

Moral responsibility was a topic that resonated among journalists at the beginning of the twentieth century, in an industrial era of self-doubt, insecurity, and journalistic extremes such as sensationalism. Journalism organizations articulated a higher responsibility and had begun instituting codes of etiquette, which became codes of ethics, as discussed by Hans Ibold and Lee Wilkins. Such written codes were part of the structure of Sigma Delta Chi and other journalism-related organizations such as the American Society of Newspaper Editors, which adopted its Canons of Journalism in 1923. Throughout the century, society's demands for accuracy and high standards became so strong that by the 1970s various mass media units added ombudsmen and media critics, and publicly awarded darts and laurels to the best and worst journalism. Some states, such as Minnesota, unsuccessfully attempted to codify journalism's codes of ethics.

After 1908, journalism would change professionally, organizationally, and intellectually. Although the field was without licensing unlike other professional fields—licensing journalists was prohibited under the First Amendment as a form of prior restraint—a university education meant official intellectual recognition. An academic curriculum in journalism would substitute for a licensed clinical approach for teaching the practical demands of the field along with its intellectual foundations. The curriculum encompassed not only the necessary skills of journalism, advertising, and management but also the history of the field, its ethical principles, and its jurisprudence. Too, a program of study would also include journalism's place in a democracy and its societal connections. The floodgate immediately opened for new scholarly endeavors.

The earliest journalism faculty added to the scant offerings of books about journalism in 1908. The need for journalism textbooks and scholarship was present, and journalism faculty immediately filled the void. With libel a major area of contention, Walter Williams wrote *Missouri Laws Affecting Newspapers* in 1912; five years later Frederick W. Lehman released *The Law—The Newspaper.*

For decades afterwards, journalism academics wrote more books with a greater focus on journalism's various components and its intellectual underpinnings. Major studies came as well from other members of the academic community who also focused on various aspects of journalism. These studies included writings about the news process (Walter Lippmann, 1922), the immigrant press (Robert E. Park, 1921), the small-town newspaper (Robert S. Lynn, 1929), and free expression (Zechariah Chaffee, 1941). None of these authors belonged to a journalism faculty. Now, a century later, scholars in all parts of the academy examine journalism; for example, sociologists study journalism concepts, beliefs, and processes; political scientists examine the multiple connections between media, governments, and the public; psychologists study the media's effects on their audiences; English department faculty analyze magazines or other journalism as literature; and American Studies researchers scrutinize how the producers as well as their products impact our nation's culture and society.

After 1908, journalists, whether publishers, reporters, editors, copyeditors, artists, advertisers, public relations agents, or engravers, printers, and production managers, joined other professions as part of the twentieth century's growing middle class. They were followed by other journalists in newer forms of journalism in the twenty-first century. Rising income levels helped. In 1908, big-city journalists were paid from $40 to $60 a week, while their rural brothers and sisters were paid $5 to $20. A century later their counterparts were often being paid some 15 to 57 percent more in terms of today's dollars. Journalism as a profession had raised the economic as well as societal status of practitioners.

Journalism became a "legitimate" calling, valued and ranked with other professions. The field's internal publications, its journals, newsletters, and Web sites, provided members with means of self-expression and offered reflection about their work. The ever-expanding journalism associations pushed particular ideas about their role and tried to make sense of what journalists did and why it was important. Fiercely, journalists pointed to their service to society, their connection to free expression, the significance of a free press and the free speech clauses in the First Amendment of the U.S. Constitution, and advocated journalism's importance to a free democratic society, especially after World War I's legal inhibitions against dissent.

To recognize the best of the best, Missouri began academic honorary organizations such as Kappa Tau Alpha, an academic equivalent of Phi Beta Kappa. It is no accident that departments and schools of journalism sought a means to highlight those who excelled as role models for their neophyte adherents. Visiting professionals gave lectures, conducted workshops, and taught classes. The University of Missouri began Editorial Week in 1909, headlined by well-known muckraking editor Will Irwin, who subsequently critiqued journalism itself in a fifteen-part series.[4] Outside speakers that could inspire as well as challenge the profession became part of Missouri's annual Journalism Week and its sessions with renowned honor medalists.

Distinguished merit in journalism would be celebrated nationally, too. In 1917, Pulitzer Prizes based at Columbia University's School of Journalism began to recognize the best work within American journalism.[5] During the twentieth century, various other kinds of awards were given annually in every area of journalism, in states and geographical regions, as well as nationally. The profession of journalism offered a culture with an expected set of values and responses with acknowledgment of the most meritorious.

During the twentieth century, other parts of the culture focused upon journalism, too. Plays, autobiographies, books, and films would laud the best and pan the worst. They included the popular play *The Front Page* (1928) and a later film based on that work (1931), and the offshoot *My Girl*

4. Will Irwin, "The American Newspaper," *Collier's Weekly* beginning January 21, 1911.
5. The *New York Tribune* received recognition for its anniversary editorial on the sinking of the *Lusitania*, and Herbert Bayard Swope, *New York World*, received the reporting award for his series, "Inside the German Empire."

Walter Williams poses with Dean Talcott Williams of the Columbia University School of Journalism at an organizing conference for journalism educators at elite journalism schools. Date unknown. Courtesy of the University of Missouri Archives.

Friday (1940). Later cinema depictions about journalism concerned broadcast news, libel, news sources, and accuracy: *Network* (1976) and *Absence of Malice* (1981), and then *The Insider* (1999) and *Shattered Glass* (2003). Popular television series involving the day-to-day operations of journalism included the 1970s *Mary Tyler Moore Show* and its spinoff, *Lou Grant*.

A book, *All the President's Men* (1974) by Pulitzer Prize–winning investigative journalists Bob Woodward and Carl Bernstein, also was made into a popular film (1976) and showed not just the power of journalism but also journalism's important connection to a democracy. More and more college students majored in journalism and mass communications, with enrollment in some programs increasing threefold after the 1974 Watergate flood of news stories. Investigative reporting grew and a new organization founded in 1975, the Investigative Reporters and Editors (IRE), set standards and recognized merit. Yet, the usual news process was affected, resulting in the pesky problem of relying on unnamed sources when accountability was demanded.

After 1908, not only did print media change, but so too would modern journalism in all its manifestations. In subsequent years, journalism came to encompass the new technologies of radio, television, cable television, and the Internet with its Web sites, blogs, and individual interactive sites. Universities began including the newest media forms under journalism or mass communication studies as separate departments, sequences, or programs, although the academic offerings often lagged behind the new technologies.

While journalism evolved into new technologies, it also converged into organizations that promoted common purposes among journalists, and between journalism and other institutions. At the beginning of the twentieth century, magazines in particular found common cause with big business, with each side benefiting from national advertising campaigns directed at readers / consumers, as Janice Hume discussed in her chapter on magazines in 1908. Community newspapers and state press associations came together for agreed-upon principles and academic education, as noted in chapters by William Taft and Stephen Banning; Washington correspondents and other groups of journalists formed their own organizations with membership benefits.

The year 1908 signaled the start of the National Press Club (NPC), open, however, only to white male correspondents. In the wake of the civil rights movement, the club eventually included minorities, and in 1985 the all-male NPC merged with the female Woman's National Press Club to become the Washington Press Club.

In the years after 1908, definitions of news varied from one era to another, one region to another, and one medium to another. For all news media, politics and business remained constant topics. News consistently emphasized timeliness, the new and unusual, and the important. By the end of the twentieth century conflict became an important element of the general news definition, often sought, and sometimes overriding other news values. The late nineteenth-century emphasis on sensationalism in coverage of sex, crime, and scandal would more or less continue throughout the twentieth century. As a proven money-maker, sensationalism rose in prominence in the large-city tabloids of the 1920s, again in the 1960s and 1970s supermarket tabloids, returned in full force in the 1990s, and continued into the new century. With the rise of visual media, the focus on celebrities increased, with close coverage of their lives, their actions, and their foibles. The results were entertaining and spilled over into television broadcasts and Web site videos.

Investigative reporting arose during reform eras. The early twentieth-century muckrakers highlighted not just wrongdoing, but the plight of those who had been ignored: immigrants and minorities. Once the muckraking era declined, it became difficult to have aggressive investigative journalism until the public's desire for reform grew again. During the 1960s and the 1970s, the nation was again troubled, this time with civil rights and the Vietnam War. Investigations since that era have included exposure of government and industry greed, agency incompetence and health hazards, and food and toy safety. Many investigations demanded lengthy stories, even a series of lengthy stories, and were usually found in large-city newspapers or magazines.

Yet, magazines changed during the twentieth century. After their golden era in the late nineteenth century and early twentieth century, when they had millions of readers, general-audience magazines such as *Life, Look,* and the *Saturday Evening Post* were struggling by midcentury and had ceased publication by 1972 after national advertisers switched to television. By then, magazines had already begun to specialize and focus on personal interests, such as sports, pulp fiction, hobbies, fashion, and health. Specialized media continued, and now the newest media have Web sites that do what these targeted publications once did.

But with newer venues of journalism, with specific personalized interests and specialized media, less-emphasized types of news coverage became more prominent, particularly in areas of entertainment and sports. In 1908 there was newspaper coverage of entertainment and live artistic performances, albeit not much in smaller newspapers, as Scott Fosdick elaborates in his chapter on the arts. News of sporting events was present in the newspapers of 1908 as well, as Tracy Everbach relates in her chapter. While entertainment and sports remain a part of newspaper coverage, other media forms like radio and cable television emphasize these areas, and by 2008 entire Web sites and blogs were devoted to the arts and sports.

The journalistic standards of 1908, such as accuracy and fairness, continued, but the ideal of objectivity became more prominent. This meant that journalists were to be neutral, reporting the news without prejudice, opinions, or personal involvement. More and more, the aim was to avoid value-laden terms and to seek balance by reporting only facts gathered from reliable sources. For many journalists, the ideal came into question after the media manipulations of Senator Joseph McCarthy and others, and with the rise of alternative forms of journalism such as the 1960s literary journalism and the new muckraking or investigative journalism. The concept of objectivity receded in journalism schools by the end of the century, as scholars examined why objectivity remains an unrealized ideal. They found that the final news product is unavoidably impacted by journalists' habits, traditions, and inherent biases that relate to story selection, while news sources themselves promote their own agendas and emphasize a particular ideology. A century later, balance remains as an important news parameter.[6]

The issues of 1908 fermented throughout the next century, especially concerning journalism work. Labor emerged as a vital force for newspapers, especially urban newspapers, fueled by immigration, urbanization, and financial concerns, as discussed in Bonnie Brennen's chapter on labor. Ethical debates about payment methods, such as the impact of the pay-for-space system, continued until salaries became standard, as noted in Betty Winfield's chapter on press coverage of politicians. By the 1930s the Newspaper Guild represented the concerns of editorial workers, and typographical unions negotiated to change low wages and abysmal working conditions. The fight for newspaper workers' rights continued through the 1970s, with up to thirty or forty strikes per year.[7] As the number of newspapers diminished by the end of the twentieth century, strikes lessened and the loss of revenue could cause the newspaper to close, as happened with the *Pittsburgh Press* in 1992. In the midst of so many new communication technologies that replaced workers, organized union power in the newspaper industry lessened. The labor issues of the twenty-first century now concern age discrimination, sexual harassment, and downsizing.

The labor force itself has changed much in a century. In its first semester in the fall of 1908, the Missouri School of Journalism included no minorities and only six women among its enrollment of sixty-four, and its three full-time faculty members were all white males, as noted in both the Maurine Beasley chapter on women and Earnest Perry and Aimee Edmondson's chapter on African Americans. A century later, women made up almost two-thirds of students in journalism and mass communication programs nationally, and at Missouri a good third of the faculty were female. In 1908, there were no African Americans or other minorities, and only one international student had been admitted at Missouri. In 2008, 13 percent of Mis-

6. Fred Fedler, "News Concepts," in Margaret Blanchard, ed., *History of the Mass Media of the United States, An Encyclopedia,* 428–29.
7. Mary Alice Shaver, "Newspaper Labor Organizations," in Blanchard, ed., *History of the Mass Media in the United States,* 447–48.

souri School of Journalism students were minorities; 8 percent were African Americans, and another 5 percent were international students, reflecting Missouri's longtime connection to international journalism, as John Merrill and Hans Ibold traced in their chapter. The student demographics do not reflect the journalism industry management profile of media owners, editors, and publishers, or news directors and managers, nor the fact that newspapers continue to lose women and minority readers at rapid rate.

Since 1968 academic units have made a concerted effort to reflect the nation's demographics in the training and hiring of journalists. A major reason was the Kerner Commission's report about the 1967 urban racial riots. That study found that the mass media failed to analyze and report adequately on racial problems, primarily because the reporting was from the perspective of a white man's world, which included journalism schools and industry. Since then, both university journalism programs and the mass media industry have made a greater attempt to educate as well as hire more women and minorities. Newer professional organizations have been founded to reflect racial and gender interests. Too, by the 1990s, accreditation for journalism and communication departments, programs, and schools required that efforts be made to sensitize students not only to "a multi-cultural, multi-ethnic, multi-racial society, but also to an otherwise diverse society."[8]

Since 1908, and particularly after World War II, research efforts at journalism and mass communications programs expanded in volume and scope. A new generation of journalism leaders had been affected by their wartime government research experiences in the World War II Office of Facts and Figures. Their academic units put in place seminars and research courses, which increased by 496 percent from 1941 to 1951.[9] Scholars such as Wilbur Schramm (Iowa, Illinois, Stanford), along with others, founded communication studies with a research emphasis on process and effects. They added to previous efforts to generate new knowledge and train academic professionals. Midwestern universities, including Missouri in 1921, had already begun graduate programs in journalism by the 1920s and 1930s.[10] In 1935 Columbia University became a professionally oriented graduate school, with a preference to those students who had bachelors' degrees in liberal arts.[11] The numbers of graduate students rose into the thousands, with an especially rapid increase following World War II. In

8. Dickson, *Mass Media Education in Transition*, 248.

9. Ibid., 31.

10. Maurine E. Votaw, who received a master's degree in journalism from Missouri in 1921, helped set up a journalism program at St. John's University in Shanghai in 1924. Farrar, *A Creed for My Profession*, 167.

11. Dickson, *Mass Media Education in Transition*, 27.

2008, 220 master's students were studying at Missouri, 40 percent of whom were international students.

Doctoral degrees in journalism and then mass communications grew rapidly after World War II, impacting teaching as well as the research about the field. By 1998, most full professors in journalism and mass communication held doctorate degrees. By the end of the century, Fedler et al. found that the percentages of journalism/mass communication faculty with doctoral degrees who taught in professional tracks ranged from 67 percent for those in advertising and public relations to 77 percent for those in broadcasting. At least 80 percent of those who taught institutional courses, such as ethics, mass media and society, law, and theory, held doctoral degrees.[12]

Doctoral degrees in journalism had been around for more than seventy years. Missouri was among the earliest, awarding its first doctoral degree in journalism to Robert Lloyd Housemen, who wrote his 1934 dissertation on early Montana territorial journalism as a reflection of the American frontier and the new Northwest. Journalism history was a main area of study for Missouri doctoral students, especially after the hiring of Frank Luther Mott in 1941, yet the social sciences grew prominent there and elsewhere in the field after World War II. By 2007, there were thirty doctoral students studying at Missouri.

For both undergraduate and graduate education, certain standards remain in place a century later. The goals from the time of Benjamin Harris's original newspaper, *Publick Occurrences,* included truthful reporting and belief in the newspaper as a public trust. The aim was for accuracy and an attempt to overcome the "spirit of lying." The 1908 classroom had the consistent aim of truth, fairness, and accuracy. These ideals were articulated within related journalism organizations and honorary societies. After World War I, bylines would acknowledge the writer's responsibility and accountability. For graduate programs, peer-reviewed research would come to serve a similar purpose as researchers also sought accountability and legitimacy in upholding the ideal of seeking truth.

What was journalism in 1908 had changed vastly a century later. Despite the U.S. population more than tripling in the century after 1908, from 92 million in the 1910 census to 300 million in 2008, the number of daily newspapers dropped almost in half, from about 2,600 in 1908 to 1,480 in 2000. Unlike the lively competing newspaper world of 1908, today, outside of a few large cities, there are few competing newspapers in the same local market. Now, citizens rely far more upon non-newspaper sources of news, including the Internet, magazines, radio, television, and cable.

12. Ibid., 114.

In 1908, newspaper ownership was consolidating, with papers merging within local markets and chains growing across markets, as Fred Blevens discussed in his chapter on the industry. The trend continues today. Just as Frank Munsey predicted in 1905, monopolies have formed within many of the news media. Yet, not even Munsey could have forecast the movement away from community local newspapers inherent in the late twentieth-century consolidations. The economic support system for journalism has grown from the early postal connection of the eighteenth century, to the nineteenth-century government contracts for printing and legal notices, to the era surrounding 1908 in which corporate journalism and chain ownership was beginning, to the monopolies of today. Rather than community service as a public utility, community journalism has become more and more a part of the monopolies. Local communities are the hardest hit for coverage of their community events and celebrations, as well as of their neighborhood human interest stories, those intimate, sweet stories of life, as once cited by William Allen White.

Distant owners often own both the broadcast stations and the newspapers in one market. Despite public outcries to the contrary, a corporate Federal Communication Commission has assisted in licensing multi-media in the same market to a single, nonlocal owner: cable, radio, television, and now cell phone towers. The media's surveillance function greatly lessens when there are no local journalists to alert the public to an environmental or weather disaster. Another issue is whether a democratic society is compromised when journalism's local watchdog role is weakened by the absence of local owners to guard against local and regional as well as national government malfeasance, lying, and corruption.

It is not evident that the crystal-ball gazers of 1908 saw the other media that would soon arise from then embryonic inventions: a first experimental radio transmission, an electron tube for alternating current, the transmission of a photograph by telegraphic circuit, the jumpy early motion pictures and nickelodeon renditions to video, and the mechanical adding machines that would later become calculators and then computers. Journalism schools and departments slowly noticed the new technologies, and began broadening their curriculums to include the embryonic newsreels and halftones as well as graphics, drawings, and portrait plates. With hands-on practice, students learned the new technologies, in classes in photoengraving by 1914 at Missouri, in radio by 1929 at Washington State College, and in television by the 1950s at the University of Southern California.[13]

13. Ibid., 42–45.

The year 1908 represented a turning point in "the look" of the printed media, as Lora England Wegman discussed in her chapter. Front pages stacked with seven to eight columns containing as many as sixteen to twenty-four stories have been replaced by front pages with four to five columns, headlines across an entire page, and no more than five to seven stories. If there were any photos in 1908, they were gray portrait headshots; a century later fullspread color action scenes and action shots dominate, with more surrounding white space for design and improved readability.

For more than a century, the industry as well as the academy has argued about whether journalism is a craft or a profession. Views about the journalism curriculum remain split on whether to focus on the vocational aspects of journalism by teaching the craft, or to emphasize the institutional and theoretical aspects of the field. Following World War II, the divide came to be called the "Green Eye Shades versus Chi-Squares." Those arguments about journalism as an academic field continue today, ranging from Michael Lewis's July 1993 article in the *New Republic*, "J-School Ate My Brain," to President Lee Bollinger's twenty-first-century questions about the future direction of Columbia's journalism school prior to the hiring of a new dean. In 2007, a major journal discussed once again "Becoming a Journalist,"[14] as did Hugh W. de Burgh in an article about journalism as a serious academic discipline.[15] Perhaps journalism will be forever attempting to find itself in the midst of new technologies and new definitions.

The one constant has been the aim for professionalism, no matter what curriculum changes are made. Attempts to define professionalism became part of the culture of journalism. By merging professionalism with academia, that vision of more than a century ago, a prescription was offered for the betterment of the field. While this approach promoted recognition of the best elements of journalism, in one sense the culture of professionalism may have also lessened creativity and innovation in the adoption of new technologies to meet the industry's current needs. It also takes individualism to make changes; uniqueness to move a field forward. Now, for the most part, particular standards are anticipated. There is an expectation for a particular process for production, for the completing of a product, and for the style and tone and makeup of the product. For many, any divergence would be deviant and should therefore be discounted or stifled. No wonder so many journalism schools and departments were slow to recognize

14. Simon Frith and P. Meech, "Becoming a Journalist," *Journalism* 8, no. 2 (2007): 137–64.

15. Hugh W. deBurgh, "Skills Are Not Enough: The Case for Journalism as an Academic Discipline," *Journalism* 4, no. 1 (2003): 95–112.

the impacts of radio, television, cable, the Internet, and blogs and interactive journalism.

Professionalism in journalism, no matter what form it took, has become and will continue to be the aim. Professionalism tied the university training with industry and the production of journalism. Professionalism was the hope as well as the plan to gain legitimacy for the field, for improving what had been into the ideal of what could be. It is that dream of professionalism on the cusp of change that encompasses this book about how journalism was changed during that year of 1908.

About the Contributors

Stephen Banning, an Assistant Professor at the Slane College of Communication, Bradley University, did his doctorate at Southern Illinois University at Carbondale, his master's at the Missouri School of Journalism, and his bachelor degree at Cedarville University. His professional work was in radio, television, public relations, and advertising. A specialist in advertising, Banning has published extensively on media theory and third-person effects.

Maurine Beasley, a specialist in women and journalism, recently published *First Ladies and the Press: The Unfinished Partnership for the Media Age* (2005) and coauthored *Taking Their Place: A Documentary History of Women and Journalism* (2002). A professor of journalism at the Philip Merrill College of Journalism, University of Maryland, she is a former staff writer for the *Washington Post.* Her bachelors' degrees are from the University of Missouri in journalism and history, her master's degree from Columbia University, and her Ph.D. from George Washington University.

Fred Blevens, Associate Dean and Professor in the School of Journalism and Mass Communication at Florida International University, is past president of the American Journalism Historians Association. For nearly twenty years, he was a journalist at metropolitan newspapers in Florida, New Jersey, Pennsylvania, and Texas. He finished his Ph.D. at Missouri in 1995. In 2001, he was recognized as a national Teacher of the Year by the Freedom Forum.

Bonnie Brennen taught in the Missouri School of Journalism from 1999 to 2004, and is the Temple University Associate Provost for Academic Affairs. She is the author of *For the Record: An Oral History of Rochester, New*

York Newsworkers (2001), and coeditor, with Hanno Hardt, of *Picturing the Past: Media, History and Photography* (1999) and *Newsworkers: Toward a History of the Rank and File* (1995). Her current research focuses on cultural aspects of media history.

Caryl Cooper is University of Alabama Associate Dean and Associate Professor in the College of Communication and Information Sciences at the University of Alabama. She teaches advertising and mass communication history courses. Cooper began her advertising career at Doyle, Dane, Bernbach in New York City and has worked at television and radio stations. Cooper received her Ph.D. from the Missouri School of Journalism in 1996.

Sandy Davidson, University of Missouri Associate Professor of Journalism and Adjunct Associate Professor of Law, is the attorney for the *Columbia Missourian* (formerly the *University Missourian*). Her academic writings include "From Spam to Stern: Advertising Law and the Internet," in *Advertising and the Internet: Theory and Research* (2007) and "Journalism: The Lifeblood of a Democracy," coauthored with Betty Houchin Winfield in *What Good Is Journalism?* (2007).

Aimee Edmondson, a University of Missouri Ph.D. candidate, will be an assistant professor at the University of Ohio beginning in August 2008. A reporter for twelve years in Louisiana, Georgia, and Tennessee, Edmondson's dissertation is a study of libel law during the civil rights movement.

Tracy Everbach, an assistant professor at the University of North Texas, earned a Ph.D. in journalism from the University of Missouri in 2004. Her research focuses on gender and the newsroom, women in media, and journalism history. She is a former reporter for the *Dallas Morning News*.

Scott Fosdick, San Jose State University Assistant Professor, worked as a drama critic and arts editor in Chicago, New Jersey, and Baltimore before earning his doctorate in theater at Northwestern University. He taught at the Missouri School of Journalism for six years before becoming director of the magazine program at San José State University in 2005.

Berkley Hudson, University of Missouri Assistant Professor, earned his degrees from the University of Mississippi, Columbia University, and the University of North Carolina at Chapel Hill where he received his doctorate. His twenty-five years of professional newspaper and magazine experience includes working for the *Providence Journal* and the *Los Angeles Times*.

Janice Hume, an associate professor at the University of Georgia's Grady College of Journalism and Mass Communication, teaches magazine writing, magazine management, and media history. She is author of *Obituaries in American Culture,* coauthor of *Journalism in a Culture of Grief,* and has published articles in *Journalism and Mass Communication Quarterly, Journalism History, American Journalism,* and the *Journal of Popular Culture.* Before receiving her Ph.D. from the University of Missouri she was lifestyle and arts editor at the *Mobile* (Ala.) *Register.*

Hans Ibold, a University of Missouri Ph.D. candidate, will be an Assistant Professor at Indiana University. He looks at media and cultural globalization, with an emphasis on the role of the Internet in Central Asia. In the industry, he worked as an arts editor, technology reporter, and Web editor.

John Merrill, University of Missouri Professor Emeritus, was on the Missouri journalism faculty from 1964 until 1980, and from 1991 until 2000. Holder of four degrees—in English, journalism, mass communication, and philosophy—Merrill has written and edited thirty books and numerous articles. He taught and lectured in some sixty countries and six U.S. universities, received the Missouri Honor Medal in journalism, and is in the Journalism Hall of Fame at three universities. He has five children, nine grandchildren, and one great-grandson.

Earnest Perry, an associate professor of journalism and chair of Journalism Studies at the Missouri School of Journalism, has research interests on African American press history, specifically the black press during the first half of the twentieth century. He has published articles on history and media management in several journals including *American Journalism, Journalism History,* and *Journalism and Mass Communication Quarterly.*

William H. Taft, University of Missouri Professor Emeritus and a native Missourian, earned his bachelor's degree from nearby Westminster College before coming to the Missouri School of Journalism in 1937, where he earned his B.J. and M.A. degrees. In 1956 he returned as a faculty member, retiring in 1981. Taft's research focused on the Missouri newspaper scene and the Missouri Press Association, which named him to the Missouri Newspaper Hall of Fame. He also earned the University of Missouri top journalism honor medal award and the university's Faculty-Alumni Medal. Westminster named him for its alumni achievement recognition. He and his wife, Myrtle, just celebrated their sixty-seventh wedding anniversary. They have three children.

Lora England Wegman is the presentation editor at the *Columbia Daily Tribune* in Columbia, Mo. She earned a master of arts degree from the Missouri School of Journalism in 2006 and a bachelor's degree in communication from Truman State University in Kirksville, Mo., in 2000.

Lee Wilkins, University of Missouri Professor, focuses on how journalists make ethical decisions. Currently editor of the *Journal of Mass Media Ethics,* she coauthored *The Moral Media: How Journalists Reason about Ethics* and coedited the *Handbook of Mass Media Ethics* (2008). Wilkins earned her B.A. and B.J. from the University of Missouri (1971). In 1998, she won the Kemper Award, the University of Missouri's highest teaching honor.

Betty Houchin Winfield, University of Missouri Curators' Professor, has written more than one hundred papers, articles, and book chapters about the news process, uses of history, White House newsgathering, and news management and political images. Author or coauthor of four books, including the award-winning *FDR and the News Media* (1990, 1994), Winfield was the recipient of the University of Missouri's system-wide Thomas Jefferson award, and served as a Jefferson fellow, 1998–1999. Her bachelor's degree is from the University of Arkansas, her master's degree from the University of Michigan, and her Ph.D. from the University of Washington.

Index

Page numbers in italics refer to photographs.